Competitive Strategy

Pearson

At Pearson, we have a simple mission: to help people make more of their lives through learning.

We combine innovative learning technology with trusted content and educational expertise to provide engaging and effective learning experience that serve people wherever and whenever they are learning.

We enable our customers to access a wide and expanding range of market-leading content from world-renowned authors and develop their own tailor-made book. From classroom to boardroom, our curriculum materials, digital learning tools and testing programmes help to educate millions of people worldwide — more than any other private enterprise.

Every day our work helps learning flourish, and wherever learning flourishes, so do people.

To learn more, please visit us at: www.pearson.com/uk

Competitive Strategy

Selected chapters from:

Exploring Strategy: Text and Cases
Eleventh Edition
Gerry Johnson, Richard Whittington, Kevan Scholes, Duncan Angwin and
Patrick Regnér

Harlow, England • London • New York • Boston • San Francisco • Toronto • Sydney • Dubai • Singapore • Hong Kong
Tokyo • Seoul • Taipei • New Dehli • Cape Town • São Paulo • Mexico City • Madrid • Amsterdam • Munich • Paris • Milan

Pearson
KAO Two
KAO Park
Harlow
Essex CM17 9NA

And associated companies throughout the world

Visit us on the World Wide Web at:
www.pearson.com/uk

© Pearson Education Limited 2018

Compiled from:

Exploring Strategy: Text and Cases
Eleventh Edition
Gerry Johnson, Richard Whittington, Kevan Scholes, Duncan Angwin and Patrick Regnér
ISBN 978-1-292-14512-9
© Pearson Education Limited 2014, 2017 (print and electronic)

ISBN 978-1-787-26752-7

Printed and bound in Great Britain by Ashford Colour Press, Gosport, Hampshire.

CONTENTS

Competitive Strategy

1

INTRODUCING STRATEGY

Strategic position

Strategic choices

Strategy in action

Learning outcomes

After reading this chapter you should be able to:

- Summarise the strategy of an organisation in a '*strategy statement*'.

- Distinguish between *corporate*, *business* and *functional* strategies.

- Identify key issues for an organisation's strategy according to the *Exploring Strategy Framework*.

- Understand different people's roles in *strategy work*.

- Appreciate the importance of different *organisational contexts*, *academic disciplines* and *theoretical lenses* to practical strategy analysis.

Key terms

business-level strategy

corporate-level strategy

Exploring Strategy Framework

functional strategies

mission statement

objectives

statements of corporate values

strategic choices

strategic position

strategy

strategy in action

strategy lenses

strategy statements

three-horizons framework

vision statement

1.1 INTRODUCTION

Claudia, a junior at a leading firm of strategy consultants, had just arrived with two senior colleagues at the headquarters of a medium-sized company considering its next strategic move. The CEO began the meeting by outlining the business the company was in and some of the history behind the firm's significant success in European markets. The recent entry into Europe of new aggressive competitors threatened their performance and the Board was wondering whether the company should globalise. The CEO then asked how the consultants might approach this problem. The consulting partner explained they would carry out a systematic strategic analysis of the company's situation and Claudia knew this would be her responsibility – to gather and analyse appropriate data. She would need to understand how the company had been so successful to date, the challenge posed by competitors and the broader opportunities and threats from the wider environment. She knew she could access key company executives to understand what resources, processes and people were supporting the current strategy and also what might support international expansion. She would have to consider the direction in which the business might expand, the methods of expansion that might be most appropriate as well as other strategic options. Through this analysis, she would hope to inform the CEO's decision about what the strategy for the company might be and perhaps gain further work to help implement a strategic direction.

The problem presented by the CEO to the consultants is one of strategy. It is concerned with key issues for the future of the organisation. For instance, how should the company compete in the future with aggressive new entrants? What growth options are there for the company? If going global is a good strategy, what would be the optimal method to achieve this outcome and what might be the resourcing implications? All of these strategy questions are vital to the future survival of the organisation.

Strategy questions naturally concern entrepreneurs and senior managers at the top of their organisations. But these questions matter more widely. Middle managers also have to understand the strategic direction of their organisations, both to know how to get top management support for their initiatives and to explain their organisation's strategy to the people they are responsible for. Anybody looking for a management-track job needs to be ready to discuss strategy with their potential employer. Indeed, anybody taking a job should first be confident that their new employer's strategy is actually viable. There are even specialist career opportunities in strategy, for example like Claudia, as a strategy consultant or as an in-house strategic planner, often key roles for fast-track young managers.

This book takes a broad approach to strategy, looking at both the economics of strategy and the people side of managing strategy in practice. It is a book about 'Exploring', because the real world of strategy rarely offers obvious answers. In strategy, it is typically important to explore several options, probing each one carefully before making choices. The book is also relevant to any kind of organisation responsible for its own direction into the future. Thus the book refers to large private-sector multinationals and small entrepreneurial start-ups; to public-sector organisations such as schools and hospitals; and to not-for-profits such as charities or sports clubs. Strategy matters to almost all organisations, and to everybody working in them.

1.2 WHAT IS STRATEGY?[1]

In this book, **strategy is the long-term direction of an organisation.** Thus the long-term direction of Amazon is from book retailing to internet services in general. The long-term direction of Disney is from cartoons to diversified entertainment. This section examines the practical implication of this definition of strategy; distinguishes between different levels of strategy; and explains how to summarise an organisation's strategy in a 'strategy statement'.

1.2.1 Defining strategy

Defining strategy as the long-term direction of an organisation implies a more comprehensive view than some influential definitions. Figure 1.1 shows the strategy definitions of several leading strategy theorists: Alfred Chandler and Michael Porter, both from the Harvard Business School, Peter Drucker from Claremont University, California and Henry Mintzberg, from McGill University, Canada. Each points to important elements of strategy. Chandler emphasises a logical flow from the determination of goals and objectives to the allocation of resources. Porter focuses on deliberate choices, difference and competition. Drucker suggests that it is a theory about how a firm will win.[2] Mintzberg, however, takes the view that strategy is less certain and uses the word 'pattern' to allow for the fact that strategies do not always follow a deliberately chosen and logical plan, but can emerge in more ad hoc ways. Sometimes strategies reflect a series of incremental decisions that only cohere into a recognisable pattern – or 'strategy' – after some time.

In this book, strategy is defined as 'the long-term direction of an organisation'. This has two advantages. First, the long-term direction of an organisation can include both deliberate, logical strategy and more incremental, emergent patterns of strategy. Second, long-term direction can include both strategies that emphasise difference and competition, and strategies that recognise the roles of cooperation and even imitation.

The three elements of this strategy definition – the long term, direction and organisation – can each be explored further. The strategy of Tesla Motors illustrates important points (see Illustration 1.1):

'. . .the determination of the long-run goals and objectives of an enterprise and the adoption of courses of action and the allocation of resources necessary for carrying out these goals'
Alfred D. Chandler

'Competitive strategy is about being different. It means deliberately choosing a different set of activities to deliver a unique mix of value'
Michael Porter

'a firm's theory about how to gain competitive advantages'
Peter Drucker

'a pattern in a stream of decisions'
Henry Mintzberg

'the long-term direction of an organisation'
Exploring Strategy

Figure 1.1 Definitions of strategy

Sources: A.D. Chandler, *Strategy and Structure: Chapters in the History of American Enterprise*, MIT Press, 1963, p. 13; M.E. Porter, 'What is strategy?', *Harvard Business Review,* November–December 1996, p. 60; P.F. Drucker, 'The theory of business', *Harvard Business Review,* September–October 1994, pp. 95–106; H. Mintzberg, *Tracking Strategies: Towards a General Theory,* Oxford University Press, 2007, p. 3.

ILLUSTRATION 1.1 Tesla Motors: the future is electric!

Tesla car

Source: Jim West/Alamy Images.

The Tesla Roadster is a staggeringly quick car with a difference. There's no wheel-spin, no traction control stutter, no driveline shutter. As soon as one stamps on the throttle the driver gets 686 lbs of torque immediately, rocketing the car from 0–60 mph in 3.2 seconds and with negligible noise – the car is electric.

The Tesla Roadster is the main product of Tesla Motors. Its charismatic chairman and main funder is PayPal co-founder, and SpaceX CEO, Elon Musk. Barely a decade old, Tesla Motors is already gigantic, $33bn (£20bn, €25bn) market capitalisation and adored. It's been called 'the world's most important automotive company'[1] and the Tesla's Model S, 'the Most Loved Vehicle in America'[1] – outselling Mercedes S-class and BMW 7 series. And yet the last successful American car start-up was Ford, founded 111 years ago. How can Tesla Motors be so successful?

Tesla is the brain-child of three Silicon Valley engineers convinced by global warming arguments and looking for alternative fuel sources for cars. Co-founder Martin Eberhard asked: 'How much of the energy that comes out of the ground makes your car go a mile?'[1] He observed: 'Hydrogen fuel cells are terrible – no more efficient than gas. Electric cars were superior to everything.'[1] He then discovered a bright yellow, all-electric, two-seater bullet car with zero emissions, 'tzero', built by AC propulsion. Inspired, Eberhard kept saying to potential recruits – 'try and touch the dashboard.'[1] He would then hit the accelerator – they couldn't! With Lamborghini-level acceleration, this demonstrated electric cars didn't have to be golf carts.

But industry logic said electric cars would never succeed. GM spent $1bn (£0.6bn, €0.75bn), developing the EV-1 which was then scrapped. Battery technology had not improved in a hundred years. But Eberhard realised lithium-ion batteries were different – improving 7 per cent p.a. So Tesla was positioned to ride the current of technological history.

The founders had no experience making cars, but realised car companies now outsourced everything, even styling. Manufacturing partners were ready to be connected with; a 'fab-less' car company was possible.[3] Production began 2008. The business plan described the Roadster as 'disruptive' technology[1] – a high-end sports car with lower price and emissions than competitors – and a lower resource cost to the planet.

> **Roadster**
>
> 0–60 mph < 3.9 seconds; 100mpg; world-class handling; zero tailpipe emissions; 300 mile range; zero maintenance for 100,00 miles (other than tyres); 50% price of the cheapest competitive sports car.[1]

Tesla's strategy was:

> to enter at the high end of the market, where customers are prepared to pay a premium, and then drive down market as fast as possible to higher unit volume and lower prices with each successive model. . . . all free cash flow is plowed back into R&D to drive down the costs and bring the follow on products to market as fast as possible. When someone buys the Tesla Roadster sports car, they are actually helping pay for development of the low cost family car.[2]

Tesla aimed to provide zero emission electric power generation from their 'giga' battery factory in line with their 'overarching purpose . . . to help expedite the move from a mine-and-burn hydrocarbon economy towards a solar electric economy.'[2] In 2015, Tesla Energy was launched selling batteries for home and business use.

Edison didn't invent the light bulb, but he made it affordable and accessible through his electric system.[3] Tesla is also offering an energy system for a world of electric vehicles, homes and businesses, using batteries.

Sources: (1) E. Musk, 'The Secret Tesla Motors Master Plan (just between you and me)', 2 August 2006; (2) D. Baer, 'The making of Tesla: invention, betrayal, and the birth of the Roadster', *Business Insider*, 11 November 2014; (3) J. Suskewicz, 'Tesla's new strategy is over 100 years old', *Harvard Business Review*, May 2015.

Questions

1 How does Tesla Motor's strategy fit with the various strategy definitions in Figure 1.1?

2 What seems to account for Tesla's success?

- *The long term*. Strategies are typically measured over years, for some organisations a decade or more. The importance of a long-term perspective on strategy is emphasised by the 'three horizons' framework in Figure 1.2. The **three-horizons framework suggests organisations should think of themselves as comprising three types of business or activity, defined by their 'horizons' in terms of years.** *Horizon 1* businesses are basically the current core activities. In the case of Tesla Motors, Horizon 1 includes the original Tesla Roadster car and subsequent models. Horizon 1 businesses need defending and extending, but the expectation is that in the long term they will likely be flat or declining in terms of profits (or whatever else the organisation values). *Horizon 2* businesses are emerging activities that should provide new sources of profit. For Tesla, that might include the new mega-battery business. Finally, there are *Horizon 3* possibilities, for which nothing is sure. These are typically risky research and development (R&D) projects, start-up ventures, test-market pilots or similar: at Tesla, these might be further solar electric initiatives, rockets and space transportation. For a fast-moving organisation like Tesla, *Horizon 3* might generate profits a few years from the present time. In a pharmaceutical company, where the R&D and regulatory processes for a new drug take many years, *Horizon 3* might be a decade ahead. While timescales might differ, the basic point about the 'three-horizons' framework is that managers need to avoid focusing on the short-term issues of their existing activities. Strategy involves pushing out Horizon 1 as far as possible, at the same time as looking to Horizons 2 and 3.

- *Strategic direction*. Over the years, strategies follow some kind of long-term direction or trajectory. The strategic direction of Tesla Motors is from the original electric car to a diversified set of solar power offerings. Sometimes a strategic direction only emerges as a coherent pattern over time. Typically, however, managers and entrepreneurs try to set the direction of their strategy according to long-term *objectives*. In private-sector businesses, the objective guiding strategic direction is usually maximising profits for shareholders. However, profits do not always set strategic direction. First, public-sector and charity organisations may set their strategic direction according to other objectives: for example, a sports club's objective may be to move up from one league to a higher one. Second, even in the private sector profit is not always the sole criterion for strategy. Thus family

Figure 1.2 Three horizons for strategy

Note: 'profit' on the vertical axis can be replaced by non-profit objectives; 'business' can refer to any set of activities; 'time' can refer to a varying number of years.

Source: M. Baghai, S. Coley and D. White, *The Alchemy of Growth*, Texere Publishers, 2000, Figure 1.1, p. 5.

businesses may sometimes sacrifice the maximisation of profits for family objectives, for example passing down the management of the business to the next generation. The objectives behind strategic direction always need close scrutiny.

- *Organisation.* In this book, organisations are not treated as discrete, unified entities. Organisations involve many relationships, both internally and externally. This is because organisations typically have many internal and external *stakeholders,* in other words people and groups that depend on the organisation and upon which the organisation itself depends. Internally, organisations are filled with people, typically with diverse, competing and more or less reasonable views of what should be done. At Tesla, co-founder and original CEO Martin Eberhard was fired by new Chairman Elon Musk. In strategy, therefore, it is always important to look *inside* organisations and to consider the people involved and their different interests and views. Externally, organisations are surrounded by important relationships, for example with suppliers, customers, alliance partners, regulators and investors. For Tesla, relationships with investors and advertisers are crucial. Strategy therefore is also vitally concerned with an organisation's external *boundaries:* in other words, questions about what to include within the organisation and how to manage important relationships with what is kept outside.

Because strategy typically involves managing people, relationships and resources, the subject is sometimes called 'strategic management'. This book takes the view that managing is always important in strategy. Good strategy is about the practicalities of managing as well as the analysis of strategising.

1.2.2 The purpose of strategy: mission, vision, values and objectives

What is a strategy for? Harvard University's Cynthia Montgomery[3] argues that the core of a strategist's job is defining and expressing a clear and motivating purpose for the organisation. Even for private-sector organisations this is generally more than simple profit-maximisation as long-term prosperity and employee motivation usually require expressions of purpose that go beyond just profits. According to Montgomery, the stated purpose of the organisation should address two related questions: *how* does the organisation make a difference; and *for whom* does the organisation make that difference? If the stakeholders of an organisation can relate to such a purpose it can be highly motivating. Indeed, research by Jim Collins and Jerry Porras suggests that the long-run success of many US corporations – such as Disney, General Electric or 3M – can be attributed (at least in part) to the clear guidance and motivation offered by such statements of purpose.[4]

There are four ways in which organisations typically define their purpose:

- A **mission statement** aims to provide employees and stakeholders with clarity about what the organisation is fundamentally there to do. This is often expressed in the apparently simple but challenging question: 'What business are we in?' Two linked questions that can clarify an organisation's 'business' are: 'What would be lost if the organisation did not exist?'; and 'How do we make a difference?' Though they do not use the term 'mission statement', Collins and Porras[5] suggest that understanding the fundamental mission can be done by starting with a descriptive statement of what the organisation actually does, then repeatedly delving deeper into the organisation purpose by asking 'why do we do this?' They use the example of managers in a gravel and asphalt company arriving at the conclusion that its mission is to make people's lives better by improving the quality of built structures. At Southampton University the mission includes educating students, training the next generation of researchers and addressing social issues.

- **A vision statement is concerned with the future the organisation seeks to create.** The vision typically expresses an aspiration that will enthuse, gain commitment and stretch performance. So here the question is: 'What do we want to achieve?' Porras and Collins suggest managers can identify this by asking: 'If we were sitting here in twenty years what do we want to have created or achieved?' They cite the example of Henry Ford's original vision in the very early days of automobile production that the ownership of a car should be within the reach of everyone. For the Swedish music site Spotify, the vision is to become 'the Operating System of music', a universal platform for listening just as Microsoft is for office software.

- **Statements of corporate values communicate the underlying and enduring core 'principles' that guide an organisation's strategy and define the way that the organisation should operate.** For example, Alphabet (previously Google) famously includes in its values 'you can be serious without a suit', 'fast is better than slow' and 'don't be evil'. It is important that these values are enduring, so a question to ask is: 'Would these values change with circumstances?' And if the answer is 'yes' then they are not 'core' and not 'enduring'. An example is the importance of leading-edge research in some universities. Whatever the constraints on funding, such universities hold to the enduring centrality of research. On the other hand, as Alphabet has grown and diversified, some critics wonder whether the company still abides by its principle of 'don't be evil' (see Chapter 13 end case).

- **Objectives are statements of specific outcomes that are to be achieved.** These are often expressed in precise financial terms, for instance, the level of sales, profits or share valuation in one, two or three years' time.[6] Organisations may also have quantifiable market-based objectives, such as market share, customer service, repeat business and so on. Sometimes objectives focus on the basis of competitive advantage: for example, low-cost airlines such as RyanAir set objectives on turnaround time for their aircraft because this is at the core of their distinctive low-cost advantage. Increasingly, organisations are also setting objectives referred to as 'the triple bottom line', by which is meant not only economic objectives such as those above, but also environmental and social objectives to do with their corporate responsibility to wider society (see Section 5.4.1).

Although visions, missions and values may be liable to become bland and too wide-ranging,[7] they can offer more enduring sources of direction and motivation than the concrete nature of objectives. It is therefore crucial that vision, mission and values are meaningful when included in strategy statements.

1.2.3 Strategy statements

David Collis and Michael Rukstad[8] at the Harvard Business School argue that all entrepreneurs and managers should be able to summarise their organisation's strategy with a 'strategy statement'. **Strategy statements should have three main themes: the fundamental *goals* (mission, vision or objectives) that the organisation seeks; the *scope* or domain of the organisation's activities; and the particular *advantages* or capabilities it has to deliver all of these.**

Mission, vision and objectives have been described in Section 1.2.2 so here we concentrate on the other two main themes, *scope* and *advantage,* with examples of all five given in Illustration 1.2:

- *Scope.* An organisation's scope or domain refers to three dimensions: customers or clients; geographical location; and extent of internal activities ('vertical integration'). For a university, scope questions are two-fold: first, which academic departments to have (a business

ILLUSTRATION 1.2 Strategy statements

Both Samsung Electronics, the Korean telecommunications, computing and TV giant, and Southampton University, a leading British university, publish a good deal about their strategies.

Samsung Electronics

At Samsung, we follow a simple business philosophy: to devote our talent and technology to creating superior products and services that contribute to a better global society.

Every day, our people bring this philosophy to life. Our leaders search for the brightest talent from around the world, and give them the resources they need to be the best at what they do. The result is that all of our products – from memory chips that help businesses store vital knowledge to mobile phones that connect people across continents – have the power to enrich lives. And that's what making a better global society is all about.

As stated in its new motto, Samsung Electronics' vision [. . .] is, 'Inspire the World, Create the Future'. This new vision reflects Samsung Electronics' commitment to inspiring its communities by leveraging Samsung's three key strengths: 'New Technology', 'Innovative Products' and 'Creative Solutions'. As part of this vision, Samsung has mapped out a specific plan of reaching $400 billion in revenue and becoming one of the world's top five brands by 2020. To this end, Samsung has also established three strategic approaches in its management: 'Creativity', 'Partnership' and 'Talent'.

As we build on our previous accomplishments, we look forward to exploring new territories, including health, medicine, and biotechnology. Samsung is committed to being a creative leader in new markets, becoming No. 1 business in the Global IT industry and in the Global top 5.

Southampton University strategy

The university's core mission is to change the world for the better. It is an exceptional place whose people achieve remarkable things. We are a world-leading, research-intensive university, with a strong educational offering, renowned for our innovation and enterprise. Our strategy is about our aspirations – building our reputation and being simply better than our competitors.

We will increase our rankings to be in the top 10 (UK) and top 100 internationally. This will increase our reputation, which will increase our ranking.

A reputation for delivering excellence and an exemplary student experience will lead to greater demand from the best student applicants, sustained support from research funders and strong support from our alumni.

We aim to achieve:

1 *Collegiality*: providing excellent staff experience, improving management and leadership throughout, developing agile governance, increasing risk appetite.

2 *Internal quality*: improve student experience to amongst the best in the UK's National Student Survey, develop high quality systems and infrastructure, improve quality of research applications, develop £5m+ strategic partnerships, raise admission standards, increase international student numbers, improve student employability, recruit and retain high quality staff.

3 *National and international recognition*: improve league table rankings and reputation, improve quality of education, grow international alumni community, deliver impactful research.

4 *Sustainability*: deliver the ability to invest, develop sustainable smooth income, improve research overhead recovery, improve productivity, increase revenue from other sources.

Sources: Edited extract from the University of Southampton *Simply Better: The University Strategy*, www.southampton.ac.uk.

Questions

1 Construct short strategy statements covering the goals, scope and advantage of Samsung and the Southampton University. How much do the different private- and public-sector contexts matter?

2 Construct a strategy statement for your own organisation (university, sports club or employer). What implications might this statement have for change in your organisation?

school, an engineering department and so on); second, which activities to do internally themselves (vertically integrate) and which to externalise to subcontractors (for example, whether to manage campus restaurants in-house or to subcontract them).

- *Advantage.* This part of a strategy statement describes how the organisation will achieve the objectives it has set for itself in its chosen domain. In competitive environments, this refers to the *competitive* advantage: for example, how a particular company or sports club will achieve goals in the face of competition from other companies or clubs. In order to achieve a particular goal, the organisation needs to be better than others seeking the same goal. In the public sector, advantage might refer simply to the organisation's capability in general. But even public-sector organisations frequently need to show that their capabilities are not only adequate, but superior to other rival departments or perhaps to private-sector contractors.

Collis and Rukstad suggest that strategy statements covering goals, scope and advantage should be no more than 35 words long. *The three themes are deliberately made highly concise.* Brevity keeps such statements focused on the essentials and makes them easy to remember and communicate. Thus for Tesla, a strategy statement might be: 'To accelerate the advent of a sustainable solar economy by developing and incorporating superior battery-based technologies into compelling mass market electric products and bringing them to market as soon as possible.' The strategy statement of Swedish multinational group IKEA is a little more specific: 'To create a better everyday life for the many people [by offering] a wide range of well-designed, functional home furnishing products at prices so low that as many people as possible will be able to afford them.' Of course, such strategy statements are not always fulfilled. Circumstances may change in unexpected ways. In the meantime, however, they can provide a useful guide both to managers in their decision-making and to employees and others who need to understand the direction in which the organisation is going. The ability to give a clear strategy statement is a good test of managerial competence in an organisation.

As such, strategy statements are relevant to a wide range of organisations. For example, a small entrepreneurial start-up can use a strategy statement to persuade investors and lenders of its viability. Public-sector organisations need strategy statements not only for themselves, but to reassure clients, funders and regulators that their priorities are the right ones. Voluntary organisations need persuasive strategy statements in order to inspire volunteers and donors. Thus organisations of all kinds frequently publish materials relevant to such strategy statements on their websites or annual reports. Illustration 1.2 provides published materials on the strategies of two very different organisations: the technology giant Samsung from the private sector and Southampton University in the UK from the public sector.

1.2.4 Levels of strategy

So far we have considered an organisation as a whole, but inside an organisation, strategies can exist at three main levels.

- **Corporate-level strategy is concerned with the overall scope of an organisation and how value is added to the constituent businesses of the organisational whole.** Corporate-level strategy issues include geographical scope, diversity of products or services, acquisitions of new businesses, and how resources are allocated between the different elements of the organisation. For Tesla, moving from car manufacture to battery production for homes and businesses is a corporate-level strategy. Being clear about corporate-level strategy is important: determining the range of businesses to include is the basis of other strategic decisions, such as acquisitions and alliances.

- **Business-level strategy is about how the individual businesses should compete in their particular markets** (this is often called 'competitive strategy'). These might be stand-alone businesses, for instance entrepreneurial start-ups, or 'business units' within a larger corporation. Business-level strategy typically concerns issues such as innovation, appropriate scale and response to competitors' moves. For Tesla this means rolling out a lower cost electric car to build volume and capture market share in advance of potential competitor entry. In the public sector, the equivalent of business-level strategy is decisions about how units (such as individual hospitals or schools) should provide best-value services. Where the businesses are units within a larger organisation, business-level strategies should clearly fit with corporate-level strategy.

- **Functional strategies are concerned with how the components of an organisation deliver effectively the corporate- and business-level strategies in terms of resources, processes and people.** For example, Tesla continues to raise external finance to fund its rapid growth: its functional strategy is partly geared to meeting investment needs. In most businesses, successful business strategies depend to a large extent on decisions that are taken, or activities that occur, at the functional level. Functional decisions need therefore to be closely linked to business-level strategy. They are vital to successful strategy implementation.

This need to link the corporate, business and functional levels underlines the importance of *integration* in strategy. Each level needs to be aligned with the others. The demands of integrating levels define an important characteristic of strategy: strategy is typically *complex*, requiring careful and sensitive management. Strategy is rarely simple.

1.3 THE *EXPLORING STRATEGY* FRAMEWORK

This book is structured around a three-part framework that emphasises the interconnected nature of strategic issues. The *Exploring Strategy* Framework includes understanding *the strategic position* of an organisation; assessing *strategic choices* for the future; and managing *strategy in action*. Figure 1.3 shows these elements and defines the broad coverage of this book. Together, the three elements provide a practical template for studying strategic situations. The following sections of this chapter will introduce the strategic issues that arise under each of these elements of the *Exploring Strategy* Framework. But first it is important to understand why the framework is drawn in this particular way.

Figure 1.3 could have shown the framework's three elements in a linear sequence – first understanding the strategic position, then making strategic choices and finally turning strategy into action. Indeed, this logical sequence is implicit in the definition of strategy given by Alfred Chandler (Figure 1.1) and many other textbooks on strategy. However, as Henry Mintzberg recognises, in practice the elements of strategy do not always follow this linear sequence. Choices often have to be made before the position is fully understood. Sometimes too a proper understanding of the strategic position can only be built from the experience of trying a strategy out in action. The real-world feedback from launching a new product is often far better at uncovering the true strategic position than remote analysis carried out in a strategic planning department at head office.

The interconnected circles of Figure 1.3 are designed to emphasise this potentially non-linear nature of strategy. Position, choices and action should be seen as closely related, and in practice none has priority over another. It is only for structural convenience that this book divides its subject matter into three sections; the book's sequence is not meant to suggest that the process of strategy must follow a logical series of distinct steps. The three

Figure 1.3 The *Exploring Strategy* Framework

circles are overlapping and interdependent. The evidence provided in later chapters will suggest that strategy rarely occurs in tidy ways and that it is better not to expect it to do so.

However, the *Exploring Strategy* Framework does provide a comprehensive and integrated schema for analysing an organisation's position, considering the choices it has and putting strategies into action. Each of the chapters can be seen as asking fundamental strategy questions and providing the essential concepts and techniques to help answer them. Working systematically through questions and answers provides the basis for persuasive strategy recommendations.

1.3.1 Strategic position

The **strategic position** is concerned with the impact on strategy of the macro-environment, the industry environment, the organisation's strategic capability (resources and competences), the organisation's stakeholders and the organisation's culture. Understanding these five factors is central for evaluating future strategy. These issues, and the fundamental questions associated with them, are covered in the following five chapters of Part I of this book:

- *Macro-environment*. Organisations operate in complex multi-level environments. At the macro level, organisations are influenced by political, economic, social, technological, ecological and legal forces. The macro-environment varies widely in terms of its dynamism. The fundamental question here relates to the *opportunities* and *threats* available to the organisation in complex, changing environments. Chapter 2 provide key frameworks to help in focusing on priority issues in the face of environmental complexity and dynamism.

- *Industry environment*. At the industry level of analysis, competitors, suppliers and customers present challenges to an organisation. A fundamental question is: how can an organisation manage industry forces? Industry environments can vary widely in their attractiveness and present *opportunities* and *threats*. Chapter 3 provides key frameworks to help identify major forces at work in different industries.

- *Strategic capability.* Each organisation has its own strategic capabilities, made up of its *resources* (e.g. machines and buildings) and *competences* (e.g. technical and managerial skills). The fundamental question on capability regards the organisation's *strengths* and *weaknesses* (for example, where is it at a competitive advantage or disadvantage?). Are the organisation's capabilities adequate to the challenges of its environment and the demands of its goals? Chapter 4 provides tools and concepts for analysing such resources and capabilities.

- *Stakeholders.* There are many actors who hold a 'stake' in the future of every organisation – not just owners, but employees, customers, suppliers and more. The fourth fundamental question then is: how can the organisation be aligned around a common purpose? An organisation's key stakeholders should define its purpose. Understanding their different interests to identify this purpose is important. *Corporate governance* then matters as it translates this purpose into strategy: how to ensure that managers stick to the agreed purpose? Questions of purpose and accountability raise issues of *corporate social responsibility* and *ethics:* is the purpose an appropriate one and are managers sticking to it? Chapter 5 provides concepts for addressing these issues of purpose.

- *Culture.* Organisational cultures can also influence strategy. So can the cultures of a particular industry or particular country. These cultures are typically a product of an organisation's *history*. The consequence of history and culture can be *strategic drift*, a failure to create necessary change. A fundamental question here, therefore, is: how does culture fit with the required strategy? Chapter 6 demonstrates how managers can analyse, challenge and sometimes turn to their advantage the various cultural influences on strategy.

The *Exploring Strategy* Framework (Illustration 1.1) points to the following positioning issues for Tesla Motors. What is the future of the company given the growing social, political, ecological and legal demands for businesses to be environmentally sustainable? Are its distinctive capabilities really valued sufficiently by consumers to provide a financial return to investors and to allow sustained investment in further innovative products? How will Tesla cope with rising competition from car industry giants who are now selling electric and hybrid cars?

1.3.2 Strategic choices

Strategic choices involve the options for strategy in terms of both the *directions* in which strategy might move and the *methods* by which strategy might be pursued. For instance, an organisation might have a range of strategic directions open to it: the organisation could diversify into new products; it could enter new international markets; or it could transform its existing products and markets through radical innovation. These various directions could be pursued by different methods: the organisation could acquire a business already active in the product or market area; it could form alliances with relevant organisations that might help its new strategy; or it could try to pursue its strategies on its own. Typical strategic choices, and the related fundamental questions, are covered in the five chapters that make up Part II of this book, as follows:

- *Business strategy and models.* There are strategic choices in terms of how the organisation seeks to compete at the individual business level. For example, a business unit could choose to be the lowest cost competitor in a market, or the highest quality. The fundamental question here, then, is what strategy and what business model should a company use to compete? Key dilemmas for business-level strategy, and ways of resolving them, are discussed in Chapter 7.

- *Corporate strategy and diversification.* The highest level of an organisation is typically concerned with issues of corporate scope, in other words, which businesses to include in the portfolio. This relates to the appropriate degree of *diversification,* with regard to products offered and markets served. Corporate-level strategy is also concerned with internal relationships, both between business units and with the corporate head office. Chapter 8 provides tools for assessing diversification strategies and the appropriate relationships within the corporate portfolio.

- *International strategy.* Internationalisation is a form of diversification, but into new geographical markets. Here the fundamental question is: where internationally should the organisation compete? Chapter 9 examines how to prioritise various international options and key strategies for pursuing them.

- *Entrepreneurship and innovation.* Most existing organisations have to innovate constantly simply to survive. Entrepreneurship, the creation of a new enterprise, is an act of innovation too. A fundamental question, therefore, is whether the organisation is innovating appropriately. Chapter 10 considers key choices about innovation and entrepreneurship, and helps in selecting between them.

- *Mergers, acquisitions and alliances.* Organisations have to make choices about methods for pursuing their strategies. Many organisations prefer to build new businesses with their own resources. Other organisations develop by acquiring other businesses or forming alliances with complementary partners. The fundamental question in Chapter 11, therefore, is whether to buy another company, ally or to go it alone.

Again, issues of strategic choice are live in the case of Tesla Motors (Illustration 1.1). The *Exploring Strategy* Framework asks the following kinds of questions here. Should Tesla continue to produce new higher volume cheaper cars or remain specialised? How far should it widen the scope of its businesses: is producing batteries for homes really helping or detracting from car production? Where should Tesla innovate next?

1.3.3 Strategy in action

Managing **strategy in action** is about how strategies are formed and how they are implemented. The emphasis is on the practicalities of managing. These issues are covered in the five chapters of Part III, and include the following, each with their own fundamental questions:

- *Strategy performance and evaluation.* Managers have to decide whether existing and forecast performance is satisfactory and then choose between options that might improve it. The fundamental evaluation questions are as follows: are the options *suitable* in terms of matching opportunities and threats; are they *acceptable* in the eyes of significant stakeholders; and are they *feasible* given the capabilities available? Chapter 12 introduces a range of financial and non-financial techniques for appraising performance and evaluating strategic options.

- *Strategy development processes.* Strategies are often developed through formal *planning* processes. But sometimes the strategies an organisation actually pursues are *emergent* – in other words, accumulated patterns of ad hoc decisions, bottom-up initiatives and rapid responses to the unanticipated. Given the scope for emergence, the fundamental question is: what kind of strategy process should an organisation have? Chapter 13 addresses the question of whether to plan strategy in detail or leave plenty of opportunities for emergence.

- *Organising.* Once a strategy is developed, the organisation needs to organise for successful implementation. Each strategy requires its own specific configuration of *structures* and *systems.* The fundamental question, therefore, is: what kinds of structures and systems are required for the chosen strategy? Chapter 14 introduces a range of structures and systems and provides frameworks for deciding between them.

- *Leadership and strategic change.* In a dynamic world, strategy inevitably involves change. Managing change involves *leadership,* both at the top of the organisation and lower down. There is not just one way of leading change, however: there are different *styles* and different *levers* for change. So the fundamental question is: how should the organisation manage necessary changes entailed by the strategy? Chapter 15 therefore examines options for managing change, and considers how to choose between them.

- *Strategy practice.* Inside the broad processes of strategy development and change is a lot of hard, detailed work. The fundamental question in managing this work is: who should do what in the strategy process? Chapter 16 thus provides guidance on which *people* to include in the process; what *activities* they should do; and which *methodologies* can help them do it. These kinds of practicalities are a fitting end to the book and essential equipment for those who will have to go out and participate in strategy work themselves.

With regard to strategy in action, the *Exploring Strategy* Framework raises the following kinds of questions for Tesla. How will Tesla return value to shareholders going forwards? How will the rate of innovation at Tesla be maintained? Should Tesla move towards a more disciplined strategy development process rather than depend on the vision of Elon Musk? Does Tesla need more structure and systems? As Tesla grows, how should any changes that may be necessary be managed?

Thus the *Exploring Strategy* Framework offers a comprehensive way for analysing an organisation's position, considering alternative choices, and selecting and implementing strategies. In this sense, the fundamental questions in each chapter provide a comprehensive checklist for strategy. These fundamental questions are summed up in Table 1.1. Any assessment of an organisation's strategy will benefit from asking these questions systematically. The frameworks for answering these and related questions can be found in the respective chapters.

The logic of the *Exploring Strategy* Framework can be applied to our personal lives as much as to organisations. We all have to make decisions with long-run consequences for our futures and the issues involved are very similar. For example, in pursuing a career strategy, a job-seeker needs to understand the job market, evaluate their strengths and weaknesses, establish the range of job opportunities and decide what their career goals really are (positioning issues). The job-seeker then narrows down the options, makes some applications

Table 1.1 The strategy checklist

Sixteen fundamental questions in strategy		
Strategic position	Strategic choices	Strategy in action
• What are the macro-environmental opportunities and threats? • How can the organisation manage industry forces? • How are stakeholders aligned to the organisational purpose? • What resources and capabilities support the strategy? • How does culture fit the strategy?	• How should business units compete? • Which businesses to include in a portfolio? • Where should the organisation compete internationally? • Is the organisation innovating appropriately? • Should the organisation buy other companies, ally or go it alone?	• Are strategies suitable, acceptable and feasible? • What kind of strategy-making process is needed? • What are the required organisation structures and systems? • How should the organisation manage necessary changes? • Who should do what in the strategy process?

and finally gets an offer (choice issues). Once the job-seeker has chosen a job, he or she sets to work, adjusting their skills and behaviours to suit their new role (strategy in action). Just as in the non-linear, overlapping *Exploring Strategy* Framework, experience of the job will frequently amend the original strategic goals. Putting a career strategy into action produces better understanding of strengths and weaknesses and frequently leads to the setting of new career goals.

1.4 WORKING WITH STRATEGY

Strategy itself is a kind of work, and it is something that almost all levels of management have to engage in, not just top decision-makers. Middle and lower-level managers have to understand their organisation's strategic objectives and contribute to them as best they can. Managers have to communicate strategy to their teams, and will achieve greater performance from them the more convincing they are in doing so. Indeed, as responsibility is increasingly decentralised in many organisations, middle and lower-level managers play a growing part in shaping strategy themselves. Because they are closer to the daily realities of the business, lower-level managers can be a crucial source of ideas and feedback for senior management teams. Being able to participate in an organisation's 'strategic conversation' – engaging with senior managers on the big issues facing them – is therefore often part of what it takes to win promotion.[9]

For many managers, then, strategy is part of the job. However, there are specialist strategists as well, in both private and public sectors. Many large organisations have in-house strategic planning or analyst roles.[10] Typically requiring a formal business education of some sort, strategic planning is a potential career route for many readers of this book, especially after some functional experience. Strategy consulting has been a growth industry in the last decades, with the original leading firms such as McKinsey & Co., the Boston Consulting Group and Bain joined now by more generalist consultants such as Accenture, IBM Consulting and PwC, each with its own strategy consulting arm.[11] Again, business graduates are in demand for strategy consulting roles, such as that of Claudia in the opening example.[12]

The interviews in Illustration 1.3 give some insights into the different kinds of strategy work that managers and strategy specialists can do. Galina, the manager of an international subsidiary, Chantal, a strategy consultant, and Paul, heading a strategy office in a not-for-profit organisation, all have different experiences of strategy, but there are some common themes also. All find strategy work stimulating and rewarding. The two specialists, Chantal and Paul, talk more than Galina of analytical tools such as scenario analysis, sensitivity analysis and hypothesis testing. Galina discovered directly the practical challenges of real-world strategic planning, having to adapt the plan during the first few years in the UK. She emphasises the importance of flexibility in strategy and the value of getting her managers to see the 'whole picture' through involving them in strategy-making. But Chantal and Paul too are concerned with much more than just analysis. Chantal emphasises the importance of gaining 'traction' with clients, building consensus in order to ensure implementation. Paul also realises that delivering recommendations is just the beginning of the strategy process and getting buy-in from key stakeholders is critical for implementation. He sees strategy and delivery as intimately connected, with people involved in delivery needing an understanding of strategy to be effective, and strategists needing to understand delivery.

ILLUSTRATION 1.3   Strategists

For Galina, Chantal and Paul, strategy is a large part of their jobs.

Galina

At the age of 33, after a start in marketing, Galina became managing director of a Russian-owned British IT company. As well as developing the strategy for her local business, she has to interact regularly with headquarters: 'Moscow is interested in the big picture, not just the details. They are interested in the future of the business.'

She had to adapt substantially the subsidiary's strategic plans:

'When we first came here, we had some ideas about strategy, but soon found the reality was very different to the plans. The strategy was not completely wrong, but in the second stage we had to change it a lot: we had to change techniques and adapt to the market. Now we are in the third stage, where we have the basics and need to focus on trends, to get ahead and be in the right place at the right time.'

Galina works closely with her management team on strategy, taking them on an annual 'strategy away-day' (see Chapter 16): 'Getting people together helps them see the whole picture, rather than just the bits they are responsible for. It is good to put all their separate realities together.'

Galina is enthusiastic about working on strategy:

'I like strategy work, definitely. The most exciting thing is to think about where we have come from and where we might be going. We started in a pub five years ago and we have somehow implemented what we were hoping for then. Strategy gives you a measure of success. It tells you how well you have done.'

Her advice is: 'Always have a strategy – have an ultimate idea in mind. But take feedback from the market and from your colleagues. Be ready to adjust the strategy: the adjustment is the most important.'

Chantal

Chantal is in her early thirties and has worked in Paris for one of the top three international strategy consultancies since graduating in business. Consulting was attractive to her originally because she liked the idea of helping organisations improve. She enjoys strategy consulting because 'I like solving problems. It's a bit like working on a mystery case: you have a problem and then you have to find a solution to fit the company, and help it grow and to be better.'

The work is intellectually challenging:

'Time horizons are short. You have to solve your case in two to three months. There's lots of pressure. It pushes you and helps you to learn yourself. There are just three to four in a team, so you will make a significant contribution to the project even as a junior. You have a lot of autonomy and you're making a contribution right from the start, and at quite a high level.'

Consulting work can involve financial and market modelling (see Chapters 3 and 12), interviewing clients and customers, and working closely with the client's own teams. Chantal explains:

'As a consultant, you spend a lot of time in building solid fact-based arguments that will help clients make business decisions. But as well as the facts, you have to have the ability to get traction. People have to agree, so you have to build consensus, to make sure that recommendations are supported and acted on.'

Chantal summarises the appeal of strategy consulting: 'I enjoy the learning, at a very high speed. There's the opportunity to increase your skills. One year in consulting is like two years in a normal business.'

Paul

In his early forties, Paul is a UK ex-pat in Saudi Arabia heading up a key part of the Strategy and Planning Office in a large hospital with a multi-million pound investment responsibility.

'Rational linear analysis is very important here. We have an abundance of data from all the major consultancies and a number of high-profile US academic advisors and need to assemble it for forecasting and trend analysis purposes. A great deal of time is taken crafting documents for key stakeholders. Informally we used a range of strategy tools and techniques including statistical analysis, scenario analysis (see Chapter 2), sensitivity analysis (see Chapter 12), hypothesis testing (see Chapter 16) and also carry out many internal surveys to monitor implementation progress.'

Paul has been surprised by the sheer amount of time and effort needed to consult key internal and external stakeholders personally: 'I have to consult every project manager and director and, more importantly, politically powerful and rich external stakeholders, regardless of their knowledge – and they have to be flattered to get buy-in.'

What Paul likes about the job is making a difference by 'changing people's perceptions, getting powerful individuals to make decisions and understand the reasons – rather than hiding behind endless committees (see Chapter 16).'

Source: interviews (interviewees anonymised).

Questions

1   Which of these strategy roles appeals to you most – manager of a business unit in a multinational, strategy consultant or in-house strategy specialist? Why?

2   What would you have to do to get such a role?

Strategy, therefore, is not just about abstract organisations. It is about linking analysis with implementation on the ground. It is complex work that real people do. An important aim of this book is to equip readers to do this work better.

1.5 STUDYING STRATEGY

This book is both comprehensive and serious about strategy. To understand the full range of strategy issues – from analysis to action – it is important to be open to the perspectives and insights of key disciplines such as economics, finance, sociology and psychology. To be serious about strategy means to draw as far as possible on rigorous research about these issues. This book aims for an evidence-based approach to strategy, hence the articles and books referenced at the end of each chapter.[13]

This book therefore covers equally the three main branches of strategy research: conventionally, these are known as strategy *context*, strategy *content* and strategy *process*. In terms of the *Exploring Strategy* Framework (Figure 1.3), context broadly relates to positioning, content to choice and process to action. Each of these branches contains various research streams whose lessons can be readily applied to practical questions of strategy issues. Figure 1.4 shows the three branches and their respective research streams: these are listed in the approximate historical order of their emergence as strong research streams, the arrows representing the continuously developing nature of each. In more detail, the three branches and the characteristic analytical approaches of their main research streams are as follows:

- *Strategy context* refers to multiple layers of environment, internal and external to organisations. All organisations need to take into account the opportunities and threats of their external environments. *Macro-environmental analysis* has been an enduring theme in strategy with early recognition of multiple pressures upon industries in the 1960s. Subsequently, researchers have focused upon various additional themes including institutional pressures establishing the 'rules of the game' within which companies operate. *Industry analysis* took off as a research tradition in the early 1980s, when Michael Porter showed

Figure 1.4 Strategy's three branches

how the tools of economics could be applied to understanding what makes industries attractive (or unattractive) to operate in.[14] From the 1980s too, *cultural analysts* have used sociological insights into human behaviour to point to the importance of shared cultural understandings about appropriate ways of acting. In the internal context, cultural analysts show that strategies are often influenced by the organisation's specific culture. In the external context, they show how strategies often have to fit with the surrounding industry or national cultures. *Resource-based view* researchers focus on internal context, looking for the unique characteristics of each organisation.[15] According to the resource-based view, the economic analysis of market imperfections, the psychological analysis of perceptual or emotional biases, and the sociological analysis of organisational cultures should reveal the particular characteristics (resources) that contribute to an organisation's specific competitive advantages and disadvantages.

- *Strategy content* concerns the content (or nature) of different strategies and their probability of success. Here the focus is on the merits of different strategic options. *Strategy and performance* researchers started by using economic analysis to understand the success of different types of diversification strategies. This research continues as the enduring central core of the strategy discipline, with an ever-growing list of issues addressed. For example, contemporary strategy and performance researchers examine various new innovation strategies, different kinds of internationalisation and all the complex kinds of alliance and networking strategies organisations adopt today. These researchers typically bring a tough economic scrutiny to strategy options. Their aim is to establish which types of strategies pay best and under what conditions. They refuse to take for granted broad generalisations about what makes a good strategy.

- *Strategy process,* broadly conceived, examines how strategies are formed and implemented. Research here provides a range of insights to help managers in the practical processes of managing strategy.[16] From the 1960s, researchers in the *strategic planning* tradition have drawn from economics and management science in order to design rational and analytical systems for the planning and implementing of strategy. However, strategy involves people: since the 1980s, *choice and change* researchers have been pointing to how the psychology of human perception and emotions, and the sociology of group politics and interests, tend to undermine rational analysis.[17] The advice of these researchers is to accept the irrational, messy realities of organisations, and to work with them, rather than to try to impose textbook rationality. Finally, *strategy-as-practice* researchers have recently been using micro-sociological approaches to closely examine the human realities of formal and informal strategy processes.[18] This tradition focuses attention on how people do strategy work, and the importance of having the right tools and skills.

From the above, it should be clear that studying strategy involves perspectives and insights from a range of academic disciplines. Issues need to be 'explored' from different points of view. A strategy chosen purely on economic grounds can easily be undermined by psychological and sociological factors. On the other hand, a strategy that is chosen on the psychological grounds of emotional enthusiasm, or for sociological reasons of cultural acceptability, is liable to fail if not supported by favourable economics. As underlined by the four strategy lenses to be introduced later, one perspective is rarely enough for good strategy. A complete analysis will typically need the insights of economics, psychology and sociology.

1.6 EXPLORING STRATEGY FURTHER

So far we have stressed that strategic issues are typically complex, best explored from a number of points of views. There is no simple, universal rule for good strategy. This section introduces two further ways of exploring strategy: one depending on context, the other depending on perspective.

1.6.1 Exploring strategy in different contexts

Although the basic elements of the *Exploring Strategy* Framework are relevant in most circumstances, how they play out precisely is likely to differ according to organisational contexts. To return to Illustration 1.2, both Samsung and Southampton University share some fundamental issues about how to compete and what activities they should have in their portfolio. However, for a Korean electronics company and a British university, the role of institutions, particularly government, varies widely, affecting the freedom to choose and the ability to change. In applying the *Exploring Strategy* Framework, it is therefore useful to ask what kinds of issues are likely to be particularly significant in the specific context being considered. To illustrate, this section shows how issues arising from the *Exploring Strategy* Framework can vary in three important organisational contexts.

- *Small businesses.* With regard to positioning, small businesses will certainly need to attend closely to the environment, because they are so vulnerable to change. But, especially in small entrepreneurial and family businesses, the most important positioning issue will often be strategic purpose: this will not necessarily just be profit, but might include objectives such as independence, family control, handing over to the next generation and maybe even a pleasant lifestyle. The range of strategic choices is likely to be narrower: for a small business, acquisitions may not be affordable, though they may have to decide whether to allow themselves to be acquired. Some issues of strategy in action will be different, for example strategic change processes will not involve the same challenges as for large, complex organisations.

- *Multinational corporations.* In this context, positioning in a complex global marketplace will be very important. Each significant geographical market may call for a separate analysis of the business environment. Likewise, operating in many different countries will raise positioning issues of culture: variations in national culture imply different demands in the marketplace and different managerial styles internally. Strategic choices are likely to be dominated by international strategy questions about which geographical markets to serve. The scale and geographical reach of most multinationals point to significant issues for strategy-in-action, particularly those of organisational structure and strategic change.

- *Public sector and not-for-profits.* Positioning issues of competitive advantage will be important even in these contexts, but have a different flavour. Charitable not-for-profits typically compete for funds from donors; public-sector organisations, such as schools and hospitals, often compete on measures such as quality or service. The positioning issue of purpose is likely to be very important too. In the absence of a clear, focused objective such as profit, purpose in the public sector and not-for-profits can be ambiguous and contentious. Strategic choice issues may be narrower than in the private sector: for example, there may be constraints on diversification. Strategy in action issues often need close attention, leadership and change typically being very challenging in large public-sector organisations.

In short, while drawing on the same basic principles, strategy analysis is likely to vary in focus across different contexts. As the next section will indicate, it is often helpful therefore to apply different lenses to strategy problems.

1.6.2 Exploring strategy through different 'strategy lenses'

Exploring means looking for new and different things. Exploring strategy involves searching for new angles on strategic problems. A comprehensive assessment of an organisation's strategy needs more than one perspective. We introduce 'the strategy lenses' as distinct, theoretically-informed perspectives on strategy. **The strategy lenses are ways of looking at strategy issues differently in order to generate additional insights.** Different perspectives will help you criticise prevailing approaches and raise new issues or solutions. Thus, although drawn from academic theory, the lenses should also be highly practical in the job of doing strategy.

The four lenses are described fully at the end of Part I, after you have had a chance to take on board some key strategy frameworks for analysing strategic position. We shall return to them as well through brief *commentaries* at the end of Parts II and III. The following is therefore just a brief introduction to the lenses:

- *Strategy as design* views strategy development as 'designed' in the abstract, as an architect might design a building using pens, rulers and paper. Taking a design lens to a strategic problem means valuing hard facts and objectivity. It's about being systematic, analytical and logical.

- *Strategy as experience* recognises that an organisation's future strategy is often heavily influenced by its experience and that of its managers. Taken-for-granted assumptions and ways of doing things, embedded in people's personal experience and in organisational culture, will drive strategy. Strategy is likely to build on rules of thumb, appeals to precedent, standard fixes, biases and routines of key decision-makers.

- *Strategy as variety.*[19] Neither of the above lenses is likely to uncover radical new ideas in strategy as a design approach risks being too rigid and top-down and experience builds too much on the past. The variety lens sees strategy as emergent from within and around organisations as new ideas bubble up through an unpredictable process in response to an uncertain and changing environment.

- *Strategy as discourse* focuses attention on the ways managers use language to frame strategic problems, make strategy proposals, debate issues and then finally communicate strategic decisions. Strategy discourse becomes a tool for managers to shape 'objective' strategic analyses in their favour and to gain influence, power and legitimacy – strategy 'talk' matters.

None of these lenses is likely to offer a complete view of a strategic situation. The point of the lenses is to encourage the exploration of different perspectives: first from one point of view and then from another. This might help in recognising how otherwise logical strategic initiatives might be held back by cultural experience, unexpected ideas and self-interested strategy discourse.

SUMMARY

- Strategy is the *long-term direction* of an organisation.

- The work of strategy is to define and express the purpose of an organisation through its *mission*, *vision*, *values* and *objectives*.

- Ideally a *strategy statement* should include an organisation's *goals*, *scope* of activities and the *advantages* or *capabilities* it brings to these goals and activities.

- *Corporate-level strategy* is concerned with an organisation's overall scope; *business-level strategy* is concerned with how to compete; and *functional strategy* is concerned with how corporate- and business-level strategies are actually delivered.

- The *Exploring Strategy* Framework has three major elements: understanding the *strategic position*, making *strategic choices* for the future and managing *strategy in action*.

- Strategy work is done by *managers* throughout an organisation, as well as specialist *strategic planners* and *strategy consultants*.

- Research on strategy *context*, *content* and *process* shows how the analytical perspectives of economics, finance, sociology and psychology can all provide practical insights for approaching strategy issues.

- Although the fundamentals of strategy may be similar, strategy varies by *organisational context*, for example, small business, multinational or public sector.

- Strategic issues can be viewed critically from a variety of perspectives, as exemplified by the four *strategy lenses* of *design*, *experience*, *variety* and *discourse*.

WORK ASSIGNMENTS

✻ Denotes more advanced work assignments.
* Refers to a case study in the Text and Cases edition.

1.1 Drawing on Figure 1.2 as a guide, write a strategy statement for an organisation of your choice (for example, the Airbnb end of chapter case, or your university), drawing on strategy materials in the organisation's annual report or website.

1.2 Using the *Exploring Strategy* Framework of Figure 1.3, map key issues relating to strategic position, strategic choices and strategy in action for either the Airbnb or Glastonbury* cases, or an organisation with which you are familiar (for example, your university).

1.3 Go to the website of one of the major strategy consultants such as Bain, the Boston Consulting Group or McKinsey & Co. (see reference 11 below). What does the website tell you about the nature of strategy consulting work? Would you enjoy that work?

1.4✻ Using Figure 1.3 as a guide, show how the elements of strategic management differ in:

(a) a small or family business (e.g. Adnams*)

(b) a large multinational business (e.g. SABMiller or AB InBev in the Megabrew* case, Kraft Foods in the Mondelez* case)

(c) a non-profit organisation (e.g. Aurizon or King Faisal Hospital*).

RECOMMENDED KEY READINGS

It is always useful to read around a topic. As well as the specific references below, we particularly highlight:

- Two stimulating overviews of strategic thinking in general, aimed particularly at practicing managers, are C. Montgomery, *The Strategist: Be the Leader your Business Needs*, Harper Business, 2012; and R. Rumelt, *Good Strategy/Bad Strategy: the Difference and Why it Matters*, Crown Business, 2011.

- Two accessible articles on what strategy is, and might not be, are M. Porter, 'What is strategy?', *Harvard Business Review*, November–December 1996, pp. 61–78; and F. Fréry, 'The fundamental dimensions of strategy', *MIT Sloan Management Review*, vol. 48, no. 1 (2006), pp. 71–75.

- For contemporary developments in strategy practice, consult business newspapers such as the *Financial Times, Les Echos* and the *Wall Street Journal* and business magazines such as *Business Week, The Economist, L'Expansion* and *Manager-Magazin*. Several of these have well-informed Asian editions. See also the websites of the leading strategy consulting firms: www.mckinsey.com; www.bcg.com; and www.bain.com.

REFERENCES

1. The question 'What is strategy?' is discussed in R. Whittington, *What Is Strategy – and Does it Matter?*, International Thomson, 1993/2000; and M.E. Porter, 'What is strategy?', *Harvard Business Review*, November–December 1996, pp. 61–78.

2. T. Zenger, 'What is the theory of your firm?', *Harvard Business Review*, June 2013, pp. 72–80.

3. Cynthia A. Montgomery, 'Putting leadership back into strategy', *Harvard Business Review*, January 2008, pp. 54–60.

4. See J. Collins and J. Porras, *Built to Last: Successful Habits of Visionary Companies*, Harper Business, 2002.

5. J. Collins and J. Porras, 'Building your company's vision', *Harvard Business Review*, September–October 1996, pp. 65–77.

6. See Sayan Chatterjee, 'Core objectives: clarity in designing strategy', *California Management Review*, vol. 47, no. 2 (2005), pp. 33–49. For some advantages of ambiguity, see J. Sillince, P. Jarzabkowski and D. Shaw, 'Shaping strategic action through the rhetorical construction and exploitation of ambiguity', *Organization Science*, vol. 22, no. 2 (2011), pp. 1–21.

7. For example, see B. Bartkus, M. Glassman and B. McAfee, 'Mission statements: are they smoke and mirrors?', *Business Horizons*, vol. 43, no. 6 (2000), pp. 23–8.

8. D. Collis and M. Rukstad, 'Can you say what your strategy is?' *Harvard Business Review*, April 2008, pp. 63–73.

9. F. Westley, 'Middle managers and strategy: microdynamics of inclusion', *Strategic Management Journal*, vol. 11, no. 5 (1990), pp. 337–51.

10. For insights about in-house strategy roles, see D. N. Angwin, S. Paroutis and S. Mitson, 'Connecting up strategy: are strategy directors a missing link?' *California Management Review*, vol. 51, no. 3 (2009), pp. 74–94.

11. The major strategy consulting firms have a wealth of information on strategy careers and strategy in general: see www.mckinsey.com; www.bcg.com; www.bain.com.

12. University careers advisers can usually provide good advice on strategy consulting and strategic planning opportunities. See also www.vault.com.

13. For reviews of the contemporary state of strategy as a discipline, see J. Mahoney and A. McGahan, 'The field of strategic management within the evolving science of strategic organization', *Strategic Organization*, vol. 5, no. 1 (2007), pp. 79–99; and R. Whittington, 'Big strategy/small strategy', *Strategic Organization*, vol. 10, no. 3 (2012), pp. 263–68.

14. See M.E. Porter, 'The Five Competitive Forces that shape strategy', *Harvard Business Review*, January 2008, pp. 57–91.

15. The classic statement of the resource-based view is J. Barney, 'Firm resources and sustained competitive advantage', *Journal of Management*, vol. 17, no. 1 (1991), pp. 91–120.

16. A recent review of strategy process research is H. Sminia, 'Process research in strategy formation: theory, methodology and relevance', *International Journal of Management Reviews*, vol. 11, no. 1 (2009), pp. 97–122.

17. Psychological influences on strategy are explored in a special issue of the *Strategic Management Journal*, edited by T. Powell, D. Lovallo and S. Fox: 'Behavioral strategy', vol. 31, no. 13 (2011).

18. For a review of strategy-as-practice research, see E. Vaara and R. Whittington, 'Strategy-as-practice: taking social practices seriously', *Academy of Management Annals*, vol. 6, no. 1 (2012), pp. 285–336.

19. In earlier editions, this lens was called the 'ideas lens'.

The rise of a unicorn – Airbnb

Duncan Angwin

Airbnb logo
Source: Russell Hart/Alamy Images.

A unicorn is a mythical animal that has been described since antiquity as a horse with a large pointed spiral horn. Legend has it unicorns are very rare and difficult to tame. It is a name that has been adopted by the US venture capital industry to denote a start-up company whose valuation exceeds $1bn (£0.6bn, €0.75bn). Airbnb, founded in 2007, was one of these rare and valuable unicorns, already valued at $25bn in 2015. How could this start-up become so successful, so fast?

Origins

The original founders of Airbnb, Joe Gebbia and Brian Chesky, first met at Rhode Island School of Design. Five years later, both aged 27, they were struggling to pay their rent when a design conference came to San Francisco. All the hotels were fully booked, so they set up a simple website with pictures of their loft-turned-lodging space – complete with three air mattresses on the floor and the promise of a home-cooked breakfast in the morning. This site got them their first three paying guests at $80 each. It dawned on them this could be the start of something big. They both wanted to be entrepreneurs and Brian already had some experience having designed a cushion for back sufferers and built a website.[1] Next day they created a website, www.airbedandbreakfast.com.

They decided to target conferences and festivals across America, getting local people to list their rooms on a website created by former flatmate and computer programmer, Nathan Blecharczyk. In the summer of 2008, Barack Obama was due to speak in Denver at the Democratic Party National Convention. Eighty thousand people were expected to attend and Joe and Brian thought there would be a shortage of hotel rooms. They rushed to complete their website in time and recorded 800 listings in one week. However, it did not make any money. To survive they had to make use of their entrepreneurial skills, buying cereal in bulk and designing packaging such as 'Obama's O's' and 'Cap'n McCain' cereal; jokey references to the two Presidential candidates of the year. However, they soon added a payment facility to their website allowing them to charge up to 15 per cent of the booking (the host pays 3 per cent and the traveller between 6 and 12 per cent). By April 2009, they were breaking even.

Growth

Attracting funding for their start-up was not easy. Investors saw Gebbia and Cesky purely as designers, which did not fit the traditional start-up profile. Funders thought there would not be much demand for listings that mostly advertised sleeping on airbeds.

Nonetheless, in 2009 Airbnb received its first funding of $20,000 from angel investor, Paul Graham, co-founder of Y Combinator (a start-up mentoring programme), who was impressed with their inventiveness and tenacity. The company was renamed Airbnb and it provided an app and website that connects people seeking lodging with renters who have listed their personal houses, apartments, guest rooms on either platform. Further funding followed: in November 2010 Airbnb raised an additional $7.2m. This allowed the company to expand to 8000 cities worldwide, to increase the number of employees to 500 and to move out of the founders' flat – where staff had been making sales calls from the bathroom and holding conferences in the kitchen – to offices in the design district of San Francisco. The early history of Airbnb is illustrated in Figure 1.

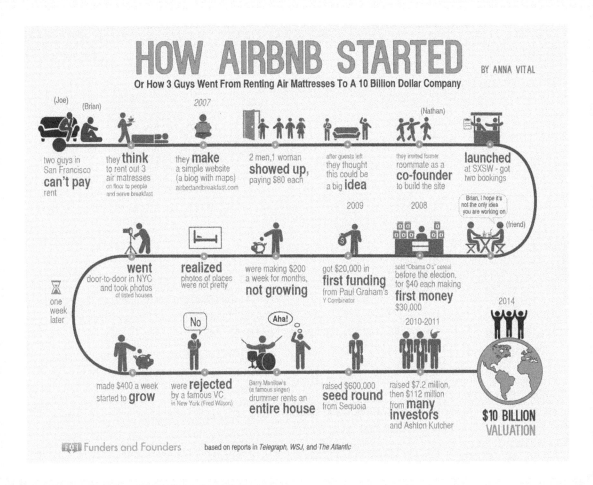

Figure 1 Airbnb early growth story

Source: Funders and Founders, Inc., image courtesy of Anna Vital.

However, in 2010 Airbnb was experiencing sluggish listings in New York. Joe and Brian booked spaces with 24 hosts and flew out to try to understand the problem. They soon realised hosts were doing a very poor job of presenting their properties. They immediately rented a $5000 camera and took as many photos of New York apartments as possible. Listings in the city suddenly doubled. From there on hosts could automatically schedule a professional photographer. This was an immediate hit and by 2012 there were 20,000 freelance photographers being employed by Airbnb around the world. The photos also built trust for guests as they verified addresses. The company also introduced Airbnb Social Connections, which leverages users' social graphs via Facebook Connect. This shows whether friends have stayed with the host or are friends with the host and it allows guests to search for hosts based on other characteristics, like alma mater. Again this reassured potential guests.

Further venture funding of $112m was received in July 2011. Airbnb expanded through acquisitions with a deal in Germany and the purchase of their largest UK-based competitor Crashpadder just in time for the 2012 Summer Olympics in London. Offices were opened in Paris, Barcelona and Milan. Airbnb's growth was explosive with a higher valuation than Hyatt and Wyndham hotel groups by 2014 and more guest nights booked than Hilton Hotels (see Figure 2). By 2016 Airbnb was valued at $25bn – more than any other hotel group. The company justified its valuation by claiming that, when its price ($25bn) to sales ratio of 27.8 (based on estimated sales of $900m for 2015) is divided by its high growth rate of 113 per cent per year, the resulting value for the group is broadly in line with the sector.[2] Airbnb forecasts $10bn of revenues by 2020, with $3bn of profits before tax.

Airbnb proved attractive to guests and hosts as its listings were far superior to others available at the time, such as Craigslist – they were more personal, with better descriptions and nicer photos that made them more appealing for people searching for vacation rentals. The rooms provided by Airbnb were also cheaper than equivalent ones at hotels and had more of a personal flavour. For instance, in a recent stay in Paris a user noted the host

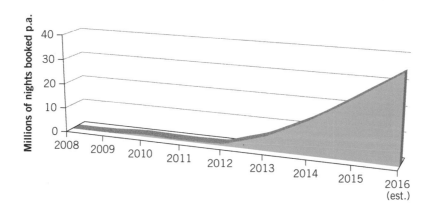

Figure 2 Guest nights booked

had left a selection of food in the refrigerator, a bottle of wine on the counter for her guests and a welcoming note suggesting good places nearby to eat out and convenience shops. Staying in another person's apartment makes the visitor feel far more at home than an anonymous hotel room. For many young guests and hosts, Airbnb fitted into the contemporary sharing culture exemplified by Easy car club, where users can rent their car to others, and Girl Meets Dress, that allows girls to borrow and lend their dresses for special occasions. For hosts, rents provide a source of income to help pay for soaring accommodation costs in many major cities.

Managing growth

Founder and CEO Brian Chesky penned a memo in 2013 to his top management team, as follows:[3]

Hey team,

Our next team meeting is dedicated to Core Values, which are essential to building our culture. It occurred to me that before this meeting, I should write you a short letter on why culture is so important to [co-founders] Joe, Nate, and me.

. . . In 2012, we invited Peter Thiel [a major investor] to our office. This was late last year, and we were in the Berlin room showing him various metrics. Midway through the conversation, I asked him what was the single most important piece of advice he had for us.

He replied, 'Don't f*** up the culture.'

This wasn't what we were expecting from someone who just gave us $150m. I asked him to elaborate on this. He said one of the reasons he invested in us was our

culture. But he had a somewhat cynical view that it was practically inevitable once a company gets to a certain size to 'f*** it up.'

Accordingly, the company began to manage its culture more deliberately. For example, Joe Gebbia had become concerned that as the company grew, it had become less open to dialogue. To encourage more discussion, he invented the notion of 'elephants, dead fish and vomit'. As Gebbia explains: 'Elephants are the big things in the room that nobody is talking about, dead fish are the things that happened a few years ago that people can't get over, and vomit is that sometimes people just need to get something off their mind and you need someone to just sit there and listen'.[4] All three need to be aired. Airbnb also established a series of annual meetings called One Airbnb, bringing together employees (called 'Airfam') from all around the world to the San Francisco base for four-day conferences at which everyone can meet the founders, discuss strategy and also talk about both their work roles and their hobbies. The company has 'ground control' staff in every office in the world dedicated to making the company culture 'come alive', organising pop-up birthday celebrations, anniversary parties or baby showers. The company is rigorous in its recruitment policy, committed to hiring 'missionaries, not mercenaries'.

At the same time, founders Joe Gebbia, Brian Chesky and Nathan Blecharczyk had begun to ask themselves again: 'What is our mission? What is the big idea that truly defines Airbnb?'. As they recalled in their own words: 'It turns out the answer was right in front of us. For so long, people thought Airbnb was about renting houses. But really, we're about home. You see, a house is just a space, but a home is where you belong. And what makes this global community so special is that for the very first time, you can belong anywhere. That is the idea at the core of our company.'[5]

Airbnb in 2016

In 2016, Airbnb had over 1.5 million listings in 34,000 cities in 192 countries, with 40 million total guests. Anyone anywhere in the world can list spare space from a room to a tree house, from a castle to an island in Fiji, with prices ranging from $50 to $2000 per night. Airbnb received 30 million page views per month. The headquarters' walls were covered with world maps dotted with hundreds of coloured pins, charting world domination. Airbnb was so popular that one of their rooms was booked every two seconds.[6]

The company was now focused on the whole travel trip with an emphasis on delivering local experiences. This focus on hospitality was not just about where you stay, but what you do – and whom you do it with – while you're there. To this end they introduced Airbnb Neighbourhoods and local lounges, partnering with local coffee shops that can offer free wifi, a comfortable setting and local guidebooks. They also acquired a small start-up that connects guests with locals who can answer their questions. They also offer cleaning services.

Airbnb was providing a strong challenge to hotels with prices 30–80 per cent lower than local operators. San Francisco hotels were having to slash prices to protect their occupancy rates. Incumbents in the industry fought back by arguing Airbnb were dangerous and unsafe in terms of health and safety and quality assurance as it was unregulated. Although one must have a permit to rent for under 30 days, San Francisco residents were still illegally listing personal homes and apartments. Similar problems were being experienced in New York where an 'illegal hotel law' was passed preventing people from subletting apartments for less than 29 days. There was also a question mark over hosts not paying tax on earnings.

During 2016, Airbnb redesigned its website and apps with subtle animations and flashier imagery. This huge rebranding represented a transition from a hotel service to a lifestyle brand. Airbnb wanted their logo to be seen on a variety of products, houses and businesses, so people understood that owners supported their ideal and their brand. Airbnb's focus was now firmly on 'belonging'. This rebranding may not have been before time, as competition

was brewing in the US from vacation rental site HomeAway Inc. (owned by Expedia), Roomorama, HouseTrip, Flipkey and Travel Advisor holiday rentals. Indeed, websites have sprung up such as www.airbnbhell.com that list a string of internet accommodation providers. Nonetheless, at the time of writing Airbnb was rumoured to be the hottest IPO (an initial public offering of its stock to investors) tip for 2016.

References
1. Salter, J. (2012) 'Airbnb: The story behind the $1.3bn room-letting website', *The Telegraph*, 7 September; Lee, A. (2013) 'Welcome to The Unicorn Club: learning from billion-dollar startups', *TechCrunch*, 2 November, https://techcrunch.com/2013/11/02/welcome-to-the-unicorn-club/
2. A ratio of price /sales to revenue growth rate gives Airbnb a figure of 24.6 against Marriott at 19.2, Wyndham at 34.1 and Expedia at 12.2 (Guest post, ' Why that crazy-high AirBnB valuation is fair, www.valuewalk.com, 1 January 2016).
3. https://medium.com/@bchesky/dont-fuck-up-the-culture-597cde9ee9d4\#.5wd5kwtdm.
4. B. Clune, 'How Airbnb is building its culture through belonging', *Culture Zine*.
5. http://blog.airbnb.com/belong-anywhere/.
6. Zacks.com, 'Investing in resting: is Airbnb a top 2016 IPO candidate?', 11 December 2015.

Questions

1 Sticking to the 35-word limit suggested by Collis and Rukstad in Section 1.2.3, what strategy statement would you propose for Airbnb?

2 Carry out a 'three-horizons' analysis (Section 1.2.1) of Airbnb, in terms of both existing activities and possible future ones. How might this analysis affect its future strategic direction?

3 Using the headings of environments, strategic capability, strategic purpose and culture seen in Section 1.3.1, identify key positioning issues for Airbnb and consider their relative importance.

4 Following on from the previous questions and making use of Section 1.3.2, what alternative strategies do you see for Airbnb?

5 Converting good strategic thinking into action can be a challenge: examine how Airbnb has achieved this by considering the elements seen in Section 1.3.3?

2

BUSINESS STRATEGY AND MODELS

2.1 INTRODUCTION

This chapter is about two fundamental strategic choices: what business strategy and what business model should a company, business unit or other organisation adopt in its market? Business strategy questions are fundamental both to stand-alone small businesses and to all the many business units that typically make up large diversified organisations. Business strategies are about how to compete in a marketplace so that a restaurant for instance has to decide a range of issues such as menus, décor and prices in the light of local competition from other restaurants. Similarly, large diversified corporations typically include many decentralised 'strategic business units' in different product or market areas each with its own business strategy depending on the specific needs of their served market. A **strategic business unit (SBU) supplies goods or services for a distinct domain of activity** (sometimes these SBUs are called 'divisions' or 'profit centres'). For example, Nestlé's ice-cream SBU has to decide how to compete against smaller and local artisanal companies with new imaginative flavours and different customer focus, distribution channels and pricing. These kinds of business strategy issues are distinct from the question as to whether Nestlé should own an ice-cream business in the first place: this is a matter of corporate strategy, the subject of Chapter 8.

Another important choice is to identify the relationship between the value created for customers and other participants, the organisational activities that create this value and how the organisation and other stakeholders can capture value from this – a *business model*. For instance, Amazon was a pioneer with its e-commerce business model that contrasted with bricks-and-mortar retailers. It involved a different customer offering, arrangement of its activities and structure of revenues and costs compared to the traditional retailing model. Over time, however, business models get established and many other retailers also entered into e-commerce. This shows that organisations need to consider what business model to build on; established or new ones or both.

Business strategy and business models are not just relevant to the private business sector. Charities and public-sector organisations also compete and have business models. Thus charities compete between each other for support from donors. Public-sector organisations also need to be 'competitive' against comparable organisations in order to satisfy their stakeholders, secure their funding and protect themselves from alternative suppliers from the private sector. Schools compete in terms of examination results, while hospitals compete in terms of waiting times, treatment survival rates and so on. Likewise, these sectors need to consider what value is created for whom and how organisational activities contribute to this in a business model. Although some of the detailed implications may vary between sectors, wherever comparison is possible with other similar organisations, basic principles of business strategy and models are likely to be relevant. Very few organisations can afford to be demonstrably inferior to peers. Most have to make choices on key competitive variables such as costs, prices and quality.

Figure 2.1 shows the main three themes around business strategy that provide the structure for the rest of the chapter:

- *Generic competitive strategies,* including cost leadership, differentiation, focus and hybrid strategies.
- *Interactive strategies,* building on the notion of generic strategies to consider interaction with competitors, especially in *hypercompetitive environments,* and including both *cooperative strategies* and *game theory.*
- *Business models,* including the three basic components of *value creation, value configuration* and *value capture.*

Figure 2.1 Business strategy

2.2 GENERIC COMPETITIVE STRATEGIES

This section introduces the competitive element of business strategy, with cooperation addressed particularly in Section 2.4. **Competitive strategy is concerned with how a company, business unit or organisation achieves competitive advantage in its domain of activity.** Competitive strategy therefore involves issues such as costs, product and service features and branding. In turn, **competitive advantage is about how a company, business unit or organisation creates value for its users which is both greater than the costs of supplying them and superior to that of rivals.** Competitive advantages should underpin competitive strategies. There are two important features of competitive advantage. To be *competitive* at all, an organisation must ensure that customers see sufficient value that they are prepared to pay more than the costs of supply. To have an *advantage,* the organisation must be able to create greater value than competitors. In the absence of a competitive advantage, an organisation's competitive strategy is always vulnerable to competitors with better products or offering lower prices.

Michael Porter[1] argues that there are two fundamental means of achieving competitive advantage. An organisation can have structurally lower *costs* than its competitors. Or it can have products or services that are *differentiated* from competitors' products or services in ways that are so valued by customers that it can charge higher prices that cover the additional costs of the differentiation. In defining competitive strategies, Porter adds a further dimension based on the *scope* of customers that the business chooses to serve. Businesses can choose to focus on narrow customer segments, for example a particular demographic group such as the youth market. Alternatively, they can adopt a broad scope, targeting customers across a range of characteristics such as age, wealth or geography.

Porter's distinctions between cost, differentiation and scope define a set of 'generic' strategies: in other words, basic types of strategy that hold across many kinds of business situations. These three generic strategies are illustrated in Figure 2.2. In the top left-hand corner is a strategy of *cost leadership,* as exemplified in the British food and grocery market by retailers such as Lidl. Waitrose, in contrast, pursues a strategy of *differentiation*, offering

Figure 2.2 Three generic strategies

a range of quality, fresh and environmentally-friendly products focused on the upper market with relatively higher prices. Porter distinguishes between cost focus and differentiation focus, but for him narrow scope is such a distinctive fundamental principle that these two are merely variations on the same basic theme of narrowness. For example, delicatessens target a relatively narrow group of higher-end customers with their high food quality and provenance. They thus often achieve a higher price for their distinctive products through their *differentiation focus* strategy. On the other hand, the product lines of the major supermarkets, like Tesco, target shoppers who are simply looking for good-value standard products for their families, a *cost focus* strategy. The rest of this section discusses these three generic strategies in more detail.

2.2.1 Cost-leadership strategy

Cost-leadership strategy involves becoming the lowest-cost organisation in a domain of activity. For example, Ryanair pursues a relentless low-cost strategy in the European airline industry. The airline saves costs in virtually every aspect of its operation from purchasing a single type of aircraft (without reclining seats) to selling tickets primarily online (over 90 per cent of sales) to low employee costs (second lowest in Europe). There are four key *cost drivers* that can help deliver cost leadership, as follows:

- *Input costs* are often very important, for example labour or raw materials. Many companies seek competitive advantage through locating their labour-intensive operations in countries with low labour costs. Examples might be service call centres in India or manufacturing in South East Asia and China. Location close to raw material sources can also be advantageous, as for example the Brazilian steel producer CSN which benefits from its own local iron-ore facilities.

- *Economies of scale* refer to how increasing scale usually reduces the average costs of operation over a particular time period, perhaps a month or a year. Economies of scale are important wherever there are high fixed costs. Fixed costs are those costs necessary for a

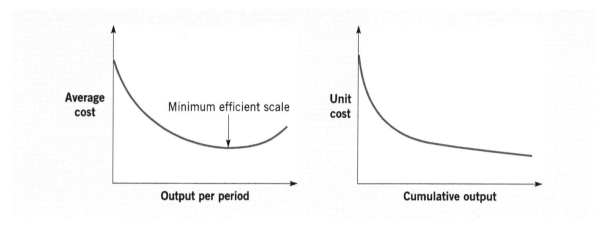

Figure 2.3 Economies of scale and the experience curve

level of output: for example, a pharmaceutical manufacturer typically needs to do extensive R&D before it produces a single pill. Economies of scale come from spreading these fixed costs over high levels of output: the average cost due to an expensive R&D project halves when output increases from one million to two million units. Economies of scale in purchasing can also reduce input costs. The large airlines, for example, are able to negotiate steep discounts from aircraft manufacturers. For the cost-leader, it is important to reach the output level equivalent to the *minimum efficient scale*. Note, though, that *diseconomies of scale* are possible. Large volumes of output that require special overtime payments to workers or involve the neglect of equipment maintenance can soon become very expensive. As to the left in Figure 2.3, therefore, the economies of scale curve is typically somewhat U-shaped, with the average cost per unit actually increasing beyond a certain point.

- *Experience*[2] can be a key source of cost efficiency. The *experience curve* implies that the cumulative experience gained by an organisation with each unit of output leads to reductions in unit costs (see Figure 2.3 to the right). For example, for many electronic components per unit costs can drop as much as 95 per cent every time the accumulated volume doubles. There is no time limit: simply the more experience an organisation has in an activity, the more efficient it gets at doing it. The efficiencies are basically of two sorts. First, there are gains in labour productivity as staff simply learn to do things more cheaply over time (this is the specific *learning curve* effect). Second, costs are saved through more efficient designs or equipment as experience shows what works best. The experience curve has three important implications for business strategy. First, entry timing into a market is important: early entrants into a market will have experience that late entrants do not yet have and so will gain a cost advantage. Second, it is important to gain and hold market share, as companies with higher market share have more 'cumulative experience' simply because of their greater volumes. Finally, although the gains from experience are typically greatest at the start, as indicated by the steep initial curve to the right in Figure 2.3, improvements normally continue over time. Opportunities for cost reduction are theoretically endless. Figure 2.3 compares the experience curve (to the right) and economies of scale (to the left) in order to underline the contrast here. Unlike scale, where diseconomies appear beyond a certain point, the experience curve implies at worst a flattening of the rate of cost reduction. However, completely new production technologies can potentially introduce even steeper experience effects and further improved cost savings.

- *Product/process design* also influences cost. Efficiency can be 'designed in' at the outset. For example, engineers can choose to build a product from cheap standard components rather than expensive specialised components. Organisations can choose to interact with customers exclusively through cheap web-based methods, rather than via telephone or stores. Organisations can also tailor their offerings in order to meet the most important customer needs, saving money by ignoring others. In designing a product or service, it is important to recognise *whole-life costs*: in other words, the costs to the customer not just of purchase but of subsequent use and maintenance. In the photocopier market, for example, Canon eroded Xerox's advantage (which was built on service and a support network) by designing a copier that needed far less servicing.

Porter underlines two tough requirements for cost-based strategies. First of all, the principle of competitive advantage indicates that a business's cost structure needs to be *lowest* cost (i.e. lower than all competitors'). Having the second-lowest cost structure implies a competitive disadvantage against somebody. Competitors with higher costs than the cost-leader are always at risk of being undercut on price, especially in market downturns. For businesses competing on a cost basis, cost leadership is always more secure than being second or third in terms of costs. The US financial investments company Vanguard is a good example of this as discussed in Illustration 2.1 (see also Illustration 6.3).

The second requirement is that low cost should not be pursued in total disregard for quality. To sell its products or services, the cost-leader has to be able to meet market standards. For example, low-cost Chinese car producers exporting to Western markets need to offer not only cars that are cheap, but cars that meet acceptable norms in terms of style, safety, service network, reliability, resale value and other important characteristics. Cost-leaders have two options here:

- *Parity* (in other words, equivalence) with competitors in product or service features valued by customers. Parity allows the cost-leader to charge the same prices as the average competitor in the marketplace, while translating its cost advantage wholly into extra profit (as in the second column of Figure 2.4). The Brazilian steel producer CSN, with its cheap iron-ore sources, is able to charge the average price for its steel, and take the cost difference in greater profit.

Figure 2.4 Costs, prices and profits for generic strategies

ILLUSTRATION 2.1   Vanguard's low-cost strategy comes to Europe

The US company Vanguard pioneered a distinct low-cost strategy in the mutual fund industry and is now exporting it worldwide.

Mutual funds are managed by investment companies that raise money from multiple customers and invest the money in a group of assets (stocks, bonds, money market instruments, etc.). Each customer, often as part of a retirement plan, then owns shares that represent a portion of the holdings of the fund. They are charged an annual fee or 'expense ratio' that covers investment advisory fees, administrative costs, distribution fees and other operating expenses. The traditional way of competing in the industry was by actively managed and differentiated investments that tried to generate as high returns as possible and thus being able to charge higher fees. The emphasis was on the business performance end of the business by offering differentiated funds with higher returns. Vanguard instead focused on the cost end of the business and offered customers considerably lower annual fees and costs. Most comparisons showed that Vanguard's fees or expense ratios were 65–80 per cent less than the industry average depending on investment asset. The company also launched the industry's first index mutual fund that passively followed a stock market index without ambitions to generate a better performance than the market, but which outperformed many actively managed funds.

Vanguard has started to export its low-cost focus to Europe, and their non-US assets have more than doubled in the last six years, reaching over $90bn (€68bn, £54bn) in Europe. 'Lowering the cost of investing is in our DNA,' blogged Tom Rampulla, former head of Vanguard Europe. Their low-cost strategy involved several components. First, unlike competitors it did not need to make a profit. Tim Buckley, chief investment officer explained:

'We are not a listed company. We're a mutual company. We're owned by our clients. So when we make a profit, we have two choices. We can roll that profit back into the business or we can pay it out to our owners, our clients, in the form of lower expenses. Over the years we have lowered expenses and that has attracted more clients.'[1]

Second, Vanguard distributed their funds directly to customers and did not need to pay commissions of around eight per cent to brokers. Third, the company had internalised investment advisory functions of the funds at cost instead of using external investment advisors that would charge a premium. Fourth, Vanguard relied on a no-nonsense thrifty organisational culture where managers were incentivised to control cost and no one, not even senior executives, flew first class. Fifth, the company had only a few retail centres and spent less on advertising than anyone else in the industry. Last, but not least, as one of the largest asset managers globally they gained large economies of scale.

By 2015, the next step for Vanguard was to do to the financial advisory services industry what they had done to the mutual fund industry. Based on webcam chats and other cost reductions, the aim was to offer advisory services at a fraction of the cost of competitors. They would charge annually 0.3 per cent on assets compared to the industry average of one per cent, according to Vanguard CEO Bill McNabb:[2]

'Can we provide really super-high quality advice at a very low cost and do that in a very large way, and change the market? I think we can. We continue to think of our primary mission to reduce the complexity and cost of investing across the board.'

Sources: (1) D. Oakley, *Financial Times*, 4 March 2015. (2) S. Foley, *Financial Times*, 8 December 2014.

Questions

1 What type of competitive strategy, low-cost, differentiation, focus or hybrid, would you suggest as a way of competing with Vanguard?

2 Using webcam chats is one approach to lower costs in financial advisory services as indicated above. What other ways could there be to lower costs to support a low-cost strategy?

- *Proximity* (closeness) to competitors in terms of features. Where a competitor is sufficiently close to competitors in terms of product or service features, customers may only require small cuts in prices to compensate for the slightly lower quality. As in the third column in Figure 2.4, the proximate cost-leader still earns better profits than the average competitor because its lower price eats up only a part of its cost advantage. This proximate cost-leadership strategy might be the option chosen initially by Chinese car manufacturers in export markets, for example.

2.2.2 Differentiation strategy

The principal alternative to cost leadership is differentiation.[3] **Differentiation strategy involves uniqueness along some dimension that is sufficiently valued by customers to allow a price premium.** For example, German manufacturer Miele pursues a differentiation strategy in the domestic appliance industry. Their European manufactured, high-quality and durable dishwashers, washing machines and stoves are targeted towards higher income households at a price premium. Relevant points of differentiation vary between markets. Within each market too, businesses may differentiate along different dimensions. Thus in clothing retail, competitors may differentiate by store size, locations or fashion. In cars, competitors may differentiate by safety, style or fuel efficiency. Where there are many alternative dimensions that are valued by customers, it is possible to have many different types of differentiation strategy in a market. Thus, even at the same top end of the car market, BMW and Mercedes differentiate in different ways, the first typically with a sportier image, the second with more conservative values. In brief, there are various aspects to consider in pursuing a differentiation strategy and below are three primary differentiation drivers to consider:

- *Product and service attributes*. Certain product attributes can provide *better or unique features* than comparable products or services for the customer. For example, the Dyson vacuum cleaner with its unique technology provides customers with a better suction performance compared to competitors. The possibilities of product differentiation are, however, virtually endless and only limited by the creativity of an organisation. They may include differences in colour, design, speed, style, taste, etc. For vacuum cleaners, other companies may, for example, differentiate themselves on the basis of user convenience or design rather than suction performance. Product innovation and introduction can also be a basis of differentiation. Apple has been able to charge considerable premiums by continuously launching novel products with superior technologies, design and consumer interfaces, including the iPod, iPhone and iPad.

  In building a basis for differentiation it is vital to identify clearly the customer on whose needs the differentiation is based. This is not always straightforward, as discussed in Section 3.4.2. For example, for a newspaper business, the customers could be readers (who pay a purchase price), advertisers (who pay for advertising), or both. Finding a distinctive means of prioritising customers can be a valuable source of differentiation. Considering competitors' offerings is also important when identifying a basis for differentiation and the strategy canvas provides one means of mapping various kinds of differentiation (see Section 3.4.3).

- *Customer relationships*. Besides more tangible differences in product and service characteristics, differentiation can rely on the relationship between the organisation providing the product and the customer. This often relates to how the product is perceived by the customer. The perceived value can increase through *customer services and responsiveness*. This can include distribution services, payment services or after-sales services among other things. For example, Zalando, Europe's leading online retailer for fashion and shoes, offers not only free shipping to the customer but free returns and a 'bill-me-later' service. Products can also be differentiated for the individual customer through *customisation*. This is the case for a variety of consumer goods from athletic shoes to cars, but also for business-to-business goods like enterprise software. For example, the German software company SAP not only sells its standardised software packages, but customises these to meet specific customer needs. Finally, *marketing and reputation,* including emotional and psychological aspects, that an organisation projects can be another basis for differentiation. Starbucks, for example, can charge a premium price for its coffee not only because of its product differences but also because of the ambiance and image that the company displays at its outlets. Building on brand image is common for products that otherwise are difficult to differentiate. This is a foundation for Coca Cola's differentiation strategy for example.

- *Complements.* Differentiation can also build on linkages to other products or services. The perceived value of some products can be significantly enhanced when consumed together with other product or service complements compared to consuming the product alone. This complementarity was discussed in Chapter 3 as these complements can be vital for the profit potential of an industry (see Section 3.2.6). Apple has created the complement services iTunes and App Store free of charge for the consumer, which differentiate its products (iPhone, iPad, etc.) with the possibility to charge a premium. Considering how customers benefit from consuming two products or services in tandem is thus another possible way to differentiate. More generally, this can be thought of as a way of bundling products and services together to increase the value for the customer.

There is an important condition for a successful differentiation strategy. Differentiation allows higher prices, but usually this comes at a cost. To create valuable differentiation typically involves additional investments, for example in R&D, branding or staff quality. The differentiator can expect that its costs will be higher than those of the average competitor. But, as in the fourth column of Figure 2.4, the differentiator needs to ensure that the additional costs of differentiation do not exceed the gains in price. It is easy to add on additional costs in ways that are not valued sufficiently by customers. The historic failures under British ownership of the luxury car companies Rolls-Royce and Bentley against top-end Mercedes cars are partly attributable to the expensive crafting of wood and leather interiors, the full cost of which even wealthy customers were not prepared to pay for. Just as cost-leaders should not neglect quality, so should differentiators attend closely to costs, especially in areas irrelevant to their sources of differentiation. Volvo's differentiation strategy in the Indian bus market in Illustration 2.2 also involved keeping an eye on costs besides differentiation.

2.2.3 Focus strategy

Porter distinguishes focus as the third generic strategy, based on competitive scope. A **focus strategy targets a narrow segment or domain of activity and tailors its products or services to the needs of that specific segment to the exclusion of others.** Focus strategies come in two variants, according to the underlying sources of competitive advantage, cost or differentiation. In air travel, Ryanair follows a *cost focus strategy,* targeting price-conscious travellers with no need for connecting flights. In the domestic detergent market, the Belgian company Ecover follows a *differentiation focus strategy*, gaining a price premium over rivals on account of its ecological cleaning products targeted at environmental conscious customers.

The focuser achieves competitive advantage by dedicating itself to serving its target segments better than others that are trying to cover a wider range of segments. Serving a broad

ILLUSTRATION 2.2   Volvo's different Indian buses

Volvo has a strategy to sell buses at nearly four times the prevailing market price.

The Indian bus market has long been dominated by two subsidiaries of major Indian conglomerates: Tata Motors and Ashok Leyland. They made simple coaches on a design that had hardly changed for decades. On top of a basic truck chassis, the two companies bolted a rudimentary coach body. Engines were a meagre 110–120 horsepower, and roared heartily as they hauled their loads up the steep roads. Mounted at the front, the heat from the over-strained engines would pervade the whole bus. Air conditioning was a matter of open windows, through which the dust and noise of the Indian roads would pour. Suspension was old-fashioned, guaranteeing a shaky ride on pot-holed roads. Bags were typically slung on the top of the bus, where they were easily soiled and at high risk of theft. But at least the buses were cheap, selling to local bus companies at around Rs 1.2m (€15,000, £12,000, $19,500).

In 1997, Swedish bus company Volvo entered, with buses priced at Rs 4m, nearly four times as much as local products. Akash Passey, Volvo's first Indian employee, commissioned a consultancy company to evaluate prospects. The consultancy company recommended that Volvo should not even try. Passey told the *Financial Times*: 'My response was simple – I took the report and went to the nearest dustbin and threw it in.' Passey entered the market in 2001 with the high-priced luxury buses.

Passey used the time to develop a distinctive strategy. His product had superior features. Volvo's standard engines were 240–250 hp and mounted at the back, ensuring a faster and quieter ride. Air conditioning was standard of course. The positioning of the engine and the specific bus design of the chassis meant a roomier interior, plus storage for bags internally. But Passey realised this would not be enough. He commented to the *Financial Times*: 'You had to do a lot of things to break the way business is done normally.'

Volvo offered post-sale maintenance services, increasing life expectancy of buses from three to ten years, and allowing bus operating companies to dispense with their own expensive maintenance workshops. Free training was given to drivers, so they drove more safely and took more care of their buses. The company advertised the benefits of the buses direct to customers in cinemas, rather than simply promoting them to the bus operators. Faster, smoother and more reliable travel allowed the bus operators to increase their ticket prices for the Volvo buses by 35 per cent.

Business people and the middle classes were delighted with the new Volvo services. Speedier, more comfortable journeys allowed them to arrive fresh for meetings and potentially to save the costs of overnight stays. Tata and Ashok Leyland both now produce their own luxury buses, with Mercedes and Isuzu following Volvo into the market. Nonetheless, the phrase 'taking a Volvo' has become synonymous with choosing a luxury bus service in India, rather as 'hoover' came to refer to any kind of vacuum cleaner.

A new state-of-the-art bus factory was opened in Bangalore 2008 and after further investments in 2012 it doubled the annual capacity to 1,500 buses per year. As Volvo's most efficient bus factory worldwide it started to export buses to Europe three years later. In 2016, Volvo continued its distinctive strategy and became the first bus company in India to manufacture and sell hybrid buses running on an electric motor and battery as well as diesel.

Sources: Adapted from J. Leahy, 'Volvo takes a lead in India', *Financial Times*, 31 August 2009; M. Lalatendu, 'Hybrid Volvo bus for Navi Mumbai', *The Hindu*, 15 February 2016.

Questions

1 Rank the elements of Passey's strategy for Volvo in order of importance. Could any have been dispensed with?

2 How sustainable is Volvo's luxury bus strategy?

range of segments can bring disadvantages in terms of coordination, compromise or inflexibility. Focus strategies are, therefore, able to seek out the weak spots of broad cost-leaders and differentiators:

- *Cost focusers* identify areas where broader cost-based strategies fail because of the added costs of trying to satisfy a wide range of needs. For instance, in the UK food retail market, Iceland Foods has a cost-focused strategy concentrated on frozen and chilled foods, reducing costs against discount food retailers with a wider product range and more diverse suppliers which have all the complexity of fresh foods and groceries as well as their own frozen and chilled food ranges.

- *Differentiation focusers* look for specific needs that broader differentiators do not serve so well. Focus on one particular need helps to build specialist knowledge and technology, increases commitment to service and can improve brand recognition and customer loyalty. For example, ARM Holdings dominates the world market for mobile phone chips, despite being only a fraction of the size of the leading microprocessor manufacturers, AMD and Intel, which also make chips for a wide range of computers.

Successful focus strategies depend on at least one of three key factors:

- *Distinct segment needs.* Focus strategies depend on the distinctiveness of segment needs. If segment distinctiveness erodes, it becomes harder to defend the segment against broader competitors. For example, Tesla Motors currently targets a narrow segment with its expensive premium electric vehicles. However, if the boundaries become blurred between Tesla's focus on electric cars used by affluent environmentally conscious consumers and electric cars used by general consumers it could become easier for competitors to also attack this distinctive niche.

- *Distinct segment value chains.* Focus strategies are strengthened if they have distinctive value chains that will be difficult or costly for rivals to construct. If the production processes and distribution channels are very similar, it is easy for a broad-based differentiator to push a specialised product through its own standardised value chain at a lower cost than a rival focuser. In detergents, Procter & Gamble cannot easily respond to the Belgian ecologically friendly cleaning products company Ecover because achieving the same environmental soundness would involve transforming its purchasing and production processes.

- *Viable segment economics.* Segments can easily become too small to serve economically as demand or supply conditions change. For example, changing economies of scale and greater competition have eliminated the traditional town-centre department stores from many smaller cities, with their wider ranges of different kinds of goods from hardware to clothing.

2.2.4 Hybrid strategy

Porter warned that managers face a crucial choice between the generic strategies of cost leadership, differentiation and focus. According to him, it would be unwise to blur this choice. As earlier, the lowest-cost competitor can always undercut the second lowest-cost competitor. For a company seeking advantage through low costs, therefore, it makes no sense to add extra costs by half-hearted efforts at differentiation. For a differentiator, it is self-defeating to make economies that jeopardise the basis for differentiation. For a focuser, it is dangerous to move outside the original specialised segment, because products or services tailored to one set of customers are likely to have inappropriate costs or features for the new target customers. Porter's argument was that managers are generally best to choose which generic strategy they are pursuing and then sticking to it. Otherwise there would be a danger of being *stuck in the middle,* doing no strategy well.

However, Porter's early argument for pure generic strategies was controversial and it has later been acknowledged that a hybrid type of strategy is possible under certain circumstances. A **hybrid strategy combines different generic strategies.** For example, American Southwest Airlines pursues a low-cost strategy with their budget and no-frills offering. However, its brand also signals differentiation based on convenience including frequent departures and friendly service. Another example in the airline industry is Singapore Airlines with a differentiation strategy based on passenger comfort, attentive personal service and amenities. This is, however, combined with a lowest-cost position among its key competitors based on low maintenance costs, standardisation and outsourcing of various activities. Some companies start out with one strategy that is later combined with another. McDonald's first followed a product differentiation strategy, but later its fast-food leader position allowed the company to emphasise scale and low costs as well.

As Porter himself acknowledges there may also be particular circumstances in which the strategies can be combined:[4]

- *Organisational separation.* It is possible for a company to create separate strategic business units (SBUs), each pursuing different generic strategies and with different cost structures. The challenge, however, is to prevent negative spill-overs from one SBU to another. For example, a company mostly pursuing differentiated strategies is liable to have high head office costs that the low-cost SBUs will also have to bear. On the other hand, a cheap cost-leader might damage the brand value of a sister SBU seeking differentiation. Because of these kinds of trade-offs, it can be very difficult to pursue different generic strategies within a single set of related businesses. Despite the success of Singapore Airlines, Europe's leading airline Lufthansa has struggled to combine its low-cost subsidiaries, Eurowings, with its traditional higher-service core business.

- *Technological or managerial innovation.* Sometimes technological innovations allow radical improvements in both cost and quality. Internet retailing reduces the costs of bookselling, at the same time as increasing differentiation by greater product range and, through online book reviews, better advice. Managerial innovations are capable of such simultaneous improvements too. The Japanese car manufacturers' introduction of Total Quality Management led to reductions in production line mistakes that both cut manufacturing costs and improved car reliability, a point of successful differentiation.

- *Competitive failures.* Where competitors are also stuck in the middle, there is less competitive pressure to remove competitive disadvantage. Equally, where a company dominates a particular market, competitive pressures for consistency with a single competitive strategy are reduced.

Hybrid strategies are, however, complex and should be pursued with caution. They require careful considerations as the fundamental trade-off between low cost and differentiation has to be resolved. Porter's warning about the danger of being stuck in the middle provides a useful discipline for managers. It is very easy for them to make incremental decisions that compromise the basic generic strategy. As profits accumulate, the successful cost-leader will be tempted to stop scrimping and saving. In hard times, a differentiator might easily cut back the R&D or advertising investments essential to its long-term differentiation advantage. Consistency with generic strategy provides a valuable check for managerial decision-making. The next section provides a helpful tool in calibrating generic and hybrid strategies.

2.2.5 The Strategy Clock

The Strategy Clock provides another way of approaching generic strategies (see Figure 2.5), one which gives more scope for *hybrid* strategies.[5] The Strategy Clock has two distinctive features. First, it is focused on prices to customers rather than costs to the organisation: because prices are more visible than costs, the Strategy Clock can be easier to use in comparing competitors. Second, the circular design of the clock allows for more continuous choices than Michael Porter's sharp contrast between cost leadership and differentiation: there is a full range of incremental adjustments that can be made between the 7 o'clock position at the bottom of the low-price strategy and the 2 o'clock position at the bottom of the differentiation strategy. Organisations may travel around the clock, as they adjust their pricing and benefits over time.

The Strategy Clock identifies three zones of feasible strategies, and one zone likely to lead to ultimate failure:

- *Differentiation (zone 1).* This zone contains a range of feasible strategies for building on high perceptions of product or service benefits among customers. Close to the 12 o'clock position is a strategy of *differentiation without price premium*. Differentiation without a price premium combines high-perceived benefits and moderate prices, typically used to gain market share. If high benefits also entail relatively high costs, this moderate pricing strategy would only be sustainable in the short term. Once increased market share has been achieved, it might be logical to move to *differentiation with price premium* closer to a 1 or 2 o'clock position. Movement all the way towards the 2 o'clock position is likely to involve a focus strategy. Such a *focused differentiation* strategy targets a niche where the higher prices and reduced benefits are sustainable, for instance because of a lack of competition in a particular geographical area.

Figure 2.5 The Strategy Clock

Source: Adapted from D. Faulkner and C. Bowman, *The Essence of Competitive Strategy,* Prentice Hall, 1995.

- *Low-price (zone 2)*. This zone allows for different combinations of low prices and low perceived value. Close to the 9 o'clock position, a standard *low-price* strategy would gain market share by combining low prices with reasonable value (at parity with competitors). To be sustainable, this strategy needs to be underpinned by some cost advantage, such as economies of scale gained through increased market share. Without such a cost advantage, cuts in benefits or increases in prices become necessary eventually. A variation on the standard low-price strategy is the *no-frills* strategy, close to the 7 o'clock position. No-frills strategies involve both low benefits and low prices, similar to low-cost airlines such as Ryanair.

- *Hybrid strategy (zone 3)*. A distinctive feature of the Strategy Clock is the space it allows between low-price and differentiation strategies.[6] Hybrid strategies involve both lower prices than differentiation strategies and higher benefits than low-price strategies. Hybrid strategies are often used to make aggressive bids for increased market share. They can also be an effective way of entering a new market, for instance overseas. Even in the case of innovations with high benefits, it can make sense to price low initially in order to gain experience curve efficiencies or lock-in through network effects (see Section 3.2.6). Some companies sustain hybrid strategies over long periods of time: for example, furniture store IKEA, which uses scale advantages to combine relatively low prices with differentiated Swedish design (see end of chapter case).

- *Non-competitive strategies (zone 4)*. The final set of strategies occupies a zone of unfeasible economics, with low benefits and high prices. Unless businesses have exceptional strategic lock-in, customers will quickly reject these combinations. Typically these strategies lead to failure.

The Strategy Clock's focus on price, and its scope for incremental adjustments in strategy, provides a more dynamic view on strategy than Porter's generic strategies. Instead of organisations being fairly fixed in terms of either a cost or a differentiation strategy, they can move around the clock. For example, an organisation might start with a *low-price* strategy to gain market share, later shift to a higher-priced *differentiation with premium* strategy in order to reap profits, and then move back to a *hybrid* strategy in order to defend itself from new entrants. However, Porter's generic strategies do remind managers that costs are critical. Unless an organisation has some secure cost advantage (such as economies of scale), a hybrid strategy of high-perceived benefits and low prices is unlikely to be sustainable for long.

2.3 INTERACTIVE STRATEGIES

Generic strategies need to be chosen, and adjusted, in the light of competitors' strategies. If everybody else is chasing after cost leadership, then a differentiation strategy might be sensible. Thus business strategy choices *interact* with those of competitors. This section starts by considering business strategy in the light of competitor moves, especially in hypercompetition. It then addresses the option of cooperation and closes with game theory, which helps managers choose between competition and more cooperative strategies.

2.3.1 Interactive price and quality strategies

Richard D'Aveni depicts competitor interactions in terms of movements against the variables of price (the vertical axis) and perceived quality (the horizontal axis), similar to the Strategy Clock: see Figure 2.6.[7] Although D'Aveni applies his analysis to the very fast-moving environments he terms 'hypercompetitive' (see Section 3.3.1), similar reasoning applies wherever competitors' moves are interdependent.

(i) Differentiator (D) improves quality

(ii) Mid-point business (M) counter-attacks on price

Figure 2.6 Interactive price and quality strategies

Note: axes are not necessarily to linear scales.

Source: Adapted with the permission of The Free Press, a Division of Simon & Schuster, Inc., from *Hypercompetition: Managing the Dynamics of Strategic Maneuvering* by Richard D'Aveni with Robert Gunther. Copyright © 1994 by Richard D'Aveni. All rights reserved.

Figure 2.6 shows different organisations competing by emphasising either low prices or high quality or some mixture of the two. Graph (i) starts with a 'first value line', describing various trade-offs in terms of price and perceived quality that are acceptable to customers. The cost-leading firm (here L) offers relatively poor perceived quality, but customers accept this because of the lower price. While the relative positions on the graph should not be taken literally, in the car market this cost-leading position might describe some of Hyundai's products. The differentiator (D) has a higher price, but much better quality. This might be Mercedes. In between, there are a range of perfectly acceptable combinations, with the mid-point firm (M) offering a combination of reasonable prices and reasonable quality. This might be Ford. M's strategy is on the first value line and therefore entirely viable at this stage. On the other hand, firm U is uncompetitive, falling behind the value line. Its price is higher than M's, and its quality is worse. U's predicament is typical of the business that is 'stuck in the middle', in Porter's terms. U no longer offers acceptable value and must quickly move back onto the value line or fail.

In any market, competitors and their moves or counter-moves can be plotted against these two axes of price and perceived value. For example, in graph (i) of Figure 2.6, the differentiator (D) makes an aggressive move by substantially improving its perceived quality while holding its prices. This improvement in quality shifts customer expectations of quality right across the market. These changed expectations are reflected by the new, second value line (in green). With the second value line, even the cost-leader (L) may have to make some improvement to quality, or accept a small price cut. But the greatest threat is for the mid-point competitor, M. To catch up with the second value line, M must respond either by making a substantial improvement in quality while holding prices, or by slashing prices, or by some combination of the two.

However, mid-point competitor M also has the option of an aggressive counter-attack. Given the necessary capabilities, M might choose to push the value line still further outwards, wrong-footing differentiator D by creating a third value line that is even more demanding in terms of the price-perceived quality trade-off. The starting point in graph (ii) of Figure 2.6 is all three competitors L, M and D successfully reaching the second value line (uncompetitive U has disappeared). However, M's next move is to go beyond the second value line by making radical cuts in price while sustaining its new level of perceived quality. Again, customer expectations are changed and a third value line (in red) is established. Now it is differentiator D that is at most risk of being left behind, and it faces hard choices about how to respond in terms of price and quality.

Plotting moves and counter-moves in these terms underlines the dynamic and interactive nature of business strategy. Economically viable positions along the value line are always in danger of being superseded as competitors move either downwards in terms of price or outwards in terms of perceived quality. The generic strategies of cost leadership and differentiation should not be seen as static positions, but as dynamic trajectories along the axes of price and quality.

A more detailed example of the sequence of decisions and possible options involved in competitive interaction is given in Figure 2.7.[8] This illustrates the situation of a business facing a low-price competitor, for example a high-cost Western manufacturer facing possible attack by cheap imports from Asia. There are three key decisions:

- *Threat assessment*. The first decision point is whether the threat is substantial or not. If there is a threat, the high-cost organisation should not automatically respond to a low-price competitor by trying to match prices: it is likely to lose a price war with its existing cost structure. The high-cost organisation needs a more sophisticated response.

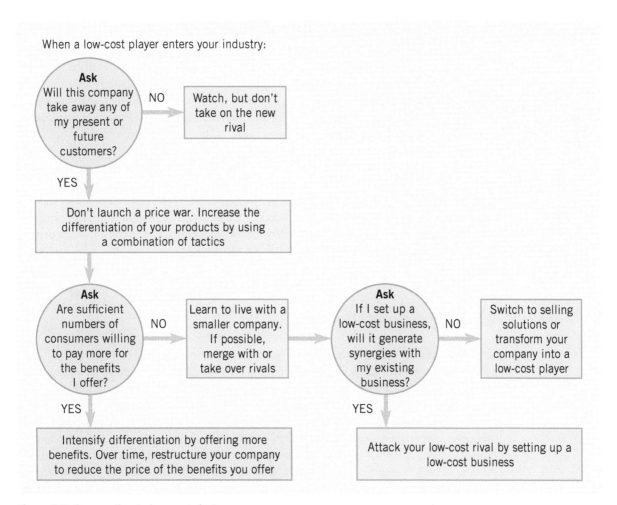

Figure 2.7 Responding to low-cost rivals

Source: Reprinted by permission of *Harvard Business Review*. Exhibit from 'A framework for responding to low-cost rivals' by N. Kumar, December 2006. Copyright © 2006 by the Harvard Business School Publishing Corporation. All rights reserved.

- *Differentiation response.* If there are enough consumers prepared to pay for them, the high-cost organisation can seek out new points of differentiation. For example, a Western manufacturer may exploit its closeness to local markets by improving service levels. At the same time, unnecessary costs should be stripped out. If increased differentiation is not possible, then more radical cost solutions should be sought.

- *Cost response.* Merger with other high-cost organisations may help reduce costs and match prices through economies of scale. If a low-cost business is synergistic with (in other words, has benefits for) the existing business, this can be an effective platform for an aggressive cost-based counter-attack. If there is neither scope for further differentiation or synergy between the existing business and a possible new low-cost business, then the existing business must sooner or later be abandoned. For a Western manufacturer, one option might be to outsource all production to low-cost operators, simply applying its design and branding expertise. Another option would be to abandon manufacturing in favour of becoming a 'solutions provider', aggregating manufactured components from different suppliers and adding value through whole-systems design, consultancy or service.

Equivalent decisions would have to be made, of course, by a low-price competitor facing a differentiator. When Apple entered the phone market with its expensive iPhone, established handset manufacturers had first to decide whether Apple was a serious long-term threat, and then choose how far they should either match the iPhone's features or increase the price differential between their products and Apple's expensive ones.

According to Richard D'Aveni, these kinds of moves and counter-moves are a constant feature of hypercompetitive environments. As in Section 3.3.1, hypercompetition describes markets with continuous disequilibrium and change, for example popular music or consumer electronics. In these conditions, it may no longer be possible to plan for sustainable positions of competitive advantage. Indeed, planning for long-term sustainability may actually destroy competitive advantage by slowing down response. Managers have to be able to act faster than their competitors.

Successful competitive interaction in hypercompetition thus demands speed and initiative rather than defensiveness. Richard D'Aveni highlights four key principles: first, that an organisation has to be willing to cannibalise the basis of its own old advantage and success; second, that smaller moves can create a series of temporary advantages; third, that surprise, unpredictability, even apparent irrationality can be important; and, finally, that an organisation might signal particular moves, but then do something else (see Section 2.3.3 on game theory below).

2.3.2 Cooperative strategy

So far the emphasis has been on competition and competitive advantage. However, the competitive moves and counter-moves in the previous section make it clear that sometimes competition can escalate in a way that is dangerous to all competitors. It can be in the self-interest of organisations to restrain competition. Moreover, advantage may not always be achieved just by competing. Collaboration between some organisations in a market may give them advantage over other competitors in the same market, or potential new entrants. Collaboration can be explicit in terms of formal agreements to cooperate, or tacit in terms of informal mutual understandings between organisations. In short, while organisations need to avoid illegal collusion, business strategy includes cooperative options as well as competitive ones.[9] *Tacit collusion,* where companies agree on a certain strategy without any explicit communication between them, is not uncommon; for example agreeing to avoid price competition. It is facilitated by industries or sectors with few competitors, homogenous products and high entry barriers.

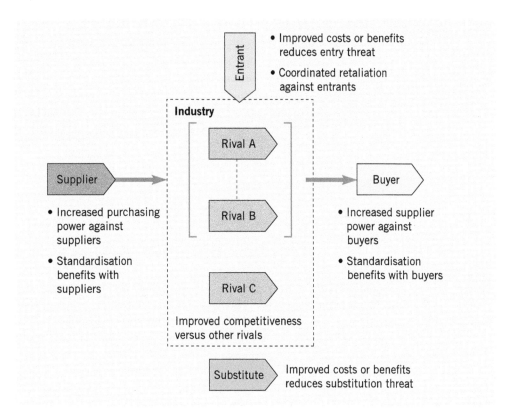

Figure 2.8 Cooperating with rivals

Source: Adapted from *Competitive Strategy: Techniques for Analysing Industries and Competitors,* The Free Press by Michael E. Porter. Copyright © 1980, 1998 by The Free Press. All rights reserved.

Figure 2.8 illustrates various kinds of benefits from cooperation between firms in terms of Michael Porter's five forces of buyers, suppliers, rivals, entrants and substitutes (see Section 3.2). Key benefits of cooperation are as follows:

- *Suppliers.* In Figure 2.8, cooperation between rivals A and B in an industry will increase their purchasing power against suppliers. Sometimes this increased cooperation is used simply to squeeze supplier prices. However, cooperation between rivals A and B may enable them to standardise requirements, allowing suppliers to make cost reductions to all parties' benefit. For example, if two car manufacturers agreed on common component specifications, their suppliers could gain economies through production of the standardised part on a greater scale (this kind of *complementarity* is discussed in Section 3.2.6).

- *Buyers.* Conversely, cooperation between rivals A and B will increase their power as suppliers vis-à-vis buyers. It will be harder for buyers to shop around. Such *collusion* between rivals can help maintain or raise prices, though it may well attract penalties from competition regulators. On the other hand, buyers may benefit if their inputs are standardised, again enabling reductions in costs that all can share. For example, if food manufacturers supplying a retailer agree on common pallet sizes for deliveries, the retailer can manage its warehouses much more efficiently.

- *Rivals.* If cooperative rivals A and B are getting benefits with regard to both buyers and suppliers, other competitors without such agreements – in Figure 2.8, rival C – will be at a competitive disadvantage. Rival C will be in danger of being squeezed out of the industry.

- *Entrants.* Similarly, potential entrants will likely lack the advantages of the combined rivals A and B. Moreover, A and B can coordinate their retaliation strategies against any new entrant, for example by cutting prices by the same proportions in order to protect their own relative positions while undermining the competitiveness of the new entrant.

- *Substitutes.* Finally, the improved costs or efficiencies that come from cooperation between rivals A and B reduce the incentives for buyers to look to substitutes. Steel companies have cooperated on research to reduce the weight of steel used in cars, in order to discourage car manufacturers from switching to lighter substitutes such as aluminium or plastics.

Further kinds of cooperation will be considered under alliance strategy in Section 11.4.

2.3.3 Game theory

Game theory provides important insights into competitor interaction.[10] The 'game' refers to the kinds of interactive moves two players make in a game of chess. **Game theory encourages an organisation to consider competitors' likely moves and the implications of these moves for its own strategy.** Game theorists are alert to two kinds of interaction in particular. First, game theorists consider how a *competitor response* to a strategic move might change the original assumptions behind that move: for example, challenging a competitor in one area might lead to a counter-attack in another. Second, game theorists are sensitive to the *strategic signals,* or messages, their moves might convey to competitors, for example with regard to how fiercely they seem willing to defend their position in a particular market. In the light of possible attacks and counter-attacks, game theorists often advise a more cooperative approach than head-to-head competition.

Game theory is particularly relevant where competitors are *interdependent*. Interdependence exists where the outcome of choices made by one competitor is dependent on the choices made by other competitors. For example, the success of price cuts by a retailer depends on the responses of its rivals: if rivals do not match the price cuts, then the price-cutter gains market share; but if rivals follow the price cuts, nobody gains market share and all players suffer from the lower prices. Anticipating competitor counter-moves is clearly vital to deciding whether to go forward with the price-cutting strategy.

There are two important guiding principles that arise from interdependence:

- *Get in the mind of the competitors.* Strategists need to put themselves in the position of competitors, take a view about what competitors are likely to do and choose their own strategy in this light. They need to understand their competitors' game-plan to plan their own.
- *Think forwards and reason backwards.* Strategists should choose their competitive moves on the basis of understanding the likely responses of competitors. Think forwards to what competitors might do in the future, and then reason backwards to what would be sensible to do in the light of this now.

Game theory insights can be gained through two methods. On the one hand, *war gaming* is helpful where it is important to get stakeholders to deeply appreciate each other's positions through actually playing out their respective roles, and where there is uncertainty about the range of outcomes. Illustration 2.3 provides a public policy example of war gaming and using game theory principles when changing and improving public-sector services. On the other hand, *mathematical game theory* is useful where there is a clear but limited range of outcomes and the values associated with each outcome can be reasonably quantified.

One of the most famous illustrations of mathematical game theory is the *prisoner's dilemma*. Game theorists identify many situations where organisations' strategic decisions are similar to the dilemma of two prisoners accused of serial crimes together and being interrogated in separate prison cells without the possibility of communicating with each other.

ILLUSTRATION 2.3	Game theory in practice in the public sector

Game theory and war gaming can provide insights when changing and improving public sector services.

Game theory has not become a common strategic tool. It has often been considered too theoretical and focused on single solutions to be able to cope with real-world messy managerial problems. However, it has been proposed that instead of using game theory to predict a single optimal solution it can be used to generally understand advantages and disadvantages with different strategic options.

When public-sector organisations try to change and improve public services they frequently need to partner with and interact with a variety of organisations. They need to collaborate with other public-sector organisations, with private companies and not-for-profit organisations. Success therefore depends not only on the public-sector organisation itself, but on several other partners. This requires an insight into partners' intentions and how they may behave. This is central to game theory – understanding what strategic options different players have, what their objectives are and how they will act under different circumstances.

The basic principles of game theory can thus be used to evaluate changes and improvements of public-sector services. The English National Health Service (NHS) has, for example, used war games to better prepare them for government reforms. War gaming began as a military preparation that places players in the positions of different actors (e.g. enemies or allies), and asks them to play out a sequence of moves and counter-moves as if they were the actors themselves. A basic principle underlying the game is that to know your enemy you must become your enemy in the play. Another consideration is that you need to test your own plan and strategy in confrontation with the (played) enemy.

In a war game for healthcare systems, teams are assigned to play the role of different stakeholders including payers, hospitals, physician groups, regulators and suppliers. In a first round the teams are then asked to respond to a given challenge. The actions each team can consider are stipulated by the game's rules, which are based on realistic rules of the healthcare system. In subsequent rounds each team reacts to the moves the other teams have made. Through several rounds every team acts on its own strategies and reacts

to the moves of other teams. The aim is not primarily to determine a winner, but to develop new insights. War games make participants think carefully about how they would act, react to and interact with others under specific conditions. In this way, participants gain a better understanding of other players' perspectives and possible actions. This helps them to anticipate how various actors will behave under different conditions. The participants also gain a better understanding of their own organisation's strengths and weaknesses in interactions with others.

The principles of game theory can thus be of more general assistance and Timothy Meaklim in the *Guardian* has suggested that public organisations and their leaders should:

1 Be knowledgeable about partners, their strategies, needs and decision-making
2 Be flexible adjusting their own strategies or objectives to meet the overall aim
3 Develop clear lines of partnership communication and decision-making
4 Share the power equally between parties
5 Get agreement on partnership operation and benefits
6 Consider own roles and motives for engaging with the partnership
7 Create partner trust.

Sources: Partly adapted from T. Meaklim, 'Game theory: what prisoners and stags can teach public leaders',*The Guardian*, 27 November 2013 and *International Journal of Leadership in Public Services*, 9(1/2), 2013, pp. 22–31; E. Bury, J. Horn and D. Meredith, 'How to use war games as a strategic tool in health care', *Health International*, 11, 2011, pp. 28–37.

Questions

1 Besides the public sector, can you think of other business situations where war games could be useful?
2 War games could possibly play a role when preparing for strategic change at a university. What stakeholders or players would be relevant and what would their interests be?

The prisoners have to decide on the relative merits of: (i) loyally supporting each other by refusing to divulge any information to their interrogators; and (ii) seeking an advantage by betraying the other. If both stay silent, they might get away with most of their crimes and only suffer some lesser punishment, perhaps for just one or two offences. The interrogators, though, will tempt each of them to divulge full information by offering them their freedom if only they betray their fellow criminal. However, if both betray, then the judge is unlikely to be grateful for the confessions, and will punish them for all their crimes. The dilemma for each of the prisoners is how much to trust in their mutual loyalty: if they both refuse to divulge, they can both get away with the lesser punishment; on the other hand, if one is sure that the other will not betray, it makes even more sense to betray the loyal one as that allows the betrayer to go totally free. The two prisoners are clearly interdependent. But because they cannot communicate, they each have to get in the mind of the other, think forwards to what they might do, and then reason backwards in order to decide what their own strategy should be – stay silent or betray.

The prisoner's dilemma has its equivalence in business where there are two major players competing head-to-head against each other in a situation of tight interdependence. This is the position of Airbus and Boeing in the aircraft business, Sony and Microsoft in the games market, or British Airways and Virgin in transatlantic travel. It would be relevant to the strategic decisions of two such interdependent companies in a range of situations: for example, if one company was thinking about making a major investment in an innovative new product that the other company could match. For two such competitors to communicate directly about their strategies in these situations would likely be judged illegal by the competition authorities. They therefore have to get into each other's minds, think forwards and reason backwards. How will the other company act or react and, in the light of that, what strategy is best?

The kind of situation two interdependent competitors could get into is represented in the prisoner's dilemma matrix of Figure 2.9. Suppose the two main aircraft manufacturers Airbus and Boeing were both under pricing pressure, perhaps because of falling demand. They each have to decide whether to announce radical price cuts or to hold their prices up. If both choose to hold their prices, neither gets an advantage over the other and they both get the returns represented in the top left-hand quadrant of Figure 2.9: for the sake of illustration, each might earn profits of €500m. However, if one competitor pursues the radical price cuts on its own while the other does not, the pattern of returns might be quite different: the radical price-cutter attracts a significantly larger share of airline customers and earns €700m profits through spreading fixed costs over greater sales, while the market-share-losing competitor earns only €100m (as represented in the top-right and bottom-left quadrants).

Figure 2.9 Prisoner's dilemma game in aircraft manufacture

This situation might tempt one of the competitors to choose radical price cuts for two reasons: first, there is the prospect of higher profits; but, second, there is the risk of the other competitor cutting prices while leaving it behind. The problem is that if each reason in the same way, the two competitors will *both* cut prices at once. They will thus set off a price war in which neither gains share and they both end up with the unsatisfactory return of just €300m (the bottom-right quadrant).

The dilemma in Figure 2.9 is awkward because cooperation is simultaneously attractive and difficult to achieve. The most attractive strategy for Airbus and Boeing jointly is for them both to hold their prices, yet in practice they are likely to cut prices because they must expect the other to do so anyway. A distinctive feature of game theory is that it frequently highlights the value of a more cooperative approach to competitor interaction, rather than aggressive competition. The cooperation need not be in the form of an explicit agreement: cooperation can be tacit, supported by the recognition of mutual self-interest in not attacking each other head-to-head. Game theory therefore encourages managers to consider how a 'game' can be transformed from lose–lose competition to win–win cooperation. There are various principles to consider here. If players know that their interaction will be repeated this can encourage cooperation. Signalling by responding quickly and aggressively and deterring unwanted strategic moves by competitors can also encourage cooperation and so can a strong commitment to a particular strategy.

2.4 BUSINESS MODELS

Business models have become increasingly popular as internet-based companies like Airbnb, Spotify and Uber have conquered the world with their new models. They are particularly useful when explaining more complex business interrelationships that generate value and profits for more parties than just a buyer and seller. Consequently, the business model concept is commonly discussed in relation to strategy today. Building on David Teece's work, this chapter carefully distinguishes business models from business strategy.[11] A **business model describes a value proposition for customers and other participants, an arrangement of activities that produces this value, and associated revenue and cost structures.**[12] When entrepreneurs in new start-ups have entered old industries with new business models in recent years they have frequently changed industry dynamics and competition in radical ways. The new models often involve more complex interrelationships than traditional models and create value for participants besides the customer and generate profits for more parties than the seller. This shows that both entrepreneurs and managers, whose organisations may be threatened by new start-ups, need to understand business models. Illustration 2.4 discusses how Uber's business model has revolutionised the taxi industry globally. The remainder of this section first discusses three fundamental elements of business models and then some typical business model patterns.

2.4.1 Value creation, configuration and capture

Business models describe business transactions and interrelationships between various parties and are best explained in terms of three interrelated components (see Figure 2.10).[13] The first emphasises *value creation*; a proposition that addresses a specific customer segment's needs and problems and those of other participants. The second component is the *value configuration* of the resources and activities that produce this value. The final *value capture* part explains revenue streams and cost structures that allow the organisation and other stakeholders to gain a share of the total value generated.[14]

ILLUSTRATION 2.4   Uber's ubiquitous business model

The on-demand transportation service that has revolutionised the taxi industry.

With a market value of $50bn (£30bn, €37.5bn) Uber has been predicted to become the world's dominant transportation company without owning a single vehicle. Since its start in San Francisco 2009, it has quickly expanded to over 60 countries and 340 cities worldwide. It now employs 4000, adds 50,000 new partner drivers a month and makes one million trips each day. The company is growing at exponential rates and has received $10bn of equity funding so far. Co-founder and CEO Travis Kalancik claims that they are doubling its size every six months.

Uber's smartphone app is at the centre of their business model. Customers download the app, create an account and put in their credit card information. By tapping the app they request a car and a notification is sent to the nearest driver who can accept or reject the ride and, if rejected, it is sent to another driver in the area. Customers can track the estimated time of arrival and the meter via the app. Payment is made to Uber via the app with a later payment to the driver. The customer gets an option to rate the driver and the driver also has the option to rate the customer.

Through the Uber app customers can search, book, pay and rate the taxi service. They are offered a convenient, reliable and fast taxi service either through luxury rides, priced less than conventional limousine services (Uber Black), or through regular rides priced less than normal taxi fares (UberPop or UberX). The value for drivers is an extra source of income and flexible working hours. The review and rating system is a key difference compared to regular taxis. Customers can avoid drivers with low ratings and drivers can avoid passengers with low ratings.

The basic resources of Uber include their technological platform and app, but they do not own any cars or employ any drivers. Drivers own the cars and are self-employed and apply to Uber to become a driver. Uber's activities are configured to match customers with a nearby driver and car. In addition to matchmaking, the platform and app includes pricing and payment, car tracking and review systems. Uber thus structures the value for both customers and drivers through the development of sophisticated software and algorithms that optimise matchmaking, pricing and reviews for different cities and local markets.

Uber captures their profit and value by typically taking a 20 per cent cut on all rides except for special promotions to customers and/or drivers and in areas where they face competition from similar services. Besides generating a margin, these revenues should cover their expenses to cover R&D, technology development, marketing, local infrastructure and own local employees in each city.

Even though the business model has been a success, there are several significant challenges. The UberPOP service has faced regulatory pushbacks in several European countries and even been forced to shut down in some markets. Uber is also facing an increasing number of competitors with similar business models; Lyft is a significant competitor in the USA and Didi Kuaidi is ahead of Uber in China. As CEO Travis Kalancik explains:

'We're profitable in the USA, but we're losing over $1 billion a year in China.'

Sources: M. Ahmed, 'Uber: Backseat driver', *Financial Times*, 16 September 2015; A. Damodaran, 'A disruptive cab ride to riches: The Uber payoff', *Forbes*, 6 October 2014; J. Narvey, 'Travis Kalanick speaks out: Uber's CEO on risk, regulation, and women in tech', *Betakit*, 16 February 2016.

Questions ∕

1 In terms of Figure 2.10, what are Uber's value creation, value configuration and value capturing?

2 If you were the head of a traditional taxi company, how could you change your business model to compete with Uber?

Value creation

What is offered to what customer segment?

- Customer needs and problems: value and benefit
- Target customer and market segment
- Value for other participants

Value configuration

How is the value proposition structured?

- Composition and selection of resources and activities
- Linkages between and system of activities
- Identifies what participants perform what activities

Value capture

Why does the model generate a margin?

- Revenue stream and payments
- Cost structure and drivers
- Apportion of value between stakeholders

Figure 2.10 Business model components

The business model of the San Francisco-based accommodation broker Airbnb, for example, *creates value* for both the customers that rent the apartment, house or private room and for the hosts that offer their homes for rent. The Airbnb website conveniently provides a platform for exchange activities between the hosts and guests. These activities are *configured* via the web platform so that hosts list, describe and present pictures of their homes and customers are thus offered a wide selection of accommodation to choose from and rent. A review system of both accommodations and guests is available to build references and prevent deception. Finally, both hosts and Airbnb *capture value* from this business model. Hosts receive guest payments and Airbnb gets a 6–12 per cent commission fee on guest reservations, a three per cent to process the payment to the host and also guest credit card processing fees. This points managers and entrepreneurs to three basic and interdependent attributes of business models:

- *Value creation.* A key part of a business model describes what is offered and how value is thus created for the various parties involved: customers, partners and other participants. The main concern here is thus the targeted customer segment and how their needs are fulfilled and their problems solved, but also how to create value for any other parties involved.

- *Value configuration.* A second component explains how various interdependent resources and activities in the value chain underlie the value proposition, for example technology, equipment, facilities, brands, managerial processes, etc. (for a discussion of the value chain see Section 4.4.2). These factors are part of an activity system that not only explains what activities create value, but how they are linked and what participants perform them (for activity systems see Section 4.4.3). While this system is centred on the organisation it can also involve activities conducted by customers, partners, and other participants.[15]

- *Value capture.* A business model also describes the cost structure of resources and activities and the revenue stream from customers and any other parties. In addition, this component shows how the value created will be apportioned between the organisation and any other stakeholders involved. For a company, then, this last component also describes how profit is made while for non-for-profits and the public sector there are of course no expectations of financial gain.[16]

Two points need to be emphasised here:

- First, once established in an industry, business models are often taken for granted. All businesses rely on business models, but as they mature and become standardised they are rarely questioned. Until Airbnb and others started their services few thought about or challenged the 'hotel business model' and how value creation, configuration and capture were interrelated in this model. There may have been efforts to change individual model components, increasing customer value by differentiation, for example, but few changed the whole model and all of the relationships between the components as Airbnb did. Business models thus often become institutionalised and part of an industry's 'recipe' (see Section 6.3.2).

- Second, while competitors may share business models their business strategy can still differ. Walmart, for example, shares the same discount retailer model with several competitors, but has a distinct low cost strategy. Likewise, Airbnb in the example above have the same business model as Wimdu and other competitors. However, Airbnb's extensive selection of accommodations from close to one million listings in 34,000 cities in 200 countries surpasses any competitor and thus differentiates them. Because of this size both customers and hosts are likely to prefer Airbnb over competitors as guests are offered more accommodations and hosts more guests. In addition, the more customers that use their service the better it is for every customer in their network of guests and hosts and Airbnb can thus build on network effects (see Section 3.2.6 for network effects).

2.4.2 Business model patterns

Even though business model patterns often become established within industries over time, companies use them competitively. New entrants often use new business models to be able to compete successfully with established players. Dell, for example, entered the PC and laptop industry many years ago based on a different business model compared to the established one. Instead of going via the middlemen of retailers and wholesalers as HP, IBM and others did, they sold directly to customers. It is thus important for managers to understand what type of business model pattern their businesses built on and how it may differ from other competitors. It should be noted, however, that business model patterns are described at various levels of detail and sometimes only emphasise one or two business model components, such as value capturing.[17] There are many business models around, but three typical patterns include the following:

- *Razor and blade.* This is perhaps the most well-known business model pattern, but its primary focus is on the value capture component, which makes it more of a revenue model. It builds on Gillette's classic model of selling the razors at a very low price and the compatible replacement blades at a quite high price.[18] This model of selling two technically interlinked products separately is quite common. For example, mobile operators offering consumers a cheap or even a free mobile phone and then catching them through a two-year fee-based subscription plan. In other industries it is the services, maintenance and parts that are priced expensively while the basic product is sold at relatively low margins. This is, for example, the case for ink-jet printers; they are sold at relatively low prices, but manufacturers make their margins on selling expensive ink. It is also common in industrial goods with an emphasis on expensive services; for example, Rolls Royce and GE and others in the jet engine industry and Otis and Schindler and other players in the elevator industry.

- *Freemium.* This business model pattern name comes from combining 'free' and 'premium' and it primarily relates to online businesses. It refers to how a basic version of a service or product is offered for free so as to build a high volume of customers and eventually

THINKING DIFFERENTLY | Transient rather than sustainable advantage

Some question to what extent sustainable competitive advantage is possible at all in today's fast-changing world.

Section 2.4.1 indicated that in hypercompetitive environments it may not be possible to form business strategies that provide for sustainable competitive advantage. Some argue that the era of sustainability in competitive advantage is over altogether as most industries today are too turbulent. It is claimed that competitors and customers have become too unpredictable to form any single long-term strategy. Companies with strong and long-lasting positions like IKEA, GE and Unilever are argued to be exceptions. In this view then, it is a waste of effort to invest in sustainable advantages; better to invest in a series of *transient advantages*.[19]

In this new era managers thus need to constantly start new strategic initiatives and have a portfolio of several transient competitive advantages. They need to think of advantages as fleeting and going through a life cycle. Each competitive advantage has a launch stage that identifies an opportunity and raises resources to capitalise on it. Next is a ramp up period in which the business is brought to scale, which leads into a phase of exploitation where market shares and profits are gained. Finally, there is a phase of inevitable erosion as competitors enter and weaken the advantage, which may force the company to exit. A company thus needs to catch new advantages continuously as old ones expire; freeing up resources from the old to invest in the new. Even if each advantage is temporary a portfolio of several different advantages would always provide an advantage somewhere. Hence, if managers continuously start strategic initiatives and build many transient advantages they could still get ahead of competitors.

> **Question**
>
> If IKEA chose not to build on sustainable competitive advantage, how could they build on many transient advantages?

convince a portion of the customers to buy a variety of premium services. Revenue is generated by the premium buying customers. Often only a small portion of the total volume of users, their revenues can be enough for the provider and they can also be used to attract even more users. The photo sharing service Flickr by Yahoo uses this business model pattern. Flickr offers the basic service of uploading and sharing photos for free while generating revenues through extra services for a subscription fee including unlimited uploading and storing of photos. Flickr also uses contextual advertising and cooperation with retail chains and other photo service companies besides subscription fees to generate revenue. Other online businesses that use this business model are the business-oriented social networking service LinkedIn, the video chat and voice call service Skype and the streaming music service Spotify. The aim of freemium, however, is not only to convince premium customers, but to attract a larger volume of customers as the value of the service increases with more users, which means that the enterprise can gain network effects based on a large installed base of adopters (see Section 3.2.6 for network effects).

- *Multi-sided platforms.* This business model pattern brings together two or more distinct, but interdependent groups of customers on one platform. They are interdependent as the platform is of value to each group of customers only if the other group of customers is also present. There are many different enterprises and markets that rely on this pattern (see for example Illustration 2.4), and video games consoles are a typical example. The players are on one side of the platform and favour consoles with a wide variety of games. This makes them dependent on the other side of the platform, the game developers, which in turn favour platforms with a large enough customer group to regain their development costs for the games. This shows that the value of the platform increases for both customer types as more customers use it. It suggests a network effect as each customer has a positive effect on the value of the product or platform for other customers (see Section 3.2.6). Web search companies like Google also rely on a similar pattern. For them the two sides of the platform involve consumer searchers on the one hand and advertisers that sponsor links on the search website on the other. The more searchers that use Google the better for advertisers and the better data for Google to refine search results and the better quality of the searches the better for consumers.

SUMMARY

- Business strategy is concerned with seeking competitive advantage in markets at the *business* rather than *corporate* level.
- Porter's framework and the Strategy Clock define various *generic strategies*, including *cost leadership*, *differentiation*, *focus* and *hybrid* strategies.
- In *hypercompetitive* conditions sustainable competitive advantage is difficult to achieve and competitors need to carefully consider moves and counter-moves.
- *Cooperative strategies* may offer alternatives to competitive strategies or may run in parallel.
- *Game theory* encourages managers to get in the mind of competitors and think forwards and reason backwards.
- A *business model* describes the business logic of an enterprise including the domains of *value creation*, *value configuration* and *value capture*.

WORK ASSIGNMENTS

✱ Denotes more advanced work assignments.
* Refers to a case study in the Text and Cases edition.

2.1 What are the advantages and what are the disadvantages of applying principles of business strategy to public-sector or charity organisations? Illustrate your argument by reference to a public-sector organisation of your choice.

2.2 Using either Porter's generic strategies or the Strategy Clock, identify examples of organisations following strategies of differentiation, low cost or low price, and stuck-in-the-middle or hybrid. How successful are these strategies?

2.3✱ You have been appointed personal assistant to the chief executive of a major manufacturing firm, who has asked you to explain what is meant by 'differentiation' and why it is important. Write a brief report addressing these questions.

2.4✱ Choose a company that you are familiar with (e.g. Spotify, Netflix, Apple). How do the business model components (value creation, configuration and capture) apply to the company?

2.5✱ Drawing on Section 2.3.2 (on cooperative strategies) write a report for the chief executive of a business in a competitive market (e.g. pharmaceuticals* or Formula One*) explaining when and in what ways cooperation rather than direct competition might make sense.

Integrative assignment

2.6✱ Applying game theory ideas from Section 2.3.3 to issues of international strategy (Chapter 9), how might a domestic player discourage an overseas player from entering into its home market?

RECOMMENDED KEY READINGS

- The foundations of the discussions of generic competitive strategies are to be found in the writings of Michael Porter, which include *Competitive Strategy* (1980) and *Competitive Advantage* (1985), both published by Free Press.

- Hypercompetition, and the strategies associated with it, are explained in Richard D'Aveni, *Hypercompetitive Rivalries: Competing in Highly Dynamic Environments*, Free Press, 1995.

- There is much written on game theory, but a good deal of it can be rather inaccessible to the lay reader. Exceptions are R. McCain, *Game Theory: a Non-technical Introduction to the Analysis of Strategy*, South Western, 2003; and P. Ghemawat, *Games Businesses Play*, MIT Press, 1998.

- There is considerably less written on business models, but one introduction including a long list of various business model types is O. Gassman, K. Frankenberger and M. Csik, *The Business Model Navigator*, Pearson, 2014.

REFERENCES

1. This section draws heavily on M. Porter, *Competitive Advantage*, Free Press, 1985. For a more recent discussion of the generic strategies concept, see J. Parnell, 'Generic strategies after two decades: a reconceptualisation of competitive strategy', *Management Decision*, vol. 48, no. 8 (2006), pp. 1139–54.

2. P. Conley, *Experience Curves as a Planning Tool*, available as a pamphlet from the Boston Consulting Group. See also A.C. Hax and N.S. Majluf, in R.G. Dyson (ed.), *Strategic Planning: Models and Analytical Techniques*, Wiley, 1990.

3. B. Sharp and J. Dawes, 'What is differentiation and how does it work?', *Journal of Marketing Management*, vol. 17, nos 7/8 (2001), pp. 739–59, reviews the relationship between differentiation and profitability.

4. C. Markides and C. Charitou, 'Competing with dual business models: a contingency approach', *Academy of Management Executive,* vol. 18, no. 3 (2004), pp. 22–36.

5. See D. Faulkner and C. Bowman, *The Essence of Competitive Strategy*, Prentice Hall, 1995.

6. For empirical support for the benefits of a hybrid strategy, see E. Pertusa-Ortega, J. Molina-Azorín and E. Claver-Cortés, 'Competitive strategies and firm performance: a comparative analysis of pure, hybrid and "stuck-in-the-middle" strategies in Spanish firms', *British Journal of Management*, vol. 20, no. 4 (2008), pp. 508–23.

7. R. D'Aveni, *Hypercompetition: Managing the Dynamics of Strategic Maneuvering*, Free Press, 1994.

8. This analysis is based on N. Kumar, 'Strategies to fight low cost rivals', *Harvard Business Review*, vol. 84, no. 12 (2006), pp. 104–13.

9. Useful books on collaborative strategies are Y. Doz and G. Hamel, *Alliance Advantage: The Art of Creating Value through Partnering*, Harvard Business School Press, 1998; C. Hutham (ed.), *Creating Collaborative Advantage*, Sage, 1996; and D. Faulkner, *Strategic Alliances: Cooperating to Compete*, McGraw-Hill, 1995.

10. For readings on game theory, see B. Nalebuff and A. Brandenburger, *Co-opetition*, Profile Books, 1997; R. McCain, *Game Theory: A Non-technical Introduction to the Analysis of Strategy*, South Western, 2003; and, for a summary, S. Regan, 'Game theory perspective', in M. Jenkins and V. Ambrosini (eds), *Advanced Strategic Management: a Multi-Perspective Approach*, 2nd edn, Palgrave Macmillan, 2007, pp. 83–101. A more recent practical example is in H. Lindstädt and J. Müller, 'Making game theory work for managers', *McKinsey Quarterly*, December 2009.

11. For discussion about business models and how they differ from business strategy, see D.J. Teece, 'Business models, business strategy and innovation', *Long Range Planning*, vol. 43, no. 2 (2010), pp. 172–94; J. Magretta, 'Why business models matter', *Harvard Business Review*, May 2002, pp. 86–92; C. Zott and A. Raphael, 'The fit between product market strategy and business model: implications for firm performance', *Strategic Management Journal*, vol. 29, no. 1 (2008), pp.1–26; and H. Chesbrough and R.S. Rosenbloom, 'The role of the business model in capturing value from innovation: evidence from Xerox Corporation's technology spin-off companies' *Industrial and Corporate Change*, vol. 11, no. 3 (2002), pp. 529–55.

12. In earlier editions we did not emphasise the first value proposition part, but emphasised the arrangement of activities and the revenues and cost structure (business models were discussed in Chapter 9 in the last two editions).

13. Please note that the business model literature is quite young and fragmented. For a couple of reviews of the literature, see C. Zott, A. Raphael and L. Massa, 'The business model: recent developments and future research', *Journal of Management*, vol. 37, no. 4 (2011), pp. 1019–42; and A. Osterwalder, Y. Pinneur and C. Tucci, 'Clarifying business models: origins, present, and future of the concept', *Communications of AIS*, vol. 16, article 1 (2005). For a debate of the value of business models, see R.J. Arend, 'The business model: present and future – beyond a skeumorph', *Strategic Organization*, vol. 11, no. 4 (2013), pp. 390–402; C. Baden-Fuller and V. Mangematin, 'Business models: a challenging agenda', *Strategic Organization*, vol. 11, no. 4 (2013), pp. 418–27; and C. Zott and A. Raphael, 'The

business model: a theoretically anchored robust construct for strategic analysis', *Strategic Organization*, vol. 11, no. 4 (2013), pp. 403–11.

14. For another division of business model components and a description of a wide range of business models, see O. Gassmann, K. Frankenberger and M. Csik, *The Business Model Navigator*, Pearson, 2014.

15. For a discussion about activity systems in business models, see C. Zott and A. Raphael, 'Business model design: an activity system perspective', *Long Range Planning*, vol. 43, no. 2 (2010), pp. 216–26; and R. Casadesus-Masanell and J.E. Ricart, 'From strategy to business models and onto tactics', *Long Range Planning*, vol. 43, no 2 (2010), pp. 195–215.

16. For a discussion of business models for sustainability that also includes non-for profits, see B. Cohen and J. Kietzmann, 'Ride on! Mobility business models for the sharing economy', *Organization & Environment*, vol. 27, no. 3 (2014) pp. 279–96.

17. There are thus multiple labels around and diverse patterns are often combined into a single business model for a particular enterprise. Airbnb's model is an example of this. On the one hand, it is often referred to as a 'multi-sided platform model' as they connect hosts and guests (see this models' specifications below in the text). On the other hand, it is sometimes also called a 'peer to peer model' as it is based on cooperation among individuals who are connected via an app, website or some other online or communication service.

18. The model is sometimes also referred to as a 'cross-subsidisation' model as one basic product is inexpensive and sold at a discount, while the second dependent product or service needed to get the basic product functional is sold at a considerably higher price. Others refer to it as a 'bait and hook' pattern as it lures in consumers in.

19. R. Gunther McGrath, 'Transient advantage', *Harvard Business Review*, vol. 91, no. 6 (2013), pp. 62–70.

The IKEA approach

Kevan Scholes*

'Our business model is to offer a wide range of well-designed, functional home furnishing products at prices so low that as many people as possible will be able to afford them.'

This was the headline in IKEA's yearly summary report for year ending 31 August 2015.[1] It reported a revenue increase of 11.2 per cent to €32.7bn (£26.2bn, $42.5bn),[2] profits of €3.5bn and share gains in most markets. IKEA continued to be the world's largest home furnishings company with some 9500 products in 375 stores in 28 countries.[3] The company had 172,000 co-workers (of which 40,000 were in production and distribution).

The home furnishings market[4]

By the late 2000s home furnishings was a huge market worldwide with retail sales in excess of $US600bn in items such as furniture, household textiles and floor coverings. More than 50 per cent of these sales were in furniture stores. Table 1 compares the geographical spread of the market and IKEA sales by region.

IKEA's competitors

The home furnishings market was highly fragmented with competition occurring locally rather than globally and included competitors of several types:

- Multinational furniture retailers (like IKEA) all of whom were considerably smaller than IKEA. These included, for example, the Danish company Jysk (turnover €2.9bn).
- Companies specialising in just part of the furniture product range and operating in several countries – such as Alno from Germany in kitchens.
- Multi-branch retail furniture outlets whose sales were mainly in one country, such as DFS in the UK. The US

market was dominated by such players (e.g. Bed, Bath & Beyond Inc. with revenues of some $US12bn).
- Non-specialist companies that carried furniture as part of a wider product range. In the UK, the largest operator was the Home Retail Group whose subsidiary Argos offered some 53,000 general merchandise products through its network of 840 stores and online sales. It was number one in UK furniture retailing. General DIY companies such as Kingfisher (through B&Q in the UK and Castorama in France) were attempting to capture more of the bottom end of the furniture market.
- Small and/or specialised retailers and/or manufacturers. These accounted for the biggest share of the market in Europe.

In 2014, it was estimated that the UK market was about £10.2bn[7] of which IKEA had £1.7bn share (16.7 per cent).

IKEA's approach

IKEA had been founded by Ingvar Kamprad in 1943 in the small Swedish town of Älmhult and opened its first furniture store 1958. The company's success had been achieved through the now legendary IKEA business approach – revolutionary in the furnishing industry of its early years (see Table 2). The guiding business philosophy of Kamprad was that of improving the everyday life of people by making products more affordable. This was achieved by massive (more than 20 per cent) reductions in sales prices vs competitors which, in turn, required aggressive reductions in IKEA's costs.

Reasons for success

In his book *The IKEA Edge*[8] published in 2011, Anders Dahlvig reflected on the reasons for IKEA's success

Table 1 The geographical spread of the market and of IKEA sales by region

	Europe (incl. Russia)	Americas	Asia/Pacific
% of global market[5]	52	29	19
% of IKEA sales[6]	72	18	10

*This case was prepared by Kevan Scholes, Emeritus Professor of Strategic Management at Sheffield Business School. It is intended as a basis for class discussion and not as an illustration of good or bad management practice. Copyright Kevan Scholes 2016. Not to be reproduced or quoted without permission.

Table 2 IKEA's 'upside-down' approach

Element of the approach	Traditional furniture retailer	IKEA
Design	Traditional	Modern (Swedish)
Target households	Older, established	Families with children
Style of shop	Small specialist shops	All furnishing items in big stores
Location	City centre	Out-of-town
Product focus	Individual items	'Room sets'
Marketing	Advertising	Free catalogue (213 million in 32 languages in 2015)
Price	High	Low
Product assembly	Ready assembled	Flat pack – self-assembly
Sourcing	Local	Global
Brand	Manufacturers'	IKEA
Financial focus	Gross margin	Sales revenue
Overheads	Often high	Frugal – no perks

before, during and after his period as CEO (1999–2009). He felt IKEA had five success criteria:

'1. Design, function, and quality at low prices; 2. Unique (Scandinavian) design; 3. Inspiration, ideas, and complete solutions; 4. Everything in one place; 5. "A day out", the shopping experience. . . . You may well say that they are similar to those of most companies. The difference, in my opinion, is that IKEA is much better at delivering on these customer needs than are other retailers. . . . Most competitors focus on one or at most two of these customer needs. High-street shops focus on design and inspiration. Out-of-town low-cost retailers focus on price. Department stores focus on choice. The real strength of IKEA lies in the combination of all five.'[9]

IKEA's competitive strategy

Dahlvig explained IKEA's approach to competition:

'You can choose to adapt your company's product range to the markets you are operating in, or you can choose to shift the market's preference toward your own range and style. IKEA has chosen the latter. By doing this, the company can maintain a unique and distinct profile. This is, however, a more difficult path to follow.[10] . . . A significant understanding of the customer's situation at home is the basis for IKEA's product development.[11] . . . For most competitors, having the lowest price seems to mean being five to ten per cent cheaper than the competition on comparable products. At IKEA, this means being a minimum 20 per cent cheaper and often up to 50 per cent cheaper than the competition.'[12]

Managing the value chain

Dahlvig explained that IKEA's strategy crucially requires the 'design' and control of their wider value chain in detail:

'The secret is the control and coordination of the whole value chain from raw material, production, and range development, to distribution into stores. Most other companies working in the retail sector have control either of the retail end (stores and distribution) or the product design and production end. IKEA's vertical integration makes it a complex company compared to most, since it owns both production, range development, distribution, and stores.[13] . . . This included backward integration by extending the activities of Swedwood (IKEA's manufacturing arm) beyond furniture factories, into control over the raw materials, saw mills, board suppliers, and component factories.'[14]

Global expansion

Despite IKEA's strong global position when Dahlvig took over as CEO, he felt there was need for improvement. Earlier growth had come from going 'wide but thin' with limited market shares, but now they would go 'deep' and concentrate on their existing markets.[15]

He explained his reasoning:

'Why make the change? . . . the competition had been very fragmented and local in nature. However, many of the very big retail companies were shifting strategy. From being local, they were looking to a global expansion, not least in the emerging markets like China, Russia, and Eastern Europe . . . [and] broadening their product range . . . with much more muscle than IKEA's traditional competitors. . . . One way to dissuade them from entering into the home furnishing arena was to aggressively reduce prices and increase the company's presence with more stores in all local markets in the countries where IKEA was operating. . . . Another reason for the shift in strategy was cost efficiency. Growing sales in existing stores is the most cost-efficient way to grow the company.'[16]

China and India

Around 70 per cent of IKEA stores are still in Europe and expansion into Asia was crucial, but the company had come to realise that emerging markets could be particularly challenging. As head of research Mikael Ydholm remarked: 'The more far away we go from our culture, the more we need to understand, learn, and adapt.'[17]

IKEA first opened in China in 1998 and today it is the company's fastest growing market. They now have eight of its ten biggest stores there. The Chinese market was extremely challenging for a company that had built global success through standardisation.[18] The main problems were that in emerging markets IKEA products were expensive relative to local competitors and the consumer shopping expectations were centred on small, local shops and personal service. IKEA thus had to be flexible and presented an image as exclusive Western Europian interior design specialists – popular with younger, affluent, city dwellers. Their shops were smaller than usual for IKEA and typically nearer city centres. Because DIY was not well developed in China they offered home delivery and assembly services. Catalogues were only available *in store*. Crucially, stores were allowed to source almost 50 per cent locally (against company average of about 25 per cent) in order to keep prices competitive.

The Chinese experience would be useful when IKEA entered India. It was announced in 2012 that IKEA was to invest €1.5bn opening 25 stores over 15 to 20 years[19] with the first store opened in Hyderabad 2017. However, India also proved challenging as a third of a retailer chains' merchandise had to be produced locally. IKEA had huge problems to find producers that could live up to their strict corporate social responsibility requirements.

New leadership

Michael Ohlsson succeeded Dahlvig as CEO in 2009 – having already worked for IKEA for 30 years. In turn, he was succeeded in 2013 by another internal appointee – Peter Agnefjäll (18 years at IKEA).

Despite extremely challenging economic conditions after the global financial crash of 2008, the company's success continued with revenue reaching €21.8bn, €27.6bn and €32.7bn in 2009, 2012 and 2015, respectively, with the goal to reach €50bn by 2020. However, the market was changing as IKEA expanded into more countries (43 by 2015).

Growing IKEA and reaching more customers

Although the IKEA approach remained central to the company's strategy, the yearly report for financial year 2015[20] explained how new challenges were being addressed.

'We want to be even more accessible to the many people. This means working hard to ensure we make it easier for customers to shop with us, wherever and whenever they want to visit our stores and shopping centres, or our website and apps.

Shopping centres

We now operate 40 shopping centres and 25 retail parks [in 14 countries] and we have 20 projects in the pipeline across several markets. These family-friendly shopping centres have an IKEA store as one of the main attractions.

Online

Online sales through our website and apps exceeded €1 billion in FY15. [*There were 1.9bn visits to* IKEA.com *and 54 million hits on the IKEA catalogue app – in each case an increase of about 20 per cent from 2014.*] Currently we offer online shopping in 13 of our 28 retail countries. We are continually exploring how we can expand and improve the ways our customers can find out about our products and be inspired by our range through digital channels, such as website, apps and catalogue.

Pick-up and order points

Our three new pick-up and order points in Spain, Norway and Finland enable customers to see and buy selected products from our range, as well as collect pre-ordered purchases.'

Based on their unique approach and the more recent ingredients mentioned above, IKEA continued to take over the world with the same vision as always. CEO Peter Agnefjäll confirmed:

'We're guided by a vision to create a better everyday life for the many people. That is what steers us, motivates us – that is our role . . . We feel almost obliged to grow.'[21]

Questions

1 Identify where (in their value system) and how IKEA have achieved cost leadership.

2 Identify how IKEA have achieved differentiation from their competitors.

3 Explain how IKEA tries to ensure that their 'hybrid' strategy remains sustainable and does not become 'stuck-in-the-middle'.

4 How would you explain IKEA's business model in terms of value creation, configuration and capture?

Suggested Video Clip

http://fortune.com/video/2015/03/10/
ikeas-secret-to-global-success/

Notes and References

1. 'IKEA Group Yearly Summary FY15' from IKEA website (www.ikea.com).
2. The revenue figure consists of €31.9bn sales and €0.8bn rental income on retail property.
3. IKEA had a presence in 43 countries if retail, distribution and production are all included.
4. Data in this section comes from the IKEA website 2015 and from the Data Monitor report on Global Home Furnishings Retail Industry Profile (Reference Code: 0199-2243 Publication date: April 2008).
5. 2008.
6. 2015.
7. British Furniture Manufacturers (www.bfm.org.uk).
8. Anders Dahlvig, *The Ikea Edge,* McGraw Hill, 2011.
9. Ibid., page 62.
10. Ibid., page 63.
11. Ibid., page 63.
12. Ibid., page 74.
13. Ibid., page 75.
14. Ibid., page 83.
15. Ibid., page 120.
16. Ibid., page 123.
17. B. Kowitt, 'How Ikea took over the world', *Fortune,* 15 March, 2015.
18. U. Johansson and A. Thelander, 'A standardised approach to the world? IKEA in China', *International Journal of Quality and Service Sciences,* vol. 1, no. 2 (2000), pp. 199–219.
19. N. Bose and M. Williams, 'Ikea to enter India, invest 1.5 bln euros in stores', Reuters, 23 June 2012.
20. See endnote 1.
21. See endnote 17.

3

MACRO-ENVIRONMENT ANALYSIS

Learning outcomes

After reading this chapter you should be able to:

- Analyse the broad macro-environment of organisations in terms of *political, economic, social, technological, ecological* and *legal* factors (*PESTEL*).

- Evaluate different approaches to environmental *forecasting*.

- Construct alternative *scenarios* in order to address possible environmental changes.

Key terms

forecasting

key drivers

macro-environment

organisational field

PESTEL analysis

scenarios

3.1 INTRODUCTION

The environment creates both opportunities and threats for organisations. Some organisations have been transformed by environmental change: think how traditional cable and satellite TV services such as Comcast and Sky are being challenged by the digital technologies of players such as Netflix or Amazon. Some organisations have sprung suddenly to global scale: take for example the end of chapter case, the Alibaba trading company, whose massive growth in less than two decades has been facilitated by a combination of new technologies, Chinese political and economic change and international regulations. Although the future can never be predicted perfectly, it is clearly important that entrepreneurs and managers try to analyse their environments as carefully as they can in order to anticipate and – if possible – take advantage of such environmental changes.

Environments can be considered in terms of a series of 'layers', as summarised in Figure 3.1. This chapter focuses on organisations' *macro-environments,* the outermost layer. **The macro-environment consists of broad environmental factors that impact to a greater or lesser extent many organisations, industries and sectors.** For example, the effects of macro-environmental factors such as the internet, economic growth rates, climate change and aging populations go far beyond one industry or sector, impacting a wide range of activities from tourism to agriculture. The *industry,* or *sector,* makes up the next layer within this broad macro-environment. This layer consists of organisations producing the same sorts of products or services, for example the automobile industry or the healthcare sector. The third layer is that of specific *competitors and markets* immediately surrounding organisations. For a company like Nissan, this layer would include competitors such as Ford and Volkswagen; for a hospital, it would include similar facilities and particular groups of patients. Whereas this chapter focuses on the macro-environment, Chapter 3 will analyse industries and sectors and competitors and markets. Chapters 4 and 5 examine the individual organisations at the heart of Figure 3.1.

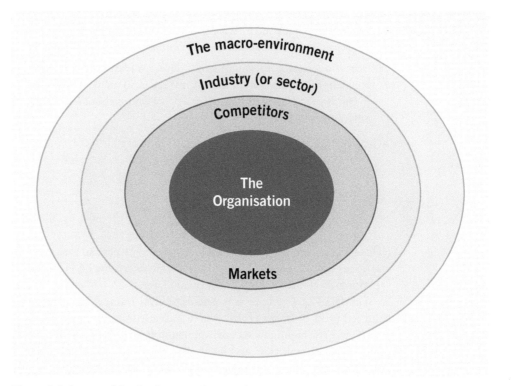

Figure 3.1 Layers of the business environment

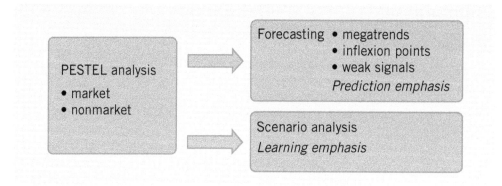

Figure 3.2 Analysing the macro-environment

Macro-environmental changes can often seem too big, complex or unpredictable for managers to grasp. The result is that changes can creep up on them until it is too late to avoid threats or take advantage of opportunities. Thus many traditional retailers, banks and newspapers were slow to seize the opportunities of the internet; many oil and steel producers underestimated the potential impact of China's slowing economic growth. While managers are always liable to some biases and inertia (see Chapter 5), this chapter introduces a number of analytical tools and concepts that can help keep organisations alert to macro-environmental change. The point is to minimise threats and to seize opportunities. The chapter is organised in three main sections:

- *PESTEL* factors which examine macro-environmental factors according to six key types: political, economic, social, technological, ecological and legal. These factors include both *market* and *nonmarket* aspects.

- *Forecasting,* which aims to predict, with varying degrees of precision or certainty. Macro-environmental forecasting draws on PESTEL analysis and often makes use of three conceptual tools: *megatrends, inflexion points* and *weak signals.*

- *Scenario analysis,* a technique that develops plausible alternative views of how the environment might develop in the future. Scenario analysis differs from forecasting because it avoids predictions about the future; it is more about *learning* different possibilities for environmental change.

The structure of this chapter is summarised in Figure 3.2.

3.2 PESTEL ANALYSIS

This section introduces a key tool for analysing the broad macro-environment of an organisation: PESTEL analysis. Providing a wide overview, PESTEL is likely to feed into both environmental forecasts and scenario analyses.

The PESTEL framework is one of several frameworks (including the similar 'PEST' and 'STEEPLE' frameworks) which categorise environmental factors into key types.[1] **PESTEL analysis highlights six environmental factors in particular: political, economic, social, technological, ecological and legal.** This list underlines that the environment includes not only the economics of markets, but also *nonmarket* factors. Organisations need to consider both market and nonmarket aspects of strategy:[2]

- The *market environment* consists mainly of suppliers, customers and competitors. These are environmental participants with whom interactions are primarily economic. Here, companies typically compete for resources, revenues and profits. Pricing and innovation are often key strategies here. The market environment is discussed extensively in Chapter 3, but issues such as economic cycles are also considered in this chapter (Section 3.2.2).

- The *nonmarket environment* involves primarily the social, political, legal and ecological factors, but can also be impacted by economic factors. Key participants in the nonmarket environment are not just other businesses, but non-governmental organisations (NGOs), politicians, government departments, regulators, political activists, campaign groups and the media. In the nonmarket environment, organisations need to build reputation, connections, influence and legitimacy. Lobbying, public relations, networking and collaboration are key nonmarket strategies.

Nonmarket factors are obviously important for government and similar organisations reliant on grants or subsidies, for example schools, hospitals and charities. However, nonmarket factors can be very important for business organisations too. For example, nonmarket factors are particularly important where the government or regulators are powerful (for instance in the defence and healthcare sectors); where consumer sensitivities are high (for instance in the food business); or in societies where political, business and media elites are closely interconnected (typically smaller countries, or countries where the state is powerful).

The following sections consider each of the PESTEL elements in turn, providing key analytical concepts and frameworks for each. Meanwhile, Illustration 3.1 on oil giant BP provides examples of various PESTEL factors, showing how in practice they often inter-relate.

3.2.1 Politics

The political element of PESTEL highlights the role of the state and other political factors in the macro-environment. There are two important steps in political analysis: first, identifying the importance of political factors; second carrying out political risk analysis.

Figure 3.3 is a matrix that distinguishes two variables helpful to identifying the importance of political factors:

- The role of the *state*. In many countries and sectors, the state is often important as a direct economic actor, for instance as a customer, supplier, owner or regulator of businesses.

- Exposure to *civil society* organisations. Civil society comprises a whole range of organisations that are liable to raise political issues, including political lobbyists, campaign groups, social media or traditional media.

To take an example from Figure 3.3, the defence industry faces a highly politicised environment. Defence companies typically have high direct state involvement: national armed services are of course key customers, while states are often owners of their national defence companies. At the same time, defence companies are often highly exposed to groups from civil society, for instance campaigners against the international arms trade. By contrast, food companies face less direct state involvement: most food companies are privately-owned and operate in private-sector markets. However, the political environment is still important for food companies, as they are typically exposed to pressures from civil society in the form of fair trade campaigners, labour rights organisations and health lobbying groups. Pressures from civil society organisations can increase state involvement by demanding additional regulation, for instance health standards for food products. Canals are often state-owned but nowadays are not highly exposed to political pressures from civil society organisations. Industries can rapidly change positions: thus revelations about internet monitoring by

ILLUSTRATION 3.1   BP's PESTEL

In 2016, the world's oil industry was facing a toughening macro-environment.

A PESTEL analysis can be done using published sources (e.g. company annual reports, media articles and consultants' reports) or more extensively by direct discussion with managers, customers, suppliers, consultants, academics, government officials and financial analysts. It is important not to rely just on a firm's managers, who may have limited views. A PESTEL analysis of the world oil industry in 2016 based on published sources shows a preponderance of threats over opportunities. In the figure above, the scale of Opportunities and Threats on each of the PESTEL dimensions is indicated by the relative extent of the bars. Just taking 12 issues for illustration, the figure shows more and longer bars on the Threats side than the Opportunities side. Thus:

- *Political.* Global instability raised potential threats to supply and distribution, with tensions in oil-producing regions such as Russia and the Middle East, and in major oil-consuming regions, such as the South China Sea. Short-term, prices were depressed by Saudi Arabian policy to maintain output despite declining demand: oil prices had halved during 2015. The main opportunity was various measures of government support, particularly in favour of shale oil production in China and the West.
- *Economic.* During 2014–15, the world had recorded declining economic growth, with only a modest upturn forecast for 2016. High growth regions such as India and Africa still offered opportunities and Western oil companies were reducing their costs through mergers.

- *Social.* In the West, car usage is declining; in the USA, the number of car passenger miles has fallen by more than 10 per cent since 2007.
- *Technological.* More fuel-efficient cars were also reducing demand, with average miles per gallon improving by 40 per cent since the early 1980s. More positively, technology offered oil producers opportunities to reduce costs: e.g. more efficient production using digital sensors.
- *Ecological.* Climate change raised indirect legal and political threats, but also posed direct threats, as global warming changed demand patterns and threatened production and distribution infrastructure with more extreme weather events.
- *Legal.* Oil companies were facing higher legal penalties for pollution: in 2015, BP had to pay $18.7bn (£11.2bn, €14bn) in fines for the Deepwater Horizon disaster. Global agreements such as the 2015 Paris Climate Change Conference were increasing legal measures to promote decarbonisation.

Questions

1 In the light of this analysis, what strategic options would you advise a Western oil producer such as Shell or BP to consider?

2 Have the Opportunities and Threats changed since 2016? How would you update this analysis?

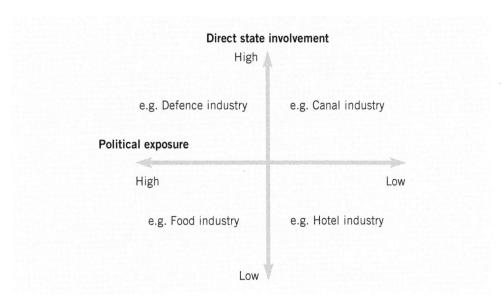

Figure 3.3 The political environment

national security agencies has placed companies such as Apple and Facebook much more under scrutiny by governments, civil liberties groups and consumers.

Organisations that face politicised environments need to carry out *political risk analysis,* the analysis of threats and opportunities arising from potential political change. There are two key dimensions to political risk analysis:[3]

- The *macro–micro* dimension. The macro dimension of political risk refers to the risks associated with whole countries – for instance China, France or Nigeria. Many specialist organisations publish relative rankings of countries' macro political risks. Western European countries are typically ranked low in terms of macro political risk, as even changes of government following elections do not bring fundamental change. On the other hand, some Middle Eastern countries rank high in terms of macro political risk, because changes of government there can be sudden and radical.[4] However, there is also an important micro dimension of political risk, relating to the specific risk of particular organisations or sectors within a country. It is important to distinguish between macro political risk and specific micro-level risk. China is typically ranked medium political risk on the macro dimension, but for some Japanese companies operating there the micro dimension is higher and variable. For many Chinese consumers, resentment of Japan is strong and Japanese car companies are from time to time targeted by nationalist boycotts.

- The *internal–external* dimension. The internal dimension of political risk relates to factors originating within the countries, for example government change or pressure from local campaigning groups. These can be relatively easy to monitor, requiring attention to election dates and opinion polls, for example. However, there are also external political risks, the knock-on effects of events occurring outside particular countries' national boundaries. For example, a fall in oil prices driven by the internal politics of Saudi Arabia is liable to have negative economic and political impacts on other big oil-producing countries such as Russia and Venezuela. On the other hand, oil price falls can produce political benefits in energy-importing countries such as India or Japan. External political risk analysis involves careful analysis of economic, political and other linkages between countries around the world.

3.2.2 Economics

The macro-environment is also influenced by macro-economic factors such as currency exchange rates, interest rates and fluctuating economic growth rates around the world. It is important for an organisation to understand how its markets are affected by the prosperity of the economy as a whole. Managers should have a view on how changing exchange rates may affect viability in export markets and vulnerability to imports. They should have an eye to changing interest rates over time, especially if their organisations have a lot of debt. They should understand how economic growth rates rise or fall over time. There are many public sources of economic forecasts that can help in predicting the movement of key economic indicators, though these are often prone to error because of unexpected economic shocks.[5]

A key concept for analysing macro-economic trends is the *economic cycle*. Despite the possibility of unexpected shocks, economic growth rates have an underlying tendency to rise and fall in regular cycles. These cycles can also link to other important economic variables. For example, severe downturns in economic growth are often followed by falls in interest rates and exchange rates. Awareness of cycles reinforces an important pattern in the macro-environment: good economic times do not last forever, while bad economic times lead eventually to recovery. The key is to identify cyclical turning points.

Overall cycles in economic growth are made up of three principal sub-cycles, each of varying length (and named after the economists who originally identified them):[6]

- *The Kitchin or 'stock' cycle* is the shortest cycle, tending to last about three to four years from one cyclical peak to the next. This short cycle is driven by the need for firms to build up stocks of raw materials and parts as economies emerge from recessions. The build-up of stocks gives an additional boost to economic growth for a year or so, but the boost fades as firms no longer need to build their stocks. As economic growth slows, firms tend to run down their stocks by buying-in less, which reinforces the downward trend. A Kitchin cycle turning point comes when stocks are totally run down and firms fuel the upturn by building-up stocks again.

- *The Juglar or 'investment' cycle* is a medium-term cycle, typically stretching over 7–11 years. The cycle is driven by surges of investment in capital equipment, for instance plant and machinery. The Juglar downturn comes once these investments have been made across an economy and firms are able to cut back on further investment until the equipment is worn out. These investment cut-backs drain demand from the economy. The economy only reaches a new turning-point when wear and tear or innovation forces firms to spend again by investing in a new generation of capital equipment.

- *The Kuznets or 'infrastructure' cycle* is the longest, lasting between 15 and 25 years. These cycles follow the life-spans of infrastructural investments, for example in housing or transport. Kuznets cycles are triggered by initial surges of infrastructure investment, which then ease off as infrastructural needs are met, perhaps for a decade or so. The cyclical upturn comes when the last generation of infrastructure is worn out or outdated, and a new surge of investment is required.

The three sub-cycles add together to determine overall cycles of economic growth. Thus in Figure 3.4, year 1 corresponds with simultaneous low-points in all three of the Kitchin, Juglar and Kuznets cycles: this could be expected to be a very bad year for economic growth. Year 8, on the other hand, corresponds with low growth on both the Kitchin and Juglar cycles, but an approaching peak in the Kuznets cycles: this would be a less bad year.

Managers making long-term strategic decisions should assess where they stand in the overall economic cycle. For example, it might be tempting after several years of rising growth to launch major investments in new capacity. Such new capacity might not be needed in the

Figure 3.4 Economic cycles

subsequent slowdown. On the other hand, two or three years of slowing growth might make firms over-cautious about new investment. As the economy recovers in the following years, rivals who had invested in extra capacity or innovation might be able to seize the advantage, leaving over-cautious firms struggling to catch up. In assessing the economic environment, therefore, it is crucial not to assume that current economic growth rates will continue.

Some industries are particularly vulnerable to economic cycles. For example:

- *Discretionary spend* industries. In industries where purchasers can easily put off their spending for a year or two, there tend to be strong cyclical effects. Thus housing, restaurants and cars tend be highly cyclical because many people can choose to delay or curtail spending on these for a while. After a period of curtailed spending, there is liable to be a strong upturn as pent-up demand is finally released into the market.

- *High fixed cost* industries. Industries such as airlines, hotels and steel suffer from economic downturns because high fixed costs in plant, equipment or labour tend to encourage competitive price-cutting to ensure maximum capacity utilisation when demand is low. For example, an airline might try to fill its seats in the face of falling demand simply by offering cheap tickets. If its competitors do the same, the resulting price-war will result in low profits for all the airlines.

3.2.3 Social

The *social* elements of the macro-environment have at least two impacts upon organisations. First, they can influence the specific nature of demand and supply within the overall economic growth rate. Second, they can shape the innovativeness, power and effectiveness of organisations.

In the first place, there are a number of key aspects of the social environment that can shape demand and supply. These can be analysed under the following four headings:

- *Demographics*. For example, the ageing populations in many Western societies create opportunities and threats for both private and public sectors. There is increasing demand for services for the elderly, but diminishing supplies of young labour to look after them.

- *Distribution*. Changes in wealth distribution influence the relative sizes of markets. Thus the concentration of wealth in the hands of elites over the last 20 years has constrained some categories of 'middle-class' consumption, while enlarging markets for certain luxury goods.

- *Geography*. Industries and markets can be concentrated in particular locations. In the United Kingdom, economic growth has in recent decades been much faster in the London area than in the rest of the country. Similarly, industries often form 'clusters' in particular locations: thus there are high concentrations of scientists and engineers in California's Silicon Valley (see also Chapter 10).[7]

- *Culture*. Changing cultural attitudes can also raise strategic challenges. For example, new ethical attitudes are challenging previously taken-for-granted strategies in the financial services industry. Changing cultural attitudes can be linked to changing demographics. Thus the rise of 'digital natives' (generations born after the 1980s, and thus from childhood immersed in digital technologies) is changing expectations about media, consumption and education.

A second important social aspect of the macro-environment is organisational networks, with significant implications for innovativeness, power and effectiveness. These networks are frequently described as 'organisational fields'.[8] An **organisational field is a community of organisations that interact more frequently with one another than with those outside the field.** These organisational fields are partly *economic* as they include competing organisations within the industry or sector, as well as customers and suppliers in the marketplace (see Chapter 3). However, the concept of organisational fields also emphasises *social* interactions with other organisations and actors that exercise an influence on the focal organisation. These might include political organisations such as governments and campaign groups, legal entities such as regulators, and other social groups, such as professions and trade unions. Sometimes key actors in the field might even be particularly influential individuals, for example politicians. The organisational field is therefore much broader than just industries or markets. Because of the importance of social networks, managers need to analyse the influence of a wide range of organisational field members, not just competitors, customers and suppliers.

Networks and organisational fields can be analysed by means of *sociograms,* maps of potentially important social (or economic) connections.[9] For a new hi-technology enterprise, important network connections might be links to leading universities, powerful firms and respected venture capitalists, for example. Maps can help assess the effectiveness of networks and identify who is likely to be most powerful and innovative within them. Three concepts help to understand effectiveness, power and innovativeness:

- *Network density* typically increases network effectiveness. Density refers to the number of interconnections between members in the network map. Effectiveness is increased by density because the more interconnections there are, the better the communication of new ideas between network members. Everybody is talking to each other, and nobody with potentially useful information is isolated.

- *Central hub positions,* where a particular organisation is responsible for connecting many network members, are relatively powerful within a network. Hubs have power because network members rely on them for interconnection with other members. Hubs are also potentially innovative because they can collect ideas from the whole network, and they hear about what is going on in one part of the network before most other parts.

- *Broker positions,* where a particular organisation connects otherwise separate groups of organisations, are associated with innovativeness. Brokers' innovation advantage stems from their ability to link the most valuable information from one group of organisations with the most valuable information from the other group. Because they provide the connection between the two groups, they are able to exploit this combination of information before anybody else.

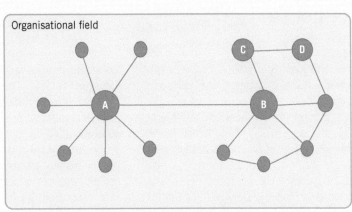

A is a more central hub than B; both A and B are brokers; B's immediate network is denser than A's.

Figure 3.5 Sociogram of social networks within an organisational field

Figure 3.5 provides an illustrative sociogram of two organisations' networks, A and B. Together these networks constitute a shared organisational field, although there are two relatively distinct groups within it. Because they link the two groups of organisations, organisation A and B can both be seen as brokers. Moreover, organisation A occupies a central hub position in its immediate network, connecting to seven other organisations, including organisation B. Organisation B is also a hub, though it links directly to only five organisations: to connect with organisation D, for instance, it passes through organisation C. Because organisation B is a less central hub, the sociogram suggests that it is likely to be relatively less powerful and innovative in its immediate group than organisation A. On the other hand, organisation B is likely to be more powerful and innovative than organisation C, because of its hub position and its role as broker. Moreover, although organisation B might be relatively less powerful and innovative in its group than organisation A, the overall effectiveness of its group might be greater than organisation A's. Organisation B's immediate network is denser, with more interconnections between individual members: all B's group have at least two or three connections. This density of connections means that ideas are more likely to pass quickly between group members, saving the problems involved in always going through a central hub. In this sense, organisation B may individually have less advantage relative to its group than organisation A, but collectively its network may perform better.

Sociograms can be drawn for key people as well as organisations: individuals are often the link between organisations anyway. Personal networks are important in many societies, for example the network of former consultants at the elite McKinsey & Co. consulting firm, or networks of company directors, or the interpersonal *guanxi* networks that prevail in China. Illustration 3.2 describes the network that has emerged from the armed service backgrounds of many Israeli entrepreneurs. The crucial issue in analysing social networks is how hub positions, brokering roles and network density are likely to affect a particular organisation's power, innovativeness and overall effectiveness.

Some organisational fields can be characterised as 'small worlds'.[10] *Small worlds* exist where the large majority of a network's members is closely connected, either just one step away (as C is from B in Figure 3.5) or one or two more steps away (as D is from B). Small

ILLUSTRATION 3.2   Intelligence Unit 8200 and the small world of Israeli hi-tech

Israel, a nation of just eight million people, exports more than $6bn worth of cybersecurity products a year, accounting for about 10 per cent of the global cybersecurity market. At the heart of this success is Unit 8200, the largest unit of the Israeli Defence Force and the equivalent of America's National Security Agency.

Unit 8200's alumni have produced more hi-tech start-ups per capita than the University of Stanford. Some of the successful companies originating with Unit 8200 include Check Point, with 2900 employees and a pioneer in Virtual Private Networks; NICE Systems, with 2700 employees and a pioneer in telephone recording technology; and Palo Alto Networks, with 3000 employees and a pioneer in computer firewall technology. Unit 8200 recruits are drawn from young Israelis doing their national military service: because this is compulsory only for Jews, few Arabs join. Recruitment into Unit 8200 is highly selective (in the Israeli Defence Force, only pilot training is harder to enter) and favours skilled computer science students and linguists. Recruits come disproportionately from the richer and more highly educated Tel Aviv area of Israel, and from elite schools such as Leyada, the semi-private Hebrew University High School in Jerusalem (where the founder of Check Point was a student). Alumni of Unit 8200 go not only into hi-tech business; many pursue successful careers in politics, the judiciary, the media and academia. For example, the former CEO of NICE Systems became director general of the Israeli Ministry of Finance.

Unit 8200's young recruits are intensively trained and work long hours in small groups applying the latest technology to security matters that might involve life and death. To maximise security, Unit 8200's technology systems – from analytics to data mining, intercept and intelligence management – are designed and built in-house. This experience prepares Unit 8200 alumni well for futures in hi-tech business. Avi Hasson, Chief Scientist at the Israeli Economy Ministry and himself an alumnus of Unit 8200, describes the working environment: 'When it comes to managing a startup, Unit 8200 is a fantastic school. . . . The unit encourages independent thought. It's something that was adopted later by many companies, a little like the culture in Google, in which good ideas can come from anywhere.'

Because recruitment in hi-tech tends to favour a 'buddy-system', alumni are often sought out for employment by other alumni. Experience of this intense, elitist organisation in the formative years of youth creates strong social bonds. The 8200 alumni association has more than 15,000 members, and hosts networking events and community outreach programmes, including start-up accelerators.

By 2020, Unit 8200 is due to move adjacent to the Advanced Technology Park at Be'er Sheva in southern Israel's Negev Desert. In 2013, Israel's President Benjamin Netanyahu had declared that Be'er Sheva would become the 'cybercenter of the Western hemisphere'. Be'er Sheva already had the advantage of the local Ben-Gurion University and its Cyber Security Research Centre. The National Cyber Bureau, a newly created agency advising the government on cyber policies, moved to Be'er Sheva in 2015. Companies already with operations in the Advanced Technology Park included many leading foreign firms such as Deutsche Telecom, IBM, Lockheed Martin, Oracle, PayPal and EMC. Venture capital firm JVP, with more than $1bn (£0.6bn, € 0.75bn) funding available, was also running a local 'cyberincubator' for start-ups. One of its first ventures was sold to PayPal.

Sources: *Haaretz*, 18 April and 24 April 2015; *Financial Times*, 10 July 2015; *TechCrunch*, 20 March 2015.

Questions

1 Identify at least one important hub and one important broker in the Unit 8200 network.

2 If you were a foreign cybersecurity company, what would you do to access Israel's expertise?

worlds typically give members a good deal of protection and effectiveness, due to their density. However, outsider organisations (for example foreign firms) will have difficulty penetrating small world networks on their own, and will typically require the help of insiders. Small worlds are particularly likely in societies where economic activity is geographically concentrated or where social elites share common backgrounds (for example, the French elite is often characterised as living in the same exclusive parts of Paris and as graduating from the same higher education institutions, the so-called Grandes Ecoles). Thus an important aspect of social analysis is the extent of small worlds in the macro-environment.

3.2.4 Technology

Further important elements within the macro-environment are *technologies* such as the internet, nanotechnology or new composite materials, whose impacts can spread far beyond single industries. As in the case of internet streaming, new technologies can open up opportunities for some organisations (e.g. Spotify and YouTube), while challenging others (traditional music and broadcasting companies). Chapter 10 will discuss specific strategies surrounding innovative new technologies in more detail.

Meanwhile, it is important to carry out the macro-environmental analysis of technology in order to identify areas of potential innovative activity. There are five primary indicators of innovative activity:[11]

- *Research & development budgets.* Innovative firms, sectors or countries can be identified by the extent of spending on research, typically reported in company annual reports and government statistics.

- *Patenting activity.* Firms active in patenting new technologies can be identified on national patent registers, the most important being the United States Patents and Trademarks Office.

- *Citation analysis.* The potential impact of patents and scientific papers on technology can be measured by the extent to which they are widely cited by other organisations, with data available from Google Scholar for instance.

- *New product announcements.* Organisations typically publicise their new product plans through press releases and similar media.

- *Media coverage.* Specialist technology and industry media will cover stories of the latest or impending technologies, as will various social media.

Although there is some variation between firms, sectors and countries in how far their innovative activity is reflected by these kinds of indicators, generally they will help to identify areas of rapid technological change and locate centres of technological leadership. For example, an analysis for the new material graphene (a material just one atom thick, but both strong and highly flexible) reveals that the annual number of published scientific papers multiplied by four between 2010 and 2014. Clearly graphene is likely to be of growing importance in the coming years. However, technological leadership is not clear. Western Europe accounts for 34 per cent of the scientific papers, but just 9 per cent of the patents. China accounts for 40 per cent of the patents and Samsung is the single firm with the largest number of patents. In terms of graphene application areas, patenting is greatest in electronics and composite materials.[12]

Many organisations also publish technology roadmaps for their sectors going forward.[13] *Technology roadmaps* project into the future various product or service demands, identify technology alternatives to meet these demands, select the most promising alternatives and then offer a timeline for their development. Thus they provide good indicators of future technological developments. Figure 3.6 provides a simplified technology roadmap for

Figure 3.6 Technology roadmap for graphene technology in electronics
Source: Substantially simplified from A. Ferrari, 'Science and technology roadmap for graphene', *Nanoscale,* vol. 7 (2015), pp. 4598–810 (Figure 121, p. 4759).

applications of graphene in electronics, both components and circuits and electronic systems. The roadmap suggests that tests of graphene devices in live animals and humans will be underway by 2018, with products like drug-screening devices and ultra-sensitive sensors emerging around 2020. This kind of roadmap has implications that go beyond the electronics industry, to include pharmaceuticals and every sector where detecting product characteristics is important, from retails to logistics.

3.2.5 Ecological

Within the PESTEL framework, *ecological* stands specifically for 'green' macro-environmental issues, such as pollution, waste and climate change. Environmental regulations can impose additional costs, for example pollution controls, but they can also be a source of opportunity, for example the new businesses that emerged around mobile phone recycling.

When considering ecological issues in the macro-environment, there are three sorts of challenges that organisations may need to meet:[14]

- *Direct pollution obligations* are an obvious challenge, and nowadays typically involve not just cleaning up 'at the end of the pipe' (for example, disposing of waste by-products safely), but also minimising the production of pollutants in the first place. Having clean processes for supply, production and distribution is generally better than managing the consequences of polluting after the fact.

- *Product stewardship* refers to managing ecological issues through both the organisation's entire value chain and the whole life cycle of the firm's products. Stewardship here might involve responsibility for the ecological impact of external suppliers or final end-users. It will also involve responsibility for what happens to products at 'end of life', in other words how they are disposed of when consumers have no more use for them. Thus car manufacturers are increasingly responsible for the recycling and safe disposal of old cars.

- *Sustainable development* is a criterion of increasing importance and refers not simply to reducing environmental damage, but to whether the product or service can be produced indefinitely into the future. This sustainability criterion sets constraints on the over-exploitation of particular sources of raw materials, for instance in developing countries, and often raises issues regarding the economic and social well-being of local communities.

In assessing the macro-environment from an ecological point of view, all three criteria of pollution, stewardship and sustainability need typically to be considered.

The extent to which these ecological criteria are important to organisations relies on three contextual sources of pressure, the first two arising directly from the macro-environment:

- *Ecological.* Clearly ecological issues are more likely to be pressing the more impactful they are: a chemical company may have more to worry about than a school. However, there are three less obvious characteristics to consider. First, ecological issues become more salient the more *certain* they are. For example, as doubts have reduced about the facts of global warming, so the pressures on organisations to act on it have increased. Pressures are also likely to be greater the more *visible* ecological issues are: aircraft pollution is more salient as an issue than shipping pollution because aircraft are more obvious to ordinary citizens than pollution done far out to sea. Similarly, the *emotivity* of the issue is liable to be a factor: threats to polar bears generally get more attention than threats to hyenas.

- *Organisational field.* Ecological issues do not become salient just because of their inherent characteristics. The extent of pressure is influenced by how ecological issues interact with the nature of the organisational field. An organisational field with highly *active* regulators or campaign groups will clearly give saliency to ecological issues. However, high levels of field *interconnectedness* will also increase the importance of ecological issues: within densely interconnected networks, it is harder to hide damaging behaviour and peer pressure to conform to ecological standards is greater.

- *Internal organisation.* The personal *values* of an organisation's leadership will clearly influence the desire to respond to ecological issues. Actual responsiveness will rely on the effectiveness of managerial *systems* that promote and monitor behaviours consistent with ecological obligations.

Although ecological issues can exercise unwelcome pressure, there are potentially strong organisational motives to respond. As in Figure 3.7, the three kinds of contextual pressure can satisfy a variety of motives. Fundamentally, there is of course a sense of ecological *responsibility:* thus the personal values of the organisation's leaders might stimulate ecological initiatives, or routine production systems might reduce pollution. However, another outcome can be *legitimacy,* as reflected in regulatory compliance and a good reputation with consumers. Finally, responding to ecological issues can even enhance *competitiveness.* For example, minimising waste in production processes for pollution reasons can reduce costs. Green products are attractive in the marketplace and often command a price premium.

3.2.6 Legal

The final element in a PESTEL analysis of the macro-environment refers to *legal* aspects. These can cover a wide range of topics: for example, labour, environmental and consumer regulation; taxation and reporting requirements; and rules on ownership, competition and corporate governance. In recent years, the relaxation of legal constraints through deregulation has created many new business opportunities, for example for low-cost airlines and

Figure 3.7 Contexts and motives for ecological issues

Source: Substantially adapted from P. Bansal and K. Roth, 'Why companies go green: a model of ecological responsiveness', *Academy of Management Journal,* vol. 43, no. 4 (2000), pp. 717–36 (Figure 2, p. 729).

'free schools' in various countries. However, regulations can also handicap organisations: Illustration 3.3 shows how the taxi-hailing app company Uber ran into important legal issues as it entered new markets and regulators struggled to keep up with the new technology.

Legal issues form an important part of the *institutional environment* of organisations, by which is meant the formal and informal 'rules of the game'.[15] This concept of institutional environment suggests that it can be useful in a PESTEL analysis to consider not only formal laws and regulations but also more informal norms: the 'L' can be stretched to cover all types of rule, formal and informal. Informal rules are patterns of expected ('normal') behaviour that are hard to ignore. Thus, regardless of the law, there are fairly explicit norms regarding proper respect for the ecological environment. Organisations ignoring these norms would risk outrage amongst consumers or employees, regardless of the legal situation.

Formal and informal rules vary sufficiently between countries to define very different institutional environments, sometimes known as 'varieties of capitalism'.[16] These *varieties of capitalism* have implications for the ways in which business and management are done in those environments and the prospects for success, both for insiders and for outsiders. Although every country differs in detail, three broad varieties of capitalism have been identified, whose formal and informal rules lead to different ways of doing business:

- *Liberal market economies* are institutional environments where both formal and informal rules favour competition between companies, aggressive acquisitions of one company by another and free bargaining between management and labour. Companies in these liberal market economies tend to raise funds from the financial markets and company ownership is either entrepreneurial or, for older companies, widely dispersed amongst many shareholders. These economies tend to support radical innovation and are receptive to foreign firms. Although neither is perfectly representative, the United States and the United Kingdom correspond broadly to this type of institutional environment.

- *Coordinated market economies* encourage more coordination between companies, often supported by industry associations or similar frameworks. There are legal and normative constraints on hostile acquisitions on the one hand, and various supports for consensual

ILLUSTRATION 3.3   Uber drives into trouble

The Uber taxi-hailing company has often run up against local regulations.

The inspiration for the Uber's taxi-hailing app came on a snowy night in Paris in 2008, when co-founders Travis Kalanick and Garrett Camp couldn't find a cab. Uber began business in Kalanick's home state of California, launching in San Francisco in 2011. With early funding from renowned investment bank Goldman Sachs and Google Ventures, Uber expanded rapidly. At the end of 2015, the company was able to celebrate its billionth ride. It was operating in about 400 cities around the world, from Abu Dhabi to Zurich.

Uber's hectic growth was in part aimed at pre-empting competitors. It is technically fairly easy to launch a local taxi-hailing app. Some of Uber's regional competitors grew rapidly, for example Lyft in the USA, Didi Kuaidi in China, Ola in India and GrabTaxi in Southeast Asia. In December 2015, these four rivals to Uber declared a strategic alliance, promising to share technologies and offer common services to customers travelling from one region to another.

The pursuit of growth has frequently got Uber into legal trouble. There are three areas in which Uber's strategy is particularly controversial. First, there is the contention that the company does not employ its drivers, but just offers a technology platform on which drivers and passengers freely interact. With drivers considered independent contractors, the company appears absolved from costly obligations such as insurance, minimum wages, overtime pay and pensions. This has helped Uber undercut the prices of traditional taxi services: in New York, the traditional yellow cabs saw a 14 per cent drop in business after the local launch of Uber. In several localities, including its home state of California, the independent contractor status of Uber's drivers has faced legal challenges, leading to local bans or fines.

Second, by comparison with becoming a licensed taxi-driver, it is relatively easy for people to become Uber drivers. This creates safety risks, with cases of Uber drivers even assaulting passengers. In 2015, an Uber driver in Delhi was convicted of raping a passenger. Uber was accused of failing to conduct adequate background checks after it emerged the rapist had been previously accused of assaulting women. The victim lodged a lawsuit in San Francisco (later dropped) and Uber was temporarily banned by the Delhi local authorities.

A third source of controversy is Uber's apparent aggression. The motto of the company's growth team is: 'it is easier to ask for forgiveness than permission'. Uber is often careless of local regulations. Local officials regarded by Uber as obstructive have allegedly become the targets of systematic attack. A hostile official in Virginia, United States, was flooded with emails and calls after Uber distributed his personal contact information to all of its users in the state. A senior vice president of Uber was widely reported to have suggested that Uber hire a team with a million-dollar budget to dig into the personal lives and backgrounds of media reporters critical of Uber: the company was obliged to disown the suggestion. During a bitter dispute in Portland, Oregon, the transportation commissioner called Uber management 'a bunch of thugs'.

In early 2016, CEO Travis Kalanick gave his view of Uber's approach to the *Times of India*: The way of an entrepreneur is the way of an adventurer. . . . . It can be conveyed as aggressive, but it is doing things people think is against conventional wisdom. . . . Ultimately, all rules have to bend towards people and progress.

Main sources: Financial Times, 15 September 2015; Times of India, 19 January 2016; Forbes, 17 August 2015.

Questions

1 Using the concept of 'varieties of capitalism', in which countries would you expect Uber to be most successful and in which less so?

2 What are the costs and benefits of Uber's aggressive approach to growth?

and collective arrangements between management and labour on the other. Companies in these coordinated market economies tend to rely on banks for funding, while family ownership is often common. These economies support steady innovation over the long-run and, because of coordination networks, are typically less easy for foreign firms to penetrate. Again, neither is perfectly representative, but Germany and Japan correspond broadly to this type of institutional environment.

- *Developmental market economies* tend to have strong roles for the state, which will either own or heavily influence companies that are important for national economic development. Formally or informally, the state will often encourage private-sector firms to coordinate between themselves and with national economic policy-makers. Labour relations may be highly regulated. Banks, often state-owned, will be a key source of funding. Long-term, infrastructural and capital-intensive projects may be favoured, but foreign firms will often be at a disadvantage. Although each is very different in its own way, Brazil, China and India all have aspects of this developmental market economy environment.

A macro-environmental analysis of any particular country should therefore include an assessment of the local variety of capitalism and the extent to which it favours particular kinds of firm and strategy.

3.2.7 Key drivers for change

The previous sections have introduced a variety of concepts and frameworks for analysing each of the PESTEL factors, particularly at a macro-level. As can be imagined, analysing these factors, together with their interrelationships, can produce long and complex lists of issues. Rather than getting overwhelmed by a multitude of details, it is necessary to step back to identify the *key drivers for change* in a particular context. **Key drivers for change are the environmental factors likely to have a high impact on industries and sectors, and the success or failure of strategies within them.**

Key drivers thus translate macro-environmental factors to the level of the specific industry or sector. Thus social and legislative changes discouraging car use might have different and greater effects on supermarkets than, for example, retail banks. Identifying key drivers for change in an industry or sector helps managers to focus on the PESTEL factors that are most important and which must be addressed most urgently. Without a clear sense of the key drivers for change, managers will not be able to take the strategic decisions that allow for effective responses: to return to the example above, the supermarket chain might address reduced car use by cutting the number of out-of-town stores and investing in smaller urban and suburban sites. It is important that an organisation's strategists consider each of the key drivers for change, looking to minimise threats and, where possible, seize opportunities.

3.3 FORECASTING

In a sense, all strategic decisions involve forecasts about future conditions and outcomes. Thus a manager may decide to invest in new capacity because of a forecast of growing demand (condition), with the expectation that the investment will help capture increased sales (outcome). PESTEL factors will feed into these forecasts, for example in tracking economic cycles or mapping future technologies. However, accurate forecasting is notoriously difficult. After all, in strategy, organisations are frequently trying to surprise their competitors. Consequently, **forecasting takes three fundamental approaches based on varying degrees** of certainty: single-point, range and multiple-futures forecasting. This section explains these three approaches and also introduces some key concepts that help explore the direction of future change.

3.3.1 Forecast approaches

The three approaches to forecasting are explored in the following and illustrated in Figure 3.8:[17]

- *Single-point forecasting* is where organisations have such confidence about the future that they will provide just one forecast number (as in Figure 3.8(i)). For instance, an organisation might predict that the population in a market will grow by 5 per cent in the next two years. This kind of single-point forecasting implies a great degree of certainty. Demographic trends (for instance the increase in the elderly within a particular population) lend themselves to these kinds of forecasting, at least in the short term. They are also often attractive to organisations because they are easy to translate into budgets: a single sales forecast figure is useful for motivating managers and for holding them accountable.

- *Range forecasting* is where organisations have less certainty, suggesting a range of possible outcomes. These different outcomes may be expressed with different degrees of probability, with a central projection identified as the most probable (the darkest shaded area in Figure 3.8(ii)), and then a range of more remote outcomes given decreasing degrees of likelihood (the more lightly shaded areas). These forecasts are often called 'fan charts', because the range of outcomes 'fans out' more widely over time, reflecting growing uncertainty over the longer term. These 'fan charts' are often used in economic forecasting, for example economic growth rates or inflation.

- *Alternative futures forecasting* typically involves even less certainty, focusing on a set of possible yet distinct futures. Instead of a continuously graduated range of likelihoods, alternative futures are discontinuous: they happen or they do not, with radically different outcomes (see Figure 3.8(iii)). These alternatives might result from fundamental policy decisions. For example, for a country facing possible exit from a currency union (for instance the Euro), outcome A might reflect the consequences for growth or unemployment of staying in the union; outcome B might reflect the consequences of exiting the union; and outcome C would be a further alternative outcome, consequent on a decision

Figure 3.8 Forecasting under conditions of uncertainty

that followed the initial decision pointing towards outcome B (for instance, to adopt trade barriers as well as to exit the currency union). For a business, outcome A might represent expected sales if a competitor business did not invest in a new machine or similar capacity; outcome B is a consequence of the competitor making that investment; and outcome C is a consequence of the competitor both making that investment and then slashing prices to make full use of the new capacity. It is possible to put probabilities to each of these outcomes too: for example, outcome A might have a 40 per cent probability, while outcomes B and C would be 30 per cent each. These kinds of alternative futures are often fed into scenario analyses (see Section 3.4), though not as simple forecasts.

3.3.2 Directions of change

It is helpful in forecasting to keep an eye on the fundamental directions of likely change. Managers need to check their forecasts are consistent with major trends and to be alert to possible turning points. Three concepts help focus both on major trends and on possible turning points that might invalidate existing forecasts:

- *Megatrends* are large-scale political, economic, social, technological, ecological or legal movements that are typically slow to form, but which influence many other activities and views, possibly over decades.[18] A megatrend typically sets the direction for other factors. Thus the social megatrend towards ageing populations in the West influences other trends in social care, retail spending and housing. The megatrend towards global warming affects agriculture, tourism and, with more extreme climatic events, insurance. It is important to identify major megatrends because they influence so many other things. Forecasts should be checked for consistency with such trends.

- *Inflexion points* are moments when trends shift in direction, for instance turning sharply upwards or downwards.[19] For example, after decades of stagnation and worse, in the early twenty-first century sub-Saharan Africa may have reached an inflexion point in its economic growth, with the promise of substantial gains in the coming decade or so. Internet retailing may also have put urban shopping on a path to significant decline in advanced economies. Inflexion points are likely to invalidate forecasts that extrapolate existing trends. Clearly it is valuable to grasp the inflexion point at the moment when trends just start to turn, in order either to take advantage of new opportunities early or to act against escalating decline as soon as possible.

- *Weak signals* are advanced signs of future trends and are particularly helpful in identifying inflexion points.[20] Typically these weak signals are unstructured and fragmented bits of information, often perceived by observers as 'weird'. A weak signal for the worldwide financial crisis that began in 2008 was the rise in mortgage failures in California the previous year. An early weak signal foreshadowing the current success of Asian business schools was the first entry of the Hong Kong University of Science and Technology into the *Financial Times*' ranking of the top 50 international business schools in the early 2000s. It is important to be alert to weak signals, but it is also easy to be overwhelmed by 'noise', the constant stream of isolated and random bits of information without strategic importance. Some signs of truly significant weak signals (as opposed to mere noise) include: the repetition of the signal and the emergence of some kind of pattern; vehement disagreement among experts about the signal's significance; and an unexpected failure in something that had previously worked very reliably.

3.4 SCENARIO ANALYSIS

Scenarios offer plausible alternative views of how the macro-environment might develop in the future, typically in the long term. Thus scenarios are not strategies in themselves, but alternative possible environments which strategies have to deal with. Scenario analysis is typically used in conditions of high uncertainty, for example where the environment could go in several highly distinct directions.[21] However, scenario analyses can be differentiated from alternative futures forecasting (Section 3.3.1), as scenario planners usually avoid presenting alternatives in terms of finely calculated probabilities. Scenarios tend to extend too far into the future to allow probability calculations and besides, assigning probabilities directs attention to the most likely scenario rather than to the whole range. The point of scenarios is more to learn than to predict. Scenarios are used to explore the way in which environmental factors inter-relate and to help keep managers' minds open to alternative possibilities in the future. A scenario with a very low likelihood may be valuable in deepening managers' understanding even if it never occurs.

Illustration 3.4 shows an example of scenario planning for information technology to 2030, published by the international advisory firm Gartner. Rather than incorporating a multitude of factors, Gartner focused on two key drivers which are clearly differentiated on the dimensions of the *scenario cube* in terms of having (i) high potential impact; (ii) high uncertainty; (iii) high independence from each other (see Figure 3.9 and below). The first of these two drivers are technological, in other words the extent to which information technologies are more interconnected; the second is regulatory, with regard to the extent to which technologies are controlled. Both of these drivers may produce very different futures, which can be combined to create four internally consistent scenarios for the next decade and a half. Gartner does not predict that one scenario will prevail over the others, nor do they allocate relative probabilities. Prediction would close managers' minds to alternatives, while probabilities would imply a spurious kind of accuracy over this period of time.

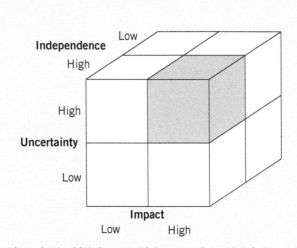

Select key drivers in the high-impact, high-uncertainty, high-independence box

Figure 3.9 The scenario cube: selection matrix for scenario key drivers

ILLUSTRATION 3.4 — Datatopia?

In 2014, Gartner, a leading information technology and research company, published a major report on four scenarios for IT developments to 2030.

Gartner had identified a major switch to digitisation of products and services in the world and wanted to consider the alternative implications of this change. Accordingly, the company used crowdsourcing to get ideas for future scenarios, bringing in 132 responses from volunteers across the world. The most frequent terms in the responses were initially analysed using a word cloud, in which words such as 'privacy' and 'trust' and 'personalization' were prominent. Next a form of PESTEL analysis was used to group assumptions by different factors, subdividing them into 'utopian' (positive) and 'dystopian' (negative) groups. Gartner then derived two basic dimensions for scenario analysis:

1 The extent to which the world would be 'connected' or 'conflicted'. In a connected world, technologies would interact easily with each other, and goals would be aligned. In a conflicted world, technologies would often be used to block each other, with conflicting goals.
2 The extent to which the world would be 'controlled' or run 'amok'. In a controlled world, society would be able to manage the direction of technological developments, but in an 'amok' world, technologies would run beyond society's control.

These two dimensions yielded four scenario stories, as summarised in the figure below. Briefly, the four scenarios were as follows:

1 *Society, Inc.* extends today's world, in which big corporations and governments control reams of data about individuals. Surveillance will be the norm and privacy disappears. Both organisations' and individuals' data will be regulated (independent storage mechanisms such as USB sticks might even be banned).
2 *Sorcerer's Apprentice* takes its title from the Disney story in which brooms come to life but run out of control. Technologies can talk to each other, so that people's identities will be easy to track. Regulation of data usage will continuously be behind what new entrepreneurial companies dream up for their own profit.
3 *Digital Wild West* describes a world where public outcry over data abuses stimulates new technologies that protect individuals, for instance widespread use of encryption. Companies will charge fees for privacy, a form of 'protection money'.
4 *Datatopia* is a utopian scenario in which privacy problems are solved by new technologies such as randomly fragmented storage, with personal keys necessary to reintegrate the information. All information is protected by copyright law. All activities – from power to parking – will be 'smart'.

Source: Adapted from Gartner Inc., 'Last Call for Datatopia . . . Boarding Now! Four future scenarios on the role of information and technology in society, business and personal life, 2030', 2014.

Questions

1 Which scenario would companies like Google and Facebook most desire and which would they most fear?

2 What are the implications of these scenarios for industries outside information technology, for example publishing and hotels?

	Conflicted	Connected
Control	Society, Inc. 'Whatever'	Datatopia 'Aspiring creativity'
Amok	Digital Wild West 'State of nature'	Sorcerer's Apprentice 'Ruled by machines'

Source: Adapted from Gartner Inc. (2014), p. 6.

Figure 3.10 The scenario process

While there are many ways to carry out scenario analyses, the process often follows five basic steps (summarised in Figure 3.10):[22]

- *Defining scenario scope* is an important first step in the process. Scope refers to the subject of the scenario analysis and the time span. For example, scenario analyses can be carried out for a whole industry globally, or for particular geographical regions and markets. While businesses typically produce scenarios for industries or markets, governments often conduct scenario analyses for countries, regions or sectors (such as the future of health-care or higher education). Scenario time spans can be either a decade or so (as in Illustration 3.4) or perhaps just five years ahead. The appropriate time span is determined partly by the expected life of investments. In the energy business, where oil fields, for example, might have a life span of several decades, scenarios often cover 20 years or more.

- *Identifying the key drivers for change* comes next. Here PESTEL analysis can be used to uncover issues likely to have a major *impact* upon the future of the industry, region or market. In the information technology, key drivers range from regulation to innovation. The *scenario cube* (Figure 3.9) helps identify the most significant key drivers. As well as the size of impact, the scenario cube underlines two additional criteria for key drivers: *uncertainty,* in order to make different scenarios worthwhile (there's no point in developing alternative scenarios when only one outcome is likely); and *mutual independence,* so that the drivers are capable of producing significantly divergent or opposing outcomes (there's no point in considering factors individually if they lead to the same outcome anyway). In the oil industry, for example, political stability in the oil-producing regions is one major uncertainty; another is the development of new exploration technologies, enabling the quick and efficient identification of new oil fields. These could be selected as key drivers for scenario analysis because both are uncertain and regional stability is not closely correlated with technological advance.

- *Developing scenario 'stories'*. As in films, scenarios are basically stories. Having selected opposing key drivers for change, it is necessary to knit together plausible stories that incorporate both key drivers and other factors into a coherent whole. These stories are often encapsulated with striking titles: for example, oil company Shell launched two opposing scenarios entitled simply 'Oceans' and 'Mountains', the first describing a more free-market world with solar power important, the second a more government-led world, with gas power important.[23] Striking titles help to communicate scenarios and embed them in strategic discussions (see also Illustration 3.4).

- *Identifying impacts* of alternative scenarios on organisations is the next key stage of scenario building. For example, in Illustration 3.4, the possibility of private data would pose major challenges to companies making their living from the assembly, analysis and sale of data. It is important for an organisation to carry out *robustness checks* in the face of each plausible scenario and to adapt strategies that appear vulnerable and develop contingency plans in case they happen.

THINKING DIFFERENTLY — The crowdsourced forecast

Do we need experts to forecast anymore?

We usually think of forecasts as the product of small groups of experts. But there is a different way. Forecasts can be 'crowdsourced', using the collective judgement of many different kinds of people, not just experts. There are two principal ways of using the 'wisdom of crowds' in forecasting: prediction markets and internet media analysis.

Prediction markets are markets designed specifically to combine the scattered information of many participants into values (for instance, market prices or betting odds) that can be used to make predictions about specific future events.[24] An example is the Iowa Electronic Market (IEM) for betting on the outcome of American Presidential elections. Market participants buy a contract that pays a dollar if, for instance, a Democrat wins the election. The more money participants are prepared to pay for that contract, the more likely it appears that a Democrat will indeed win that election. Google uses similar prediction markets to forecast the success of possible new products: if many people within the company are prepared to bet on their

success, then probably the new products will indeed turn out well. The bets of many employees may be more reliable than the self-interested forecasts of the product's own developers.

Internet media such as Twitter and Google can also provide forecasts, drawing on the inputs of many thousands of users. For example, Google Trends analyses the frequency with which people search about flu symptoms to predict the onset of flu epidemics. Others analyse the mix of positive and negative sentiments expressed by ordinary people in Twitter feeds to forecast the direction of financial markets, up or down.[25] Data about what people are interested in, or how they feel, provides valuable clues to what will happen next.

Question

Why might experts make bad forecasters in the case of (i) Presidential elections; (ii) new product developments?

- *Monitor progress.* Once the various scenarios are drawn up, organisations should monitor progress over time, to alert themselves to whether and how developments actually fit scenario expectations. Here it is important to identify indicators that might give early warning about the final direction of environmental change, and at the same time set up systems to monitor these. Effective monitoring of well-chosen indicators should facilitate prompt and appropriate responses. In Illustration 3.4, a clear indicator of a coming Sorcerer's Apprentice world would be relaxation of data-protection laws.

Because debating and learning are so valuable in the scenario-building process, and they deal with such high uncertainty, some scenario experts advise managers to avoid producing just three scenarios. Three scenarios tend to fall into a range of 'optimistic', 'middling' and 'pessimistic'. Managers naturally focus on the middling scenario and neglect the other two, reducing the amount of organisational learning and contingency planning. It is therefore typically better to have two or four scenarios, avoiding an easy mid-point. It does not matter if the scenarios do not come to pass: the value lies in the process of exploration and contingency planning that the scenarios set off.

SUMMARY

- Environmental influences can be thought of as layers around an organisation, with the outer layer making up the *macro-environment,* the middle layer making up the *industry or sector* and the inner layer *strategic groups* and *market segments.*

- The macro-environment can be analysed in terms of the *PESTEL factors* – political, economic, social, technological, ecological and legal.

- Macro-environmental trends can be *forecast* according to different levels of uncertainty, from single-point, through ranges to multiple-futures.

- A PESTEL analysis helps identify *key drivers of change,* which managers need to address in their strategic choices. Alternative *scenarios* about the future can be constructed according to how the key drivers develop.

WORK ASSIGNMENTS

✱ Denotes more advanced work assignments.
∗ Refers to a case study in the Text and Cases edition.

3.1 For an organisation of your choice, carry out a PESTEL analysis and identify key opportunities and threats. Use Illustration 3.1 as a model. For simplicity, choose an organisation that is focused on a limited number of industries.

3.2 For your own country, or any other country with which you are familiar, look up the political risk as assessed by Aon, the Economist Intelligence Unit or similar (see references in endnote 4). How far do you agree with this assessment?

3.3 For the last year or two, review the forecasts for economic growth made by key forecasting organisations such as the OECD or the World Bank (see references in endnote 5). How accurate were they? What accounts for any difference between forecast and outcomes?

3.4✱ For the same organisation as in 3.1, and using Illustration 3.4 as a model, construct four scenarios for the evolution of its macro-environment (or main industry or sector). What implications are there for the organisation's strategy?

Integrative assignment

3.5 Carry out a full analysis of an industry or sector of your choice (using for example PESTEL and scenarios). Draw also on the five forces and strategic groups analyses of Chapter 3. Consider explicitly how the industry or sector is affected by globalisation (see Chapter 9, particularly Figure 9.2 on drivers) and innovation (see Chapter 10, particularly Figure 10.5 on product and process innovation).

RECOMMENDED KEY READINGS

- For an overview of techniques for thinking ahead, see P. Tetlock and D. Gardner, *Superforecasting: The art and science of prediction,* Crown, 2015. For approaches to how environments change, see K. van der Heijden, *Scenarios: The art of strategic conversation,* 2nd edn, Wiley, 2005; and R. Ramírez, J.W. Selsky and K. Van der Heijden (eds), *Business Planning for Turbulent Times: New methods for applying scenarios,* Taylor & Francis, 2010.

- A collection of academic articles on PEST, scenarios and similar is the special issue of *International Studies of Management and Organization,* vol. 36, no. 3 (2006), edited by Peter McKiernan.

REFERENCES

1. PESTEL is an extension of PEST (Politics, Economics, Social and Technology) analysis, taking more account of ecological ('green') and legal issues. PEST is sometimes called STEP analysis. PESTEL is sometimes called PESTLE and is also sometimes extended to STEEPLE in order to include Ethical issues. For an application of PEST analysis to the world of business schools, see H. Thomas, 'An analysis of the environment and competitive dynamics of management education', *Journal of Management Development,* vol. 26, no. 1 (2007), pp. 9–21.

2. D. Bach and D. Allen, 'What every CEO needs to know about nonmarket strategies', *Sloan Management Review,* vol. 51, no. 3 (2010), pp. 41–8; J. Doh, T. Lawton and T. Rajwani, 'Advancing nonmarket strategy research: institutional perspectives in a changing world', *Academy of Management Perspectives,* August (2012), pp. 22–38.

3. I. Alon and T. Herbert, 'A stranger in a strange land: micro political risk and the multinational firm,' *Business Horizons,* vol. 52, no. 2 (2009), pp. 127–37; J. Jakobsen, 'Old problems remain, new ones crop up: political risk in the 21st century', *Business Horizons,* vol. 53, no. 5 (2010), pp. 481–90.

4. Organisations such as the insurance company Aon, and economic media such as the Economic Intelligence Unit and Euromoney, publish regular rankings of country political risk.

5. Macroeconomic forecasts can be found at: http://www.oecd.org/eco/outlook/; http://www.imf.org/external/; http://www.worldbank.org/.

6. For a summary, see B. de Groot and P.H. Franses, 'Stability through cycles', *Technological Forecasting and Social Change,* vol. 75, no. 3 (2008), pp. 301–11. Economists sometimes also highlight the 50-year long Kondratieff 'innovation' cycle: in this perspective, the world economy may still be on the upswing of the internet innovation cycle.

7. M.E. Porter, 'Clusters and the new economics of competition', *Harvard Business Review,* vol. 76, no. 6 (1997), pp. 77–90.

8. A useful review of research on this topic is R. Suddaby, K.D. Elsbach, R. Greenwood, J.W. Meyer, and T.B. Zilber, 'Organizations and their institutional environments – bringing meaning, values, and culture back in: Introduction to the special research forum', *Academy of Management Journal,* vol. 53, no. 6 (2010), pp. 1234–40. For a more general review, see G. Johnson and R. Greenwood, 'Institutional theory and strategy' in M. Jenkins and V. Ambrosini (eds), *Strategic Management: a Multiple-Perspective Approach,* V. Palgrave, 3rd edn, 2015.

9. R.S. Burt, M. Kilduff and S. Tasselli, 'Social network analysis: foundations and frontiers on advantage', *Annual Review of Psychology,* vol. 64 (2013), pp. 527–47.

10. M.A. Sytch, A. Tatarynowicz and R. Gulati, 'Toward a theory of extended contact: the incentives and opportunities for bridging across network communities', *Organization Science,* vol. 23, no. 6 (2012), pp. 1658–81.

11. J. Hagedoorn and M. Cloodt, 'Measuring innovative performance: is there an advantage in using multiple indicators?', *Research Policy,* vol. 32, no. 8 (2003), pp. 1365–79.

12. A.C. Ferrari, F. Bonaccorso, V. Falko, K.S. Novoselov, S. Roche, P. Bøggild and S. Borini, 'Science and technology roadmap for graphene, related two-dimensional crystals, and hybrid systems', *Nanoscale,* vol. 7, no. 11 (2015), pp. 4598–810.

13. J.H. Lee, H.I. Kim and R. Phaal, 'An analysis of factors improving technology roadmap credibility: a communications theory assessment of roadmapping processes', *Technological Forecasting and Social Change,* vol. 79, no. 2 (2012), pp. 263–80.

14. S.L. Hart and G. Dowell, 'A natural-resource-based view of the firm: fifteen years after', *Journal of Management,* vol. 37, no. 5 (2010), pp. 1464–79.

15. J. Cantwell, J.H. Dunning and S.M. Lundan, 'An evolutionary approach to understanding international business activity: the co-evolution of MNEs and the institutional environment', *Journal of International Business Studies,* vol. 41, no. 4 (2010), pp. 567–86.

16. M.A. Witt, and G. Redding, 'Asian business systems: institutional comparison, clusters and implications for varieties of capitalism and business systems theory', *Socio-Economic Review,* vol. 11, no. 2 (2013), pp. 265–300; M.R. Schneider and M. Paunescu, 'Changing varieties of capitalism and revealed comparative advantages from 1990 to 2005: a test of the Hall and Soskice claims', *Socio-Economic Review,* vol. 10, no. 4 (2012), pp. 731–53.

17. U. Haran and D.A. Moore, 'A better way to forecast', *California Management Review*, vol. 57, no. (2014), pp. 5–15; H. Courtney, J. Kirkland and P. Viguerie, 'Strategy under uncertainty', *Harvard Business Review*, vol. 75, no. 6 (1997), pp. 67–79.

18. R.A. Slaughter, 'Looking for the real megatrends', *Futures*, October (1993), pp. 823–49.

19. A. Grove, *Only the Paranoid Survive*, Profile Books, 1998.

20. S. Mendonca, G. Caroso and J. Caraca, 'The strategic strength of weak signals', *Futures*, 44 (2012), pp. 218–28; P. Schoemaker and G. Day, 'How to make sense of weak signals', *Sloan Management Review*, vol. 50, no. 3 (2009), pp. 81–9.

21. For a discussion of scenario planning in practice, see R. Ramirez, R. Osterman and D. Gronquist, 'Scenarios and early warnings as dynamic capabilities to frame managerial attention', *Technological Forecasting and Strategic Change*, vol. 80 (2013), pp. 825–38. For how scenario planning fits with other forms of environmental analysis such as PESTEL, see G. Burt, G. Wright, R. Bradfield and K. van der Heijden, 'The role of scenario planning in exploring the environment in view of the limitations of PEST and its derivatives', *International Studies of Management and Organization*, vol. 36, no. 3 (2006), pp. 50–76. For the grid method, see R. Ramirez and A. Wilkinson, 'Rethinking the 2 × 2 scenario method: grid or frames?' *Technological Forecasting and Social Change*, vol. 86 (2014), pp. 254–64.

22. Based on P. Schoemaker, 'Scenario planning: a tool for strategic thinking', *Sloan Management Review*, vol. 36 (1995), pp. 25–34.

23. http://www.shell.com/global/future-energy/scenarios/new-lens-scenarios.html.

24. G. Tziralis and I. Tatsiopoulos, 'Prediction markets: an extended literature review', *Journal of Prediction Markets*, vol. 1, no. 1 (2012), pp. 75–91 and K. Matzler, C. Grabher, J. Huber and Füller, J. 'Predicting new product success with prediction markets in online communities', *R&D Management*, vol. 43, no. 5 (2013), pp. 420–32.

25. P. Wlodarczak, 'An approach for big data technologies in social media mining', *Journal of Art Media and Technology*, vol. 1, no. 1 (2015), pp. 61–6.

Alibaba – the Yangtze River Crocodile

Richard Whittington

In May 2015, the Alibaba Group – China's largest e-commerce company – got a new Chief Executive. Daniel Zhang was 43 years old, with a career in the accounting firms Arthur Andersen and PwC before joining Alibaba in 2007. Zhang's experience in international firms was reflected in an early statement: 'We must absolutely globalize,' he said during a company-wide strategy session. 'We will organize a global team and adopt global thinking to manage the business and achieve the goal of *global buy and global sell*.'

Zhang's appointment as CEO came at a difficult time. Alibaba had undergone the largest ever Initial Public Offering (IPO) on the New York Stock Exchange in September 2014, achieving a total valuation of $231bn (£138.6bn, €173.3bn). But the first quarter of 2015 had seen profits at half those of the same period in the previous year. The Group's share price was down a third from its post-IPO peak. Zhang's predecessor as CEO had been dismissed after just two years in the job.

The man who appointed Zhang was Jack Ma, founder of Alibaba just 16 years earlier. Alibaba started as China's first business-to-business portal connecting domestic manufacturers with overseas buyers. Since then, the Group had grown in many directions. 1688.com was founded for business-to-business trade within China. Alibaba's Taobao Marketplace serves small businesses and individuals. Tmall.com provides electronic shop fronts to help overseas companies such as Nike, Burberry and Decathlon to reach Chinese consumers. Juhuasuan offers daily deals on everything from toys to laptops. There is also Alipay, effectively under Ma's personal control but functioning as the Group's equivalent to PayPal, which processes 75 per cent of Group transactions. One way or another, it is possible for Alibaba's customers to trade almost anything: the American security services have even set up a sting operation on Alibaba to catch traders selling uranium to Iran. At the start of 2015, Alibaba had approaching 80 per cent of the e-commerce market in China, the largest e-commerce market in the world, and also had strong positions in Brazil and Russia. International e-commerce represented nearly 10 per cent of the company's total sales of 76.2bn Yuan in the financial year ending 2015 (about $12.3bn, £11.2bn, €8.2bn: see Table 1).

Alibaba had always had an international bent. Founder Jack Ma had started his career as an English language teacher in the city of Hangzhou, not far from Shanghai. As early as 2000, Ma had persuaded both the leading American investment bank Goldman Sachs and the Japanese internet giant Softbank to invest. The then ascendant America internet company Yahoo had bought nearly a quarter of the Group in 2005. Post-IPO, SoftBank still held 32.4 per cent of the shares and Yahoo 15 per cent. The Alibaba Group board counted as members Yahoo's founder Jerry Yang, Softbank's founder Masayoshi Son and Michael Evans, former vice-chairman of Goldman Sachs. Even so, Jack Ma was ambivalent about Western investors: 'Let the Wall Street investors curse us if they wish!,' Ma had proclaimed at a staff rally. 'We will still follow the principle of customers first, employees second and investors third!'

Strictly, overseas investors do not directly own stakes in the Alibaba Group, instead owning shares in a shell company – a so-called variable interest entity (VIE) – that has a contractual claim on Alibaba's profits. This VIE structure is a common way for Western-listed Chinese firms to get around Beijing's foreign-ownership rules. But the Chinese government could close the loophole at any

Table 1 Key statistics

	2010	2011	2012	2013	2014	2015
Alibaba Group Sales Yuan bn	6.7	11.9	20.0	34.5	52.5	76.2
Chinese GDP Yuan Tr.	40.4	48.4	53.4	58.8	63.6	66.8
Chinese ecommerce market Yuan Tr.	4.6	6.4	8.1	10.5	13.4	16.2
Per cent of Chinese using Internet	34.3	38.3	42.3	45.8	49.3	51.3

Sources: iResearchChina.com; InternetLiveStats.com; Statista.com.

time, and it gives foreign shareholders limited recourse against abuses by Chinese companies' managers. Ironically, the most notorious VIE controversy so far involved Alibaba's Jack Ma, who in 2011 separated Alipay from the rest of the Group without board approval. Ma said new Chinese regulations forced him to make the move. Yahoo was only told about the spin-off five weeks after it had happened. A fund-raising round for Alipay's new parent company valued Alipay at nearly $50bn.

Alibaba's relationship with the Chinese government is hard to read. Jack Ma insists that he has never taken loans or investment from the Chinese government or its banks: he had gone to overseas investors instead. However, given that a third of Chinese business activity is carried out within state-owned enterprises, the government is bound to be in close liaison with the dominant national player in e-commerce. Ma explained his philosophy as: 'Always try to stay in love with the government, but don't marry them.' The Alibaba Group has built up its political connections. Tung Chee-hwa, Hong Kong's first chief executive after its return to China, served on its board of directors. Alibaba has also allied with several so-called 'princelings', children of important political leaders. Princeling investors include Winston Wen, son of a former Chinese premier; Alvin Jiang, grandson of a former Chinese President; He Jinlei, son of a former Politburo member and a senior manager of the state Chinese Development Bank; and Jeffrey Zang, son of a former vice premier and a senior manager at China's state sovereign wealth fund, Citic Capital.

Given Chinese President Xi Jinping's sweeping political and economic reform campaign, there are no guarantees of Alibaba's position domestically. In 2015, princeling investor He Jinlei's older brother was under house arrest because of accusations of corruption. The beginning of the year had also seen the publication of an investigation by China's State Administration for Industry and Commerce into counterfeit goods and fake listings on the Group's Taobao site, leading to a 10 per cent fall in Alibaba's share price. Jack Ma commented on his relations with Chinese regulators: 'Over the past two years, not only was I a very controversial figure, but also these days, the disputes are bigger and bigger.' He continued, 'I, too, felt puzzled, sometimes wronged – how did things become this way?' Nonetheless, Ma promised to clean up the site. Even so, just a few months later, fake Apple Watches were on sale on Taobao weeks before their official launch in the United States.

President Xi Jinping's reform campaigns were partly in response to changing economic conditions in China. After three decades of double-digit growth, China's growth rate has slowed to around 7 per cent a year (see Table 1). Such growth is very respectable by world standards. Besides, faced with rising domestic concern about the environment, President Xi was happy to restrain the expansion of high polluting industries such as cement, coal and steel. At the same time, the Chinese government was promoting e-commerce as a key area for future economic growth. However, there were causes for concern. Many local authorities and firms had borrowed heavily on expectations of higher growth, and there were fears that financial institutions had over-lent. Some warned of a consequent crash. Moreover, it was hard to see China's growth rate picking up again, on account of an ageing population and the drying up of the traditional supply of young labour from rural villages: by 2015, the Chinese workforce was falling by about three million workers a year. Although the government relaxed the famous one-child per family rule in 2013, Chinese parents are still reluctant to have more children because of the cost of housing and a good education in the main urban centres. It is predicted that by the early 2030s, about a quarter of China's population will be over 65 (against 17 per cent in the United Kingdom). Slower economic growth in China overall is being matched by some slowing in the rate of growth of the Chinese e-commerce market (see Table 1).

At the same time, Alibaba faces greater competition. A decade ago, Alibaba had seen off an attack by American rival eBay in the Chinese market with a fierce price-war. Jack Ma had proclaimed: 'EBay is a shark in the ocean; we are a crocodile in the Yangtze River. If we fight in the ocean, we will lose, but if we fight in the river, we will win.' A combination of cultural, linguistic and government policy factors kept Western internet companies at arm's length in the Chinese market: Google has been reduced to a market share of about one per cent, while Amazon eventually chose to list on Alibaba's TMall site after a decade pushing its own venture in China.

But now Alibaba's home-market dominance is facing a local challenge from the aggressive JD.com. While Alibaba still depends on China's unreliable postal service to get its goods to customers' doors, JD.com has been more like Amazon in investing in its own distribution centres and delivery services. As a result, JD.com can promise same-day delivery in 43 of China's biggest cities. Moreover, JD.com is well-placed to benefit from the shift to smartphones for e-commerce. Tencent, China's largest social networking and online games company, has taken a 15 per cent stake in JD.com, giving the challenger access to more than 400 million users of its WeChat phone messaging app. WeChat allows users to scan product bar codes with their smartphone cameras to make instant purchases through JD.com. Alibaba too has been entering smartphone e-commerce, and in early 2015, smartphone sales accounted for half of its retail Chinese sales, twice the proportion of a year earlier. But smartphone screen-sizes are less attractive to advertisers, an important part of Alibaba's traditional PC-based business model. JD.com's domestic growth in the year to 2015 has been twice that of Alibaba's. Although JD.com was still only about 15 per cent of its rival's size, founder and chief executive Richard Liu has declared a goal of beating Alibaba to the top position: 'The competition makes the two companies stronger. I'm actually enjoying competing.'

Thus Alibaba's new chief executive Daniel Zhang faced many opportunities and threats in 2015. There were already promising signs in favour of the globalisation strategy, though. Alibaba's international flagship AliExpress had rapidly taken the number one position in Russia and the number three position in Brazil, with local users delighted to have direct access to cheap Chinese goods.

One target now is the United States, only second to China in market size. The Yangtze River crocodile is aiming to attack the ocean sharks in their home seas.

Sources: China Daily, 8 and 13 May 2015; *eMarketer,* 23 December 2014; *Financial Times,* 16 June and 9 September 2014; *South China Morning Post,* 12 February 2015; *Washington Post,* 23 November 2014. With thanks to Mariya Eranova and Robert Wright for comments on an earlier version of this case.

Questions

1 Carry out a PESTEL analysis of Alibaba at the time of the case. Evaluate the balance of opportunities and threats, using the same kind of figure as in Illustration 3.1.

2 Draw a basic sociogram of Alibaba's network (see Section 3.2.3 and Figure 3.5). Explain why this network may be useful.

4

INDUSTRY AND SECTOR ANALYSIS

Learning outcomes

After reading this chapter you should be able to:

- Use *Porter's Competitive Five Forces Framework* to analyse industries or sectors: rivalry, threat of entrants, substitute threats, customer's power and supplier power.

- On the basis of the five competitive forces and *complementors* and *network effects*, define *industry attractiveness* and identify ways of managing these.

- Understand different *industry types* and how industries develop and change in *industry life cycles* and how to make five force analyses dynamic through *comparative industry structure analysis*.

- Analyse strategic and competitor positions in terms of *strategic groups, market segments* and the *strategy canvas*.

- Use these various concepts and techniques together with those from Chapter 2 in order to recognise *threats* and *opportunities* in the industry and marketplace.

Key terms

Blue Oceans	network effects
complementors	Porter's Five Forces Framework
critical success factors	strategic groups
industry	strategic lock-in
market	strategy canvas
market segment	value net

4.1 INTRODUCTION

In the last chapter, we considered how the broad macro-environment influences opportunities and threats. The impact of these general factors tends to surface in the immediate environment of the specific industry or sector. The immediate and direct opportunities and threats of this environment are the focus of this chapter. For example, Samsung's strategy depends on the smartphone industry: here it must take account of competitors' strategies, customers' needs and the supply of phone components, for example microchips. Similarly, a hospital needs to consider actors in the healthcare sector including clients, other healthcare providers and the supply of healthcare inputs such as pharmaceuticals. This suggests that it is crucial for managers to examine the industry or sector and the actors these involve carefully in order to determine what strategy to pursue.

The focus here is thus on the middle 'industry' and 'sector' layer in Figure 2.1 (see the last chapter), which involves central actors that influence an organisation's long-term survival and success including competitors, customers or clients, and suppliers. An **industry is a group of firms producing products and services that are essentially the same.**[1] Examples are the automobile industry and the airline industry. Industries are also often described as 'sectors', especially in public services (e.g. the health sector or the education sector). Industries and sectors are often made up of several specific markets or market segments. A **market is a group of customers for specific products or services that are essentially the same (e.g. a particular geographical market).** Thus the automobile industry has markets in North America, Europe and Asia, for example.

This chapter examines three main topics and provides different frameworks and concepts for understanding the industry or sector:

- Industry analysis through the use of the *Competitive Five Forces Framework,* which examines five essential industry forces: competitors, customers, potential entrants, suppliers and substitutes. Two additional factors are *complementors* and *network effects.* Together these forces and factors provide an understanding of industry attractiveness and competitive strategy.

- Fundamental industry structures and dynamics, which include examinations of underlying economic *industry types* and how industries evolve through *industry life cycles,* which might influence changes in the five forces that can be examined with a *comparative five force analysis.*

- Competitor groups and segments including examinations of *strategic groups,* groups of organisations with similar strategies and of *market segments,* groups of customers with similar needs. This focus provides a more fine-grained understanding of competition within an industry or sector.

The structure and topics of this chapter are summarised in Figure 4.1.

Figure 4.1 Industry and sector environments: the key topics

4.2 THE COMPETITIVE FORCES

Industries vary widely in terms of their attractiveness, as measured by how easy it is for participating firms to earn high profits. A key determinant of profitability is the extent of competition and the strength of buyers and suppliers, and this varies between industries. Where competition and buyer and supplier strengths are low, and there is little threat of new competitors, participating firms should normally expect good profits. Profitability between industries can thus vary considerably; for example, the pharmaceutical industry has performed very well while others, like the airline industry, have underperformed.[2]

Porter's Five Forces Framework[3] **helps to analyse an industry and identify the attractiveness of it in terms of five competitive forces: (i) extent of rivalry between competitors (ii) threat of entry, (iii) threat of substitutes, (iv) power of buyers and (v) power of suppliers.** These five forces together constitute an industry's 'structure' (see Figure 4.2), which is typically fairly stable. Porter's main message is that where the five forces are high and strong, industries are not attractive. Excessive competitive rivalry, powerful buyers and suppliers and the threat of substitutes or new entrants will all combine to squeeze profitability.

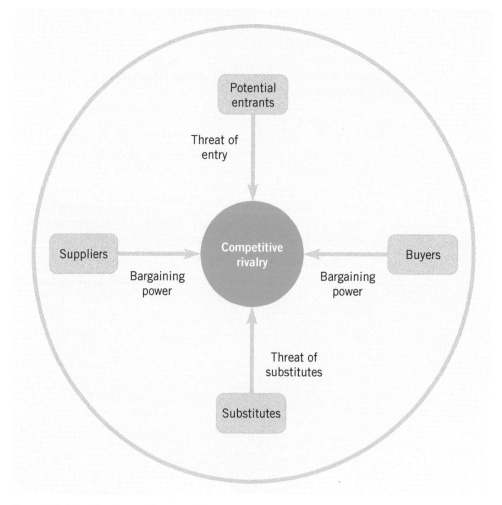

Figure 4.2 The Five Forces Framework

Source: Adapted from *Competitive Strategy: Techniques for Analyzing Industries and Competitors* by Michael E. Porter, copyright © 1980, 1998 by The Free Press. All rights reserved.

Although initially developed with businesses in mind, the five forces framework is relevant to most organisations. It can provide a useful starting point for strategic analysis even where profit criteria may not apply. In the public sector, it is important to understand how powerful suppliers can push up costs; in the charity sector, it is important to avoid excessive rivalry within the same market. Moreover, once the degree of industry attractiveness has been understood, the five forces can help set an agenda for action on the various critical issues that they identify: for example, what specific strategy to pursue in order to control excessive rivalry in a particular industry? Managers should try to finds positions where the organisation can best defend itself against strong competitive forces or where they can influence them in its favour. The rest of this section introduces each of the five forces in more detail and discusses industry definition and the implications of the forces. Illustration 4.3 at the very end of this section summarises industry and sector analysis and provides an overview of its various steps.

4.2.1 Competitive rivalry

At the centre of five forces analysis is the rivalry between the existing players – 'incumbents' – in an industry. The more competitive rivalry there is, the worse it is for incumbents. *Competitive rivals* are organisations aiming at the same customer groups and with similar products and services (i.e. not substitutes). In the European airline industry, Air France and British Airways are rivals; high-speed trains are a 'substitute' (see below). Five factors tend to define the extent of rivalry in an industry or market:

- *Competitor concentration and balance.* Where competitors are numerous or of roughly equal size or power there is the danger of intensely rivalrous behaviour as competitors attempt to gain dominance over others, through aggressive price cuts, for example. Conversely, less rivalrous industries tend to have one or two dominant organisations, with the smaller players reluctant to challenge the larger ones directly (e.g. by focusing on niches to avoid the 'attention' of the dominant companies).

- *Industry growth rate.* In situations of strong growth, an organisation can grow with the market, but in situations of low growth or decline, any growth is likely to be at the expense of a rival, and meet with fierce resistance. Low-growth markets are therefore often associated with price competition and low profitability. The *industry life cycle* influences growth rates, and hence competitive conditions: see Section 4.3.2.

- *High fixed costs.* Industries with high fixed costs, perhaps because they require high investments in capital equipment or initial research, tend to be highly rivalrous. Companies will seek to spread their costs (i.e. reduce unit costs) by increasing their volumes: to do so, they typically cut their prices, prompting competitors to do the same and thereby triggering price wars in which everyone in the industry suffers. Similarly, if extra capacity can only be added in large increments (as in many manufacturing sectors, for example a chemical or glass factory), the competitor making such an addition is likely to create short-term over-capacity in the industry, leading to increased competition to use capacity.

- *High exit barriers.* The existence of high barriers to exit – in other words, closure or disinvestment – tends to increase rivalry, especially in declining industries. Excess capacity persists and consequently incumbents fight to maintain market share. Exit barriers might be high for a variety of reasons: for example, high redundancy costs or high investment in specific assets such as plant and equipment which others would not buy.

- *Low differentiation.* In a commodity market, where products or services are poorly differentiated, rivalry is increased because there is little to stop customers switching between competitors and the only way to compete is on price. Petrol is a commodity market, for instance.

4.2.2 The threat of entry

How easy it is to enter the industry influences the degree of competition. The greater the threat of entry, the worse it is for incumbents in an industry. An attractive industry has high barriers to entry that reduce the threat of new competitors. *Barriers to entry* are the factors that need to be overcome by new entrants if they are to compete in an industry. Illustration 4.1 describes the entry barriers into the banking industry and the obstacles they provide for new entrants. Five important entry barriers are:

- *Scale and experience.* In some industries, *economies of scale* are extremely important: for example, in the production of automobiles or the advertising of fast-moving consumer goods (see Chapter 7). Once incumbents have reached large-scale production, it will be very expensive for new entrants to match them and until they reach a similar volume they will have higher unit costs. This scale effect is increased where there are high *capital investment requirements* for entry, for example research costs in pharmaceuticals or capital equipment costs in automobiles. Barriers to entry also come from *experience curve* effects that give incumbents a cost advantage because they have learnt how to do things more efficiently than an inexperienced new entrant could possibly do (see Section 7.2.1). Until the new entrant has built up equivalent experience over time, it will tend to produce at higher cost. In some industries there are 'demand or buyer side' economies of scale or *network effects* as buyers value being in a 'network' of a large number of other customers (see Section 4.2.6 below).

- *Access to supply or distribution channels.* In many industries manufacturers have had control over supply and/or distribution channels. Sometimes this has been through direct ownership (vertical integration), sometimes just through customer or supplier loyalty. In some industries this barrier has been overcome by new entrants who have bypassed retail distributors and sold directly to consumers through e-commerce (e.g. Dell Computers and Amazon).

- *Expected retaliation.* If an organisation considering entering an industry believes that the retaliation of an existing firm will be so great as to prevent entry, or mean that entry would be too costly, this is also a barrier. Retaliation could take the form of a price war or a marketing blitz. Just the knowledge that incumbents are prepared to retaliate is often sufficiently discouraging to act as a barrier.

- *Legislation or government action.* Legal restraints on new entry vary from patent protection (e.g. pharmaceuticals), to regulation of markets (e.g. pension selling), through to direct government action (e.g. tariffs). Of course, organisations are vulnerable to new entrants if governments remove such protection, as has happened with deregulation of the airline industry over the last couple of decades.

- *Incumbency advantages.* Incumbents may have cost or quality advantages not available to entrants including access to proprietary technology, raw material sources and geographical locations or an established brand identity. The medical instruments industry is, for example, protected by many patents and Coca Cola and Pepsi have brand loyalties developed over decades that few can overcome.

4.2.3 The threat of substitutes

Substitutes are products or services that offer the same or a similar benefit to an industry's products or services, but have a different nature. For example, aluminium is a substitute for steel; a tablet computer is a substitute for a laptop; charities can be substitutes for

ILLUSTRATION 4.1   Busted banking barriers?

The barriers to entry into the retail banking industry have traditionally been very high, but there are signs they could possibly be tumbling.

The high barriers to entry in financial services include two economic categories. First are the *structural* barriers due to basic industry conditions, and in this industry they include economies of scale, network effects and regulation. The last is significant; to protect the safety and stability of the financial system there are high regulatory walls. Second, incumbents may deliberately promote *strategic* barriers to keep or drive competitors out, like setting prices artificially low or spending heavily on product and brand advertising. The latter has some importance in banking, but the former does not. However, structural regulation barriers could be considered strategic in this industry as incumbents tend to exploit and lobby for them to their own advantage to keep competitors out.

In the UK, these barriers have resulted in the 'Big Five' domination: HSBC, Barclays, Royal Bank of Scotland, Lloyds and Santander. Other markets are very similar with a 'Big Five' in Canada, 'Big Threes' in Spain and the Netherlands and a 'Big Four' in Sweden. It seemed as if regulators would lower barriers to increase competition. However, in the aftermath of the 2008 financial crisis regulations have increased. The dilemma for regulators is that they have two partly conflicting objectives. First, to secure the stability of the financial system they need to increase capital requirements regulation for banks. The second aim is to deliver more efficiency and more services for customers through increased competition. To act on this second objective, regulators have started to encourage more entrants and assist them to find cracks in the barriers without totally breaking them. For example, Britain's Payment Systems Regulator has proposed that banks should cut their ownership stakes in the core payment systems as Managing Director Hannah Nixon confirms:

'There needs to be a fundamental change in the industry to encourage new entrants to compete on service, price and innovation in an open and transparent way.'

The UK's financial regulators have even launched a start-up unit to help new players to enter as Andrew Bailey, former CEO of the Prudential Regulation Authority explained:

'The New Bank Start-Up Unit builds on the work we have already done to reduce the barriers to entry for prospective banks, which has led to twelve new banks now authorised since April 2013.'

It remains to be seen if competition will increase, but adding to the regulators' aspirations is a new breed of potent rivals that may prove more powerful. Helped by new IT technologies, software and mobile banking there are over a hundred so-called 'fintech' (finance and technology) start-ups as confirmed in a Deloitte report:

'New, agile and hitherto unregulated players are emerging and are disintermediating the traditional incumbents.'

Even if incumbents also try to jump on this fintech bandwagon they may not be able to dominate it. In contrast to the flourishing fintech start-ups, they are not only behind the entry barriers, but bound by them as the report continued:

'Regulation is making it harder to innovate and grow, whilst legacy strategy, infrastructure and thinking, are preventing the existing players from responding aggressively from this threat.'

Sources: E. Robinson, *BloombergBusiness*, 16 February 2016; H. Jones, *Reuters*, 25 February 2016; Financial Conduct Authority, 20 January 2016; J. Cumbo, *Financial Times*, 6 December 2015; FCA, 25 February 2016; Deloitte, 'Digital disruption: threats and opportunities for retail financial services', 2014.

Questions

1 Evaluate the strengths of the banking industry's entry barriers according to Porter's criteria.

2 How would you evaluate the ethical behaviour of banks trying to keep competition out?

public services. Managers often focus on their competitors in their own industry, and neglect the threat posed by substitutes. Substitutes can reduce demand for a particular type of product as customers switch to alternatives – even to the extent that this type of product or service becomes obsolete. However, there does not have to be much actual switching for the substitute threat to have an effect. The simple risk of substitution puts a cap on the prices that can be charged in an industry. Thus, although Eurostar has no direct competitors in terms of train services from Paris to London, the prices it can charge are ultimately limited by the cost of flights between the two cities.

There are two important points to bear in mind about substitutes:

- *The price/performance ratio* is critical to substitution threats. A substitute is still an effective threat even if more expensive, so long as it offers performance advantages that customers value. Thus aluminium is more expensive than steel, but its relative lightness and its resistance to corrosion gives it an advantage in some automobile manufacturing applications. It is the ratio of price to performance that matters, rather than simple price.

- *Extra-industry effects* are the core of the substitution concept. Substitutes come from outside the incumbents' industry and should not be confused with competitors' threats from within the industry. The value of the substitution concept is to force managers to look outside their own industry to consider more distant threats and constraints. If the buyers' *switching costs* for the substitute are low the threat increases and the higher the threat, the less attractive the industry is likely to be.

4.2.4 The power of buyers

Buyers are the organisation's immediate customers, not necessarily the ultimate consumers. If buyers are powerful, then they can demand low prices or costly product or service improvements. *Buyer power* is likely to be high when some of the following four conditions prevail:

- *Concentrated buyers.* Where a few large customers account for the majority of sales, buyer power is increased. This is the case for items such as milk in the grocery sector in many European countries, where just a few retailers dominate the market. If a product or service accounts for a *high percentage of total purchases* of the buyer their power is also likely to increase as they are more likely to 'shop around' to get the best price and therefore 'squeeze' suppliers more than they would for more trivial purchases.

- *Low switching costs.* Where buyers can easily switch between one supplier and another, they have a strong negotiating position and can squeeze suppliers who are desperate for their business. Switching costs are typically low for *standardised and undifferentiated products* like commodities such as steel. They are also likely to be low when the buyers are *fully informed* about prices and product performance.

- *Buyer competition threat.* If the buyer has the capability to supply itself, or if it has the possibility of acquiring such a capability, it tends to be powerful. In negotiation with its suppliers, it can raise the threat of doing the suppliers' job themselves. This is called *backward vertical integration* (see Section 8.5), moving back to sources of supply, and might occur if satisfactory prices or quality from suppliers cannot be obtained. For example, some steel companies have gained power over their iron ore suppliers as they have acquired iron ore sources for themselves.

- *Low buyer profits and impact on quality.* For industrial or organisational buyers there are two additional factors that can make them price sensitive and thus increase their threat: first, if the buyer group is unprofitable and pressured to reduce purchasing costs and, second, if the quality of the buyer's product or services is little affected by the purchased product.

It is very important that *buyers* are distinguished from *ultimate consumers*. Thus for companies like Procter & Gamble or Unilever (makers of shampoo, washing powders and so on), their buyers are retailers such as Carrefour or Tesco, not ordinary consumers. Carrefour and Tesco have much more negotiating power than an ordinary consumer would have. The high buying power of such supermarkets is a strategic issue for the companies supplying them. It is often useful therefore to distinguish '*strategic customers*', powerful buyers (such as the retailers) towards whom the strategy should be primarily orientated. In the public sector, the strategic customer is typically the provider of funds, rather than the consumer of services: for a pharmaceutical company, the strategic customer is the hospital, not the patient.

4.2.5 The power of suppliers

Suppliers are those who supply the organisation with what it needs to produce the product or service. As well as fuel, raw materials and equipment, this can include labour and sources of finance. The factors increasing supplier power are the converse to those for buyer power. Thus *supplier power* is likely to be high where there are:

- *Concentrated suppliers.* Where just a few producers dominate supply, suppliers have more power over buyers. The iron ore industry is now concentrated in the hands of three main producers, leaving the steel companies, still relatively fragmented, in a weak negotiating position for this essential raw material.
- *High switching costs.* If it is expensive or disruptive to move from one supplier to another, then the buyer becomes relatively dependent and correspondingly weak. Microsoft is a powerful supplier because of the high switching costs of moving from one operating system to another. Buyers are prepared to pay a premium to avoid the trouble, and Microsoft knows it.
- *Supplier competition threat.* Suppliers have increased power where they are able to enter the industry themselves or cut out buyers who are acting as intermediaries. Thus airlines have been able to negotiate tough contracts with travel agencies as the rise of online booking has allowed them to create a direct route to customers. This is called *forward vertical integration,* moving up closer to the ultimate customer.
- *Differentiated products.* When the products or services are highly differentiated, suppliers will be more powerful. For example, although discount retailers like Walmart are extremely powerful, suppliers with strong brands, like P&G with Gillette, still have high negotiating power. Also, if there is no or few substitutes for the input the supplier group will be more powerful, like pilots' unions in the airline industry.

Most organisations have many suppliers, so it is necessary to concentrate the analysis on the most important ones or types. If their power is high, suppliers can capture all their buyers' own potential profits simply by raising their prices. Star football players have succeeded in raising their rewards to astronomical levels, while even the leading football clubs – their 'buyers' – struggle to make money.

4.2.6 Complementors and network effects

The five forces framework has to be used carefully and is not necessarily complete. Some industries may need the understanding of a 'sixth force', organisations that are complementors rather than simple competitors. **An organisation is your complementor if it enhances your business attractiveness to customers or suppliers.**[4] On the *demand side,* if customers value a product or service more when they also have the other organisation's product there is a complementarity with respect to customers. For example, app providers are complementors to Apple and other smartphone and tablet suppliers because customers value the iPhone and iPad more if there are a wide variety of appealing apps to download. This suggests that Apple and other actors in this industry need to take the app providers into consideration when forming their strategies. On the *supply side,* another organisation is a complementor with respect to suppliers if it is more attractive for a supplier to deliver when it also supplies the other organisation. This suggests that competing airline companies, for example, can be complementary to each other in this respect because for a supplier like Boeing it is more attractive to invest in particular improvements for two customers rather than one.

Complementarity implies a significant shift in perspective. While Porter's Five Forces sees organisations as battling against each other for share of industry value, complementors may *cooperate* to increase the total value available.[5] Opportunities for cooperation can be seen through a **value net: a map of organisations in a business environment demonstrating opportunities for value-creating cooperation as well as competition.** In Figure 4.3 Sony is a

* An organisation is your complementor if:
  (i) customers value your product more when they have the other organisation's product than when they have the product alone (e.g. sausage and mustard);
  (ii) it's more attractive for suppliers to provide resources to you when it's also supplying the other organisation than when it's supplying you alone (airlines and Boeing).

Note: Organisations can play more than one role. In this figure, Sony Music (publisher of AC/DC, Sade etc) is a complementor to Apple's iPod; Sony is also a supplier of batteries to the iPod; Sony also competes with its own MP3 players.

Figure 4.3 The value net

complementor, supplier and competitor to Apple's iPod. Sony and Apple have an interest in cooperating as well as competing.

Customers may not only value a product more if they also have another product or service as discussed above, but if other customers use the same product or service. When this is the case the product or service shows network effects or network externalities. **There are network effects in an industry when one customer of a product or service has a positive effect on the value of that product for other customers.** This implies that the more customers that use the product, the better for everyone in the network.[6] For example, the value of the online auction site eBay increases for a customer as the network of other sellers and buyers grows on the site. The more goods that are offered on the site, the better for customers and this makes eBay's site and services more attractive to users than smaller competitors. Network effects are very important for Facebook too (see in Illustration 4.2). Network effects can make an industry structurally attractive with high barriers to entry, low intensity of rivalry and power over buyers as entrants and rivals can't compete with other companies' larger networks and buyers become locked into them. If these effects are present in an industry they need to be carefully considered in addition to the five forces when trying to understand industry structure and strategic positioning.[7] For hardware and software computer products the number of users in a network is often referred to as an 'installed base'.

In some industries complementors and network effects work in tandem. In the smart-phone and tablet industries, for example, they operate in two steps. First, app providers are complementors to Apple as customers are more attracted to the iPhone and iPad if there are many apps. Second, when more customers are attracted to these products the network of users grows, which increases the user value even further. For Apple then the complementary app providers attract more users and this in turn provide for network effects that attract even further users. Other industries where competitors need to consider both complementors and network effects are video gaming (e.g. Nintendo) and computer operating systems industries (e.g. Microsoft).

Both complementors and network effects can create lock-ins. **Strategic lock-in is where users become dependent on a supplier and are unable to use another supplier without substantial switching costs.**[8] Strategic lock-in is related to the concept of path dependency (see Section 6.2.1) and is particularly valuable to differentiators. With customers securely locked in, it becomes possible to keep prices well above costs. For example, customers that bought music on Apple's iTunes store could earlier only play it on Apple's own iPod players. To switch to a Sony player would mean losing access to all the iTunes music previously purchased. Network effects can also create lock-in because when more and more users use the same product and technology it becomes more expensive to switch to another product or service. Sometimes companies are so successful that they create an industry standard under their own control. Microsoft built this kind of proprietary standard with its Windows operating system, which holds more than 90 per cent of the market. For a business to switch to another operating system would mean retraining staff and translating files onto the new system, while perhaps creating communications problems with network members (such as customers or suppliers) who had stuck with Windows.

4.2.7 Defining the industry

The first step in an industry analysis is to define the industry and there are several issues to consider here. First, and most generally, the industry must not be defined too broadly or narrowly. For example, if an entrepreneur considers starting a taxi business in Stockholm it would be much too broad to define the industry as 'the personal

ILLUSTRATION 4.2   Facebook's network fears

Considering Facebook's dominance they should have nothing to fear, but internet history is littered with fast rising and fast falling social networks.

A Statista survey found that with 1.5 billion users Facebook is not only the largest social network globally, but they control the second, third and seventh largest networks: WhatsApp (900m users), Facebook Messenger (800m) and Instagram (400m). It seems they are well ahead of everyone else in network effects and have created high switching costs for users to move to another social network. When users have built up a set-up of perhaps hundreds of friends and have archives of their whole life including photos they don't easily switch to another company and network just because it's something fresh.

Nevertheless, despite Facebook's clear lead, history shows it's far from obvious that any social network incumbent can stay relevant and dominate long term. Friendster pioneered the online community in 2002, three years before Facebook, and gained over three million users within a year; attracting tens of millions of users at its height. It was, however, soon overtaken by MySpace that appealed to even more and younger users with their more hip feature-filled environment including music and music videos. By 2008, it was the leading US social networking site with over 75 million users and consistently ahead of Facebook in traffic. However, soon Facebook started to attract teenagers with their new features with corresponding losses for MySpace. This overview illustrates that networks can quickly gain millions of users and huge valuations, but can just as quickly face slowing growth, users leaving in millions and final implosion. Further back in internet history, there are several other implosions of those with social network ambitions: BBS, CompuServe, AOL, etc.

Founder and CEO Mark Zuckerberg has, however, seen the threats and taken action. Instagram was acquired in 2012 when they were becoming the biggest mobile photo-sharing service with many younger users posting content there rather than on Facebook's own web-based photo service. Next was WhatsApp, the biggest messaging service globally; it was bought in 2014 as users started to move their activities to mobile platforms. To fence off LinkedIn they have launched 'Facebook at Work'. Not even Google has managed to remove Facebook from the social networking throne. Google's first social networking effort was Buzz, based on its Gmail service, but it never managed to attract enough users. Many Facebook users tried Google's next and even bigger bet, but soon discovered that not many of their friends followed so they returned and Google Plus, although still existing in another format, also flopped.

As of 2016, Facebook remains unbeaten and has perhaps learnt from social networking history. With their current valuation they can possibly continue to make defensive acquisitions as users are attracted to competing platforms, content and media, like Snapchat. But how long will it last? Some question Facebook's staying power and claim it's quite possible they will be overtaken. However, as reported by Forbes, Mark Zuckerberg, however, only sees this as inspiration to build Facebook even stronger:

'This is a perverse thing, personally, but I would rather be in the cycle where people are underestimating us. It gives us latitude to go out and make big bets that excite and amaze people.'

Sources: Statista 2016; R. Waters, *Financial Times,* 29 January 2016; J. Gapper, *Financial Times,* 12 April 2015; J. Bercovici, *Forbes,* 11 September 2012; A. Liu, digitaltrends.com, 5 August 2014; R. Waters, *Financial Times,* 21 February 2014; and J. Gapper, *Financial Times,* 3 October 2013.

Questions

1 Why are network effects important for Facebook? Would you switch to another social network if it had better features even if it was considerably smaller?

2 What other social media networks and apps do you use that you think could beat Facebook? Why?

transportation industry' while 'the minicab industry in central Stockholm' would be too narrow. The first definition would include such a wide variety of actors that the analysis would become meaningless, while the second risks excluding important competitors (e.g taxi firms from the suburbs).

Secondly, the broader industry value chain needs to be considered. Different industries often operate in different parts of a value chain or value system and should be analysed separately (see Section 4.4.2 for a discussion of value systems). For example, the iron ore industry (including companies like Vale, Rio Tinto and BHP Billiton) delivers to the steel manufacturing industry (including companies like Mittal Steel and Tata Steel) that in turn deliver to a wide variety of industries such as automobiles and construction. These three stages in the broader value chain or system should be analysed separately.

Thirdly, most industries can be analysed at different levels, for example different geographies, markets and even different product or service segments within them (see Section 4.4.2 below). Thus the airline industry has different geographical markets (Europe, China and so on) and it also has different service segments within each market (e.g. leisure, business and freight). The competitive forces are likely to be different for each of these markets and segments, with distinct buyers, suppliers and barriers, etc. Michael Porter has his own rule of thumb here and suggests that you are likely dealing with distinct industries if there are differences between them in more than one force, or where differences in any force are large.[9] In brief, it is important to consider both to what extent a market is national, regional or global (see Section 9.4 for a discussion of degree of internationalisation) and if product and service segments differ.

Larger corporations are often organised based on diverse markets and segments and would thus analyse each separately. For example, Electrolux, the Swedish appliance manufacturer, organises its major appliances (refrigerators, washing machines, etc.) in regional geographical markets, but also has two global business segments (small appliances and professional products) and would analyse all of these separately. The specific strategy question or organisation at issue might also provide a good indication of how to define the industry. Sometimes there is no ideal way of drawing the industry borders. Under these circumstances, the important thing is to draw the industry borders clearly. They have to be drawn consistently when it comes to what actors are inside and outside the industry. In particularly complex cases it might be necessary to try out both more narrow definitions to identify details and broader ones to avoid overlooking important actors.

4.2.8 Implications of the Competitive Five Forces

The Competitive Five Forces Framework provides several useful insights into the forces and actors at work in the industry or market environment of an organisation. The objective is more than simply listing the strength of the forces and their underlying driving factors. The ultimate aim is rather to determine whether the industry is a good one to compete in or not and to what extent there are strategic positions where an individual organisation can defend itself against strong competitive forces, can exploit weak ones or can influence the forces in its favour. The aim of the five force analysis is thus an assessment of the *attractiveness* of the industry and any possibilities to *manage strategies* in relation to the forces to promote long-term survival and competitive advantage. These considerations make up the last three steps in an industry analysis together with an assessment of industry change, which is discussed in the next section. See Illustration 4.3 for the different steps in an industry analysis. When each of the five forces has been evaluated, the next step is thus to understand the implications of these:

- *Which industries to enter (or leave)?* One important purpose of the five forces framework is to identify the relative attractiveness of different industries: industries are attractive when the forces are weak. In general, entrepreneurs and managers should invest in industries where the five forces work in their favour and avoid, or disinvest from, markets where they are strongly unfavourable. Entrepreneurs sometimes choose markets because entry barriers are low: unless barriers are likely to rise quickly, this is precisely the wrong reason to enter. Here it is important to note that just one significantly adverse force can be enough to undermine the attractiveness of the industry as a whole. For example, powerful buyers can extract all the potential profits of an otherwise attractive industry structure by forcing down prices. Chapter 8 further examines these *strategic choices* and *corporate strategy* and what to consider when deciding to invest into or divest out of various industries.

- *How can the five forces be managed?* Industry structures are not necessarily fixed, but can be influenced by deliberate managerial strategies. Managers should identify strategic positions where the organisation best can defend itself against strong competitive forces, can exploit weak ones or can influence them. As a general rule, managers should try to influence and exploit any weak forces to its advantage and neutralise any strong ones. For example, if barriers to entry are low, an organisation can raise them by increasing advertising spending to improve customer loyalty. Managers can buy up competitors to reduce rivalry and to increase power over suppliers or buyers. If buyers are very strong, an organisation can try to differentiate products or services for a specific customer group and thus increase their loyalty and switching costs. Managing and influencing industry structure involves many issues relating to *strategic choices* and *business strategy* and will be a major concern of Chapter 7.

- *How are competitors affected differently?* Not all competitors will be affected equally by changes in industry structure, deliberate or spontaneous. If barriers are rising because of increased R&D or advertising spending, smaller players in the industry may not be able to keep up with the larger players, and be squeezed out. Similarly, growing buyer power is likely to hurt small competitors most. Strategic group analysis is helpful here (see Section 4.4.1).

Although originating in the private sector, five forces analysis can have important implications for organisations in the public and charity sectors too. For example, the forces can be used to adjust the service offer or focus on key issues. Thus it might be worth switching managerial initiative from an arena with many crowded and overlapping services (e.g. social work, probation services and education) to one that is less rivalrous and where the organisation can do something more distinctive. Similarly, strategies could be launched to reduce dependence on particularly powerful and expensive suppliers, for example energy sources or high-shortage skills.

4.3 INDUSTRY TYPES AND DYNAMICS

The five forces framework is the most well-known strategy tool for industry analysis, but it has to be used carefully. First, industry types and their underlying economic characteristics should be considered as there will have major implications on industry attractiveness and what competitive strategies are available. Second, even though industry structures are

ILLUSTRATION 4.3 Steps in an industry analysis

There are several important steps in an industry analysis before and after analysing the five forces.

Emily wants to start a coffee shop and perhaps even try to grow the business into several outlets. She needs to consider the following steps and questions:

1 **Define the industry clearly.** Do the actors in the industry face the same buyers, suppliers, entry barriers and substitutes?
   - *Vertical scope*: What stages of the industry value chain/system?
   - *Product or service scope*: What products or services? Which ones are actually parts of other, separate industries? What segments?
   - *Geographic scope*: local, national, regional or global competition?

Emily should consider that many diverse businesses serve coffee. They include not only local cafés and coffee shop chains, but fast food chains, kiosks and restaurants. The definition also depends on whether Emily intends to start in an urban or rural area.

2 **Identify the actors of each of the five forces and, if relevant, define different groups within them and the basis for this.** Which are the . . .
   - competitors that face the same competitive forces? (compare point 1 above)
   - buyers and buyer groups (e.g. end customers vs intermediaries, individual vs organisational)?
   - suppliers and supplier groups (e.g. diverse supplier categories)?
   - potential entrants?
   - substitutes?

Provided there is a clear industry definition the identification of the actors for each force should be rather straightforward for Emily, but groups within them need to be considered. On the supplier side, for example, they include not only inputs like coffee but also the location of the premises and labour supply.

3 **Determine the underlying factors and total strength of each force.**
   - Which are the main underlying factors for each force? Why?
   - Which competitive forces are strong? Which are weak? Why?

Not all underlying factors on the five force checklists will be equally relevant for Emily. With respect to buyers, for example, the products' degree of standardisation and prices matters most, while others are less important.

4 **Assess the overall industry structure and attractiveness.**
   - How attractive is the industry? Why?
   - Which are the most important competitive forces? Which control profitability?
   - Are more profitable competitors better positioned in relation to the five forces?

For Emily several of the forces are quite strong, but some are relatively more important for profitability. In addition, some competitors, like large coffee chains, are better positioned versus the five forces than others.

5 **Assess recent and expected future changes for each force.**
   - What are the potential positive/negative changes? How likely are they?
   - Are new entrants and/or competitors changing the industry structure in any way?

For example, Emily needs to consider the proliferation of coffee chains during the last few years and that pubs and bakers have improved their coffee offerings lately. Maybe she can also spot possible changes in consumer trends and growth.

6 **Determine how to position your business in relation to the five forces.** Can you:
   - exploit any of the weak forces?
   - neutralise any of the strong forces?
   - exploit industry change in any way?
   - influence and change the industry structure to your advantage?

To cope with the forces Emily could possibly identify a concept that would attract a certain group of customers even if buyers have many choices in urban areas. This could neutralise threats from competition and entry somewhat and perhaps provide loyalty from some customers.

Sources: M.E. Porter, 'The five competitive forces that shape strategy', *Harvard Business Review,* vol. 86, no. 1 (2008), pp. 58–77; J. Magretta, *Understanding Michael Porter: The Essential Guide to Competition and Strategy,* Harvard Business Review Press, 2012.

Questions

1 Help Emily and go through each step above. Answer the questions and make a complete analysis. What is your assessment of the industry?

2 Based on your analysis: How should Emily handle the different forces? What strategic options should she consider?

often stable they do change, and some can be in flux for considerable periods of time. This suggests that basic industry types and industry dynamics in competitive forces need to be considered. This section thus first examines fundamental industry types and then industry change and dynamics.

4.3.1 Industry types

The five forces framework builds on theories in economics[10] and it helps to identify main types of industry structure. These vary from consolidated industries with just one or a few firms with high profitability to fragmented ones with many, sometimes thousands, as firms with lower profitability (see Table 4.1). In practice, particular industries are typically not pure representatives of these types, but none the less it is helpful to have these broad categories in mind in order to compare the attractiveness of industries and likely broad patterns of competitive behaviour within them. Three basic types are:

- *Monopoly industries.* A monopoly is formally an industry with just one firm with a unique product or service and therefore no competitive rivalry. Because of the lack of choice between rivals and few entrants, there is potentially very great power over buyers and suppliers. This can be very profitable. Firms can still have monopoly power where they are simply the dominant competitor: for example, Google's 65 per cent share of the American search market gives it price-setting power in the internet advertising market. Some industries are monopolistic because of economies of scale: water utility companies are often monopolies in a particular area because it is uneconomic for smaller players to compete. For this reason, the government sometimes gives one firm the right to be the only supplier of a product or service. Other industries are monopolistic because of 'network effects', where a product is more valuable because of the number of other people using it: Facebook and Microsoft Office are so powerful precisely because so many are already users.[11] See Illustration 4.2 for a discussion of Facebook's dominance.

- *Oligopoly industries.* An oligopoly is where just a few often large firms dominate an industry, with the potential for limited rivalry and threat of entrants and great power over buyers and suppliers. With only a few competitors the actions of any one firm are likely highly influential on the others: therefore all firms must carefully consider the actions of all others. The iron ore market is an oligopoly, dominated by Vale, Rio Tinto and BHP Billiton. In theory, oligopoly can be highly profitable, but much depends on the extent of

Table 4.1 Industry types

Industry structure	Characteristics	Competitive five forces threats
Monopoly	– One firm – Often unique product or service – Very high entry barriers	Very low
Oligopoly	– Few competitors – Product and service differences vary – High entry barriers	Varies
Perfect competition	– Many competitors – Very similar products or services – Low entry barriers	Very high

rivalrous behaviour, the threat of entry and substitutes and the growth of final demand in key markets. Oligopolistic firms have a strong interest in minimising rivalry between each other so as to maintain a common front against buyers and suppliers.[12] Where there are just two oligopolistic rivals, as for Airbus and Boeing in the civil airline industry, the situation is a *duopoly*.

- *Perfectly competitive industries.* Perfect competition exists where barriers to entry are low, there are countless equal rivals each with close to identical products or services, and information about prices, products and competitors is perfectly available. Competition focuses heavily on price, because products are so similar and competitors typically cannot fund major innovations or marketing initiatives to make them dissimilar. Under these conditions, firms are unable to earn more profit than the bare minimum required to survive. Agriculture often comes close to perfect competition (e.g. potatoes, apples, onions, etc.) and so do street food vendors in major cities. Few markets, however, are absolutely perfectly competitive. Markets are more commonly slightly imperfect so that products can be differentiated to a certain degree and with information not completely available for everyone. A number of small firm service industries have this character, like restaurants, pubs, hairdressers, shoe repairs, but also the shampoo, cereal and toothpaste markets.[13]

It has also been argued that there are '*hypercompetitive industries*'. Hypercompetition occurs where the frequency, boldness and aggression of competitor interactions accelerate to create a condition of constant disequilibrium and change.[14] Under hypercompetition, rivals tend to invest heavily in destabilising innovation, expensive marketing initiatives and aggressive price cuts, with negative impacts on profits. Hypercompetition often breaks out in otherwise oligopolistic industries. Competitive moves under conditions of hypercompetition are discussed in Section 7.3.1.

Industry structures change over time and industries can evolve from one type to another depending on the macro-environment and the degree of industry maturity with consequences for competitive force strengths. These industry dynamics are discussed next.

4.3.2 Industry structure dynamics

Industry structure analysis can easily become too static: after all, structure implies stability.[15] However, industries are not always stable. To begin with, industry borders can change over time and this needs to be considered when first defining an industry. For example, many industries, especially in high-tech arenas, are converging. Convergence is where previously separate industries begin to overlap or merge in terms of activities, technologies, products and customers.[16] Technological change has brought convergence between the telephone, photographic and the PC industries, for example, as mobile phones have become smartphones and include camera and video, emailing and document editing functions. Hence, companies that once were in separate industries, like Samsung in mobile phones, Sony in cameras and Microsoft in PC software, are now in the same smartphone industry.

As discussed in the previous chapter, the broader macro-environment also tends to influence the more specific industry environment through changes in the industry structure. These key drivers for change are likely to alter the industry, and scenario analyses can be used to understand possible impacts (see Section 2.4). An illustration of changing industry structure, and the competitive implications of this, is provided by Illustration 4.4 on the UK charity and public sector. This sub-section examines two additional approaches to understanding change in industry structure: the *industry life-cycle* concept and *comparative five forces analyses*.

ILLUSTRATION 4.4   Consolidation across the UK charity and public sectors

Consolidating the structure of the UK charity sector and of public-sector organisations may help improve efficiency and services.

The UK charity sector is fragmented with over 180,000 charities including multiple charities for similar causes; 700 charities for blindness, 900 for the armed forces, 500 for animal welfare, etc. These charities compete for the same fund-raising and resources and some argue that fragmentation has resulted in questionable fund-raising techniques, poor governance and outdated business processes. It has therefore been proposed that restructuring and consolidation of the sector is needed to help improve efficiency and services. As stated in a report of the Charity Commission, the regulator for charities in England and Wales:

'Some people believe that there are too many charities competing for too few funds and that a significant amount of charitable resource could be saved if more charities pooled their resources and worked together . . . '[1]

Consolidation of charities has started and, according to one report,[2] 129 charities carried out mergers with a transfer of £110m (€132m, $165m) to form new organisations in 2014/15. While many of the mergers or takeovers are smaller – an average of £2.4m income – there have been larger strategic deals. For example, Addaction (focused on drug and alcohol problems) took mental health provider KCA and Breast Cancer Campaign and Breakthrough Breast Cancer joined forces. Many small charities are forced into takeovers due to financial distress because of the overcrowded sector. Leisure trusts have been very active consolidators with three of the top ten deals, representing 5 per cent of all leisure trusts in England and Wales. Despite this, consolidation activity is still at an early stage as reported in *The Good Merger Index* (2013/14):

'The emerging picture was one of a small number of large transformative mergers, and a comparatively long-tail of local small mergers.'[2]

Richard Litchfield writing for *Charity Times* commented that:

'This shows trustees aren't proactively exploring merger and giving their charities space to think

strategically about the future. Boards should look objectively at their charity's position in an increasingly volatile sector, and plan in the best interest of beneficiaries – could we maximise our reach and impact by joining forces, and indeed are our services better housed elsewhere?'[3]

The public sector is also changing to increase efficiencies and improve services. One significant merger was the creation in 2013 of the combined Scottish Fire and Rescue Service, enabling a budget saving of £13m.[4] This new national service for Scotland involved the merger of the eight former local fire authorities. The NHS has also experienced considerable consolidation activities. For example, 25 mental health trusts in London have been consolidated into ten that also work in a network of partnership with each other.

Charity and public-sector consolidations are not without problems, however, and, as with private-sector mergers, integration difficulties can be severe. Nevertheless, there are also other forms of collaborations that offer opportunities to find efficiencies and improved services across charities and public-sector organisations. For example, joint procurement, sharing facilities, equipment and administration and combining different service deliveries to clients.

Sources: (1) 'RS 4a – Collaborative working and mergers: Summary', http://www.charitycommission.gov.uk/publications/rs4a.asp; (2) *The Good Merger Index*, Eastside Primetimers, 2014/15 and 2013/14; (3) R. Litchfield, *Charity Times*, 'Trustees need more help looking at mergers', 13 November 2015; (4) 'Fire and rescue collaboration', Grant Thornton, 26 March 2014.

Questions

1 How would you describe the current charity industry structure? How could it change if consolidation increases and what would be the benefits and disadvantages?

2 Which of Porter's five forces are creating problems for the UK's charity sector?

The industry life cycle

The industry life-cycle concept proposes that industries start small in their development or introduction stage, then go through a period of rapid growth (the equivalent to 'adolescence' in the human life cycle), culminating in a period of 'shake-out'. The final two stages are first a period of slow or even zero growth ('maturity'), and then the final stage of decline ('old age'). The power of the five forces typically varies with the stages of the industry life cycle.[17]

The *development stage* is an experimental one, typically with few players, little direct rivalry and highly differentiated products. The five forces are likely to be weak, therefore, though profits may actually be scarce because of high investment requirements. The next stage is one of *high growth*, with rivalry low as there is plenty of market opportunity for everybody. Low rivalry and keen buyers of the new product favour profits at this stage, but these are not certain. Barriers to entry may still be low in the growth stage, as existing competitors have not built up much scale, experience or customer loyalty. Suppliers can be powerful too if there is a shortage of components or materials that fast-growing businesses need for expansion. The *shake-out stage* begins as the market becomes increasingly saturated and cluttered with competitors (see Illustration 4.4). Profits are variable, as increased rivalry forces the weakest competitors out of the business. In the *maturity stage,* barriers to entry tend to increase, as control over distribution is established and economies of scale and experience curve benefits come into play. Products or services tend to standardise, with relative price becoming key. Buyers may become more powerful as they become less avid for the industry's products and more confident in switching between suppliers. Profitability at the maturity stage relies on high market share, providing leverage against buyers and competitive advantage in terms of cost. Finally, the *decline stage* can be a period of extreme rivalry, especially where there are high exit barriers, as falling sales force remaining competitors into dog-eat-dog competition. However, survivors in the decline stage may still be profitable if competitor exit leaves them in a monopolistic position. Figure 4.4 summarises some of the conditions that can be expected at different stages in the life cycle.

Figure 4.4 The industry life cycle

It is important to avoid putting too much faith in the inevitability of life-cycle stages. One stage does not follow predictably after another. First, industries vary widely in the length of their growth stages. For example, many internet-based industries have matured quickly and moved through the stages in less than a decade, like online travel and dating services. Second, some industries can rapidly 'de-mature' through radical innovation. Thus the telephony industry, based for nearly a century on fixed-line telephones, rejuvenated rapidly with the introduction of mobile and internet telephony. Likewise, since the mobile telephony industry matured it has later been revived by the introduction of smartphones and smartwatches. Anita McGahan of Toronto University warns of the 'maturity mindset', which can leave many managers complacent and slow to respond to new competition.[18] Managing in mature industries is not necessarily just about waiting for decline. However, even if the various stages are not inevitable, the life-cycle concept does remind managers that conditions are likely to change over time. Especially in fast-moving industries, five forces analyses need to be reviewed quite regularly.

Comparative industry structure analyses

The previous section raised the issue of how competitive forces may change over time. The industry life cycle thus underlines the need to make industry structure analysis dynamic. This implies that we not only need to understand the current strength of the competitive forces, but how it may change over time. One effective means of doing this is to compare the competitive five forces over time in a simple 'radar plot'.

Figure 4.5 provides a framework for summarising the power of each of the five forces on five axes. Power diminishes as the axes go outwards. Where the forces are low, the total area enclosed by the lines between the axes is large; where the forces are high, the total area enclosed by the lines is small. The larger the enclosed area, therefore, the greater is the profit potential. In Figure 4.5, the industry at Time 0 (represented by the red lines) has relatively low rivalry (just a few competitors) and faces low substitution threats. The threat of entry is moderate, but both buyer power and supplier power are relatively high. Overall, this looks like only a moderately attractive industry to invest in.

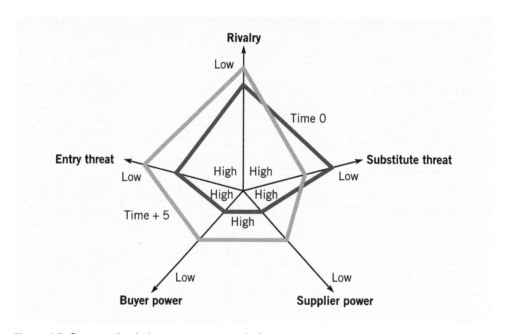

Figure 4.5 Comparative industry structure analysis

However, given the dynamic nature of industries, managers need to look forward, perhaps using scenario analysis. Figure 4.5 represents five years forward by the green lines. Managers are predicting in this case some rise in the threat of substitutes (perhaps new technologies will be developed). On the other hand, they predict a falling entry threat, while both buyer power and supplier power will be easing. Rivalry will reduce still further. This looks like a classic case of an industry in which a few players emerge with overall dominance. The area enclosed by the green lines is large, suggesting a relatively attractive industry. For a firm confident of becoming one of the dominant players, this might be an industry well worth investing in.

Comparing the five forces over time on a radar plot thus helps to give industry structure analysis a dynamic aspect. Similar plots can be made to aid diversification decisions (see Chapter 8), where possible new industries to enter can be compared in terms of attractiveness. The lines are only approximate, of course, because they aggregate the many individual elements that make up each of the forces into a simple composite measure. Notice too that if one of the forces is very adverse, then this might nullify positive assessments on the other four axes: for example, an industry with low rivalry, low substitution, low entry barriers and low supplier power might still be unattractive if powerful buyers were able to demand highly discounted prices. With these warnings in mind, such radar plots can nonetheless be both a useful device for initial analysis and an effective summary of a final, more refined and dynamic analysis.

4.4 COMPETITORS AND MARKETS

An industry or sector may be too high a level to provide for a detailed understanding of competition. The five forces can impact differently on different kinds of players, which requires a more fine-grained understanding. For example, Hyundai and Porsche may be in the same broad industry (automobiles), but they are positioned differently: they are protected by different barriers to entry and competitive moves by one are unlikely to affect the other. It is often useful to disaggregate. Many industries contain a range of companies, each of which have different capabilities and compete on different bases. Some of these competitor differences are captured by the concept of *strategic groups*. Customers too can differ significantly and these can be captured by distinguishing between different *market segments*. Thinking in terms of different strategic groups and market segments provides opportunities for organisations to develop highly distinctive positionings within broader industries. Besides disaggregating the analysis of industry competition, these approaches may help in understanding how value is created differently by different competitors. Competitor differences, both actual and potential, including the identification of entirely new market spaces can also be analysed using the *strategy canvas* and '*Blue Ocean*' thinking, the last topic in this section.

4.4.1 Strategic groups[19]

Strategic groups are organisations within the same industry or sector with similar strategic characteristics, following similar strategies or competing on similar bases. These characteristics are different from those in other strategic groups in the same industry or sector. For example, in the grocery retailing industry, supermarkets, convenience stores and corner shops each form different strategic groups. There are many different characteristics that

It is useful to consider the extent to which organisations *differ* in terms of **characteristics** such as:

Scope of activities

- Extent of product (or service) diversity
- Extent of geographical coverage
- Number of market segments served
- Distribution channels used

Resource commitment

- Extent (number) of **branding**
- **Marketing effort** (e.g. advertising spread, size of salesforce)
- Extent of **vertical integration**
- Product or service **quality**
- **Technological leadership** (a leader or follower)
- **Size** of organisation

Figure 4.6 Some characteristics for identifying strategic groups

distinguish between strategic groups, but these can be grouped into two major categories (see Figure 4.6):[20] first, the *scope* of an organisation's activities (such as product range, geographical coverage and range of distribution channels used); second, the *resource commitment* (such as brands, marketing spend and extent of vertical integration). Which characteristics are relevant differs from industry to industry, but typically important are those characteristics that separate high performers from low performers.

Strategic groups can be mapped onto two-dimensional charts – for example, one axis might be the extent of product range and the other axis the size of marketing spend. One method for choosing key dimensions by which to map strategic groups is to identify top performers (by growth or profitability) in an industry and to compare them with low performers. Characteristics that are shared by top performers, but not by low performers, are likely to be particularly relevant for mapping strategic groups. For example, the most profitable firms in an industry might all be narrow in terms of product range, and lavish in terms of marketing spend, while the less profitable firms might be more widely spread in terms of products and restrained in their marketing. Here the two dimensions for mapping would be product range and marketing spend. A potential recommendation for the less profitable firms would be to cut back their product range and boost their marketing.

Figure 4.7 shows strategic groups among Indian pharmaceutical companies, with research and development intensity (R&D spend as a percentage of sales) and overseas focus (exports and patents registered overseas) defining the axes of the map. These two axes do explain a good deal of the variation in profitability between groups. The most profitable group is the Emergent globals (11.3 per cent average return on sales), those with high R&D intensity and high overseas focus. On the other hand, the Exploiter group

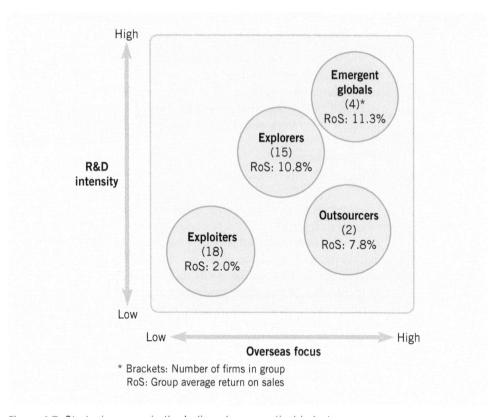

Figure 4.7 Strategic groups in the Indian pharmaceutical industry

Source: Developed from R. Chittoor and S. Ray, 'Internationalisation paths of Indian pharmaceutical firms: a strategic group analysis', *Journal of International Management*, vol. 13 (2009), pp. 338–55.

spends little on R&D and is focused on domestic markets, and enjoys only 2.0 per cent average return on sales.

This strategic group concept is useful in at least three ways:

- *Understanding competition.* Managers can focus on their direct competitors within their particular strategic group, rather than the whole industry as rivalry often is strongest between these. In general, strategic groups are influenced differently by the competitive forces and this focus thus allows for a more specific industry structure analysis. They can also establish the dimensions that distinguish them most from other groups, and which might be the basis for relative success or failure. This suggests that there may be profitability differences between different strategic groups and the differing dimensions can then become the focus of their action.

- *Analysis of strategic opportunities.* Strategic group maps can identify the most attractive 'strategic spaces' within an industry. Some spaces on the map may be 'white spaces', relatively under-occupied. In the Indian pharmaceutical industry, the white space is high R&D investment combined with focus on domestic markets. Such white spaces might be unexploited opportunities. On the other hand, they could turn out to be 'black holes', impossible to exploit and likely to damage any entrant. A strategic group map is only the first stage of the analysis. Strategic spaces need to tested carefully.

- *Analysis of mobility barriers.* Of course, moving across the strategic group map to take advantage of opportunities is not costless. Often it will require difficult decisions and rare resources. Strategic groups are therefore characterised by 'mobility barriers', obstacles to movement from one strategic group to another. These are the equivalent to barriers to entry in five forces analysis, but between different strategic groups within the same industry.

Although movement from the Exploiter group in Indian pharmaceuticals to the Emergent global group might seem very attractive in terms of profits, it is likely to demand very substantial financial investment and strong managerial skills. Mobility into the Emergent global group will not be easy. As with barriers to entry, it is good to be in a successful strategic group protected by strong mobility barriers, to impede imitation.

4.4.2 Market segments

The concept of strategic groups discussed above helps with understanding the similarities and differences in terms of competitor characteristics. Industries can also be disaggregated into smaller and specific market sections known as segments. The concept of market segment focuses on differences in *customer* needs. A **market segment**[21] **is a group of customers who have similar needs that are different from customer needs in other parts of the market.** Where these customer groups are relatively small, such market segments are often called 'niches'. Dominance of a market segment or niche can be very valuable, for the same reasons that dominance of an industry can be valuable following five forces reasoning.

Segmentation should reflect an organisation's strategy[22] and strategies based on market segments must keep customer needs firmly in mind. Therefore, two issues are particularly important in market segment analysis:

- *Variation in customer needs.* Focusing on customer needs that are highly distinctive from those typical in the market is one means of building a long-term segment strategy. Customer needs vary for a whole variety of reasons – some of which are identified in Table 4.2. Theoretically, any of these factors could be used to identify distinct market segments. However, the crucial bases of segmentation vary according to market. In industrial markets, segmentation is often thought of in terms of industrial classification of buyers: steel producers might segment by automobile industry, packaging industry and construction industry, for example. On the other hand, segmentation by buyer behaviour (e.g. direct buying versus those users who buy through third parties such as contractors) or purchase value (e.g. high-value bulk purchasers versus frequent low-value purchasers) might be more appropriate. Being able to serve a highly distinctive segment that other organisations find difficult to serve is often the basis for a secure long-term strategy.

- *Specialisation* within a market segment can also be an important basis for a successful segmentation strategy. This is sometimes called a 'niche strategy'. Organisations that have built up most experience in servicing a particular market segment should not only have lower costs in so doing, but also should have built relationships which may be difficult for others to break down. Experience and relationships are likely to protect a dominant position in a particular segment. However, precisely because customers value different things in different segments, specialised producers may find it very difficult to compete on a broader basis. For example, a small local brewery competing against the big brands on the basis of its ability to satisfy distinctive local tastes is unlikely to find it easy to serve other segments where tastes are different, scale requirements are larger and distribution channels are more complex.

Table 4.2 Some bases of market segmentation

Type of factor	Consumer markets	Industrial/organisational markets
Characteristics of people/organisations	Age, gender, ethnicity Income Family size Life-cycle stage Location Lifestyle	Industry Location Size Technology Profitability Management
Purchase/use situation	Size of purchase Brand loyalty Purpose of use Purchasing behaviour Importance of purchase Choice criteria	Application Importance of purchase Volume Frequency of purchase Purchasing procedure Choice criteria Distribution channel
Users' needs and preferences for product characteristics	Product similarity Price preference Brand preferences Desired features Quality	Performance requirements Assistance from suppliers Brand preferences Desired features Quality Service requirements

4.4.3 Critical success factors and 'Blue Oceans'

Industry or sector analysis should also include an understanding of competitors and the different ways they offer value to customers. As Michael Porter's five forces framework underlines, reducing industry rivalry involves competitors finding differentiated positions in the marketplace. W. Chan Kim and Renée Mauborgne at INSEAD propose two concepts that help think creatively about the relative positioning of competitors in the environment and finding uncontested market spaces: the strategy canvas and 'Blue Oceans'.[23]

A **strategy canvas compares competitors according to their performance on key success factors in order to establish the extent of differentiation.** It captures the current factors of competition of the industry, but also offers ways of challenging these and creatively trying to identify new competitive offerings. Figure 4.8 shows a strategy canvas for three electrical components companies. The canvas highlights the following three features:

- **Critical success factors (CSFs) are those factors that either are particularly valued by customers (i.e. strategic customers) or provide a significant advantage in terms of cost.** Critical success factors are therefore likely to be an important source of competitive advantage or disadvantage. Figure 4.8 identifies five established critical success factors in this electrical components market (cost, after-sales service, delivery reliability, technical quality and testing facilities). Note there is also a new sixth critical success factor, design advisory services, which will be discussed under the third subhead, value innovation.

- *Value curves* are a graphic depiction of how customers perceive competitors' relative performance across the critical success factors. In Figure 4.8, companies A and B perform well on cost, service, reliability and quality, but less well on testing. They do not offer any design advice. They are poorly differentiated and occupy a space in the market where

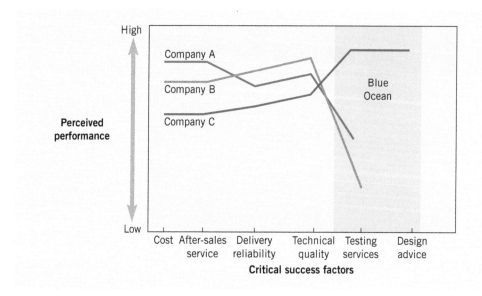

Figure 4.8 Strategy canvas for electrical components companies
Note: cost is used rather than price for consistency of value curves.
Source: Developed from W.C. Kim and R. Mauborgne, *Blue Ocean Strategy*, Harvard Business School Press, 2005.

profits may be hard to get because of excessive rivalry between the two. Company C, on the other hand, has a radically different value curve, characteristic of a 'value innovator'.

- *Value innovation* is the creation of new market space by excelling on established critical success factors on which competitors are performing badly and/or by creating new critical success factors representing previously unrecognised customer wants. Thus in Figure 4.8, company C is a value innovator in both senses. First, it excels on the established customer need of offering testing facilities for customers' products using its components. Second, it offers a new and valued design service advising customers on how to integrate their components in order for them to create better products.

A value innovator is a company that competes in 'Blue Oceans'. **Blue Oceans are new market spaces where competition is minimised.**[24] Blue Oceans contrast with 'Red Oceans', where industries are already well defined and rivalry is intense. Blue Oceans evoke wide empty seas. Red Oceans are associated with bloody competition and 'red ink', in other words financial losses. The Blue Ocean concept is thus useful for identifying potential spaces in the environment with little competition. These Blue Oceans are *strategic gaps* in the marketplace.

In Figure 4.8, company C's strategy exemplifies two critical principles of Blue Ocean thinking: *focus* and *divergence*. First, company C focuses its efforts on just two factors, testing and design services, while maintaining only adequate performance on the other critical success factors where its competitors are already high performers. Second, it has created a value curve that significantly diverges from its competitors' value curves, creating a substantial *strategic gap*, or Blue Ocean, in the areas of testing and design services. This is shrewd. For company C, beating companies A and B in the areas where they are performing well anyway would require major investment and likely provide little advantage given that customers are already highly satisfied. Challenging A and B on cost, after-sales service, delivery or quality would be a Red Ocean strategy, increasing industry rivalry. Far better is to concentrate on where a large gap can be created between competitors. Company C faces little competition for those customers who really value testing and design services, and consequently can charge good prices for them. The task for companies A and B now is to find strategic gaps of their own.

4.5 OPPORTUNITIES AND THREATS

The concepts and frameworks discussed above and in Chapter 2 should be helpful in understanding the factors in the macro-, industry and competitor/market environments of an organisation. However, the critical issue is the *implications* that are drawn from this understanding in guiding strategic decisions and choices. The crucial next stage, therefore, is to draw from the environmental analysis specific strategic opportunities and threats for the organisation. Identifying these opportunities and threats is extremely valuable when thinking about strategic choices for the future (the subject of Chapters 7 to 11). Opportunities and threats form one half of the Strengths, Weaknesses, Opportunities and Threats (SWOT) analyses that shape many companies' strategy formulation (see Section 4.4.5). In responding strategically to the environment, the goal is to reduce identified threats and take advantage of the best opportunities.

The techniques and concepts in this and the previous chapter should help in identifying environmental threats and opportunities, for instance:

- *PESTEL analysis* of the macro-environment might reveal threats and opportunities presented by technological change, or shifts in market demographics or such like factors.

- Identification of *key drivers for change* can help generate different *scenarios* for managerial discussion, some more threatening and others more favourable.

- *Porter's five forces analysis* might, for example, identify a rise or fall in barriers to entry, or opportunities to reduce industry rivalry, perhaps by acquisition of competitors.

- *Blue Ocean* thinking might reveal where companies can create new market spaces; alternatively, it could help identify success factors which new entrants might attack in order to turn 'Blue Oceans' into 'Red Oceans'.

While all these techniques and concepts are important tools for understanding environments, it is important to recognise that any analysis is likely to be somewhat subjective. Entrepreneurs and managers often have particular blinkers with regard to what they see and prioritise. Techniques and concepts can be helpful in challenging existing assumptions and encouraging broader perspectives, but they are unlikely to overcome human subjectivity and biases completely.

THINKING DIFFERENTLY | From five forces to one

A new competition view focuses on how value is created and captured.

A new 'value capture model' based on game theory aspires to replace Porter's competitive forces framework.[25] The power of his five competitive forces defines the opportunities of a firm. The new model rather emphasises how the firm's opportunities depend on how the firm, suppliers and buyers create value together. They then compete for a share of that value based on a single *competition force* that each player has.

Compared to Porter's framework, the emphasis in this model is more on how value is created between parties. The firm and its suppliers and buyers comprise a *value network* of transactions that create value to be shared among them. They then compete for their share based on the single competition force each has: suppliers compete for firms, and vice versa; firms compete for buyers and vice versa. A firm, for example, wants to make transactions with certain suppliers and customers to create value, but also to capture as much of that value as possible. The strength of each

player's competition force then depends on how many others it *could* create value with. For example, if a firm has many alternative suppliers and buyers to create value with, its competition force would go up as it can threaten to make transactions with someone else and thus bargain up its share of the value pie this way. This suggests that value creation and value appropriation are linked in this model. The more value the firm can create with various suppliers and buyers the larger portion of this value it can capture.

> **Question**
>
> How would you compare the 'value capture model' with Porter's five forces when making an industry analysis? What's the benefits and drawback of each?

SUMMARY

- The environment influence closest to an organisation includes the *industry or sector* (middle layer in Figure 2.1).
- Industries and sectors can be analysed in terms of *Porter's five forces* – barriers to entry, substitutes, buyer power, supplier power and rivalry. Together with *complementors* and *network effects*, these determine industry or sector attractiveness and possible ways of managing strategy.
- Industries and sectors are dynamic, and their changes can be analysed in terms of the *industry life cycle* and *comparative five forces radar plots*.
- Within industries *strategic group* analysis and *market segment* analysis can help identify strategic gaps or opportunities (the inner layers in Figure 2.1).
- *Blue Ocean* strategies are a means of avoiding *Red Oceans* with many similar rivals and low profitability and can be analysed with a *strategy canvas*.

WORK ASSIGNMENTS

✱ Denotes more advanced work assignments.
* Refers to a case study in the Text and Cases edition.

4.1   Drawing on Section 4.2, carry out a five forces analysis of the pharmaceutical industry* or SAB Miller's position in the brewing industry (Megabrew*). What do you conclude about that industry's attractiveness?

4.2   Drawing on Section 4.2.7, identify an industry with network effects. Consider what those might involve; why customers prefer certain services, products and companies over others; and why they may not easily switch to other services and companies.

4.3✱   Drawing on Section 4.3, and particularly using the radar plot technique of Figure 4.5, choose two industries or sectors and compare their attractiveness in terms of the five forces (a) today; (b) in approximately three to five years' time. Justify your assessment of each of the five forces' strengths. Which industry or sector would you invest in?

4.4   With regard to Section 4.4.1 and Figure 4.6, identify an industry (e.g. the motor industry or clothing retailers) and, by comparing competitors, map out the main strategic groups in the industry according to key strategic dimensions. Try more than one set of key strategic dimensions to map the industry. Do the resulting maps identify any under-exploited opportunities in the industry?

4.5✱   Drawing on Section 4.4.3, and particularly on Figure 4.8, identify critical success factors for an industry with which you and your peers are familiar (e.g. clothing retailers or mobile phone companies). Using your own estimates (or those of your peers), construct a strategy canvas comparing the main competitors, as in Figure 4.8. What implications does your strategy canvas have for the strategies of these competitors?

Integrative assignment

4.6✱   Carry out a full analysis of an industry or sector of your choice (using, for example, five forces and strategic groups). Consider explicitly how the industry or sector is affected by globalisation (see Chapter 9, particularly Figure 9.2 on drivers) and innovation (see Chapter 10, particularly Figure 10.5 on product and process innovation).

RECOMMENDED KEY READINGS

- The classic book on the analysis of industries is M.E. Porter, *Competitive Strategy*, Free Press, 1980. An updated view is available in M.E. Porter, 'The five competitive forces that shape strategy', *Harvard Business Review*, vol. 86, no. 1 (2008), pp. 58–77.

- For an in-depth discussion of how to apply Porter's Competitive Force Frameworks, see J. Magretta, *Understanding Michael Porter: The Essential Guide to Competition and Strategy*, Harvard Business Review Press, 2012.

- An influential development on Porter's basic ideas is W.C. Kim and R. Mauborgne, *Blue Ocean Strategy: How to Create Uncontested Market Space and Make Competition Irrelevant*, Harvard Business School Press, 2005.

REFERENCES

1. See M.E. Porter, *Competitive Strategy: Techniques for Analyzing Industries and Competitors*, Free Press, 1980, p. 5.
2. See endnote 1 above and see M. Porter, 'The five competitive forces that shape strategy', *Harvard Business Review*, vol. 86, no. 1 (2008), pp. 58–77; and G. Yip, T.M. Devinney and G. Johnson, 'Measuring long-term superior performance: The UK's long-term superior performers 1984-2003', *Long Range Planning*, vol. 42, no. 3 (2009), pp. 390–413. See also http://www.damodaran.com for industry profitability differences in various geographical regions.
3. An updated discussion of the classic framework is M. Porter, 'The five competitive forces that shape strategy', *Harvard Business Review*, vol. 86, no. 1 (2008), pp. 58–77 and 'Strategy and the Internet', *Harvard Business Review*, no. 3 (2001), pp. 62–78. For a discussion and guide to Porter's ideas about strategy see *Understanding Michael Porter: The Essential Guide to Competition and Strategy*, Harvard Business Review Press, 2012. C. Christensen, 'The past and future of competitive advantage', *Sloan Management Review*, vol. 42, no. 2 (2001), pp. 105–9 provides an interesting critique and update of some of the factors underlying Porter's five forces. A critical overview of Porter's thinking is also provided in R. Huggins and H. Izushi (eds), *Competition, Competitive Advantage, and Clusters: The Ideas of Michael Porter*, Oxford University Press, 2011.
4. A. Brandenburger and B. Nalebuff, 'The right game', *Harvard Business Review*, July–August 1995, pp. 57–64.
5. See K. Walley, 'Coopetition: an introduction to the subject and an agenda for research', *International Studies of Management and Organization*, vol. 37, no. 2 (2007), pp. 11–31. On the dangers of 'complementors', see D. Yoffie and M. Kwak, 'With friends like these', *Harvard Business Review*, vol. 84, no. 9 (2006), pp. 88–98.
6. For an overview of recent empirical research of strategy and network effects see D.P. McIntyre and M. Subramaniam, 'Strategy in network industries: a review and research agenda', *Journal of Management* (2009), pp 1–24. For a general discussion of the role of networks externalities and standards, see C. Shapiro and H.R. Varian, *Information Rules: a Strategic Guide to the Network Economy*, Harvard Business Review Press, 2013.
7. If network effects are present, a standard strategic advice for companies has been to move in first and grow fast to capture those effects before anyone else as this would provide an advantage over competitors, but it has recently been demonstrated that there are other issues to consider: H. Halaburda and F. Oberholzer-Gee, 'The limits of scale', *Harvard Business Review*, April 2014, pp. 95–99.
8. W.B. Arthur, 'Increasing returns and the new world of business', *Harvard Business Review*, July–August (1996), pp. 100–109. See also the concept of system lock-in in A. Hax and D. Wilde, 'The Delta Model – discovering new sources of profitability in a networked economy', *European Management Journal*, vol. 19, no. 4 (2001), pp. 379–91.
9. For an in-depth discussion of how to apply Porter's compeptive forces framework, see J. Magretta, *Understanding Michael Porter: The Essential Guide to Competition and Strategy*, Harvard Business Review Press, 2012.
10. The five forces framework builds on the structure–conduct–performance (SCP) model in industrial organisation economics. It stipulates that the industry *structure* determines firm *conduct* that in turn influences industry *performance*. SCP categorises industry structure into four main types: monopoly, oligopoly, monopolistic competition and perfect competition. See J. Lipczynski, J. Wilson and J. Goddard, *Industrial Organization: Competition, Strategy, Policy*, Prentice Hall/Financial Times, 2009.
11. D. McIntyre and M. Subramarian, 'Strategy in network industries: a review and research agenda', *Journal of Management*, vol. 35 (2009), pp. 1494–512.
12. Explicit cooperation among the firms to limit competition or cartels are prohibited in most developed nations, but there is also 'tacit collusion'. In tacit collusion, companies cooperate to reduce competition without any formal agreement. It is facilitated by a small numer of rivals, a homogenous product or service and costs and high barriers to entry. Tacit collusion can also be illegal under certain circumstances. See Lipczynski, Wilson and Goddard endnote 10.
13. Economists name these markets *'monopolistic competition'* as firms can still create a position or niche for which they have some monopoly power over pricing.
14. This definition is from R. D'Aveni, *Hypercompetition: Managing the Dynamics of Strategic Maneuvering*, Free Press, 1994, p. 2.
15. There is a discussion of the static nature of the Porter model, and other limitations in M. Grundy, 'Rethinking and reinventing Michael Porter's five forces model', *Strategic Change*, vol. 15 (2006), pp. 213–29.
16. See for example F. Hacklin, B. Battistini and G. Von Krogh, 'Strategic choices in converging industries', *MIT Sloan Management Review* vol. 51, no. 1 (2013), pp. 65–73.
17. A classic academic overview of the industry life cycle is S. Klepper, 'Industry life cycles', *Industrial and Corporate Change*, vol. 6, no. 1 (1996), pp. 119–43. See also A. McGahan, 'How industries evolve', *Business Strategy Review*, vol. 11, no. 3 (2000), pp. 1–16.
18. A. McGahan, 'How industries evolve', *Business Strategy Review*, vol. 11, no. 3 (2000), pp. 1–16.
19. For examples of strategic group analysis, see G. Leask and D. Parker, 'Strategic groups, competitive groups and performance in the UK pharmaceutical industry', *Strategic Management Journal*, vol. 28, no. 7 (2007), pp. 723–45; and W. Desarbo, R. Grewal and R. Wang, 'Dynamic strategic groups: deriving spatial evolutionary paths', *Strategic Management Journal*, vol. 30, no. 8 (2009), pp. 1420–39.
20. These characteristics are based on Porter, endnote 1 above.

21. A useful discussion of segmentation in relation to competitive strategy is provided in M.E. Porter, *Competitive Advantage*, Free Press, 1985, Chapter 7. See also the discussion on market segmentation in P. Kotler, G. Armstrong, J. Saunders and V. Wong, *Principles of Marketing*, 5th European edn, Financial Times Prentice Hall, 2008, Chapter 9.

22. For a discussion of how market segmentation needs to be broadly related to an organisation's strategy and not only narrowly focused on the needs of advertising, see D. Yankelovich and D. Meer, 'Rediscovering market segmentation', *Harvard Business Review*, February 2006, pp. 73–80.

23. W.C. Kim and R. Mauborgne, *Blue Ocean Strategy*, Boston, Harvard Business School Press, 2005.

24. W.C. Kim and R. Mauborgne, 'How strategy shapes structure', *Harvard Business Review*, September 2009, pp. 73–80.

25. M.D. Ryall, 'The new dynamics of competition', *Harvard Business Review*, vol. 91, no. 60 (2013), pp. 80–87.

Global forces and the advertising industry

Peter Cardwell

*This case is centred on the global advertising industry which faces significant strategic dilemmas driven by the rise of consumer spending in developing economies, technological convergence and pressures from major advertisers for results-based compensation. Strategy in this industry is further explored in **MyStrategyExperience** simulation (https://heuk.pearson.com/simulations/ mystrategyexperience.html).*

In the second decade of the new millennium, advertising agencies faced a number of unanticipated challenges. Traditional markets and industry operating methods, developed largely in North America and Western Europe following the rise of consumer spending power in the twentieth century, were being radically reappraised.

The industry was subject to game-changing forces from the so-called 'digital revolution' with the entry of search companies like Google, Bing and Yahoo as rivals for advertising budgets. Changing patterns in global consumer markets impacted on both industry dynamics and structure. Budgets being spent through traditional advertising agencies were being squeezed as industry rivalry intensified.

Overview of the advertising industry

Traditionally, the business objective of advertising agencies is to target a specific audience on behalf of clients with a message that encourages them to try a product or service and ultimately purchase it. This is done largely through the concept of a brand being communicated via media channels. Brands allow consumers to differentiate between products and services and it is the job of the advertising agency to position the brand so that it is associated with functions and attributes which are valued by target consumers. These brands may be consumer brands (e.g. Coca-Cola, Nike and Mercedes Benz) or business-to-business (B2B) brands (e.g. IBM, Airbus Industrie and KPMG). Some brands target both consumers and businesses (e.g. Microsoft and Apple).

As well as private-sector brand companies, governments spend heavily to advertise public-sector services such as healthcare and education or to influence individual behaviour (such as 'Don't drink and drive'). For example, the UK government had an advertising budget of £289m (€347m, $433m) in 2014. Charities, political groups, religious groups and other not-for-profit organisations also use the advertising industry to attract funds into their organisation or to raise awareness of issues. Together these account for approximately three per cent of advertising spend.

Advertisements are usually placed in selected media (TV, press, radio, internet, mobile, etc.) by an advertising agency acting on behalf of the client brand company: thus they are acting as 'agents'. The client company employs the advertising agency to use its knowledge, skills, creativity and experience to create advertising and marketing to drive consumption of the client's brands. Clients traditionally have been charged according to the time spent on creating the advertisements plus a commission based on the media and services bought on behalf of clients. However, in recent years, larger advertisers such as Coca-Cola, Procter & Gamble and Unilever have been moving away from this compensation model to a 'value' or results-based model based on a number of metrics, including growth in sales and market share.

Growth in the advertising industry

Money spent on advertising has increased dramatically over the past two decades and in 2015 was over $180 billion (€166bn, £126bn) in the USA and $569 billion worldwide. While there might be a decline in recessionary years, it is predicted that spending on advertising will exceed $719 billion globally by 2019. Over 2014–15, the Dow Jones stock price index for the American media agencies sector (of which the leading advertising agencies are the largest members) rose about 15 per cent ahead of the New York Stock Exchange average (sources: bigcharts. com and dowjones.com).

The industry is shifting its focus as emerging markets drive revenues from geographic sectors that would not have been significant 5 to 10 years ago, such as the BRICS countries and the Middle East and North Africa. This shift has seen the emergence of agencies specialising in Islamic marketing, characterised by a strong ethical responsibility to consumers. Future trends indicate the

Table 1 Global advertising expenditure by region (US$ million, currency conversion at 2011 average rates)

	2011	2012	2013	2014	2015
N America	164,516	169,277	175,024	183,075	191,130
W Europe	107,520	111,300	114,712	119,531	124,790
Asia Pacific	113,345	122,000	130,711	137,639	145,695
C & E Europe	29,243	32,284	35,514	36,691	37,305
Latin America	31,673	34,082	36,836	38,530	39,226
Africa/ME/ROW	24,150	25,941	28,044	29,334	30,625
World	**470,447**	**494,884**	**520,841**	**544,800**	**568,771**

Source: Zenith, January 2016.

strong emergence of consumer brands in areas of the world where sophisticated consumers with brand awareness are currently in the minority (see Table 1).

In terms of industry sectors, three of the top 10 global advertisers are car manufacturers. However, the two major fmcg (fast-moving consumer goods) producers, Procter & Gamble and Unilever, hold the two top spots for global advertising spend. Healthcare and beauty, consumer electronics, fast food, beverage and confectionery manufacturers are all featured in the top 20 global advertisers. The top 100 advertisers account for nearly 50 per cent of the measured global advertising economy.

Competition in the advertising industry

Advertising agencies come in all sizes and include everything from one- or two-person 'boutique' operations (which rely mostly on freelance outsourced talent to perform most functions), small to medium-sized agencies, large independents to multinational, multi-agency conglomerates employing over 190,000 people. The industry has gone through a period of increasing concentration through acquisitions, thereby creating multi-agency conglomerates such as those listed in Table 2. While these conglomerates are mainly headquartered in London, New York and Paris, they operate globally.

Large multi-agency conglomerates compete on the basis of the quality of their creative output (as indicated by industry awards), the ability to buy media more cost-effectively, market knowledge, global reach and range of services. Some agency groups have integrated vertically into higher-margin marketing services. Omnicom, through its Diversified Agency Services, has acquired printing services and telemarketing/customer care companies. Other agency groups have vertically integrated to lesser or greater degrees.

Mid-sized and smaller boutique advertising agencies compete by delivering value-added services through in-depth knowledge of specific market sectors, specialised services such as digital and by building a reputation for innovative and ground-breaking creative advertising/marketing campaigns. However, they might be more reliant on outsourced creative suppliers than larger agencies.

Many small specialist agencies are founded by former employees of large agencies, such as the senior staff breakaway from Young & Rubicam to form the agency Adam + Eve. In turn, smaller specialist agencies are often acquired by the large multi-agency conglomerates in order to acquire specific capabilities to target new sectors or markets or provide additional services to existing clients, like WPP's acquisition of a majority stake in the smaller ideas and innovation agency AKQA for $540m 'to prepare for a more digital future'.

Table 2 Top five multi-agency conglomerates: 2014, by revenue, profit before interest and tax (PBIT), number of employees and agency brands

Group name	Revenue	PBIT	Employees	Advertising agency brands
WPP (UK)	£11.5 bn	£1.662 bn	190,000	JWT, Grey, Ogilvy, Y&R
Omnicom (US)	$15.32 bn	$1.944 bn	74,000	BBDO, DDB, TBWA
Publicis Groupe (France)	€7.2 bn	€829 m	77,000	Leo Burnett, Saatchi & Saatchi, Publicis, BBH
IPG (US)	$7.54 bn	$788 m	48,700	McCann Erickson, FCB, Lowe & Partners
Havas Worldwide (France)	€1.865 bn	€263 m	11,186	Havas Conseil

Sources: WPP, Omnicom, Publicis Groupe, IPG, Havas.

Recent years have seen new competition in this industry as search companies such as Google, Yahoo and Microsoft Bing begin to exploit their ability to interact with and gain information about millions of potential consumers of branded products.

Sir Martin Sorrell, CEO of WPP, the world's largest advertising and marketing services group, has pointed out that Google will rival his agency's relationships with the biggest traditional media corporations such as TV, newspaper and magazine, and possibly even become a rival for the relationships with WPP's clients. WPP group spent more than $4bn with Google in 2015 and $1bn with Facebook. Sorrell calls Google a 'frenemy' – the combination of 'friend' and 'enemy'. Google is a 'friend' where it allows WPP to place targeted advertising based on Google analytics and an 'enemy' where it does not share these analytics with the agency and becomes a potential competitor for the customer insight and advertising traditionally created by WPP.

With the development of the internet and online search advertising, a new breed of interactive digital media agencies, of which AKQA is an example, established themselves in the digital space before traditional advertising agencies fully embraced the internet. These agencies differentiate themselves by offering a mix of web design/development, search engine marketing, internet advertising/marketing, or e-business/e-commerce consulting. They are classified as 'agencies' because they create digital media campaigns and implement media purchases of ads on behalf of clients on social networking and community sites such as YouTube, Facebook, Flickr, Instagram and other digital media.

Digital search and mobile advertising budgets are increasing faster than other traditional advertising media as search companies like Google and Facebook generate revenues from paid search as advertisers discover that targeted ads online are highly effective (see Table 3). By 2015, Google had a 55 per cent market share of the $81.6 bn spent on online search advertising globally, with Facebook also increasing its share.

Mobile ad spending on sites such as YouTube, Pinterest and Twitter continues to increase at the expense of desktop, taking a bigger share of marketers' budgets. The shift to mobile ad spending is being driven mainly by consumer demand and is predicted to be over 28 per cent of total media ad spending in the US by 2019 which is why Google has made acquisitions in this sector (see Table 4).

Table 3 Global advertising expenditure by medium (US$ million, currency conversion at 2011 average rates)

	2011	2012	2013	2014	2015
Newspapers	93,019	92,300	91,908	90,070	88,268
Magazines	42,644	42,372	42,300	40,185	39,391
Television	191,198	202,380	213,878	210,670	210,459
Radio	32,580	33,815	35,054	34,457	34,130
Cinema	2,393	2,538	2,681	2,767	2,850
Outdoor	30,945	32,821	34,554	36,143	36,324
Internet	70,518	80,672	91,516	130,019	156,543
Total	**463,297**	**486,898**	**511,891**	**544,311**	**567,956**

Note: The totals in Table 3 are lower than in Table 1, since that table includes advertising expenditure for a few countries where it is not itemised by advertising medium.
Source: Zenith, September 2015.

Table 4 US mobile ad spending 2015–2019

	2015	2016	2017	2018	2019
Mobile ad spending (US$bn)	31.59	43.60	52.76	61.20	69.15
% change	65.00%	38.00%	21.00%	16.00%	13.00%
% of digital ad spending	53.00%	63.40%	68.20%	70.70%	72.00%
% of total media ad spending	17.30%	22.70%	26.20%	28.80%	31.00%

Source: eMarketer.com.

The disruptive change in the advertising industry at the beginning of the twenty-first century started with the internet. Many industry experts believe that convergence of internet, TV, smartphones, tablets and laptop computers is inevitable, which in turn will have a further major impact on the advertising industry.

Factors that have driven competitive advantage to date may not be relevant in the future. Traditionally this industry has embodied the idea of creativity as the vital differentiator between the best and the mediocre. Individuals have often been at the heart of this creativity. With the emergence of Google, Yahoo, Facebook and Bing, influencing and changing the media by which advertising messages are being delivered, a key question is whether creativity will be more or less important in the future, in relation to breadth of services and global reach.

Sources: Zenith, September 2015, http://www.zenithoptimedia.co.uk; Advertising Age; Omnicom Group, http://www.omnicomgroup.com; WPP Group, http://www.wpp.com; Publicis, http://www.publicisgroupe. com; Interpublic Group of Companies, http://www.interpublic.com; Havas Conseils, http://www.havas.com/havas-dyn/en/; http://www. financialcontent.com; and http://www.emarketer.com. *See also* MyStrategyExperience: the Strategy Simulation designed for *Exploring Strategy*: https://heuk.pearson.com/simulations/mystrategyexperience.html.

Questions

1 Carry out a five forces analysis of the advertising industry in 2015. What is the strength of the five forces and what underlying factors drive them? What is the industry attractiveness?

2 What are the changes in the industry? Which forces are becoming more negative or positive for the major advertising agencies?

5

RESOURCES AND CAPABILITIES

5.1 INTRODUCTION

Chapters 2 and 3 emphasised the importance of the external environment of an organisation and how it can create both strategic opportunities and threats. However, it is not only the external environment that matters for strategy; there are also differences between organisations and companies that need to be taken into account. For example, manufacturers of saloon cars compete within the same industry and within the same technological environment, but with markedly different success. BMW has been relatively successful consistently; Chrysler has found it more difficult to maintain its competitive position. And others, like SAAB in Sweden, have gone out of business (even though the brand as such has been acquired by others). It is not so much the characteristics of the environment which explain these differences in performance, but differences in their company-specific *resources and capabilities*. This puts the focus on variations between companies within the same environment and industry and how they vary in their resources and capabilities arrangements. It is the strategic importance of organisations' resources and capabilities that is the focus of this chapter.

The key issues posed by the chapter are summarised in Figure 5.1. Underlying these are two key issues. The first is that organisations are not identical, but have different resources and capabilities; they are 'heterogeneous' in this respect. The second is that it can be difficult for one organisation to obtain or imitate the resources and capabilities of another. The implication for managers is that they need to understand how their organisations are different from their rivals in ways that may be the basis of achieving competitive advantage and superior performance. These concepts underlie what has become known as the **resource-based view** (RBV) of strategy (sometimes labelled the 'capabilities view') pioneered by Jay Barney at University of Utah: **that the competitive advantage and superior performance of an organisation are explained by the distinctiveness of its resources and capabilities.**[1] Resource – or capabilities – views have become very influential, but it should be borne in mind that while the terminology and concepts employed here align with these views, readers will find different terminology used elsewhere.

The chapter has four further sections:

- Section 5.2 discusses the foundations of what *resources* and *capabilities* are. It also draws a distinction between *threshold* resources and capabilities required to be able to compete in a market and *distinctive* resources and capabilities that may be a basis for achieving competitive advantage and superior performance.

Figure 5.1 Resources and capabilities: the key issues

- Section 5.3 explains the ways in which distinctive resources and capabilities can contribute to *sustained competitive advantage* (in a public-sector context the equivalent concern might be how some organisations sustain relative superior performance over time). In particular, the importance of the *Value, Rarity, Inimitability and Organisational support* (VRIO) of resources and capabilities is explained.

- Section 5.4 moves on to consider different ways resources and capabilities might be diagnosed. These include *VRIO analysis*, *value chain and system analysis*, *activity systems mapping* and *benchmarking*. The section concludes by explaining the use of *SWOT* analysis as a basis for pulling together the insights from the analyses of the environment (explained in Chapter 2 and 3) and of resources and capabilities in this chapter.

- Finally, Section 5.5 discusses some of the key issues of *dynamic capabilities* and how resources and capabilities can be developed and managed.

5.2 FOUNDATIONS OF RESOURCES AND CAPABILITIES

Given that different writers, managers and consultants use different terms and concepts, it is important to understand how concepts relating to resources and capabilities are used in this book. The **resources and capabilities of an organisation contribute to its long-term survival and potentially to competitive advantage.** However, to understand and to manage resources and capabilities it is necessary to explain their components.[2]

5.2.1 Resources and capabilities

Resources are the assets that organisations have or can call upon and capabilities are the ways those assets are used or deployed[3] (earlier editions of this text used the term 'competences' for the latter and these terms are often used interchangeably).[4] A shorthand way of thinking of this is that resources are 'what we *have*' (nouns) and capabilities are 'what we *do*' well' (verbs). Other writers use the term *intangible assets* as an umbrella term to include capabilities as well as intangible resources such as brands.

Resources and capabilities are typically related, as Table 5.1 shows. Resources are certainly important, but how an organisation employs and deploys its resources matters at least as much. There would be no point in having state-of-the-art equipment if it were not used effectively. The efficiency and effectiveness of physical or financial resources, or the people in an organisation, depend not just on their existence, but on the systems and processes by which they are managed, the relationships and cooperation between people, their adaptability, their innovative capacity, the relationship with customers and suppliers, and the experience and learning about what

Table 5.1 Resources and capabilities

Resources: what we have (nouns), e.g.		Capabilities: what we do well (verbs), e.g.
Machines, buildings, raw materials, patents, databases, computer systems	Physical	Ways of achieving utilisation of plant, efficiency, productivity, flexibility, marketing
Balance sheet, cash flow, suppliers of funds	Financial	Ability to raise funds and manage cash flows, debtors, creditors, etc.
Managers, employees, partners, suppliers, customers	Human	How people gain and use experience, skills, knowledge, build relationships, motivate others and innovate

ILLUSTRATION 5.1   Resources and capabilities

Executives emphasise the importance of resources and capabilities in different organisations.

The Australian Red Cross

To achieve the vision of improving the lives of vulnerable people, the Australian Red Cross emphasises the crucial role of capabilities in its strategic plan 'Strategy 2015'. 'Capabilities are integral to our overriding strategy to create one Red Cross,' writes CEO Robert Tickner. The Australian Red Cross distinguish between technical competency and behavioural capability. The former refers to specialist skills and may include such competencies as project management, financial management, community development, social work, administrative or information technology skills. Capabilities at the Red Cross refer to the behaviours they expect its people to demonstrate in order to be successful in achieving the objectives. The organisation aims to increasingly invest in the capabilities and skills of Red Cross people and supporters including members, branches and units, volunteers, aid workers, staff and donors. For example, this involves investing in a diverse workforce and supporter base, with strong engagement of 'young people, Aboriginal and Torres Strait Islander people, and other culturally and linguistically diverse people'. The emphasis is on people who are engaged, dynamic, innovative, entrepreneurial and motivated to realise the vision and goals.[1]

Royal Opera House, London

Tony Hall, Chief Executive of the Royal Opera House:

'"World-class" is neither an idle nor boastful claim. In the context of the Royal Opera House the term refers to the quality of our people, the standards of our productions and the diversity of our work and initiatives. Unique? Unashamedly so. We shy away from labels such as "elite", because of the obvious negative connotations of exclusiveness. But I want people to take away from here the fact that we are elite in the sense that we have the best singers, dancers, directors, designers, orchestra, chorus, backstage crew and administrative staff. We are also among the best in our ability to reach out to as wide and diverse a community as possible.'[2]

Infosys

The Indian company Infosys is a global leader in information technology, outsourcing, system integration services and IT consulting. It is listed as one of the world's most reputable companies with close to 150,000 employees worldwide. The company's 'Infosys 3.0 strategy' is taking a further step to provide more advanced IT products and services, which requires investments in new resources and capabilities.[3] Infosys CEO S.D. Shibulal: 'We continue to make focused investments in our organisational capabilities.'[4]

The strategy emphasises innovation and focuses on higher-value software. Innovation abilities are central for this, as stated on the website: 'The foundation of our innovation capability is our core lab network – Infosys Labs – and the new thinking that our team of over 600 researchers brings to the table.'[5] The strategy thus requires human resource and training capabilities including the ability to attract, employ, educate and retain new high-quality engineers. As Srikantan Moorthy, Senior Vice President and Group Head, explains: 'We are currently hiring and developing talent in the areas of cloud, mobility, sustainability, and product development. In addition, a key focus is also consultative skills. All of these are in line with our Infosys 3.0 strategy. We place significant value on continuous learning and knowledge sharing.'[6]

Sources: (1) Australian Red Cross Capability Framework, 2015; (2) Royal Opera House Annual Review 2005–6; (3) *Financial Times*, 12 August 2012; (4) Infosys Annual Report 2011–12; (5) http://www.infosys.com; (6) *SkillingIndia*, 26 September 2012.

Questions

1 Categorise the range of resources and capabilities highlighted by the executives above in terms of Section 5.2 and Table 5.1.

2 To what extent and why might these resources and capabilities be the basis of *sustained* competitive advantage?

3 Imagine you are the general manager of an organisation of your choice and undertake the same exercise as in Questions 1 and 2 above.

works well and what does not. Illustration 5.1 shows examples of how executives explain the importance of the resources and capabilities of their different organisations.

5.2.2 Threshold and distinctive resources and capabilities

A distinction also needs to be made between resources and capabilities that are at a threshold level and those that might help the organisation achieve competitive advantage and superior performance. **Threshold resources and capabilities are those needed for an organisation to meet the necessary requirements to compete in a given market and achieve parity with competitors in that market.** Without these, the organisation could not survive over time. Indeed many start-up businesses find this to be the case. They simply do not have or cannot obtain the resources or capabilities needed to compete with established competitors. Identifying threshold requirements is, however, also important for established businesses. There could be changing *threshold resources* required to meet minimum customer requirements: for example, the increasing demands by modern multiple retailers of their suppliers mean that those suppliers have to possess a quite sophisticated IT infrastructure simply to stand a chance of meeting retailer requirements. Or there could be *threshold capabilities* required to deploy resources so as to meet customers' requirements and support particular strategies. Retailers do not simply expect suppliers to have the required IT infrastructure, but to be able to use it effectively so as to guarantee the required level of service.

Identifying and managing threshold resources and capabilities raises a significant challenge because threshold levels will change as critical success factors change (see Section 3.4.3) or through the activities of competitors and new entrants. To continue the example above, suppliers to major retailers did not require the same level of IT and logistics support a decade ago. But the retailers' drive to reduce costs, improve efficiency and ensure availability of merchandise to their customers means that their expectations of their suppliers have increased markedly in that time and continue to do so. So there is a need for those suppliers continuously to review and improve their logistics resource and capability base just to stay in business.

While threshold resources and capabilities are important, they do not of themselves create competitive advantage or the basis of superior performance. They can be thought of as 'qualifiers' to be able to compete at all with competitors while distinctive resources and capabilities are 'winners' required to triumph over competitors. **Distinctive resources and capabilities are required to achieve competitive advantage.** These are dependent on an organisation having a distinctiveness or uniqueness that are of value to customers and which competitors find difficult to imitate. This could be because the organisation has *distinctive resources* that critically underpin competitive advantage and that others cannot imitate or obtain – a long-established brand, for example. Or it could be that an organisation achieves competitive advantage because it has *distinctive capabilities* – ways of doing things that are unique to that organisation and effectively utilised so as to be valuable to customers and difficult for competitors to obtain or imitate. For example, Apple has distinctive resources in mobile technology and in the powerful brand, but also distinctive capabilities in design and in understanding consumer behaviour.

Gary Hamel and C.K. Prahalad argue that distinctive capabilities or competences typically remain unique because they comprise a *bundle* of constituent skills and technologies rather than a single, discrete skill or technology. They refer to this as *core competences* and the emphasis is thus on the linked set of resources, capabilities, skills and activities.[5] In the Apple example above, it is thus the combination of the resources and capabilities that make them distinctive or core competences in Hamel's and Prahalad's words. Section 5.3 that follows discusses in more depth the role played by distinctive resources and capabilities in contributing to long-term, sustainable competitive advantage. Section 5.3.3 explores further the importance of linkages.

5.3 DISTINCTIVE RESOURCES AND CAPABILITIES AS A BASIS OF COMPETITIVE ADVANTAGE

As explained above, distinctive resources and capabilities are necessary for sustainable competitive advantage and superior economic performance. This section considers four key criteria by which resources and capabilities can be assessed in terms of them providing a basis for achieving such competitive advantage: value, rarity, inimitability and organisational support – or VRIO.[6] Figure 5.2 illustrates these four fundamental criteria and the questions they address.

5.3.1 V – value of resources and capabilities

Valuable resources and capabilities are those which create a product or a service that is of value to customers and enables the organisation to respond to environmental opportunities or threats. There are three components to consider here:

- *Taking advantage of opportunities and neutralising threats.* The most fundamental point is that to be valuable, resources and capabilities need to address opportunities and threats that arise in an organisation's environment. This points to an important complementarity with the external environment of an organisation (Chapters 2 and 3). An opportunity is addressed when a resource or capability increases the value for customers either through lowering the price or by increasing the attractiveness of a product or service. For example, IKEA has valuable resources in its cost-conscious culture and size and in its interlinked capabilities that lower its costs compared to competitors, and this addresses opportunities and customer value of low-priced designer furniture that competitors do not attend to. Using a resource and capability that do not exploit opportunities or neutralise threats does not create value and even risks decreasing revenues and increasing costs.

- *Value to customers.* It may seem an obvious point to make that resources and capabilities need to be of value to customers, but in practice it is often ignored or poorly understood. For example, managers may seek to build on resources and capabilities that *they* may see as valuable but which do not meet customers' critical success factors (see Section 3.4.3). Or they may see a distinctive capability as of value simply because it is unique, although it may not be valued by customers. Having resources and capabilities that are different from those of other organisations is not, of itself, a basis of competitive advantage.

V	**Value:** Do resources and capabilities exist that are valued by customers and enable the organisation to respond to environmental opportunities or threats?
R	**Rarity:** Do resources and capabilities exist that no (or few) competitors possess?
I	**Inimitability:** Are resources and capabilities difficult and costly for competitors to obtain and imitate?
O	**Organisational support:** Is the organisation appropriately organised to exploit the resources and capabilities?

Figure 5.2 VRIO

- *Cost.* The product or service needs to be provided at a cost that still allows the organisation to make the returns expected of it. The danger is that the cost of developing or acquiring the resources and/or capabilities to deliver what customers especially value is such that products or services are not profitable.

Managers should therefore consider carefully which of their organisation's activities are especially important in providing such value and which are of less value. Value chain analysis and activity systems mapping, explained in Sections 5.4.2 and 5.4.3, can help here.

5.3.2 R – rarity

Resources and capabilities that are valuable, but common among competitors, are unlikely to be a source of competitive advantage. If competitors have similar resources and capabilities, they can respond quickly to the strategic initiative of a rival. This has happened in competition between car manufacturers as they have sought to add more accessories and gadgets to cars. As soon as it becomes evident that these are valued by customers, they are introduced widely by competitors who typically have access to the same technology. **Rare resources and capabilities**, on the other hand, **are those possessed uniquely by one organisation or by a few others**. Here competitive advantage is longer-lasting. For example, a company can have patented products or services that give it advantage. Some libraries have unique collections of books unavailable elsewhere; a company can have a powerful brand; or retail stores can have prime locations. In terms of capabilities, organisations can have unique skills or business processes developed over time or make use of special relationships with customers or suppliers not widely possessed by competitors. However, it can be dangerous to assume that resources and capabilities that are rare will remain so. So it may be necessary to consider other bases of sustainability in competitive advantage.

5.3.3 I – inimitability

It should be clear by now that the search for resources and capabilities that provide sustainable competitive advantage is not straightforward. Having resources and capabilities that are valuable to customers and relatively rare is important, but this may not be enough. Sustainable competitive advantage also involves identifying **inimitable resources and capabilities – those that competitors find difficult and costly to imitate or obtain or substitute**. If an organisation has a competitive advantage because of its particular marketing and sales skills it can only sustain this if competitors cannot imitate, obtain or substitute for them or if the costs to do so would eliminate any gains made. Often the barriers to imitation lie deeply in the organisation in linkages between activities, skills and people.

At the risk of over-generalisation, it is unusual for competitive advantage to be explainable by differences in the tangible resources of organisations, since over time these can usually be acquired or imitated (key geographic locations, certain raw material resources, brands, etc., can, however, be exceptions). Advantage is more likely to be determined by the way in which resources are deployed and managed in terms of an organisation's activities; in other words, on the basis of capabilities.[7] For example, as indicated above, it is unlikely that an IT system will improve an organisation's competitive standing in itself, not least because competitors can probably buy something very similar on the open market. On the other hand, the capabilities to manage, develop and deploy such a system to the benefit of customers may be much more difficult and costly to imitate. Compared to physical assets and patents, capabilities tend to involve more intangible imitation barriers. In particular,

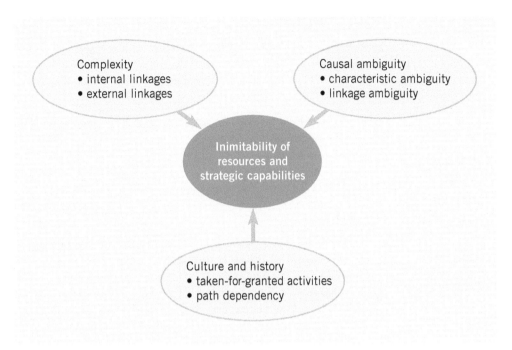

Figure 5.3 Criteria for the inimitability of resources and capabilities

they often include *linkages* that integrate activities, skills, knowledge and people both inside and outside the organisation in distinct and mutually compatible ways. These linkages can make capabilities particularly difficult for competitors to imitate, and there are three primary reasons why this may be so. These are summarised in Figure 5.3 and are now briefly reviewed.

Complexity

The resources and capabilities of an organisation can be difficult to imitate because they are complex and involve interlinkages. This may be for two main reasons:

- *Internal linkages.* There may be linked activities and processes that, together, deliver customer value. The discussion of activity systems in Section 5.4.3 below explains this in more detail and shows how such linked sets of activities might be mapped so that they can be better understood. However, even if a competitor possessed such a map, it is unlikely that it would be able to replicate the sort of complexity it represents because of the numerous interactions between tightly knit activities and decisions.[8] This is not only because of the complexity itself but because, very likely, it has developed on the basis of custom and practice built up over years and is specific to the organisation concerned. For example, companies like IKEA and Ryanair still enjoy competitive advantages despite the availability of countless case studies, articles and reports on their successes.

- *External interconnectedness.* Organisations can make it difficult for others to imitate or obtain their bases of competitive advantage by developing activities together with customers or partners such that they become dependent on them. Apple, for example, has many and intricate linkages with various app developers and actors in the music industry that others may find difficult to imitate.

Causal ambiguity[9]

Another reason why resources and capabilities might be difficult and costly to imitate is that competitors find it difficult to discern the causes and effects underpinning an organisation's advantage. This is called *causal ambiguity*. Causal ambiguity may exist in two different forms:[10]

- *Characteristic ambiguity*. Where the significance of the characteristic itself is difficult to discern or comprehend, perhaps because it is based on tacit knowledge or rooted in the organisation's culture. For example, the know-how of the buyers in a successful fashion retailer may be evident in the sales achieved for the ranges they buy year after year. But this may involve subtleties like spotting new trends and picking up feedback from pioneering customers that may be very difficult for competitors to comprehend so they will find it difficult to imitate.

- *Linkage ambiguity*. Where competitors cannot discern which activities and processes are dependent on which others to form linkages that create distinctiveness. The expertise of the fashion buyers is unlikely to be lodged in one individual or even one function. It is likely that there will be a network of suppliers, intelligence networks to understand the market and links with designers. Indeed, in some organisations the managers themselves admit that they do not fully comprehend the linkages throughout the organisation that deliver customer value. If this is so it would certainly be difficult for competitors to understand them.

Culture and history

Resources and capabilities that involve complex social interactions and interpersonal relations within an organisation can be difficult and costly for competitors to imitate systematically and manage. For example, capabilities can become embedded in an organisation's culture. Coordination between various activities occurs 'naturally' because people know their part in the wider picture or it is simply 'taken for granted' that activities are done in particular ways. We see this in high-performing sports teams or in groups of people that work together to combine specialist skills as in operating theatres. Linked to this cultural embeddedness is the likelihood that such capabilities have developed over time and in a particular way. The origins and history by which capabilities and resources have developed over time are referred to as *path dependency*.[11] This history is specific to the organisation and cannot be imitated (see Section 6.2.1). As explained in Chapter 6, there is, however, a danger that culturally embedded resources and capabilities built up over time become so embedded that they are difficult to change: they become rigidities.

5.3.4 O – organisational support

Providing value to customers and possessing capabilities that are rare and difficult to imitate provides a potential for competitive advantage. However, the organisation must also be suitably arranged to support these capabilities including appropriate organisational processes and systems.[12] This implies that in order to fully take advantage of the resources and capabilities an organisation's structure and formal and informal management control systems need to support and facilitate their exploitation (see Sections 14.1 and 14.2 for further discussions of organisational structure and systems). The question of organisational support works as an adjustment factor. Some of the potential competitive advantage can be lost if the organisation is not organised in such a way that it can fully take advantage of valuable and/or rare and/or inimitable resources and capabilities. For example, if an organisation has a unique patent underlying a product that customers value it may still not be able to convert this into a competitive advantage if it does not have the appropriate sales force to sell the product. Supporting capabilities have been labelled *complementary capabilities* as, by themselves, they are often not enough to provide for competitive advantage, but they are useful in the exploitation of other capabilities that can provide for competitive advantage.[13] In brief, even though an organisation has valuable, rare and inimitable capabilities some of its potential competitive advantage may not be realised if it lacks the organisational arrangements to fully exploit these.

In summary, and from a resource-based view of organisations, managers need to consider whether their organisation has resources and capabilities to achieve and sustain competitive advantage. To do so they need to consider how and to what extent it has capabilities which are (i) valuable, (ii) rare, (iii) inimitable and (iv) supported by the organisation. Illustration 5.2 gives an example of the challenges in meeting these criteria in the context of the internet-based company Groupon.

5.3.5 Organisational knowledge as a basis of competitive advantage

A good example of how both resources and capabilities may combine to produce competitive advantage for an organisation is in terms of organisational knowledge.[14] **Organisational knowledge is organisation-specific, collective intelligence, accumulated through formal systems and people's shared experience.**

The reasons why organisational knowledge is seen as especially important illustrate many of the points made above. As organisations become larger and more complex, the need to share what people know becomes more and more important but increasingly challenging. So organisations that can share knowledge especially well may gain advantage over those that do not. Computerised information systems are available or have been developed by organisations to codify technological, financial and market data that are *valuable* to them; indeed without which they probably could not compete effectively. However, the technology that forms the basis of information systems is hardly *rare*; it is widely available or can be developed. It is therefore less likely that organisations will achieve competitive advantage through such resources and more likely that it will be achieved through the way they manage and develop organisational knowledge more broadly. This may be to do with the capabilities they employ to utilise and develop information technology. But it is also likely to be about how they draw on and develop the accumulated and dispersed experience-based knowledge in the organisation.

The distinction between *explicit* and *tacit organisational knowledge* made by Ikijuro Nonaka and Hiro Takeuchi[15] helps explain why this is important in terms of achieving competitive advantage. Explicit or 'objective' knowledge is transmitted in formal systematic ways. It can take the form of a codified information resource such as a systems manual or files of market research and intelligence. In contrast, tacit knowledge is more personal, context-specific and therefore hard to formalise and communicate. For example, it could be the knowledge of a highly experienced sales force or research and development team; or the experience of a top management team in making many successful acquisitions. It is therefore not only distinctive to the organisation, but likely to be *difficult to imitate* or obtain for the reasons explained in Section 5.3.3 above.

Many organisations that have tried to improve the sharing of knowledge by relying on IT-based systems have come to realise that, while some knowledge can usefully be codified and built into computer-based systems, it can be very difficult to codify the knowledge that truly bestows competitive advantage.[16]

ILLUSTRATION 5.2   Groupon and the sincerest form of flattery

When a firm identifies a new market niche it must also make sure its resources and capabilities are valuable, rare, inimitable and supported by the organisation.

Chicago-based Groupon was launched in 2008 by Andrew Mason with the idea to email subscribers daily deals of heavily discounted coupons for local restaurants, theatres, spas, etc. Groupon sells a coupon for a product and takes up to half of the proceeds, which represent a big discount on the product's usual price. In return, Groupon aggregates demand from customers who receive emails or visit the website and this provides exposure and increased business for local merchants. The venture rapidly became the fastest-growing internet business ever and grew into a daily-deal industry giant. In 2010, Groupon rejected a $6bn (£3.6bn, €4.5bn) takeover bid by Google and instead went public at $10bn in November of 2011.

While Groupon's daily deals were valued by customers – the company quickly spread to over 40 countries – they also attracted thousands of copycats worldwide. Investors questioned Groupon's business and to what extent it had rare and inimitable resources and capabilities. CEO Andrew Mason denied in *Wall Street Journal* (*WSJ*) that the model was too easy to replicate:

'There's proof. There are over 2000 direct clones of the Groupon business model. However, there's an equal amount of proof that the barriers to success are enormous. In spite of all those competitors, only a handful is remotely relevant.'

This, however, did not calm investors and Groupon shares fell by 80 per cent at its all-time low. One rare asset Groupon had was its customer base of more than 50 million customers, which could possibly be difficult to imitate. The more customers, the better deals, and this would make customers come to Groupon rather than the competitors and the cost for competitors to acquire customers would go up. Further defending Groupon's competitiveness, the CEO emphasised in *WSJ* that it is not as simple as providing daily deals, but that a whole series of things have to work together and competitors would have to replicate everything in its 'operational complexity':

'People overlook the operational complexity. We have 10,000 employees across 46 countries.

We have thousands of salespeople talking to tens of thousands of merchants every single day. It's not an easy thing to build.'

Mason also emphasised Groupon's advanced technology platform that allowed the company to 'provide better targeting to customers and give them deals that are more relevant to them'. Part of this platform, however, was built via acquisitions – a route competitors possibly also could take.

If imitation is the highest form of flattery Groupon has been highly complimented, but investors have not been flattered. Andrew Mason was forced out in 2013, succeeded by the chairman Eric Lefkofsky. Even though Amazon and many other copycats left the daily-deals business, he struggled to explain how Groupon would fight off imitators and was forced to exit several international markets. In November 2015, he returned to his chairman role and was followed by Rich Williams who stated:

'As CEO, my top priority is to unlock the long-term growth potential in the business by demonstrating everything the new Groupon has to offer.'

Sources: 'Groupon shares crumble after company names new CEO', 3 November 2015, *Forbes*; 'Groupon names Rich Williams CEO', 3 November 2015, *Wall Street Journal*; All Things Digital, 2 November 2012, *Wall Street Journal*; *Financial Times*, 2 March 2013; 'Groupon and its "weird" CEO', *Wall Street Journal*, 31 January 2012.

Questions

1 Andrew Mason admits that Groupon has thousands of copycats, yet his assessment is that imitating Groupon is difficult. Do you agree?

2 Assess the bases of Groupon's resources and capabilities using the VRIO criteria (Figure 5.2 and Table 5.2).

3 If you were the new Groupon CEO, what resources and capabilities would you build on to give the company a sustainable competitive advantage?

5.4 DIAGNOSING RESOURCES AND CAPABILITIES

So far, this chapter has been concerned with explaining concepts associated with the strategic significance of organisations' resources and capabilities. This section now provides some ways in which they can be understood and diagnosed. If managers are to manage the resources and capabilities of their organisation, the sort of diagnosis explained here, the VRIO analysis tool, the value chain and system, activity systems, benchmarking and SWOT, are centrally important. If resources and capabilities are not understood at these levels, there are dangers that managers can take the wrong course of action.

5.4.1 VRIO analysis

One lesson that emerges from an understanding of the strategic importance of resources and capabilities is that it can be difficult to discern where the basis of competitive advantage lies. The strict criteria of the VRIO framework discussed above (see Section 5.3) can conveniently be used as a tool to analyse whether an organisation has resources and capabilities to achieve and sustain competitive advantage. A **VRIO analysis thus helps to evaluate if, how and to what extent an organisation or company has resources and capabilities that are (i) valuable, (ii) rare, (iii) inimitable and (iv) supported by the organisation** . Table 5.2 summarises the VRIO analysis of capabilities and shows that there is an additive effect. Resources and capabilities provide sustainable bases of competitive advantage the more they meet all four criteria. This analysis can be done for different functions in an organisation (technology, manufacturing, purchasing, marketing and sales, etc.) or more fine-grained for individual resources and capabilities (see Table 5.1). Another approach is to evaluate different sections of the value chain or system with this tool (see Section 5.4.2 below).

Sometimes it may be challenging to establish the exact competitive implication, for example when a resource or capability is on the border between sustained or temporary competitive advantage (Illustration 5.2 demonstrates this). However, for managers it is most important to distinguish between sustained or temporary competitive advantage vs competitive parity or competitive disadvantage (see Table 5.2). If it is difficult to discern whether a function or resource or capability provides for sustained competitive advantage, it may help to divide it into subparts. For example, manufacturing in itself may not provide for competitive advantage, but perhaps product engineering or design do. And even if machines and equipment generally do not provide for competitive advantage there may be a particular type of equipment that does.

5.4.2 The value chain and value system

The **value chain describes the categories of activities within an organisation which, together, create a product or service.** Most organisations are also part of a wider **value system, the set of inter-organisational links and relationships that are necessary to create a product or service.** Both are useful in understanding the strategic position of an organisation and where valuable resources and capabilities reside.

Table 5.2 The VRIO framework

| | Is the resource or capability . . . | | | |
valuable?	rare?	inimitable?	supported by the organisation?	Competitive implications
No	–	–	No	Competitive disadvantage
Yes	No	–		Competitive parity
Yes	Yes	No		Temporary competitive advantage
Yes	Yes	Yes	Yes	Sustained competitive advantage

Source: Adapted from J.B. Barney and W.S. Hesterly, *Strategic Management and Competitive Advantage*, Pearson Education, 2012.

The value chain

If organisations are to achieve competitive advantage by delivering value to customers, managers need to understand which activities their organisation undertakes that are especially important in creating that value and which are not. This can then be used to model the value generation of an organisation. The important point is that the concept of the value chain invites the strategist to think of an organisation in terms of sets of activities. There are different frameworks for considering these categories: Figure 5.4 is a representation of a value chain as developed by Michael Porter.[17]

Primary activities are directly concerned with the creation or delivery of a product or service. For example, for a manufacturing business:

- *Inbound logistics* are activities concerned with receiving, storing and distributing inputs to the product or service including materials handling, stock control, transport, etc.

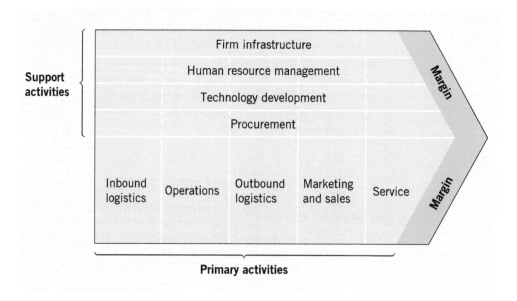

Figure 5.4 The value chain within an organisation

Source: Adapted with the permission of The Free Press, a Division of Simon & Schuster, Inc., from *Competitive Advantage: Creating and Sustaining Superior Performance* by Michael E. Porter. Copyright © 1985, 1998 by Michael E. Porter. All rights reserved.

- *Operations* transform these inputs into the final product or service: machining, packaging, assembly, testing, etc.

- *Outbound logistics* collect, store and distribute the product or service to customers; for example, warehousing, materials handling, distribution, etc.

- *Marketing and sales* provide the means whereby consumers or users are made aware of the product or service and are able to purchase it. This includes sales administration, advertising and selling.

- *Service* includes those activities that enhance or maintain the value of a product or service, such as installation, repair, training and spares.

Each of these groups of primary activities is linked to *support activities* which help to improve the effectiveness or efficiency of primary activities:

- *Procurement*. Processes that occur in many parts of the organisation for acquiring the various resource inputs to the primary activities. These can be vitally important in achieving scale advantages. So, for example, many large consumer goods companies with multiple businesses nonetheless procure advertising centrally.

- *Technology development*. All value activities have a 'technology', even if it is just know-how. Technologies may be concerned directly with a product (e.g. R&D, product design) or with processes (e.g. process development) or with a particular resource (e.g. raw materials improvements).

- *Human resource management*. This transcends all primary activities and is concerned with recruiting, managing, training, developing and rewarding people within the organisation.

- *Infrastructure*. The formal systems of planning, finance, quality control, information management and the structure of an organisation.

The value chain can be used to understand the strategic position of an organisation and analyse resources and capabilities in three ways:

- As a *generic description of activities* it can help managers understand if there is a cluster of activities providing benefit to customers located within particular areas of the value chain. Perhaps a business is especially good at outbound logistics linked to its marketing and sales operation and supported by its technology development. It might be less good in terms of its operations and its inbound logistics.

- In analysing the competitive position of the organisation by using the *VRIO analysis* for individual value chain activities and functions (see Section 5.4.2 above).

- To *analyse the cost and value of activities* of an organisation. This could involve the following steps:

  - *Identify sets of value activities*. Figure 5.4 might be appropriate as a general framework here or a value chain more specific to an organisation can be developed. The important thing is to ask (i) which separate categories of activities best describe the operations of the organisation and (ii) which of these are most significant in delivering the strategy and achieving advantage over competitors? For example, it is likely that in a branded pharmaceutical company research and development and marketing activities will be crucially important.

  - *Assess the relative importance of activity costs internally*. Which activities are most significant in terms of the costs of operations? Does the significance of costs align with the significance of activities? Which activities add most value to the final product or service (and in turn to the customer) and which do not? It can also be important to establish which sets of activities are linked to or are dependent on others and which, in effect, are self-standing. For example, organisations that have undertaken such analyses often find that central services have grown to the extent that they are a disproportionate cost and do not add value to other sets of activities or to the customer.

- *Assess the relative importance of activities externally.* How does value and the cost of a set of activities compare with the similar activities of competitors? For example, although they are both global oil businesses, BP and Shell are different in terms of the significance of their value chain activities. BP has historically outperformed Shell in terms of exploration, but the reverse is the case with regard to refining and marketing.

- *Identify where and how can costs be reduced?* Given the picture that emerges from such an analysis it should be possible to ask some important questions about the cost structure of the organisation in terms of the strategy being followed (or that needs to be followed in the future). For example, is the balance of cost in line with the strategic significance of the elements of the value chain? Can costs be reduced in some areas without affecting the value created for customers? Can some activities be outsourced (see Section 8.5.2), for example those that are relatively free-standing and do not add value significantly? Can cost savings be made by increasing economies of scale or scope; for example, through central procurement or consolidating currently fragmented activities (e.g. manufacturing units)?

The value system

A single organisation rarely undertakes in-house all of the value activities from design through to the delivery of the final product or service to the final consumer. There is usually specialisation of roles so, as Figure 5.5 shows, any one organisation is part of a wider *value system* of different interacting organisations. There are questions that arise here that build on an understanding of the value chain itself:

- The *'make or buy'* or *outsourcing* decision for a particular activity is critical: which activities most need to be part of the internal value chain because they are central to achieving competitive advantage? There may also be activities that do not generate competitive

Figure 5.5 The value system

advantage in themselves, but which the organisation needs to control as they enable the exploitation of competitive advantage in other parts of the value chain, as indicated in Section 5.3.4. Illustration 5.3 shows this in relation to the Nepalese poultry industry. Value system analysis was used by the Valley Group as a way of identifying what they should focus on in securing a steady supply of chicken and developing a more profitable structure. While their analysis resulted in integration along the value system, it is increasingly common to outsource activities as a means of lowering costs (see Section 8.5.2). Just as costs can be analysed across the internal value chain, they can also be analysed across the value system. If activities are less costly when performed by others without any adverse effects, it may make more sense to leave these to others along the value system.

- *What are the activities and cost/price structures of the value system?* Understand the entire value system and its relationship to an organisation's value chain is essential as changes in the environment may require outsourcing or integration of activities depending on changing cost/price structures. The more an organisation outsources, the more its ability to evaluate and influence the performance of other organisations in the value system may become a critically important capability in itself and even a source of competitive advantage. For example, the quality of a cooker or a television when it reaches the final purchaser is influenced not only by the activities undertaken within the manufacturing company itself, but also by the quality of components from suppliers and the performance of the distributors.

- *Where are the profit pools?*[18] **Profit pools** refer to the **different levels of profit available at different parts of the value system.** Some parts of a value system can be inherently more profitable than others because of the differences in competitive intensity (see Section 3.2.1). For example, in the computer industry microprocessors and software have historically been more profitable than hardware manufacture. The strategic question becomes whether it is possible to focus on the areas of greatest profit potential. Care has to be exercised here. It is one thing to identify such potential; it is another to be successful in it given the capabilities an organisation has. For example, engineering firms may recognise the greater profit potential in providing engineering consulting services in addition to or instead of manufacturing. Nonetheless, many have found it difficult to develop such services successfully either because their staff do not have consultancy capabilities or because their clients do not recognise the firms as having them.

- *Partnering.* Who might be the best partners in the various parts of the value system? And what kinds of relationships are important to develop with each partner? For example, should they be regarded as suppliers or should they be regarded as alliance partners (see Section 11.4)?

5.4.3 Activity systems

The discussion so far highlights the fact that all organisations comprise sets of resources and capabilities, but that these are likely to be configured differently across organisations. It is this variable configuration that makes an organisation and its strategy more or less unique. So for the strategist, understanding this matters a good deal.

VRIO and value chain analysis can help with this, but so too can understanding the more fine-grained activity systems of an organisation. As the discussion above in Section 5.3 has made clear, the way in which resources are deployed through the organisation actually takes form in the activities pursued by that organisation; so it is important to identify what these activities are, why they are valuable to customers, how the various activities fit together and how they are different from competitors'.

ILLUSTRATION 5.3   An integrated value system in the Nepalese poultry industry

Integrating the value system under complex conditions.

The Valley Group has moved from backyard farming and selling 13 kilograms of broilers' meat in 1981 to becoming the Nepal poultry market leader despite a context including decades of political insurgency, economic turmoil and social unrest. They have managed the value system and supply chain problems of Nepal's decentralised and scattered poultry-keeping activities. Gradually they have integrated various elements of the value system while leaving supplementary elements to other organisations.

The complex context, including an absence of law and order, frequent general strikes, shortage of supplies and energy and poor transport infrastructure, resulted in irregularities in the supply of commercial chicks, their feeds and medicines. The Valley Group managers recognised that various industrial customers, such as hotels and food processing firms, preferred those suppliers that could meet their steady demand for poultry products. Supply regularity thus emerged as a primary determinant of business success. The managers then vertically and horizontally integrated various parts of the value system. They developed a sustained network of reciprocal interdependence in order to ensure the quality and regularity of poultry products and services thereof, even under the difficult circumstances prevailing.

The poultry value system begins from genetic engineering that passes through the foundation stock, primary breeder (known as grandparents that produce the parent stock – the breeders), parent stock, hatcheries, farm houses, slaughter/processing houses and finally the selling outlets (see table). The primary breeder produces breeder eggs that hatch into breeder chicks, whose eggs further hatch into day-old commercial chicks. These chicks (baby chickens hatched from the breeder eggs) are raised into live broilers (reaching slaughter-weight at between five and seven weeks) in farm houses. The live broilers are then transported to slaughter/processing houses in order to portion, pack and prepare them for sales outlets.

The Valley Group integrated itself into various parts of the value system in order to secure a regular supply of live broilers to meet the steady demand for poultry products from the market. First, the difficult circumstances made it difficult for poultry farmers to receive live broilers and feed them consistently and this resulted in irregular supply. To address this problem, the Valley Group established Valley Poultry and Valley Feed in order to ensure a steady supply of chicks and feeds, respectively, to the farmers, who could then grow the chicks to live broilers on a regular basis. A second element that prevented regular supply from the farmers was that they were not confident that there would be a steady market demand for their live broilers. This resulted in the Valley Mart that buys live broilers directly from the farmers. The broilers are then slaughtered and processed and, finally, high-quality chicken, chicken sections, processed and packed items are steadily made available in Valley Cold Store.

Source: Prepared by Raj Kumar Bhattarai, Nepal Commerce Campus, Tribhuvan University.

Questions

1 Draw up a value system and value chains for another business and organisation in terms of the activities conducted within each part (see Figure 5.5).

2 Would it make sense to integrate or outsource some of the various value chain activities in this value system in relation to the focal organisation?

3 What are the strategic implications of your analysis – what would you do?

	Major actors in the poultry value system					
	Breeding farm	**Valley Poultry**	**Farmers**	**Valley Feed**	**Valley Mart**	**Valley Cold Store**
Input	Primary breeder: – Feed – Medicine and vaccine	Breeder chickens: – Feed – Medicine and vaccine	Chickens: – Feed – Medicine and vaccine	– Food grains and remains – Other items	Live broiler feed	Live broilers
Output	– Breeder eggs – Breeder chickens	– Eggs – Chicks/chickens	– Live broilers – Food grains – Remains	– Feed for poultry and cattle	Live broilers	Poultry: whole chicken, parts and processed items

Some scholars,[19] including Michael Porter, have written about the importance of mapping activity systems and shown how this might be done. The starting point is to identify what Porter refers to as 'higher order strategic themes'. In effect, these are the ways in which the organisation meets the critical success factors determining them in the industry. The next step is to identify the clusters of activities that underpin each of these themes and how these do or do not fit together. The result is a picture of the organisation represented in terms of activity systems such as that shown in Figure 5.6. It shows an activity systems map for the Scandinavian strategic communications consultancy, Geelmuyden.Kiese.[20] The core higher-order theme at the heart of its success is its knowledge, built over the years, of how effective communications can influence 'the power dynamics of decision-making processes'. However, as Figure 5.6 shows, this central theme is related to other higher-order strategic themes (rectangles) as listed below (each of which is underpinned by clusters of supporting activities; see ovals in Figure 5.6):

- The company seeks to work at a *strategic level* based on its own *in-house methodology*, prioritising those clients where such work is especially valued.

- The company takes a *clear stance on integrity of communication,* always advising openness of communication rather than suppression of information and only dealing with clients that will accept such principles.

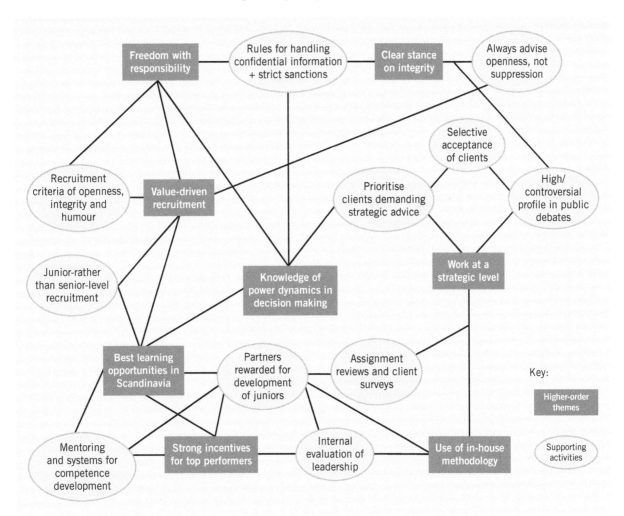

Figure 5.6 Activity systems at Geelmuyden.Kiese

- Staff are given *high degrees of freedom* but with some absolute criteria of responsibility including strict rules for handling clients' confidential information and strict sanctions if such rules are broken.

- Recruitment aims to ensure this responsibility and is carried out largely on the basis of *values of openness and integrity* but also humour. The emphasis is on recruiting junior personnel and developing them based on a mentoring system and, thus, the company believes it offers the best *learning opportunities* in Scandinavia for young consultants.

- There are *strong financial incentives* for top performance, including rewards for the development of junior personnel and based on internal evaluation of leadership qualities and performance.

When mapping activity systems four points need to be emphasised:

- *Relationship to the value chain.* The various activities represented in an activity map can also be seen as parts of a value chain. The in-house methodology is, in effect, part of Geelmuyden.Kiese's operations; its recruitment practices are a component of its human resource management; its stance on integrity and insistence on openness rather than suppression of the information part of its service offering; and so on. However, activity systems mapping encourages a greater understanding of the complexity of resources and capabilities – important if bases of competitive advantage are to be identified and managed.

- *The importance of linkages and fit.* An activity systems map emphasises the importance of different activities that create value to customers pulling in the same direction and supporting rather than opposing each other. So the need is to understand (i) the fit between the various activities and how these reinforce each other and (ii) the fit externally with the needs of clients. There are two implications:

  - The danger of *piecemeal change* or tinkering with such systems which may damage the positive benefits of the linkages that exist.

  - The consequent *challenge of managing change.* When change is needed, the implication is that change to one part of the system will almost inevitably affect another; or, put another way, change probably has to be managed over the whole system.

- *Relationship to VRIO.* It is these linkages and this fit that can be the bases of sustainable competitive advantage. In combination they may be *valuable* to clients, truly distinctive and therefore *rare*. Moreover, while individual components of an activity system might be relatively easy to imitate, in combination they may well constitute the complexity and causal ambiguity rooted in culture and history that makes them *inimitable*. Finally, there can be activities in the system that in themselves do not provide for competitive advantage, but that provide *organisational support* for other activities that do.

- *Superfluous activities.* It should also be asked if there are activities that are not required in order to pursue a particular strategy or if some activities do not contribute to value creation. If activities do not do this, why are they being pursued by the organisation? Whether Ryanair used activity mapping or not, it has systematically identified and done away with many activities that other airlines commonly undertake.

5.4.4 Benchmarking

Benchmarking is used as a means of understanding how an organisation compares with others.[21] It may be organisations that compete in the same industry, typically competitors, or other organisations that perform the same or similar functions. Many benchmarking exercises focus on outputs such as standards of product or service, but others do attempt to take account of organisational capabilities.

Broadly, there are two approaches to benchmarking:

- *Industry/sector benchmarking.* Insights about performance standards can be gleaned by comparing performance against other organisations in the same industry sector or between similar service providers against a set of performance indicators. Some public-sector organisations have, in effect, acknowledged the existence of strategic groups (see Section 3.4.1) by benchmarking against similar organisations rather than against everybody: for example, local government services and police treat 'urban' differently from 'rural' in their benchmarking and league tables. However, an overriding danger of industry norm comparisons (whether in the private or the public sector) is that the whole industry can be performing badly and losing out competitively to other industries that can satisfy customers' needs in different ways.

- *Best-in-class benchmarking.* Best-in-class benchmarking compares an organisation's performance or capabilities against 'best-in-class' performance – from whichever industry – and therefore seeks to overcome some of the above limitations. It may also help challenge managers' mindsets that acceptable improvements in performance will result from incremental changes in resources or capabilities. For example, Southwest Airlines improved refuelling time by studying the processes surrounding Formula One Grand Prix motor racing pit stops.[22]

The importance of benchmarking is, then, not so much in the detailed 'mechanics' of comparison but in the impact that these comparisons might have on reviewing resources and capabilities underlying performance. But it has two potential limitations:

- *Surface comparisons.* If benchmarking is limited to comparing outputs, it does not directly identify the reasons for relative performance in terms of underlying resources and capabilities. For example, it may demonstrate that one organisation is poorer at customer service than another, but not show the underlying reasons.

- *Simply achieving competitive parity.* Benchmarking can help an organisation to develop capabilities and create value in the same way as its competitors and those best-in-class. However, the best performance that can be expected out of this exercise is to achieve a threshold level and competitive parity. For organisations with competitive disadvantage, this can be highly rewarding, but to achieve competitive advantage an organisation needs to move further and develop its own distinctive resources and capabilities.

5.4.5 SWOT[23]

It can be helpful to summarise the key issues arising from an analysis of resources and capabilities discussed in this chapter and the analysis of the business environment discussed in Chapters 2 and 3 to gain an overall picture of an organisation's strategic position. **SWOT provides a general summary of the Strengths and Weaknesses explored in an analysis of resources and capabilities** (Chapter 4) **and the Opportunities and Threats explored in an analysis of the environment** (Chapters 2 and 3). This analysis can also be useful as a basis for generating strategic options and assessing future courses of action.

The aim is to identify the extent to which strengths and weaknesses are relevant to, or capable of dealing with, the changes taking place in the business environment. Illustration 5.4 takes the example of a pharmaceuticals firm (Pharmcare).[24] It assumes that key environmental impacts have been identified from analyses explained in Chapters 2 and 3 and that major strengths and weaknesses have been identified using the analytic tools explained in this chapter. A scoring mechanism (plus 5 to minus 5) is used as a means of getting managers to assess the interrelationship between the environmental impacts and the strengths and weaknesses of the firm. A positive (+) denotes that the strength of the company would help it take advantage of, or counteract, a problem arising from an environmental change or that

ILLUSTRATION 5.4   SWOT analysis of Pharmcare

A SWOT analysis explores the relationship between the environmental influences and the resources and capabilities of an organisation compared with its competitors.

(a) SWOT analysis for Pharmcare

	Environmental change (opportunities and threats)					
	Healthcare rationing	Complex and changing buying structures	Increased integration of healthcare	Informed patients	+	−
Strengths						
Flexible sales force	+3	+5	+2	+2	+12	0
Economies of scale	0	0	+3	+3	+6	0
Strong brand name	+1	+3	0	−1	+4	−1
Healthcare education department	+3	+3	+4	+5	+15	0
Weaknesses						
Limited capabilities in biotechnology and genetics	−1	0	−4	−3	0	−8
Ever lower R&D productivity	−3	−2	−1	−2	0	−8
Weak ICT capabilities	−3	−2	−5	−5	0	−15
Over-reliance on leading product	−2	−1	−3	−1	0	−7
Environmental impact scores	+7	+11	+9	+10		
	−9	−5	−13	−12		

(b) Competitor SWOT analyses

	Environmental change (opportunities and threats)				
	Healthcare rationing	Complex and changing buying structures	Increased integration of healthcare	Informed and passionate patients	Overall impact
Pharmcare Big global player suffering fall in share price, low research productivity and post-mega-merger bureaucracy	−2 Struggling to prove cost-effectiveness of new drugs to new regulators of healthcare rationing	+6 Well-known brand, a flexible sales force combined with a new healthcare education department creates positive synergy	−4 Weak ICT and lack of integration following mergers means sales, research and admin are all under performing	−2 Have yet to get into the groove of patient power fuelled by the internet	−2 Declining performance over time worsened after merger
Company W Big pharma with patchy response to change, losing ground in new areas of competition	−4 Focus is on old-style promotional selling rather than helping doctors control costs through drugs	−4 Traditional sales force not helped by marketing which can be unaccommodating of national differences	+0 Alliances with equipment manufacturers but little work done across alliance to show dual use of drugs and new surgical techniques	+4 New recruits in the ICT department have worked cross-functionally to involve patients like never before	−4 Needs to modernise across the whole company

(b) Competitor SWOT analyses (continued)

	Environmental change (opportunities and threats)				
	Healthcare rationing	Complex and changing buying structures	Increased integration of healthcare	Informed and passionate patients	Overall impact
Organisation X Partnership between a charity managed by people with venture capital experience and top hospital geneticists	+3 Potentially able to deliver rapid advances in genetics-based illnesses	+2 Able possibly to bypass these with innovative cost-effective drug(s)	+2 Innovative drugs can help integrate healthcare through enabling patients to stay at home	+3 Patients will fight for advances in treatment areas where little recent progress has been made	+10 Could be the basis of a new business model for drug discovery – but all to prove as yet
Company Y Only develops drugs for less common diseases	+3 Partnering with big pharma allows the development of drugs discovered by big pharma but not economical for them to develop	0 Focus on small market segments so not as vulnerable to overall market structure, but innovative approach might be risky	+2 Innovative use of web to show why products still worthwhile developing even for less common illnesses	+1 Freephone call centres for sufferers of less common illnesses Company, like patients, is passionate about its mission	+6 Novel approach can be considered either risky or a winner, or both!

Questions

1 What does the SWOT analysis tell us about the competitive position of Pharmcare within the industry as a whole?

2 How readily do you think executives of Pharmcare identify the strengths and weaknesses of competitors?

3 Identify the benefits and dangers (other than those identified in the text) of a SWOT analysis such as that in the illustration.

Source: Prepared by Jill Shepherd, Segal Graduate School of Business, Simon Fraser University, Vancouver, Canada.

a weakness would be offset by that change. A negative (−) score denotes that the strength would be reduced or that a weakness would prevent the organisation from overcoming problems associated with that change.

Pharmcare's share price had been declining because investors were concerned that its strong market position was under threat. This had not been improved by a merger that was proving problematic. The pharmaceutical market was changing with new ways of doing business, driven by new technology, the quest to provide medicines at lower cost and politicians seeking ways to cope with soaring healthcare costs and an ever more informed patient. But was Pharmcare keeping pace? The strategic review of the firm's position (Illustration 5.4a) confirmed its strengths of a flexible sales force, well-known brand name and new healthcare department. However, there were major weaknesses, namely relative failure on low-cost drugs, competence in information and communication technology (ICT) and a failure to get to grips with increasingly well-informed users.

However, in the context of this chapter, if this analysis is to be useful, it must be remembered that the exercise is not absolute but relative to its competitors. So SWOT analysis is most useful when it is comparative – if it examines strengths, weaknesses, opportunities and threats in relation to competitors. When the impact of environmental forces on competitors was analysed (Illustration 5.4b), it showed that Pharmcare was still outperforming its traditional competitor (Company W), but potentially vulnerable to changing dynamics in the general industry structure courtesy of niche players (X and Y).

There are two main dangers in a SWOT exercise:

- *Listing.* A SWOT exercise can generate very long lists of apparent strengths, weaknesses, opportunities and threats, whereas what matters is to be clear about what is really important and what is less important. So prioritisation of issues matters. Three brief rules can be helpful here. First, as indicated above, focus on strengths and weaknesses that differ in *relative* terms compared to competitors or comparable organisations and leave out areas where the organisation is at par with others. Second, focus on opportunities and threats that are directly *relevant* for the specific organisation and industry and leave out general and broad factors. Third, summarise the *result* and draw concrete conclusions.

- *A summary, not a substitute.* SWOT analysis is an engaging and fairly simple tool. It is also useful in summarising and consolidating other analysis that has been explained in this chapter and also in Chapters 2 and 3. It is not, however, a substitute for that analysis. There are two dangers if it is used on its own. The first is that, in the absence of more thorough analysis, managers rely on preconceived, often inherited and biased views. The second is again the danger of a lack of specificity. Identifying very general strengths, for example, does not explain the underlying reasons for those strengths.

SWOT can also help focus discussion on future choices and the extent to which an organisation is capable of supporting these strategies. A useful way of doing this is to use a TOWS matrix[25] as shown in Figure 5.7. This builds directly on the information in a SWOT exercise. Each box of the TOWS matrix can be used to identify options that address a different combination of the internal factors (strengths and weaknesses) and the external factors (opportunities and threats). For example, the top left-hand box prompts a consideration of options that use the strengths of the organisation to take advantage of opportunities in the business environment. An example for Pharmcare might be the re-training of the sales force to deal with changes in pharmaceuticals buying. The bottom right-hand box prompts options that minimise weaknesses and also avoid threats; for Pharmcare, this might include the need to develop its ICT systems to better service more informed patients. Quite likely this would also help take advantage of opportunities arising from changes in the buying structure of the industry (top right). The bottom left box suggests the need to use strengths to avoid threats, perhaps by building on the success of the healthcare education department to also better service informed patients.

Internal factors

	Strengths (S)	Weaknesses (W)
Opportunities (O)	**SO Strategic options** Generate options here that use strengths to take advantage of opportunities	**WO Strategic options** Generate options here that take advantage of opportunities by overcoming weaknesses
Threats (T)	**ST Strategic options** Generate options here that use strengths to avoid threats	**WT Strategic options** Generate options here that minimise weaknesses and avoid threats

External factors is positioned to the left spanning the Opportunities (O) and Threats (T) rows.

Figure 5.7 The TOWS matrix

5.5 DYNAMIC CAPABILITIES

The previous section was concerned with diagnosing resources and capabilities. This section considers what managers might do to manage and improve resources and capabilities. If resources and capabilities for competitive advantage do not exist, then managers need to consider if they can be developed. Also, if they are to provide a basis for long-term success, resources and capabilities cannot be static; they need to change. University of Berkeley economist David Teece has introduced the concept of **dynamic capabilities**, by which he means **an organisation's ability to renew and recreate its resources and capabilities to meet the needs of changing environments.**[26] He argues that the resources and capabilities that are necessary for efficient operations, like owning certain tangible assets, controlling costs, maintaining quality, optimising inventories, etc., are unlikely to be sufficient for sustaining superior performance.[27] These '*ordinary capabilities*' allow companies to be successful and earn a living now by producing and selling a similar product or service to similar customers over time, but are not likely to provide for long-term survival and competitive advantage in the future.[28]

In other words, there is a danger that capabilities and resources that were the basis of competitive success can over time be imitated by competitors, become common practice in an industry or become redundant as its environment changes. So, the important lesson is that if resources and capabilities are to be effective over time they need to change; they cannot be static. Dynamic capabilities are directed towards that strategic change. They are dynamic in the sense that they can create, extend or modify an organisation's existing ordinary capabilities. Teece suggests the following three generic types of dynamic capabilities:

- *Sensing*. Sensing implies that organisations must constantly scan, search and explore opportunities across various markets and technologies. Research and development and investigating customer needs are typical sensing activities. For example, companies in the PC operating systems industry, like Microsoft, sensed the threats from and opportunities in tablets and smartphones.

- *Seizing*. Once an opportunity is sensed it must be seized and addressed through new products or services, processes, activities, etc. Microsoft, for example, has tried to seize opportunities by launching its own tablet device and software, Surface, and by acquiring the mobile phone company Nokia (now under the brand name Microsoft Lumia).

| ILLUSTRATION 5.5 | Dynamic capabilities (and rigidities) in mobile telephone companies |

Dynamic capabilities can help firms sense and seize opportunities and reconfigure ordinary capabilities in changing environments.

Companies in the mobile telephone industry have built on their dynamic capabilities in their effort to adapt to environmental changes and dominate the market. They have identified and evaluated new opportunities (sensing); addressed these opportunities with new products (seizing); and renewed and redeployed their capabilities accordingly (reconfiguring). This is illustrated in the table.

The pioneers in mobile telephony, Ericsson and Motorola, managed to sense and explore an entirely new mobile telephony market. They satisfied and captured value in that market by recombining and redeploying telecommunication and radio capabilities. However, they got stuck in these early mobile telephone capabilities and were followed by Nokia. Nokia sensed new opportunities as it realised that mobile phones' awkward design and functionality was not suited to what had become a mass consumer and fashion market. The company seized and addressed these new opportunities, offering improved design and functionality, building on design and consumer behaviour capabilities. Finally, Apple, with a long legacy in consumer products, explored even further opportunities. Apple realised that most phones, even the new smartphones, still maintained a complex and unintuitive interface with limited multimedia functionalities. Apple addressed this by introducing an upgraded multimedia platform smartphone with an intuitive and simple interface combined with complementary services like the App Store and iTunes Music Store. Apple built on a recombination of its prior design, interface and consumer behaviour capabilities and (for them) new mobile phone capabilities.

While the dynamic capabilities of the mobile phone companies helped them adapt, they are no guarantee for keeping ahead permanently as the ordinary capabilities they developed risk becoming rigidities as markets and technologies change even further. If dynamic capabilities do not manage to detect and alleviate rigidities, competitors may emerge over time with more appropriate dynamic capabilities for the constantly changing environment.

Questions

1 What type of dynamic capabilities could help mobile phone companies like Apple and Samsung avoid becoming stuck in their old resources and capabilities?

2 Based on your own experience of using mobile and smartphones:

   a What are the possible future opportunities in mobile telephones?

   b How could they possibly be sensed and seized?

- *Reconfiguring.* To seize an opportunity may require renewal and reconfiguration of organisational capabilities and investments in technologies, manufacturing, markets, etc. For example, Microsoft's inroad into tablets, smartphones and related software and apps requires major changes in its current resources and capabilities. The company must discard some of its old capabilities, acquire and build new ones and recombine them, which may prove quite challenging.

This view of dynamic capabilities relates directly to the framework for this book: strategic position, strategic choices and strategy in action (see Figure 1.3). Sensing capabilities is to do with understanding an organisation's strategic position; seizing opportunities relates to making strategic choices; and reconfiguration is to do with enacting strategies. Illustration 5.5

Companies	Approximate time period	Product	Sensing	Seizing	Reconfiguring
Ericsson (primarily Europe) **Motorola** (primarily the USA)	Mid-1980s–late 1990s	Mobile phones	Need for mobile telephones: fixed telephony did not offer mobility	Creating the first mobile telephone systems and telephones	Creating a new mobile telephone market Acquiring and building mobile telephone capabilities
Nokia	Late 1990s–early 2000s	Mobile phones with improved design and functionality	Need for well-designed and fashionable mobile phones: existing mobile phones were close to their car-phone origins and maintained their awkward design and functionality	Upgrading the mobile phone to provide a richer experience in design, fashion and functionality	Entering the mobile telephone market Acquiring and building mobile telephony capabilities Building design and marketing capabilities
Apple	Late 2000s–	Mobile or smartphones with perfected design, functionality and interface	Need for smartphones with multimedia functionality: existing smartphones maintained a complex and unintuitive interface with limited functionalities	Upgrading the mobile phone to include an intuitive interface and multimedia functionalities containing the App store and iTunes	Entering the mobile telephone market Acquiring mobile telephony capabilities and recombining them with existing design and interface capabilities Cooperating with the music and telephone app industries

provides an example of dynamic capabilities in the context of mobile telephones, but also shows that they are no guarantee for future success.

New product development is a typical example of a dynamic capability and strategic analysis and planning is another. They both involve activities that can sense and seize opportunities and that are intended to reconfigure resources and capabilities. Outlet proliferation by chain retailers such as Starbucks or Zara is another example of a dynamic capability as it extends ordinary capabilities.[29] Dynamic capabilities may also take the form of relatively formal organisational systems, such as reorganisation,[30] recruitment and management development processes and cooperating with others through alliances or acquisitions, by which new skills are learned and developed.[31]

As Teece acknowledges, however, dynamic capabilities are likely to have 'micro-founda-tions'[32] in people's behaviour within organisations, such as the way in which decisions get taken, personal relationships and entrepreneurial and intuitive skills. This puts the focus on behaviour and the significance of beliefs, social relationships and organisational processes in capability management, which is discussed in 'Thinking Differently' at the end of the chapter.[33]

In brief, dynamic capabilities can change ordinary capabilities in case the environment changes. However, as they are focused on finding solutions beyond and outside current ordi-nary capabilities there is a trade-off and tension between the two that can make it difficult to achieve an optimal balance between them. This is sometimes referred to as exploration/exploitation trade-offs and they are further discussed in Chapter 15.

As suggested above, dynamic capabilities may take different forms and there are thus many ways in which managers might create, extend or upgrade resources and capabilities including more experimental ones.[34] Several approaches to manage resources and capabilities are discussed in other parts of this book:[35]

- *Internal capability development*. Could resources and capabilities be added or upgraded so that they become more reinforcing of outcomes that deliver against critical success factors? This might be done, for example, by:

  - *Building and recombining capabilities*. Creating entirely new capabilities that provide for competitive advantage requires entrepreneurship and intrapreneurship skills. Man-agers can build managerial systems and a culture that promote capability innovation or form new venture units outside the rules of ordinary R&D and product development (see Chapter 10).[36]

  - *Leveraging capabilities*. Managers might identify resources and capabilities in one area of their organisation, perhaps customer service in one geographic busi-ness unit of a multinational, which are not present in other business units. They might then seek to extend this throughout all the business units, but capabilities might not be easily transferred because of the problems of managing change (see Chapter 15).

  - *Stretching capabilities*. Managers may see the opportunity to build new products or services out of existing capabilities. Indeed, building new businesses in this way is the basis of related diversification, as explained in Chapter 8.

- *External capability development*. Similarly, there may be ways of developing resources and capabilities by looking externally. For example, they could be attained or developed by acquisition or entering into alliances and joint ventures (see Chapter 11).

- *Ceasing activities*. Could current activities, not central to the delivery of value to cus-tomers, be done away with, outsourced or reduced in cost? If managers are aware of the resources and capabilities central to bases of competitive advantage, they can retain these and focus on areas of cost reduction that are less significant (see Chapter 7).

- *Awareness development*. One of the lessons of this chapter is that the bases of competitive advantage often lie in the day-to-day activities that people undertake in organisations, so developing the ability of people to recognise the relevance of what they do in terms of how that contributes to the strategy of the organisation is important. This suggests that staffing policies, training and development, including developing employee's awareness of how they contribute to competitive advantage, are all central to capability deployment and development. Together with organisational learning, these issues are discussed in later chapters on organising and leading strategic change (see Chapters 14 and 15).

THINKING DIFFERENTLY   Micro-foundations of capabilities

A new view emphasises the individuals behind capabilities.

In the discussion of dynamic capabilities above (Section 5.5) it was noted that 'micro-foundations' of people's behaviour underlie them, which suggests that strategy is rooted in individual action. From this perspective then the focus is not so much on organisation's resources and capabilities as on the individuals behind them. The emphasis is on how managers' decisions and actions aggregate up to the organisational level and shape resources and capabilities.[37]

The emphasis of this alternative micro-foundations approach is thus on individuals and their social interactions and how they form organisational resources and capabilities. Instead of taking resources and capabilities as the point of departure, micro-foundations starts with individuals' beliefs, preferences, interests and activities. The focus is on the role of key individuals, particularly those at the top, and their ambitions, competences and social networks. It is these individuals' decisions and choices that determine capabilities, strategy and performance.

The focus on micro-foundations suggests that managers should not take resources and capabilities for granted. Instead, they should carefully consider how their skills, activities and choices can develop and change them. For strategy then the focus is primarily on individual managers' capabilities rather than those of the whole organisation. However, it needs to be emphasised that there are limits to how managers can influence resources and capabilities. First, they are often built over extended periods of time (see Chapter 13), even over decades, which often go beyond the tenure of individual CEOs or managers. Second, cognitive and psychological biases often put a limit to managerial judgments and achievements (see Chapter 16).

Question

Pick an organisation mentioned in this chapter (e.g. Apple, IKEA, Microsoft, Ryanair, Starbucks, Zara) or one you admire and would like to work for. What micro-foundations (e.g. individuals and their competences, skills, networks, choices, activities) do you think underlie their resources and capabilities?

SUMMARY

- To be able to compete at all in a market an organisation needs *threshold* resources and capabilities, but to achieve sustained competitive advantage they also need to be unique and *distinctive.*

- To be distinctive and provide for sustainable competitive advantage, resources and capabilities need to fulfil the *VRIO* criteria of being *Valuable*, *Rare*, *Inimitable* and *supported by the Organisation.*

- Ways of diagnosing organisational resources and capabilities include:

  - *VRIO analysis* of resources and capabilities as a tool to evaluate if they contribute to competitive advantage.

  - Analysing an organisation's *value chain* and *value system* as a basis for understanding how value to a customer is created and can be developed.

  - *Activity systems mapping* as a means of identifying more detailed activities which underpin resources and capabilities.

  - *SWOT analysis* as a way of drawing together an understanding of the strengths, weaknesses, opportunities and threats an organisation faces.

  - *Benchmarking* as a means of understanding the relative performance of organisations.

- Managers need to adapt and change resources and capabilities if the environment changes and this can be done based on *dynamic capabilities*.

WORK ASSIGNMENTS

✱ Denotes more advanced work assignments.

 * Refers to a case study in the Text and Cases edition.

5.1 Using Table 5.1 identify the resources and capabilities of an organisation with which you are familiar, your university or school, for example. Alternatively, you can answer this in relation to H&M* or Formula One* if you wish.

5.2✱ Undertake a VRIO analysis of the resources and capabilities of an organisation with which you are familiar in order to identify which resources and capabilities meet the criteria of (a) value, (b) rarity, (c) inimitability and (d) organisational support (see Section 5.3; Figure 5.2 and Table 5.2). You can answer this in relation to H&M* or Formula One* or the end of chapter case, Rocket Internet, if you wish.

5.3✱ For an industry or public service of your choice consider how the resources and capabilities that have been the basis of competitive advantage (or best value in the public sector) have changed over time. Why have these changes occurred? How did the relative strengths of different companies or service providers change over this period? Why? Did dynamic capabilities play any role? Which?

5.4 Undertake a value chain or system analysis for an organisation of your choice (referring to Illustration 5.3 could be helpful). You can answer this in relation to a case study in the book such as Ryanair* or the end of chapter case, Rocket Internet, if you wish.

5.5✱ For a benchmarking exercise to which you have access, make a critical assessment of the benefits and dangers of the approach that was taken.

Integrative assignment

5.6 Prepare a SWOT analysis for an organisation of your choice (see Illustration 5.5). Explain why you have chosen each of the factors you have included in the analysis, in particular their relationship to other analyses you have undertaken in Chapters 2 and 3. What are the conclusions you arrive at from your analysis and how would these inform an evaluation of strategy (see Chapter 12)?

RECOMMENDED KEY READINGS

- For an understanding of the resource-based view of the firm, an early and much cited paper is by Jay Barney: 'Firm resources and sustained competitive advantage', *Journal of Management,* vol. 17 (1991), pp. 99–120. An overview of RBV research is written by Jay B. Barney, David J. Ketchen Jr and Mike Wright: 'The future of resource-based theory: revitalization or decline?', *Journal of Management,* vol. 37, no. 5 (2011), pp. 1299–315.

- A comprehensive book on dynamic capabilities is written by C. Helfat, S. Finkelstein, W. Mitchell, M. Peteraf, H. Singh, D. Teece and S. Winter, *Dynamic Capabilities: Understanding Strategic Change in Organisations,* Blackwell Publishing, 2007. For a discussion of micro-foundations and dynamic capabilities, see D.J. Teece, 'Explicating dynamic capabilities: the nature and microfoundations of (sustainable) enterprise performance', *Strategic Management Journal,* vol. 28 (2007), pp. 1319–50.

- For a critical discussion of the use and misuse of SWOT analysis, see T. Hill and R. Westbrook, 'SWOT analysis: it's time for a product recall', *Long Range Planning,* vol. 30, no. 1 (1997), pp. 46–52.

REFERENCES

1. The concept of resource-based strategies was introduced by B. Wernerfelt, 'A resource-based view of the firm', *Strategic Management Journal,* vol. 5, no. 2 (1984), pp. 171–80. The seminal and most cited paper is by Jay Barney, 'Firm resources and sustained competitive advantage', *Journal of Management,* vol. 17, no. 1 (1991), pp. 99–120. There are many books and papers that explain and summarise the approach: for example, J. Barney, D.J. Ketchen Jr and M. Wright: 'The future of resource-based theory: revitalization or decline?', *Journal of Management,* vol. 37, no. 5, (2011), pp. 1299–315; and J. Barney and D. Clark, *Resource-Based Theory: Creating and Sustaining Competitive Advantage,* Oxford University Press, 2007.

2. The literature most commonly differentiates between 'resources' and 'capabilities'. See, for example, an early article by Raphael Amit and J.H. Paul Schoemaker: 'Strategic assets and organizational rent', *Strategic Management Journal,* vol. 14 (1993), pp. 33–46; and Jay Barney's book: J.B. Barney, *Gaining and Sustaining Competitive Advantage,* Addison-Wesley, 1997.

3. Please note that we use the terms 'resources' and 'capabilities' as most contemporary strategy texts do and the latter corresponds to what we in earlier editions referred to as 'competences' (earlier we also, somewhat idiosyncratically, used the umbrella term 'strategic capabilities' to refer to resources and capabilities). 'Capabilities' is commonly used in both research and in practice-oriented writings and in discussions within organisations. As Illustration 5.1 shows, organisations frequently refer to their capabilities when describing their strategies. Nevertheless, the term 'competences' is still used by some organisations and managers; 'core competences' in particular. Hence, we also refer to this latter term in the text (see also the next two endnotes).

4. Gary Hamel and C.K. Prahalad popularised the term *core competences* in the early 1990s to refer to an organisation's unique competences. See G. Hamel and C.K. Prahalad, 'The core competence of the corporation', *Harvard Business Review,* vol. 68, no. 3 (1990), pp. 79–91. Please note, however, that 'capabilities' rather than 'competences' is a more common term today (see also next endnote).

5. G. Hamel and C.K. Prahalad, 'The core competence of the corporation', *Harvard Business Review,* vol. 68, no. 3 (1990), pp. 79–91. This idea of driving strategy development from the resources and capabilities or competences of an organisation is also discussed in G. Hamel and C.K. Prahalad, 'Strategic intent', *Harvard Business Review,* vol. 67, no. 3 (1989), pp. 63–76; and G. Hamel and C.K. Prahalad, 'Strategy as stretch and leverage', *Harvard Business Review,* vol. 71, no. 2 (1993), pp. 75–84.

6. The VRIO criteria were introduced by Jay Barney in J.B. Barney, *Gaining and Sustaining Competitive Advantage,* Addison-Wesley, 1997. Originally the acronym *VRIN* was used to also emphasise non-substitutability and how competitors must not be able to substitute a valuable, rare and inimitable capability for another, but this is now encompassed in the inimitability criterion (see endnote 1; Barney, 1991). See also endnote 12 on VRIN.

7. This is borne out in a meta-study of research on RBV by S.L. Newbert, 'Empirical research on the Resource Based View of the firm: an assessment and suggestions for future research', *Strategic Management Journal,* vol. 28 (2007), pp. 121–46.

8. For an explanation of how complex capabilities and strategies contribute to inimitability, see J.W. Rivkin, 'Imitation of complex strategies', *Management Science,* vol. 46, no. 6 (2000), pp. 824–44.

9. The seminal paper on causal ambiguity is S. Lippman and R. Rumelt, 'Uncertain imitability: an analysis of interfirm differences in efficiency under competition', *Bell Journal of Economics,* vol. 13 (1982), pp. 418–38. For a summary and review of research on causal ambiguity, see A.W. King, 'Disentangling interfirm and intrafirm causal ambiguity: a conceptual model of causal ambiguity and sustainable competitive advantage', *Academy of Management Review,* vol. 32, no. 1 (2007), pp. 156–78.

10. The distinction between and importance of characteristic and linkage ambiguity is explained by A.W. King and C.P. Zeithaml, 'Competencies and firm performance: examining the causal ambiguity paradox', *Strategic Management Journal*, vol. 22, no. 1 (2001), pp. 75–99.

11. For a fuller discussion of path dependency in the context of resources and capabilities, see D. Holbrook, W. Cohen, D. Hounshell and S. Klepper, 'The nature, sources and consequences of firm differences in the early history of the semiconductor industry', *Strategic Management Journal*, vol. 21, nos 10/11, 2000, pp. 1017–42.

12. While the original framework ('VRIN') included 'non-substitutability' ('N') as a separate component, it is now encompassed by the 'Imitation' factor. Hence, in the VRIO framework 'Imitation' encompasses both direct replication of a resource and capability and substitution for it. Direct replication refers to the difficulty or impossibility of replicating resources and capabilities. Substitution refers rather to the difficulty of substituting one resource or capability for another. For example, if it is impossible to replicate a specific marketing expertise of a leading firm a competitor may instead try to substitute for it by cooperating with a marketing consultancy. If neither direct replication nor substitution via consultancy is possible then this capability is inimitable.

13. For an extensive discussion about complementary assets and capabilities, see D. Teece, 'Profiting from technological innovation', *Research Policy*, vol. 15, no. 6 (1986), pp. 285–305.

14. The knowledge-based view was pioneered by B. Kogut and U. Zander, 'Knowledge of the firm, combinative capabilities, and the replication of technology', *Organization Science*, vol. 3, no. 3 (1992), pp. 383–97. The importance of analysing and understanding knowledge is discussed in I. Nonaka and H. Takeuchi, *The Knowledge-creating Company*, Oxford University Press, 1995. More recently, Mark Easterby-Smith and Isabel Prieto have explored the relationships in 'Dynamic capabilities and knowledge management: an integrative role for learning', *British Journal of Management*, vol. 19 (2008), pp. 235–49.

15. See I. Nonaka and H. Takeuchi, endnote 14 above.

16. See S. Gabriel, 'Exploring internal stickiness', *Strategic Management Journal*, vol. 17, no. 2 (1996), pp. 27–43; and D. Leonard and S. Sensiper, 'The role of tacit knowledge in group innovation', *California Management Review*, vol. 40, no. 3 (1998), pp. 112–32.

17. An extensive discussion of the value chain concept and its application can be found in M.E. Porter, *Competitive Advantage*, Free Press, 1985.

18. The importance of profit pools is discussed by O. Gadiesh and J.L. Gilbert, 'Profit pools: a fresh look at strategy', *Harvard Business Review*, vol. 76, no. 3 (1998), pp. 139–47.

19. See M. Porter, 'What is strategy?', *Harvard Business Review*, November–December (1996), pp. 61–78; N. Siggelkow, 'Evolution towards fit', *Administrative Science Quarterly*, vol. 47, no. 1 (2002), pp. 125–59; and M. Porter and N. Siggelkow, 'Contextuality within activity systems and sustainability of competitive advantage', *Academy of Management Perspectives*, vol. 22, no. 2 (2008), pp. 34–56.

20. We are grateful for this example based on the doctoral dissertation of Bjorn Haugstad, *Strategy as the Intentional Structuration of Practice: Translation of Formal Strategies into Strategies in Practice*, submitted to the Saïd Business School, University of Oxford, 2009.

21. See R. Camp, *Benchmarking: the Search for Industry Best Practices that Lead to Superior Performance*, Quality Press, 2006.

22. See A. Murdoch, 'Lateral benchmarking, or what Formula One taught an airline', *Management Today* (November 1997), pp. 64–7. See also the Formula One case study in the case study section of this book (Text and Cases version only).

23. The idea of SWOT as a common-sense checklist has been used for many years: for example, S. Tilles, 'Making strategy explicit', in I. Ansoff (ed.), *Business Strategy*, Penguin, 1968. See also T. Jacobs, J. Shepherd and G. Johnson's chapter on SWOT analysis in V. Ambrosini (ed.), *Exploring Techniques of Strategy Analysis and Evaluation*, Prentice Hall, 1998. For a critical discussion of the (mis)use of SWOT, see T. Hill and R. Westbrook, 'SWOT analysis: it's time for a product recall', *Long Range Planning*, vol. 30, no. 1 (1997), pp. 46–52. For a more recent evaluation of the use of SWOT, see M.M. Helms and J. Nixon. 'Exploring SWOT analysis – where are we now? A review of academic research from the last decade', *Journal of Strategy and Management*, vol. 3, no. 3, 2010, pp. 215–51.

24. For background reading on the pharmaceutical industry see, for example, 'From vision to decision Pharma 2020', PWC, www.pwc.com/pharma, 2012; 'The pharmaceutical industry', Scherer, F.M., *Handbook of Health Economics*, vol. 1 (2000), part B, pp. 1297–336; 'A wake-up call for Big Pharma', *McKinsey Quarterly*, December 2011; and Gary Pisano, *Science Business*, Harvard Business School Press, 2006.

25. See H. Weihrich, 'The TOWS matrix – a tool for situational analysis', *Long Range Planning*, April 1982, pp. 54–66.

26. For summary papers on dynamic capabilities, see I. Barreto, 'Dynamic capabilities: a review of past research and an agenda for the future', *Journal of Management*, vol. 36, no. 1 (2010), pp. 256–80; C.L. Wang and P.K. Ahmed, 'Dynamic capabilities: a review and research agenda', *International Journal of Management Reviews*, vol. 9, no. 1 (2007), pp. 31–52; and V. Ambrosini and C. Bowman, 'What are dynamic capabilities and are they a useful construct in strategic management?', *International Journal of Management Reviews*, vol. 11, no. 1 (2009), pp. 29–49. The most comprehensive book on dynamic capabilities is written by C. Helfat, S. Finkelstein, W. Mitchell, M. Peteraf, H. Singh, D. Teece and S. Winter, *Dynamic Capabilities: Understanding Strategic Change in Organizations*, Blackwell Publishing, 2007.

27. David Teece has written about dynamic capabilities originally in D.J. Teece, G. Pisano and A. Shuen, 'Dynamic capabilities and strategic management', *Strategic Management Journal*, vol. 18, no. 7 (1997), pp. 509–34. More recently, he has expanded his explanation in the book *Dynamic*

Capabilities and Strategic Management – Organizing for innovation and growth, Oxford University Press, 2009.

28. A distinction is made between what is labelled 'ordinary' (sometimes called 'operational') and 'dynamic' capabilities. Sid Winter has explained the difference between ordinary (or operational) and dynamic capabilities in S.G. Winter, 'Understanding dynamic capabilities', *Strategic Management Journal*, vol. 24, no. 10 (2003), pp. 991–5 and David J. Teece, explains the linkage between them in 'The foundations of enterprise performance: dynamic and ordinary capabilities in an (economic) theory of firms', *The Academy of Management Perspectives* vol. 28, no. 4 (2014), pp. 328–52.

29. For a discussion of outlet proliferation as dynamic capability, see S.G. Winter, 'Understanding dynamic capabilities', *Strategic Management Journal*, vol. 24, no. 10 (2003), pp. 991–5.

30. See G. Stephane and R. Whittington, 'Reconfiguration, restructuring and firm performance: dynamic capabilities and environmental dynamism,' *Strategic Management Journal*, online and forthcoming, 2016.

31. For a list of examples of dynamic capabilities, see K.M. Eisenhardt and J.A. Martin, 'Dynamic capabilities: what are they?', *Strategic Management Journal*, vol. 21, no. 10/11 (2000), pp. 1105–21.

32. For a discussion of micro-foundations of capabilities and managerial beliefs, see G. Gavetti, 'Cognition and hierarchy: rethinking microfoundations of capabilities development', *Organization Science*, vol. 16 (2005) pp. 599–617; and for an overview see J.B. Barney and T. Felin, 'What are microfoundations?', *Academy of Management Perspectives*, vol. 27, no. 2 (2013), pp. 138–55.

33. For a discussion of how resources and capabilities relate to strategy practices and processes, see P. Regnér, 'Relating strategy as practice to the resource-based view, capabilities perspectives and the micro-foundations approach', D. Golsorkhi, L. Rouleau, D. Seidl and E. Vaara (eds), in *Cambridge Handbook of Strategy-as-Practice*, London, Cambridge University Press, 2015, pp. 301–316.

34. See J. Teece, 'Explicating dynamic capabilities: the nature and microfoundations of (sustainable) enterprise performance', *Strategic Management Journal*, vol. 28, no. 1, (2007), pp. 1319–50.

35. For a fuller discussion of how managers may manage resources and capabilities, see C. Bowman and N. Collier, 'A contingency approach to resource-creation processes', *International Journal of Management Reviews*, vol. 8, no. 4 (2006), pp. 191–211.

36. For a discussion of how the periphery in organisations can build radically new capabilities, see P. Regnér, 'Strategy creation in the periphery: inductive versus deductive strategy making', *Journal of Management Studies*, vol. 40, no. 1 (2003), pp. 57–82.

37. J.B. Barney and T. Felin, 'What are microfoundations?', *Academy of Management Perspectives* vol. 27, no. 2 (2013), pp. 138–55.

Rocket Internet – will the copycat be imitated?

Patrick Regnér

Introduction

Rocket Internet is a very successful Berlin-based start-up incubator and venture capital firm. It starts, develops and funds e-commerce and other online consumer businesses. With over 700 employees and an additional 30,000 across its network of portfolio companies, the firm has helped create and launch over 100 start-ups and is currently active in more than 70 companies across more than 100 countries.

The company was founded by the Samwer brothers, Alexander, Oliver and Marc. After going to Silicon Valley in the late 1990s they became inspired by the Californian entrepreneurial culture and especially eBay. The brothers contacted eBay offering to create a German version of the online auction house, but they received no reply from eBay. Instead they launched their own eBay clone, Alando. A month later they were acquired by eBay for $50m (£30m, €37.5m). This was to be their first great online success, but far from the last.

Next the brothers created Jamba, a mobile phone content platform. It was sold to VeriSign, a network infrastructure company, for $273m in 2004. Since then they have become experts in spotting promising business models, especially in the USA, and imitating and scaling them internationally quicker than the originals. This model is the basis of Rocket Internet, which was founded in 2007 and stock listed in Germany in 2014 valued at $8.2bn. Several of their ventures have been acquired by the company with the original idea (see Table 1). Two of their most high-profile ventures after Alando were CityDeal, which was sold off to American Groupon, and eDarling sold to American eHarmony.

The company has frequently been criticised for simply being a copycat machine without any original ideas, and some have even claimed it is a scam that rips off the originals. However, the question remains: if Rocket Internet has been so incredibly successful and what it does is simply copying, why has no one successfully imitated Rocket Internet yet? The brothers, through Oliver Samwer, defend their model in *Wired*:[1]

> 'But look at the reality. How many car manufacturers are out there? How many washing-machine manufacturers are there? How many Best Buys? Did someone write that Dixons copied Best Buy, or did anyone ever write that Best Buy copied Dixons, or that [German electronics retailer] Media Markt copied Dixons? No, they talk about Media Markt. They talk about Dixons. They talk about Best Buy. What is the difference? Isn't it all the same thing?'

Finance and expert teams

Rocket Internet has strong financial backup from its main investor globally, Kinnevik, a Swedish investment company with a 14 per cent stake. Other investors invest

The Samwer brothers
Source: Dieter Mayr Photography.

Company	Founded	Business	Buyer	Founded	Price, $m	Transaction date
Alando	1999	Online marketplace	eBay	1995	50	1999
cember.net	2005	Online business network	Xing	2003	6.4	2008
eDarling	2009	Online dating	eHarmony	1998	30% stake*	2010
GratisPay	2009	Virtual currency for online games	SponsorPay	2009	*na*	2010
CityDeal	2009	Discount deals for consumers	Groupon	2008	126†	2010
viversum	2003	Online astrology	Questico	2000	*na*	2010

*With option to buy more † Including a stake in Groupon

Source: Attack of the clones, *The Economist*, 6th August 2011, © The Economist Newspaper Limited, London, 2011.

directly in the start-ups and in the later growth stages, among them the American investment bank J.P. Morgan. To work with the investors and structure the financial solutions, Rocket Internet has a large team of finance experts at the Berlin headquarters.

Besides financial skills Rocket Internet also develops the concepts of new ventures, provides the technology platforms and combines various skills necessary for setting up new ventures. It has about 250 specialists working at the Berlin head office. These specialists are part of diverse expert teams. Engineering, including IT software, programming and web design skills, is essential for product development and there are around 200 engineers with access to state-of-the-art technologies.

The expert team in marketing includes experts in customer management, customer relationship marketing and online marketing. Other teams include Operations, Business Intelligence and HR. Apart from this, there is a Global Venture Development programme including a global mobile task force of entrepreneurial talents that can bring further know-how to all international markets. This task force includes venture developers with functional skills in product development, supply management, operations and online marketing. They rotate every 4–6 months to a new venture in another part of the world.

Human resource management and culture

The HR team recruit regular staff support for Rocket Internet and specialists for the expert teams and Global Venture Development programme and, not least, the founders of the ventures. Based on their entrepreneurial spirit they emphasise personal drive rather than good school grades. Head of HR, Vera Termuhlen, explains to VentureVillage.com:[2]

> 'All in all, it doesn't matter if an applicant is from an elite university. For the area of global venture development, we look for applicants that are hands-on, first-class, have analytical skills, describe themselves as entrepreneurs, have a passion for the online start-up scene along and a willingness to work internationally, often in exotic locations like the Philippines or Nigeria.'

The co-founders and managing directors of the individual ventures establish all operations, build the team around a venture, and develop the business; acting as entrepreneurs and holding personal stakes in the venture's equity. Recruiting them is central and Rocket Internet normally recruits extraordinary, ambitious MBA-level graduates with high analytic skills from within the local regions where the venture is set up. As Alexander Kudlich, Managing Director of Rocket Internet, says:[3]

> 'We are looking for those who from an analytical point of view understand the beauty of the business model, understand the rationale and understand what a huge opportunity is. Sometimes we say we are looking for analytical entrepreneurs rather than accidental billionaires.'

The company emphasises not only strong expertise, but 'a close cultural connection to Rocket Internet'. Rocket Internet has an intense entrepreneurial working culture that is highly performance driven including high pressure, long working hours, often from 09.00 to 23.00, and little job security. While this is attractive to some, the culture has also been criticised for being too tough and aggressive. Rocket Internet's Managing Director Alexander Kudlich comments on the culture:[3]

> 'I would describe our culture as very focused, we have young teams – the average age is below 30. There is no place where you get more freedom and where you can take as much responsibility as you want. The only thing we want back is accountability.'

Identification of business models and execution

While some of Rocket Internet's skills are common among other European incubators, the company is more of an international venture builder compared to most. Expertise is shared throughout the portfolio of ventures globally and its best practice can be applied across diverse business models (ranging from online fashion to payments to deals to social networking). Compared to many other incubators, the function of the headquarters is central. While entrepreneurs are hired to oversee individual ventures, overall strategy for Rocket Internet is largely shaped at the head office. The managing directors at head office lead the scanning for and identification of novel and proven online and mobile transaction-based business models that are internationally scalable. Former Managing Director Florian Heinemann explains in *Wired*: 'We take a pretty systematic look at business models that are already out there and we basically try to define whether a model suits our competence and is large enough that it's worth it for us to go in there.'

Another significant aspect of Rocket Internet's centralised model is the speed at which it can launch novel business models internationally. This is different compared to many US and European counterparts. Rocket Internet has an international infrastructure and distribution network with the capacity to build ventures on an international scale in just a few months. As Managing Director Kudlich explains in *Wall Street Journal*:[3]

'When we identify a business model we can, within a few weeks, build a platform out of our central teams. In the meantime the local Rocket offices will have hired or allocated the people who will execute on the ground . . . That gives us the speed. The combination of access to the best talent in each country combined with highly standardised or modular approach in terms of platform and systems which are rolled out by our headquarters.'

In brief, Rocket Internet specialises in execution rather than innovation. This is also how the management defend their model when they are blamed for simply being a clone machine. Oliver Samwer says that they are 'execution entrepreneurs' rather than 'pioneering entrepreneurs'.[4] Managing Director Kudlich explains to *Inc. Magazine*: 'Which is harder: to have the idea of selling shoes online or to build a supply chain and warehouse in Indonesia? Ideas are important. But other things are more important.'[5]

Paradoxically, even though Rocket Internet often builds on others' ideas, it prefers to keep its own ideas for itself as explained by Marc Samwer in the *International Herald Tribune*: 'We really don't like to speak about our investments since our track record encourages people to set up competing sites . . . Ideas travel much faster these days.'[6]

The future

Rocket Internet's success has continued. Zalando, which initially mimicked the online shoe retailing business in the USA by Zappos, now part of Amazon, has expanded into clothing and jewellery. Sales are rising rapidly: annual revenues for 2014 were $2.5bn and $94m in profit; and at its German stock listing the same year it was valued at €5.3bn. Other fashion brands have also been launched under the umbrella Global Fashion Group: Dafiti (Latin America), Jabong (India), Lamoda (Russia), Namshi (Middle East) and Zalora (South East Asia and Australia). After the IPO some investors complained that the company had become too complex to analyse and understand. In the *Financial Times*, Oliver Samwer describes it as a 'killer cocktail' including proprietary software, its training programmes and its 'matter-of-fact and objective' culture and claims: 'I don't think we have to change our successful model because of public investors'.[7]

Rocket Internet has, however, started to attract imitators of its own. One of the operations is Wimdu, a copy of the American Airbnb, which allows individual home and apartment owners to list their properties as holiday accommodation. However, Airbnb quickly formed a partnership with another Berlin incubator, Springstar, and they have since been rolling out Airbnb globally. Similarly, the original company responded swiftly when Rocket Internet imitated Fab.com, a designer deal site, with its Bamarang. Fab acquired Casacanda, a parallel European site, and quickly re-launched it as Fab internationally and Rocket Internet had to close down Bamarang. Rocket Internet is even facing imitators from within. Two of its managing directors have, together with other former employees, left to set up the Berlin incubator 'Project A Ventures'. Internationally there is also increasing competition including The Hut Group in the UK. There are thus signs that Rocket Internet may eventually be imitated itself.

Sources: G. Wiesmann, 'Zalando to set foot in seven new countries', *Financial Times*, 26 March 2012; T. Bradshaw, 'Facebook backers to take stake in Zalando', *Financial Times*, 2 February 2012; R. Levine, 'The kopy kat kids', Cnnmoney.com, 2 October 2007; *The Economist*, 'Attack of the clones', 6 August 2011 and 'Launching into the unknown', 4 October 2014.

References
1. M. Cowan, 'Inside the clone factory', *Wired* UK, 2 March 2012; http://www.economist.com/node/21525394\#.
2. J. Kaczmarek, 'An inside look at Rocket Internet', VentureVillage.com, 18 November 2012.
3. B. Rooney, 'Rocket Internet leads the clone war', *Wall Street Journal*, 14 May 2012.
4. C. Winter, 'How three Germans are cloning the web', *Bloomberg*, 1 March 2012.
5. M. Chafkin, 'Lessons from the world's most ruthless competitor', *Inc. Magazine*, 29 May 2012.
6. T. Crampton, 'German brothers break the mold', *International Herald Tribune*, 3 Decmeber 2006.
7. S. Gordon and D. McCrum, 'Rocket Internet: waiting for the lift-off, *Financial Times*, 19 October 2015.

Questions

1 Based on the data from the case (and any other sources available), use the frameworks from the chapter and analyse the resources and capabilities of Rocket Internet:

  a What are its resources and capabilities?

  b What are its threshold, distinctive and dynamic resources and capabilities?

2 Based on your initial analysis and answers to question 1, carry out a VRIO analysis for Rocket Internet. What do you conclude? To what extent does Rocket Internet have resources and capabilities with sustained competitive advantage?

3 What is the importance of the Samwer brothers? What would happen if they left or sold the company?

Suggested video clip

http://www.youtube.com/watch?v=Tq7WnzY89KE

6

ORGANISING AND STRATEGY

Evaluating

Processes

Strategy in action

Organising

Leadership and change

Practice

6.1 INTRODUCTION

Strategies only happen because people do what is required. If the American multinational retailer Walmart wants to achieve its strategy, it needs to get 2.2 million employees spread over 11,000 locations pointing in the right direction. In just the same way, a sports team has to ensure that its members coordinate their game plays. Thus strategies require organising and this involves both structures and systems. If the organisation is not consistent with the strategy, then even the cleverest strategy will fail because of poor implementation.

This chapter examines organising for successful strategy implementation. It focuses particularly on two key elements of organisational 'design': organisational structures and organisational systems. **Structures give people formally defined roles, responsibilities and lines of reporting.** These structures can be seen as the skeletons of organisations, providing the basic frameworks on which everything is built. **Systems support and control people as they carry out structurally defined roles and responsibilities.** Systems can be seen as the muscles of organisations, giving them movement and coherence.

Figure 6.1 expresses the interdependency between strategy, structure and systems. A starting principle of organisational design is that all three should support each other in a circular process of mutual reinforcement. This chapter captures the importance of mutual reinforcement between elements with the concept of *configuration,* explained in Section 6.4. However, the mutually reinforcing nature of configurations can create not only virtuous circles of performance, but also problems of control and adaptability. With regard to control, logically it seems that strategic priorities should determine structure and systems. But the circular nature of Figure 6.1 captures the potential for structures and systems to feed *into* strategy. As discussed in Section 6.2.6, structure and systems are not always the logical supports of strategy; sometimes, they shape it, consciously or not. With regard to adaptability, tightly-interlinked configurations of strategy, structure and systems can actually be a handicap. Section 6.4 will consider how configurations can be made more adaptable by fostering both *agility* and *resilience.*

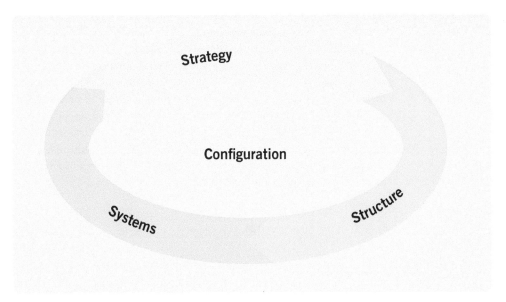

Figure 6.1 Organisational configurations: strategy, structure and systems

The chapter therefore addresses the following topics:

- *Structures,* defining the formal roles, responsibilities and lines of reporting in organisations. The chapter considers the main types of structures, including functional, divisional, matrix, project and transnational structures. Strategy and structure *fit* will be a key theme here.

- *Systems,* supporting and controlling people within and around an organisation. These systems include direct mechanisms such as performance targeting and planning, and more indirect ones such as cultural and market systems.

- *Configurations,* the mutually supporting elements that make up an organisation's design. As well as strategy, structure and systems, these elements can include staff, style, skills and superordinate goals, as encapsulated in the *McKinsey 7-S framework*.

The chapter concludes by considering new *non-hierarchical* structures and systems in Thinking Differently.

6.2 STRUCTURAL TYPES

Managers often describe their organisation by drawing an organisation chart, mapping out its formal structure. These structural charts define the levels and roles in an organisation. They are important to managers because they describe who reports to whom in terms of management and who is responsible for what in terms of activities. Thus structures can have major implications for organisational priorities and interactions in the marketplace. Structures therefore need careful alignment with strategy. One of the strategy discipline's founders, Alfred Chandler, documents how major corporations such as DuPont and General Motors nearly failed not because of ill-chosen strategies, but due to mismatches between their centralised structures and diversified strategies. He sums up the importance of fitting structure to strategy by saying: 'Unless structure follows strategy, inefficiency results.'[1] Qwikster's quick demise (Illustration 6.1) shows the perils of getting structure wrong.

This section reviews five basic structural types: functional, divisional, matrix, transnational and project.[2] Broadly, the first two of these tend to emphasise one structural dimension over another, either functional specialisms or business divisions. The three that follow tend to mix structural dimensions more evenly, for instance trying to give product and geographical units equal weight. However, none of these structures is a universal solution to the challenges of organising. Rather, the right structure depends on the particular strategic challenges each organisation faces. Researchers propose a wide number of important challenges (sometimes called 'contingencies') shaping organisational structure, including organisational size and type of technology.[3] This implies that the first step in organisational design is deciding what the key challenges facing the organisation actually are. Section 6.2.6 will particularly focus on how the five structural types fit the strategic challenges of diversification (Chapter 8), internationalisation (Chapter 9) and innovation (Chapter 10).

6.2.1 The functional structure

Even a small entrepreneurial start-up, once it involves more than one person, needs to divide up responsibilities between different people. The **functional structure divides responsibilities according to the organisation's primary specialist roles** such as production, research and

ILLUSTRATION 6.1   Structural fault: Qwikster's quick demise

Netflix's introduction of the new Qwikster structure is a multi-billion-dollar failure.

In 2011, Netflix, the USA's largest online DVD rental and internet streaming company, faced a dilemma. Internet streaming of movies was clearly a growth business, one which competitors such as Amazon were beginning to enter. On the other hand, DVD rental by mail was facing long-term decline. In September 2011, Reed Hastings, CEO and joint founder of the company, responded to the dilemma with a structural solution. He proposed to split his business into two separate parts: henceforth streaming would be done exclusively under the Netflix label, while DVD rental would be done exclusively in a new organisational unit called Qwikster. In a blog post, Hastings explained his motivation: 'For the past five years, my greatest fear at Netflix has been that we wouldn't make the leap from success in DVDs to success in streaming. Most companies that are great at something – like AOL dialup or Borders bookstores – do not become great at new things people want (streaming for us) because they are afraid to hurt their initial business. Eventually these companies realise their error of not focusing enough on the new thing, and then the company fights desperately and hopelessly to recover. Companies rarely die from moving too fast, and they frequently die from moving too slowly.'

There were other reasons for the proposed split. The DVD business requires large warehouse and logistics operations, while streaming requires large internet resources. For DVDs, competitors include Blockbuster and Redbox, whereas streaming rivals include Amazon, iTunes and cable TV companies. As a stand-alone unit, managers in the streaming business could promote their alternative model without worrying about protecting the DVD business, still the larger part of Netflix's profits overall.

For customers, though, the split was less attractive. In future, customers would have to deal with two sites to get what they had previously got through one site. The DVD site offered many more movies, and tended to have more recent releases. Movie viewing recommendations for one site would not transfer to the other site. DVD renters would no longer receive the distinctive Netflix DVD envelopes which had strong brand loyalty.

The customer response was hostile. In the month following Qwikster's launch, Netflix lost hundreds of thousands of subscribers. The Netflix share price fell more than 60 per cent, wiping out more than $3bn (£1.8bn, €2.3bn) in value. CEO Reed Hastings joked in a Facebook message that he feared poisoning by some of his investors: 'I think I might need a food taster. I can hardly blame them.'

On 10 October 2011, three weeks after the original Qwikster announcement, Hastings blogged that the new unit would not go ahead after all, and that all business would continue under the Netflix label. Hastings explained: 'There is a difference between moving quickly – which Netflix has done very well for years – and moving too fast, which is what we did in this case.' Despite his reversal of the structural change, repercussions were still being felt a year later: Netflix's market share of DVD rentals in 2012 had dropped from 35 per cent to 27 per cent, and rival Redbox had taken market leadership.

Sources: *Wall Street Journal*, 11 October 2011; *Strategy+Business*, 2 April 2012; *PC Magazine*, 17 September 2012.

Questions

1 How do the pros and cons of the Qwikster structure fit with those associated with the divisional structure (see Section 6.2.2)?

2 In the light of the planning, cultural, market and targeting systems discussed in Section 6.3, what else would Netflix have needed to do to manage the separation of the streaming business and the rental business?

Figure 6.2 A functional structure

sales. Figure 6.2 represents a typical organisation chart for such a functional organisation. This kind of structure is particularly relevant to small or start-up organisations, or larger organisations that have retained narrow, rather than diverse, product ranges. Functional structures may also be used within a multidivisional structure (see below), where the divisions themselves may split themselves up according to functional departments (as in Figure 6.2).

Figure 6.2 also summarises the potential advantages and disadvantages of a functional structure. There are advantages in that it gives senior managers direct hands-on involvement in operations and allows greater operational control from the top. The functional structure provides a clear definition of roles and tasks, increasing accountability. Functional departments also provide concentrations of expertise, thus fostering knowledge development in areas of functional specialism.

However, there are disadvantages, particularly as organisations become larger or more diverse. Perhaps the major concern in a fast-moving world is that senior managers focus too much on their functional responsibilities, becoming overburdened with routine operations and too concerned with narrow functional interests. As a result, they find it hard either to take a strategic view of the organisation as a whole or to coordinate separate functions quickly: marketing managers focus on just marketing, while operations managers focus on operations. Thus functional organisations can be inflexible, poor at adapting to change. Separate functional departments tend also to be inward-looking – so-called 'functional silos' – making it difficult to integrate the knowledge of different functional specialists.[4] Finally, because they are centralised around particular functions, functional structures are not good at coping with product or geographical diversity. For example, a central marketing department may try to impose a uniform approach to advertising regardless of the diverse needs of the organisation's various markets around the world.

6.2.2 The divisional structure

A **divisional structure is built up of separate divisions on the basis of products, services or geographical areas** (see Figure 6.3). Divisionalisation often comes about as an attempt to overcome the problems that functional structures have in dealing with the diversity mentioned

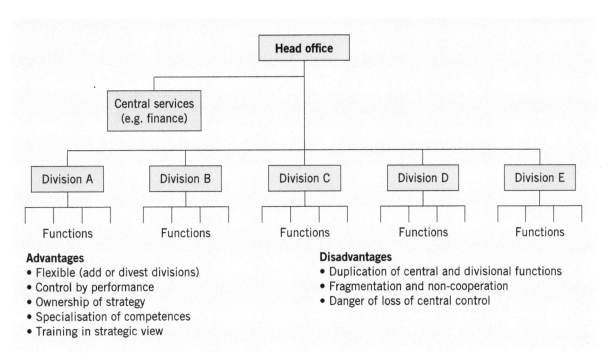

Advantages
- Flexible (add or divest divisions)
- Control by performance
- Ownership of strategy
- Specialisation of competences
- Training in strategic view

Disadvantages
- Duplication of central and divisional functions
- Fragmentation and non-cooperation
- Danger of loss of central control

Figure 6.3 A multidivisional structure

above.[5] Each division can respond to the specific requirements of its product/market strategy, using its own set of functional departments. A similar situation exists in many public services, where the organisation is structured around *service departments* such as recreation, social services and education.

There are several potential advantages to divisional structures. As self-standing business units, it is possible to control divisions from a distance simply by monitoring business performance: top management need only intervene if targets are being missed (see Illustration 6.2 on Google and Section 6.3.3). Having divisions also provides flexibility because organisations can add, close or merge divisions as circumstances change. Divisional managers have greater personal ownership for their own divisional strategies. Geographical divisions – for example, a European division or a North American division – offer a means of managing internationally (see Section 6.2.4). There can be benefits of specialisation within a division, allowing competences to develop with a clearer focus on a particular product group, technology or customer group. For managers expecting to go on to a main board position, management responsibility for a whole divisional business is good training in taking a strategic view.

However, divisional structures can also have disadvantages of three main types. First, divisions can become so self-sufficient that they are *de facto* independent businesses, but duplicating the functions and costs of the corporate centre of the company. In such cases of *de facto* independence, it may make more sense to split the company into independent businesses, and de-mergers of this type are now common. Second, divisionalisation tends to get in the way of cooperation and knowledge-sharing between business units: divisions can quite literally divide. Expertise is fragmented and divisional performance targets provide poor incentives to collaborate with other divisions. Finally, divisions may become too autonomous, especially where joint ventures and partnership dilute ownership. Here, divisions pursue their own strategies almost regardless of the needs of the corporate parent. In these cases, divisional companies become *holding companies,* where the corporate centre effectively 'holds' the various businesses in a largely financial sense, exercising little control and adding little value. Figure 6.3 summarises these potential advantages and disadvantages of a multidivisional structure.

Large and complex divisional companies often have a second tier of *subdivisions* within their main divisions. Treating smaller strategic business units as subdivisions within a large division reduces the number of units that the corporate centre has to deal with directly. Subdivisions can also help complex organisations respond to contradictory pressures. For example, an organisation could have geographical subdivisions within a set of global product divisions (see Section 6.2.4).

6.2.3 The matrix structure

A matrix structure combines different structural dimensions simultaneously, for example product divisions and geographical territories or product divisions and functional specialisms.[6] In matrix structures, staff typically report to two managers rather than one. Figure 6.4 gives examples of such a structure.

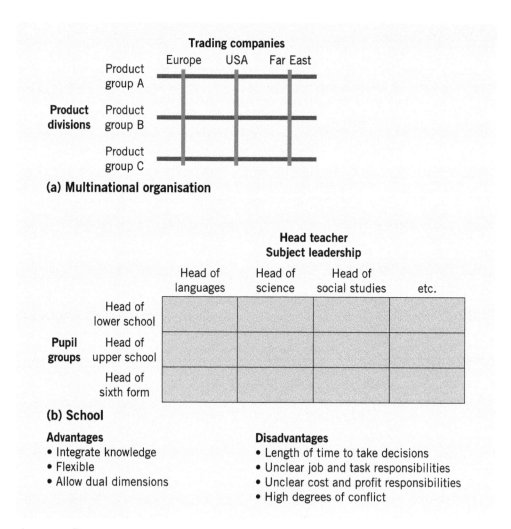

(a) Multinational organisation

(b) School

Advantages	Disadvantages
• Integrate knowledge	• Length of time to take decisions
• Flexible	• Unclear job and task responsibilities
• Allow dual dimensions	• Unclear cost and profit responsibilities
	• High degrees of conflict

Figure 6.4 Two examples of matrix structures

Matrix structures have several advantages. They promote *knowledge-sharing* because they allow separate areas of knowledge to be integrated across organisational boundaries. Particularly in professional service organisations, matrix organisations can be helpful in applying particular knowledge specialisms to different market or geographical segments. For example, to serve a particular client, a consulting firm may draw on people from groups with particular knowledge specialisms (e.g. strategy or organisation design) and others grouped according to particular markets (industry sectors or geographical regions). Figure 6.4 shows how a school might combine the separate knowledge of subject specialists to create programmes of study tailored differently to various age groups. Matrix organisations are *flexible*, because they allow different dimensions of the organisation to be mixed together. They are particularly attractive to organisations operating globally, because of the possible mix between local and global dimensions. For example, a global company may prefer geographically defined divisions as the operating units for local marketing (because of their specialist local knowledge of customers). But at the same time it may still want global product units responsible for the worldwide coordination of product development and manufacturing, taking advantage of economies of scale and specialisation. However, because a matrix structure replaces single lines of authority with multiple cross-matrix relationships, this often brings problems. In particular, it will typically take *longer to reach decisions* because of bargaining between the managers of different dimensions. There may also be *conflict* because staff find themselves responsible to managers from two structural dimensions. In short, matrix organisations are hard to control.

As with any structure, but particularly with the matrix structure, the critical issue in practice is the way it actually works (i.e. behaviours and relationships). The key ingredient in a successful matrix structure can be senior managers good at sustaining collaborative relationships (across the matrix) and coping with the messiness and ambiguity which that can bring. It is for this reason that Chris Bartlett and Sumantra Ghoshal describe the matrix as involving a 'frame of mind' as much as a formal structure.[7]

6.2.4 Multinational/transnational structures

Operating internationally adds an extra dimension to the structural challenge. As in Figure 6.5, there are essentially four structural designs available for multinationals. Three are simple extensions of the principles of the divisional structure (Section 6.2.2), so are dealt with briefly. The fourth, the transnational structure, is more complex and will be explained at more length.

The three simpler multinational structures are as follows:

- *International divisions.* An international division is a stand-alone division added alongside the structure of the main home-based business. This is often the kind of structure adopted by corporations with large domestic markets (such as in the USA or China), where an initial entry into overseas markets is relatively small-scale and does not require structural change to the original, much bigger, home businesses. For example, a Chinese car, truck and motorbike manufacturer might have separate divisions for each of its product areas in its home market of China, but run its overseas businesses in a separate 'international division' combining all three product areas together. The international division is typically run from headquarters, but not integrated with the domestic business. As in Figure 6.5, the international division is centralised, but not highly coordinated with other parts of the business.

- *Local subsidiaries.* These subsidiaries typically have most of the functions required to operate on their own in their particular local market, for example design, production and marketing. They are thus a form of geographic divisional structure. They have high

Figure 6.5 Multinational structures

local responsiveness and are loosely coordinated. A local subsidiary structure is very common in professional services such as law, accounting and advertising, where there are few economies of scale and responsiveness to local regulations, relationships or tastes is very important. This structure fits the multi-domestic strategy introduced in Section 9.4.

- *Global product divisions.* This kind of structure is often used where economies of scale are very important. Organising the design, production and marketing on the basis of global divisions rather than local subsidiaries typically maximises cost efficiency. It also helps direct central resources to targeted markets and facilitates cross-subsidisation of unprofitable geographical markets. To return to the Chinese car, truck and motorbike manufacturer, there would be just three divisions, each responsible for its particular product area across the whole world, China included. There would be very little scope for adaptation to local tastes or regulations in particular markets. In global product divisions, local responsiveness would typically be very low. This structure fits the global strategy introduced in Chapter 9. It is also similar to Google's basic structural approach (see Illustration 6.2 and Chapter 13 end case).

The international division, local subsidiary and global product division structures all have their particular advantages, whether it is managing relative size, maximising local responsiveness or achieving economies of scale. The fourth structure, however, tries to integrate the advantages of the local subsidiary structure with those of the global product divisional structure.

In terms of Figure 6.5, the **transnational structure combines local responsiveness with high global coordination**.[8] According to Bartlett and Ghoshal, transnational structures are similar to matrices but distinguish themselves by their focus on knowledge-sharing, specialisation and network management, as follows:

- *Knowledge-sharing.* While each national or regional business has a good deal of autonomy, in the transnational they should see themselves as sources of ideas and capabilities for the whole corporation. Thus a good idea that has been developed locally is offered for adoption by other national or regional units around the world.

ILLUSTRATION 6.2   Google gets a new name and a new structure

In August 2015, Google became a subsidiary of Alphabet Inc.

Google had been founded in 1998 as an internet search company by two Stanford PhD students, Larry Page and Sergey Brin. The search activities were funded by advertising (Ads). In the following years, the company had diversified radically, entering for example maps, video (YouTube) and mobile operating systems (Android). It had also established Google X, for so-called 'moonshot' initiatives such as Google Glass, which displays information on a headset (like glasses). Google Ventures invested in start-ups such as Uber. There were also acquisitions such as Nest, involved in home automation. Another major venture was Calico, a health business dedicated to extending lives through better use of information.

In August 2015, Google CEO Larry Page announced a major change of structure. A new parent company Alphabet Inc. would be created, under which Google would become a subsidiary responsible for a group of businesses (Ads, Maps, Search and so on) that would no longer report directly to Page. The Google X, Ventures, Nest and Calico subsidiaries would continue to report directly to Page. Each of the subsidiaries would have their own CEOs (Pichai, Teller, Marris, Fadell and

Levinson). Financial results would be reported for each subsidiary, instead of just consolidated for the whole as previously. Brin explained: 'Fundamentally, we believe this allows us more management scale, as we can run things independently that aren't very related. . . . In general, our model is to have a strong CEO who runs each business, with Sergey and me in service to them as needed.' News of the restructuring lifted the Google/Alphabet stock price by seven per cent, an increase worth $29bn (£17.4bn, €21.6bn).

Sources: Business Insider, 11 August 2015; *Financial Times*, 11 August 2015; *Google Press Release*, 10 August 2015.

Questions

1 In what respects is the change consistent with Alfred Chandler's phrase, 'structure follows strategy'?

2 Why do investors think that the new Alphabet structure is worth an extra $29bn?

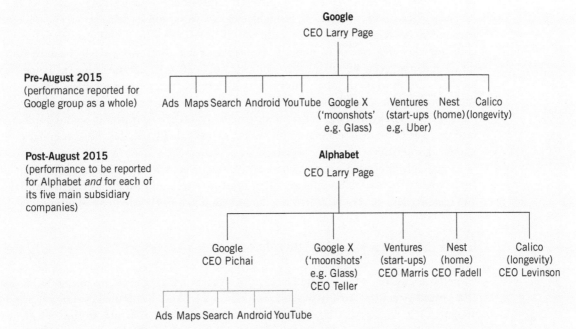

Source: Simplified from *Business Insider*, 'One chart that explains Alphabet, Google's new parent company', 11 August 2015, Wright's Media, LLC.

- *Specialisation.* National (or regional) units specialise in areas of expertise in order to achieve greater scale economies on behalf of the whole corporation. Thus a national unit that has particular competences in manufacturing a particular product, for example, may be given responsibility for manufacturing that product on behalf of other units across the world.

- *Network management.* The corporate centre has the role of managing this global network of specialisms and knowledge. It does so first by establishing the specialist role of each business unit, then sustaining the systems and relationships required to make the network of business units operate in an integrated and effective manner.

The success of a transnational corporation is dependent on the ability *simultaneously* to achieve global competences, local responsiveness and organisation-wide innovation and learning. Theoretically the transnational combines the best of local decentralisation with the best of global centralisation. However, the transnational can be very demanding of managers in terms of willingness to work not just at their national business units but for the good of the transnational as a whole. Diffuse responsibilities also make for similar complexities and control problems to those of the matrix organisation.[9]

6.2.5 Project-based structures [10]

Many organisations rely heavily on project teams with a finite life span. A **project-based structure is one where teams are created, undertake a specific project and are then dissolved.**[11] This can be particularly appropriate for organisations that deliver large and expensive goods or services (civil engineering, information systems, films) and those delivering time-limited events (conferences, sporting events or consulting engagements). The organisation structure is a constantly changing collection of project teams created, steered and glued together loosely by a small corporate group. Many organisations use such teams in a more ad hoc way to complement the 'main' structure. For example, projects or *task forces* are set up to make progress on new elements of strategy (for example acquisitions or new business initiatives) or to provide momentum where the regular structure of the organisation is not effective.

The project-based structure can be highly flexible, with projects being set up and dissolved as required. Because project teams should have clear tasks to achieve within a defined period, accountability and control are good. As project team members will typically be drawn from different departments within the firm, projects can be effective at knowledge exchange. Projects can also draw on members internationally and, because project lifespans are typically short, project teams may be more willing to work temporarily around the world. There are disadvantages, however. Organisations are prone to proliferate projects in an ill-coordinated fashion. The constant breaking up of project teams can also hinder the accumulation of knowledge over time or within specialisms.

Overall, project-based structures have been growing in importance because of their inherent flexibility. Such flexibility can be vital in a fast-moving world where individual knowledge and competences need to be redeployed and integrated quickly and in novel ways.

6.2.6 Strategy and structure fit

From the discussion so far, it should be clear that functional, divisional, matrix, transnational and project structures each have their own advantages and disadvantages. Organisational designers, therefore, have to choose structures according to the particular strategic challenges they face. As Chandler said, structures have to fit strategies.[12] This section summarises the effectiveness of the five structures in relation to three key strategies, before going on to consider specific organisation design tests.

Table 6.1 Strategy and structure fit

Strategy/structure	Functional	Multidivisional	Matrix	Transnational	Project
Diversification	*	***	**	**	**
Internationalisation	*	**	***	***	*
Innovation	**	*	**	**	***

* Stars indicate *typical* fits with each strategy, with three stars indicating good fit, two indicating medium fit and one typically less good fit. Fits may vary with industry specific conditions.

Table 6.1 summarises the typical fits between the five structural types and strategies of diversification, internationalisation and innovation (organisations and strategies vary and structures can be adjusted, so outcomes may differ in particular cases). Key points are highlighted in the following:

- *Diversification* raises the corporate strategy challenges of control and accountability within widely different businesses, as discussed in Chapter 8. Divisionalisation should allow business managers enough decentralised responsibility to enact their own strategies, while the corporate parent can exercise control by monitoring business performance. The functional structure is too centralised to allow effective diversification. Matrix structures blur accountability, as divisional business units have horizontal responsibilities as well.

- *Internationalisation* strategies raise dilemmas over global scale, horizontal coordination and local adaptation, as discussed in Section 9.4. Matrix and transnational structures are particularly effective in accommodating both sides of such dilemmas: for example, one dimension could allow for scale, the other could allow for coordination or sharing. Divisional structures tend to resolve these dilemmas more unilaterally, either allowing centralised product divisions for scale or local subsidiaries for local adaptation. They tend to be less good at horizontal coordination and sharing.

- *Innovation* strategies typically require knowledge creation and knowledge-sharing, as discussed in Chapters 4 and 10. Matrix organisations are good for horizontal sharing. Project organisations can bring together teams of relevant experts to focus intensively on innovation initiatives. The functional structure can be effective in innovation because centralisation concentrates resources, particularly research and development.

While Table 6.1 considers the typical fits between strategies and structures, Goold and Campbell provide *nine design tests* to help design tailor-made structural solutions for specific circumstances.[13] The first four tests stress fit with the key objectives and constraints of the organisation:

- The *Market-Advantage Test*. This test of fit with market strategy is fundamental, following Alfred Chandler's classic principle that 'structure follows strategy'.[14] For example, if market advantage depends on integrated services (such as research and development or information technology), then they should probably not be split between different structural units.

- The *Parenting Advantage Test*. The structural design should fit the 'parenting' role of the corporate centre (see Section 8.6). For example, if the corporate centre aims to add value as a synergy manager, then it should design a structure that places important integrative specialisms, such as marketing or research, at the centre.

- The *People Test*. The structural design must fit the people available. It is dangerous to switch completely from a functional structure to a multidivisional structure if, as is likely, the organisation lacks managers with competence in running decentralised business units.

- The *Feasibility Test*. This is a catch-all category, indicating that the structure must fit legal, stakeholder, trade union or similar constraints. For example, after scandals involving biased research, investment banks are now required by financial regulators to separate their research departments from their deal-making departments.

Goold and Campbell then propose five more tests based on good general organisational design principles, as follows:

- The *Specialised Cultures Test*. This test reflects the value of bringing together specialists so that they can develop their expertise in close collaboration with each other. A structure scores poorly if it breaks up important specialist cultures.
- The *Difficult Links Test*. This test asks whether a proposed structure will set up links between parts of the organisations that are important but bound to be strained. For example, extreme decentralisation to profit-accountable business units is likely to strain relationships with a central research and development department. Unless compensating mechanisms are put in place, this kind of structure is likely to fail.
- The *Redundant Hierarchy Test*. Any structural design should be checked in case it has too many layers of management, causing undue blockages and expense. Delayering in response to redundant hierarchies has been an important structural trend in recent years.
- The *Accountability Test*. This test stresses the importance of clear lines of accountability, ensuring the control and commitment of managers throughout the structure. Because of their dual lines of reporting, matrix structures are often accused of lacking clear accountability.
- The *Flexibility Test*. While not all organisations will face the same general rise in environmental velocity as referred to with regard to Table 6.1, a final important test is whether the design will be sufficiently flexible to accommodate possible changes in the future. Here Kathleen Eisenhardt argues for structural 'modularity' (i.e. standardisation) in order to allow easy 'patching' (i.e. transfer) of one part of the organisation to another part of the organisation, as market needs change.[15] For example, if strategic business units are similar in structural size and internal management systems throughout a large organisation, it becomes easy to transfer them from one division to another according to changing business needs.

Goold and Campbell's nine tests provide a rigorous screen for effective structures. However, it is important to realise that in practice managers do not start from scratch in choosing their organisational structures. With regard to the market advantage test, for instance, structure does not always follow logically from strategy; rather, existing structures can shape the strategy. Thus a business with an existing multidivisional structure may continue with an acquisitions and divestments strategy simply because that structure makes it easy just to keep on adding and subtracting various businesses as divisional units. Conversely, a functional organisation might be reluctant to undertake acquisitions because it is hard to integrate within its centralised structure. Thus the structure can reinforce the current strategy, regardless of whether the strategy is a good one.[16] Moreover, not only is it hard to fit strategy and structure as logic seems to dictate, but managers also have to align them with the other key part of the configuration—organisational systems. As in Figure 6.1, systems too should be designed to reinforce strategy and structure.

6.3 SYSTEMS

Structure is a key ingredient of organising for success. But structures can only work if they are supported by formal and informal organisational systems, the 'muscles' of the organisation. Systems help ensure control over strategy implementation. Small organisations may be able to rely on *direct supervision,* where a single manager or entrepreneur monitors activity in person. But larger or more complex organisations typically need more elaborate structures and systems if they are to be effective over time (though see Thinking Differently on non-hierarchical systems, at the end of this chapter). This section considers four systems specifically: planning, performance targeting, culture and internal markets.

Such systems can be subdivided in two ways. First, systems tend to emphasise either control over inputs or control over outputs. Input control systems concern themselves with the *resources* consumed in the strategy, especially financial resources and human commitment. Output control systems focus on ensuring satisfactory *results,* for example the meeting of targets or achieving market competitiveness. The second subdivision is between direct and indirect controls. Direct controls involve *close supervision* or monitoring. Indirect controls are more *hands-off,* setting up the conditions whereby desired behaviours are achieved semi-automatically. Table 6.2 summarises how the four systems of planning, performance targeting, culture and internal markets each emphasise input or output controls and direct or indirect controls.

Organisations normally use a blend of these control systems, but some will dominate over others according to the nature of strategic challenges. As we shall see, direct measures tend to require that the controllers have high levels of knowledge of what the controlled are supposed to do. In many knowledge-intensive organisations, especially those generating innovation and change, controllers rarely have a good understanding of what their expert employees are doing, nor can they easily define what they are potentially capable of doing. In these conditions, it is usually better to rely on indirect controls such as performance targeting: at least they can know when a unit has made its revenue or profitability targets. Direct control works better in simple and stable businesses, where input requirements are stable and well understood, or where key outcomes are unambiguous. Utility businesses supplying power or water might respond well to direct forms of control.

6.3.1 Planning systems

Planning systems plan and control the allocation of resources and monitor their utilisation. The focus is on the direct control of inputs. These might be simple financial inputs (as in budgeting), human inputs (as in planning for managerial succession) or long-term investments (as particularly in strategic planning). This section concentrates on strategic oversight from the corporate centre, developing the discussions in Chapters 8 and 13.

Table 6.2 Types of control systems

	Input	Output
Direct	Planning systems	Performance targeting
Indirect	Cultural systems	Internal markets

Goold and Campbell's[17] typology of three *corporate strategy styles* helps to identify the advantages and disadvantages of planning systems against other methods of corporate central oversight. The three strategy styles differ widely along two dimensions: the *dominant source of planning influence,* either top-down (from the corporate centre to the business units) or bottom-up (from the business units to the centre); and the *degree of performance accountability* for the business units, either tight or reasonably relaxed. As in Figure 6.6, the three corporate strategy styles align themselves on these two dimensions thus:

- The *strategic planning* style is the archetypal planning system, hence its name. In the Goold and Campbell sense, the strategic planning style combines both a strong planning influence on strategic direction from the corporate centre with relatively relaxed performance accountability for the business units. The logic is that if the centre sets the strategic direction, business unit managers should not be held strictly accountable for disappointing results that might be due to an inappropriate plan in the first place. In the strategic planning style, the centre focuses on inputs in terms of allocating resources necessary to achieve the strategic plan, while exercising a high degree of direct control over how the plan is executed by the businesses.

- The *financial control* style involves very little central planning. The business units each set their own strategic plans, probably after some negotiation with the corporate centre, and are then held strictly accountable for the results against these plans. This style differs from the strategic planning style in that control is against financial outputs, similar to a performance targeting system (see Section 6.3.3). If the businesses devised the plans, then they should take full responsibility for success or failure. Business unit managers in the financial control style have a lot of autonomy and typically receive high bonus payments for success. But failure may easily lead to dismissal. The financial planning style fits with the portfolio manager or restructurer roles of the corporate centre referred to in Chapter 8.

- The *strategic control* style is in the middle, with a more consensual development of the strategic plan between the corporate centre and the business units and moderate levels of business unit accountability. Under the strategic control style, the centre will typically act as coach to its business unit managers, helping them to see and seize opportunities

Figure 6.6 Strategy styles

Source: Adapted from M. Goold and A. Campbell, *Strategies and Styles,* Blackwell, 1989, Figure 3.1, p. 39.

in a supportive manner. This style often relies on strong cultural systems to foster trust and mutual understanding (see Section 6.3.3). Consequently, the strategic control style is often associated with the synergy manager or parental developer roles of the corporate centre discussed in Chapter 8.

Thus the three corporate strategy styles vary with regard to their reliance on, and application of, planning systems. The direct control of inputs characteristic of the strategic planning style is only appropriate in certain circumstances. In particular, it makes sense where there are large, risky and long-range investments to be allocated: for example, an oil company typically has to take the decision to invest in the ten-year development of an oilfield at the corporate centre, rather than risk delegating it to business units whose resources and time horizons may be limited. On the other hand, the financial control style is suitable where investments are small, relatively frequent and well understood, as typically in a mature, non-capital-intensive business. The strategic control style is suitable where there are opportunities for collaborating across businesses and there is a need to nurture new ones.

The strategic planning style (not the practice of strategic planning in general) has become less common in the private sector in recent years. The style is seen as too rigid to adapt to changing circumstances and too top-down to reflect real business circumstances on the ground. However, it is important to recognise the internal consistency of all three styles, including strategic planning. Each achieves logical combinations of accountability and strategic influence. Problems occur when organisations construct systems of planning and accountability that depart substantially from the diagonal line in Figure 6.6. Too far below the line (the 'south-west' corner) implies an excessively relaxed combination of weak direction from the centre and low accountability for the businesses. Too far above the diagonal line (the 'north-east' corner) implies a harsh combination of strong direction from the centre and strict accountability in the businesses. In the 'north-east' corner, business managers are held accountable even for mistakes that may have their origins in the centre's own plans.

6.3.2 Cultural systems

Organisations typically have distinctive cultures which express basic assumptions and beliefs held by organisation members and define taken-for-granted ways of doing things (see Chapter 6). Despite their taken-for-granted, semi-conscious nature, organisational cultures can seem a tempting means of managerial control. Managers may therefore try to influence organisational culture through various deliberate mechanisms in order to achieve the kinds of employee behaviour required by their strategy.[18] Such **cultural systems aim to standardise norms of behaviour within an organisation in line with particular objectives.** Cultural systems exercise an *indirect* form of control, because of not requiring direct supervision: it becomes a matter of willing conformity or *self*-control by employees. Control is exerted on the *input* of employees, as the culture defines the norms of appropriate effort and initiative that employees will put into their jobs.

Three key cultural systems are:

- *Selection.* Here cultural conformity may be attempted by the selection of appropriate staff in the first place. Employers look to find people who will 'fit'. Thus some employers may favour recruiting people who have already shown themselves to be 'team-players' through sport or other activities.

- *Socialisation.* Here employee behaviours are shaped by social processes once they are at work. It often starts with the integration of new staff through training, induction and mentoring programmes. It typically continues with further training throughout a career. Symbols can also play a role in socialisation, for example the symbolic example of leaders' behaviours or the influence of office décor, dress codes or language.

- *Reward*. Appropriate behaviour can be encouraged through pay, promotion or symbolic processes (e.g. public praise). The desire to achieve the same rewards as successful people in the organisation will typically encourage imitative behaviour.

It is important to recognise that organisations' cultures are not fully under formal management control. Sometimes aspects of organisational culture may persistently contradict managerial intentions, as with peer-group pressure not to respond to organisational policies. Cynicism and 'going through the motions' are common in some organisations. Sometimes the culture of an organisation may even drive its strategy (see Chapter 6). On the other hand, some cultures can bring about desired results, even without deliberate management intervention. For example, workers often form spontaneous and informal 'communities of practice', in which expert practitioners inside or even outside the organisation share their knowledge to generate innovative solutions to problems on their own initiative.[19] Examples of these informal communities of practice range from the Xerox photocopying engineers who would exchange information about problems and solutions over breakfast gatherings at the start of the day, to the programmer networks which support the development of Linux 'freeware' internationally over the internet.

6.3.3 Performance targeting systems

Performance targets focus on the *outputs* of an organisation (or part of an organisation), such as product quality, revenues or profits. These targets are often known as *key performance indicators* (KPIs) (see Chapter 12). The performance of an organisation is judged, either internally or externally, on its ability to meet these targets. However, within specified boundaries, the organisation remains free on how targets should be achieved. This approach can be particularly appropriate in certain situations:

- Within *large businesses,* corporate centres may choose performance targets to control their business units without getting involved in the details of how they achieve them (as in the financial control style in Section 6.3.1). These targets are often cascaded down the organisation as specific targets for subunits, functions and even individuals.

- In *regulated markets,* such as privatised utilities in the UK and elsewhere, government-appointed regulators increasingly exercise control through agreed key performance indicators (KPIs), such as service or quality levels, as a means of ensuring 'competitive' performance.[20]

- In *the public services,* where control of resource inputs was the dominant approach historically, governments are attempting to move control processes towards outputs (such as quality of service) and, more importantly, towards outcomes (e.g. patient mortality rates in healthcare). See Illustration 6.3 for consideration of performance targets in police, fire and ambulance services.

Many managers find it difficult to develop a useful set of targets. There are at least three potential problems with targets:[21]

- *Inappropriate measures* of performance are quite common. For example, managers often prefer indicators that are easily measured or choose measures based on inadequate understanding of real needs on the ground. The result is a focus on the required measures rather than the factors that might be essential to long-term success. In the private sector, focus on short-term profit measures is common, at the expense of investment in the long-run prosperity of the business.

ILLUSTRATION 6.3   Call fire, police and ambulance

In early 2016, fire, police and ambulance services faced proposals from the UK government for greater collaboration and even merger.

Police officers, firefighters and ambulance paramedics often work closely together in incidents such as major traffic accidents, public disorder or floods and similar natural disasters. Experiments have shown that there is scope for major efficiencies in greater cooperation, for example in the sharing of emergency call facilities or the management of vehicle fleets. It seemed to make sense to the UK government to impose upon the three services a duty of cooperation, and indeed to propose mergers between police and fire services in particular.

However, the three services have previously been controlled by very different organisation structures and have had very different performance metrics and cultures. The police are controlled by directly elected Police and Crime Commissioners for particular localities. They are a uniformed service, with a highly hierarchical quasi-militaristic structure. A key responsibility is to fight crime. The fire services are under the control of local authorities, so without direct accountability to the electorate. They too are a uniformed service, though with a somewhat less militaristic structure. Their job is to prevent and suppress fire and similar types of threat. The ambulance services are the responsibility of local health authorities and are part of the National Health Service. Paramedics see themselves as part of the caring professions.

The government minister responsible told Parliament in January 2016: 'Directly elected Police and Crime Commissioners are clearly accountable to the public and have a strong incentive to pursue ambitious reform and deliver value for money. We will enable them to take on responsibility for fire and rescue services where a local case is made.' It was estimated that savings of about £200m (€240m, $300m) could result from shared back-office activities.

Some were enthusiastic about the possibilities of merger. Adam Simmonds, Police and Crime Commissioner for Northamptonshire, told the *Daily Express* that he saw a day when ambulance services too could be placed under the Police and Crime Commissioner's remit and roles could become more interchangeable:

'You are looking at a single executive figure who has control of a wide range of public services. . . . PCCs certainly have a role to play in wider public service delivery. This merger is . . . about getting a better service for the public. Why not train the workforce in each of the services to do different bits [of each others' jobs] depending on the circumstances? . . . That is the model for the future.'

Others had reservations, especially about where back-office merger and cooperation could eventually lead to. Steve White, chairman of the Police Federation, was reported in the *Daily Express* as warning:

'We can't arrive at the situation where your home has been burgled and you don't know whether a paramedic, a fireman or a police officer is going to turn up. I don't think anybody would want a police car to turn up and then to wheel a hose out of the boot and start putting a fire out. That is utterly barmy.'

Matt Wrack, leader of the Fire Brigades Union, wrote in the *Huffington Post*:

'The fire and rescue service is a separate humanitarian service very distinct from policing. Indeed a more obvious link lies with emergency ambulance services . . . The situation is very different in relation to policing. The police have the power to arrest. Firefighters do not. This is an extremely important aspect of our relations with local communities, especially in an era when firefighters are asking to enter people's homes every day to provide safety.'

Sources: Daily Express, 31 May 2015; *Huffington Post*, 1 January 2016; *Financial Times*, 26 January 2016.

Questions

1 Consider the kinds of cultural and performance targeting systems the police, fire and ambulance services are each likely to have. How compatible are they?

2 Would you agree with Matt Wrack that the more obvious links are between ambulance and fire services?

- *Inappropriate target levels* are a common problem. Managers are liable to give their superiors pessimistic forecasts so that targets are set at undemanding levels, which can then be easily met. On the other hand, superiors may over-compensate for their managers' pessimism and end up setting excessively demanding targets. Unrealistically ambitious targets can either demotivate employees who see no hope of achieving them regardless of their effort, or encourage risky or dishonest behaviours in order to achieve the otherwise impossible.

- *Excessive internal competition* can be a result of targets focused on individual or subunit performance. Although an organisation by definition should be more than the sum of its parts, if individuals or subunits are being rewarded on their performance in isolation, they will have little incentive to collaborate with the other parts of the organisation. The struggle to meet individualistic targets will reduce the exchange of information and the sharing of resources. This kind of individualistic behaviour played a part in the fraud at UBS (Illustration 6.4).

These acknowledged difficulties with targets have led to the development of two techniques designed to encourage a more balanced approach to target-setting. The most fundamental has been the development of the balanced scorecard approach.[22] *Balanced scorecards* set performance targets according to a range of perspectives, not only financial. Thus balanced scorecards typically combine four specific perspectives: the *financial perspective*, which might include profit margins or cash flow; the *customer perspective*, which sets targets important to customers, such as delivery times or service levels; the *internal perspective*, with targets relating to operational effectiveness, such as the development of IT systems or reductions in waste levels; and finally the future-orientated *innovation and learning perspective*, which targets activities that will be important to the long-run performance of the organisation, for example investment in training or research. Attending to targets relevant to all four perspectives helps ensure that managers do not focus on one set of targets (e.g. financial) at the expense of others, while also keeping an eye to the future through innovation and learning.

A second more balanced approach to target-setting is strategy mapping, developing the balanced scorecard idea. *Strategy maps* link different performance targets into a mutually supportive causal chain supporting strategic objectives. Figure 6.7 shows an extract of a strategy map for a delivery company based on the four perspectives of finance, customers, internal processes and innovation and learning. In this map, investments in well-trained and motivated drivers under the heading of 'innovation and learning' lead to on-time deliveries under the heading of 'internal processes', and thence to satisfied customers and finally to profitable growth. The causal chain between the various targets underlines the need for balance between them: each depends on the others for achievement. Thus strategy maps help in reducing the problem of partial measures referred to above; the problems of inappropriate target levels and internal competition are not so easily resolved.

6.3.4 Market systems

Market disciplines (or *internal markets*) can be brought inside organisations to control activities internally.[23] **Market systems typically involve some formalised system of 'contracting' for resources or inputs from other parts of an organisation and for supplying outputs to other parts of an organisation.** Control focuses on outputs, for example revenues earned in successful competition for internal contracts. The control is indirect: rather than accepting detailed performance targets determined externally, units have simply to earn their keep in competitive internal markets.

Internal markets can be used in a variety of ways. There might be *competitive bidding*, perhaps through the creation of an internal investment bank at the corporate centre to support new initiatives. Also, a customer–supplier relationship may be established between a

ILLUSTRATION 6.4   Rogue banker or rogue bank?

In 2012, Kweku Adoboli was convicted for a fraud involving $2.3bn. But were his actions a product of deep-rooted systems failures at accident-prone UBS?

In 2003, Kweku Adoboli graduated from the University of Nottingham with a degree in Computer Science and Management. Seven years later, he was earning £60,000 (€72,000, $90,000) in salary and £250,000 in bonuses at the London offices of UBS, Switzerland's largest bank. In 2012, he was facing the prospect of seven years in jail, after committing one of the largest frauds in British history.

Adoboli had worked himself up at UBS from so-called back-office jobs (recording and checking trades) to a position as associate director on the elite Delta One desk at UBS. In banking, Delta One desks trade using the bank's own capital, and typically engage in high-risk and innovative deals. As early as 2008, Adoboli had started to create fictitious deals to hide some of his trading losses, taking advantage of his knowledge of back-office systems. The concealment was successful and Adoboli gained a reputation as a star trader, with lavish bonuses to match. It was only in September 2011, as one of UBS's accountants finally began to probe, that Adoboli owned up to his fraud. At that point, UBS had over $10bn at risk through his various trades.

UBS was the creation of a merger between two large Swiss banks in 1998, Union Bank of Switzerland and Swiss Bank Corporation. In 2000, the new bank merged with the leading American stockbroker Paine Webber, launching an aggressive strategy of growth. By 2006, UBS had risen from seventh-largest investment bank in terms of fees, to being one of the top four.

But this growth strategy had an underside. As the financial crisis loomed during 2007, the bank deliberately sold assets to its customers in order to reduce its own liabilities: it would later receive a $150m fine in the USA for this mis-selling. The bank had also taken aggressive positions in the fatally flawed sub-prime mortgage market during the good years, leaving it exposed to losses of $38bn. The Swiss government had to rescue the bank in 2008, firing the then chief executive, with a further 11,000 job losses following. In 2009, the bank had to pay a fine of $781m to the US government for its role in helping American citizens in tax evasion: one scheme had involved bank employees smuggling diamonds out of the country in toothpaste tubes. UBS faced another large fine ($160m) in 2011, due to the rigging of the municipal bonds derivatives market.

In this context, some observers did not think that Adoboli's fraud was an aberration. The bank had been focused on headlong growth, paying rich rewards to those who seemed to deliver it. Top management had not attended to the true merger of the three main component companies. It was commented that Adoboli's Delta One desk had just five staff, working in close proximity to each other, and presumably very aware of what each of their colleagues was doing. A former UBS investment banker told the *New York Times*:

'The problem isn't the culture. The problem is that there wasn't a culture. There are silos. Everyone is separate. People cut their own deals, and it's every man for himself. A lot of people made a lot of money that way, and it fuelled jealousies and efforts to get even better deals. People thought of themselves first, and then maybe the bank, if they thought about it at all.'

Sources: *New York Times*, 24 September 2011; *Financial Times*, 19 September 2012.

Questions

1 In this account, what elements of UBS's systems appear to have been deficient, with regard to Adoboli and more generally?

2 What roles might the merger and growth strategy have played in the various failures at UBS?

Partial Strategy Map

Figure 6.7 A partial strategy map

Source: Exhibit 1: R. Lawson, W. Stratton and T. Hatch (2005), 'Achieving strategy with scorecarding', *Journal of Corporate Accounting and Finance*, March–April, vol. 16, no. 3: p. 64.

central service department, such as training or IT, and the operating units. Typically these internal markets are subject to considerable regulation. For example, the corporate centre might set rules for *transfer prices* between internal business units to prevent exploitative contract pricing, or insist on *service-level agreements* to ensure appropriate service by an essential internal supplier, such as IT, for the various units that depend on it.

Internal markets work well where complexity or rapid change make detailed direct or input controls impractical. But market systems can create problems as well. First, they can increase bargaining between units, consuming important management time. Second, they may create a new bureaucracy monitoring all of the internal transfers of resources between units. Third, an over-zealous use of market mechanisms can lead to dysfunctional competition and legalistic contracting, destroying cultures of collaboration and relationships. These have all been complaints made against the internal markets and semi-autonomous Foundation Trust Hospitals introduced into the UK's National Health Service. On the other hand, their proponents claim that these market processes free a traditionally over-centralised health service to innovate and respond to local needs, while market disciplines maintain overall control.

6.4 CONFIGURATIONS AND ADAPTABILITY

The introduction of this chapter introduced the concept of configurations. **Configurations are the set of organisational design elements that fit together in order to support the intended strategy.** The introductory Figure 6.1 focused on the three mutually supporting elements of strategy, structure and systems, but this section will add more elements in the form of the McKinsey 7-S framework. When all the various elements fit together, they can form a self-reinforcing virtuous circle of superior performance. However, fit can also create problems of adaptability, so this section will also address issues of agility and resilience.

6.4.1 The McKinsey 7-Ss

Developed by the McKinsey consulting company, the *McKinsey 7-S framework* highlights the importance of fit between not just strategy, structure and systems, but also with staff, style, skills and superordinate goals.[24] All seven elements have to be configured together to achieve effectiveness. The elements can therefore serve as a checklist in any organisational design exercise: see Figure 6.8. Because we have already addressed strategy, structure and systems, we shall focus on the remaining four elements of the 7-S framework in the following:

- *Style* here refers to the leadership style of top managers in an organisation. Leadership styles may be collaborative, participative, directive or coercive, for instance (see Chapter 15). Managers' behavioural style can influence the culture of the whole organisation (see Chapter 6). The style should fit other aspects of the 7-S framework: for example, a highly directive or coercive style is not likely to fit a matrix organisation structure.

- *Staff* is about the kinds of people in the organisation and how they are developed. This relates to systems of selection, socialisation and reward (Section 6.3.2). A key

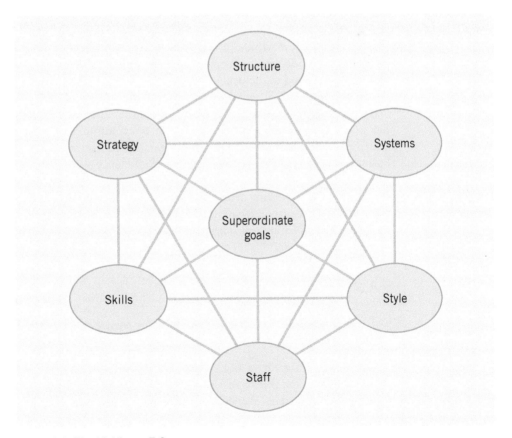

Figure 6.8 The McKinsey 7-Ss.

Source: R. Waterman, T. Peters and J. Phillips, 'Structure is not organisation', *Business Horizons*, June 1980, pp. 14–26: p. 18.

criterion for the feasibility of any strategy is: does the organisation have the people to match (see Section 12.2.4)? A common constraint on structural change is the availability of the right people to head new departments and divisions (the 'People Test': see Section 6.2.6).

- *Skills* relates to staff, but in the 7-S framework refers more broadly to capabilities in general (see Chapter 4). The concept of capabilities here raises not only staff skills but also issues to do with how these skills are embedded in and captured by the organisation as a whole. For example, how do the organisation's training schemes, information technology and reward systems transform the talents of individuals into the organisational capabilities required by the strategy?

- *Superordinate goals* refers to the overarching goals or purpose of the organisation as a whole, in other words the mission, vision and objectives that form the organisational purpose (see Chapter 1). Superordinate (i.e. overarching) goals are placed at the centre of the 7-S framework: all other elements should support these.

The McKinsey 7-S framework highlights at least three aspects of organising. First, organising involves a lot more than just getting the organisational structure right; there are many other elements to attend to. Second, the 7-S framework emphasises fit between all these elements: everything from structure to skills needs to be configured together in order to create virtuous circles of performance. Third, if managers change one element of the 7-S, the concept of fit suggests they are likely to have to change all the other elements as well in order to keep them all appropriately aligned to each other. Changing one element in isolation is liable to break the virtuous circle and make performance worse until overall fit is restored.[25]

Although the concept of configurations and the 7-S framework emphasises the value of mutual fit between elements, in practice this can cause problems in terms of adaptability. First, making everything fit tightly together makes it hard to adapt to specific needs: adjusting to the demands of one particular market is liable to spoil the configuration required to respond to the demands of all the others. One solution to this is to *subdivide* the organisation into different strategic business units, so that one unit is configured optimally according to one set of demands, while the other unit is configured optimally for the others. For example, IBM created its then revolutionary personal computer in a separate new-venture division, configured differently to the traditional mainframe computer business whose principles of hierarchy and efficiency were incompatible with the need to innovate in the new business.[26] Second, as above, configurations create problems for change: tight fits in terms of configurations can make it costly to adapt: changing just a few elements leads to performance declines unless everything else is changed in line. The concepts of agility and resilience are intended to emphasise the importance of adaptability in the face of change.

6.4.2 Agility and resilience

Two concepts help in designing organisations for greater adaptability, the first proactive, the second more after-the-fact:

- Organisational *agility* refers to the ability of organisations to detect and respond to opportunities and threats fast and easily.[27] Agile organisations anticipate environmental shifts and act on them as they emerge. Agility is important because of the growing turbulence of many environments, produced by rapid technological change for example.

- Organisational *resilience* refers to the capacity of organisations to recover from environmental shocks fast and easily after they have happened.[28] Resilient organisations

THINKING DIFFERENTLY · Beyond hierarchy?

There are alternatives to bosses and controls.

This chapter has concerned itself mostly with hierarchical structures and systems, used for top-down control. But there are less hierarchical alternatives which can work as well.

One non-hierarchical way of organising is the 'rule-of-three'.[29] Under the rule-of-three, any project within the organisation can get underway so long as three organisational members agree to do it. The project champion has to persuade two other people that the project is a valid one and worthwhile investing their own work-time into. If the champion can win support from those with the necessary skills to take it forward, the project is deemed worth backing. It does not require the approval of any manager: effectively employees 'vote with their feet'. As the project continues and perhaps attracts more members, nobody is appointed as formal project manager: instead, project 'leads' emerge by informal consensus, these leads changing as project needs evolve. Differences are normally resolved by discussion. The project goes to market when three project members deem it ready.

This rule-of-three is operated by the games company Valve, with 400 employees and responsible for the games portal Steam and games such as *Half-Life* and *Counter Strike*. Although the company operates non-hierarchically, its owner and founder Gade Newell exercises strict control over recruitment and dismissal of employees. Pay is high by industry standards and the company operates a very generous bonus policy. Bonuses are awarded non-hierarchically, according to review by peers. There are thus substantial potential benefits to getting involved in a project creating a successful new game, and large costs to investing time in one that fails. Projects that lose the support of the necessary three members are automatically closed down. Valve is estimated to be worth $2bn (£1.2bn, €1.5bn).

Question

What types of industry or sector would this model be likely to work best in, and in what types might it not work well at all?

are good at rebounding from shocks. Resilience is important because of the prevalence of unanticipated events: the collapse of key customers or suppliers, extreme weather events (tsunamis or earthquakes), or sudden changes in government policy, for instance.

Both agility and resilience are facilitated by the existence of *organisational slack*. Such organisational slack provides important spare resources. Slack supports agility by giving organisational members the extra resources necessary to look beyond the immediate business and either to experiment with future possible opportunities or to move against threats. Examples of slack resources supporting agility might be 'blue sky' research and development units or simply financial reserves capable of being used for acquisition opportunities. Similarly, slack can enhance resilience by providing spare resources that can be quickly redeployed to assist or repair parts of the organisation that have suffered an unanticipated shock. Examples of slack resources that enhance resilience might include emergency stocks, spare production capacity or under-used managers. An organisation that is perfectly configured so that everything fits tightly together is unlikely to have much organisational slack. It is therefore important in designing organisations to ask whether their structure and systems have enough slack to allow for adaptability, either in the form of agility or of resilience.

SUMMARY

- Successful organising means responding to the key challenges facing the organisation. This chapter has stressed *control*, *change*, *knowledge* and *internationalisation*.

- There are many *structural types* (e.g. functional, divisional, matrix, transnational and project). Each structural type has its own strengths and weaknesses and responds differently to the challenges of control, change, knowledge and internationalisation.

- There is a range of different organisational *systems* to facilitate and control strategy. These systems can focus on either *inputs* or *outputs* and be *direct* or *indirect*.

- The separate organisational elements, summarised in the *McKinsey 7-S framework*, should come together to form a coherent *reinforcing configuration*. But these reinforcing cycles also raise problems of *agility* and *resilience*, which can be alleviated by the presence of organisational *slack*.

WORK ASSIGNMENTS

✱ Denotes more advanced work assignments.
* Refers to a case study in the Text and Cases edition.

6.1 Go to the website of a large organisation you are familiar with and find its organisational chart (not all organisations provide these). Why is the organisation structured like this?

6.2 Referring to Section 6.2.2 on the divisional structure, consider the advantages and disadvantages of creating divisions along different lines – such as product, geography or technology – with respect to a large organisation you are familiar with or a case organisation such as Siemens A and B*, Academies/ Free Schools* or Unilever*.

6.3✱ Referring to Figure 6.7, write a short executive brief explaining how strategy maps could be a useful management system to monitor and control the performance of organisational units. Be sure to analyse both advantages and disadvantages of this approach.

6.4 As a middle manager with responsibility for a small business unit, which 'strategy style' (Section 6.3.5) would you prefer to work within? In what sort of circumstances or corporate organisation would this style not work so well for you?

Integrative assignment

6.5 Take a recent merger or acquisition (see Chapter 11), ideally one involving two organisations of roughly equal size, and analyse how the deal has changed the acquiring or merged company's organisational structure. What do you conclude from the extent or lack of structural change for the new company going forward?

RECOMMENDED KEY READINGS

- The best single coverage of this chapter's issues is in R. Daftt, *Organization Theory and Design*, 12th edn, Cengage, 2016. G. Tett, *The Silo Effect,* Little and Brown, 2015, is a very readable and stimulating perspective on what can go wrong in organising and some contemporary solutions.

- For a collection of relevant articles, see the special issue 'Learning to design organisations', R. Dunbar and W. Starbuck (eds), *Organisation Science,* vol. 17, no. 2 (2006).

- M. Goold and A. Campbell, *Designing Effective Organisations,* Jossey-Bass, 2002, provides a practical guide to organisational design issues.

REFERENCES

1. A.D. Chandler, *Strategy and Structure,* MIT Press, 1962.

2. Good reviews of recent tendencies in organisation structure are J.R. Galbraith, 'The future of organization design', *Journal of Organization Design,* vol. 1, no. 1 (2012), pp. 3–6; and N. Argyres and T. Zenger, 'Dynamics in organization structure', in A. Grandori (ed.), *Handbook of Economic Organization,* Edward Elgar, 2013.

3. For an introduction to the view that organisations should fit their structures to key challenges ('contingencies'), see B. Luo and L. Donaldson, 'Misfits in organization design: information processing as a compensatory mechanism', *Journal of Organization Design,* vol. 2, no. 1 (2013), pp. 2–10. See also R. Whittington, 'Organisational structure', in *The Oxford Handbook of Strategy,* Volume II, Oxford University Press, 2003, Chapter 28.

4. G. Tett, *The Silo Effect,* Little and Brown, 2015 is an attractive account of the dangers of segmented, silo organisations.

5. This view of divisionalisation as a response to diversity was originally put forward by A.D. Chandler, *Strategy and Structure,* MIT Press, 1962. See R. Whittington and M. Mayer, *The European Corporation: Strategy, Structure and Social Science,* Oxford University Press, 2000, for a summary of Chandler's relevance more recently.

6. For a review of current experience with matrix structures, see S. Thomas and L. D'Annunzio, 'Challenges and strategies of matrix organisations: top-level and mid-level managers' perspectives', *Human Resource Planning,* vol. 28, no. 1 (2005), pp. 39–48; and J. Galbraith, *Designing Matrix Structures that Actually Work,* Jossey-Bass, 2009.

7. See C. Bartlett and S. Ghoshal, 'Matrix management: not a structure, more a frame of mind', *Harvard Business Review,* vol. 68, no. 4 (1990), pp. 138–45.

8. C. Bartlett and S. Ghoshal, *Managing Across Borders,* 2nd edn, Harvard Business School Press, 2008.

9. Research finds that transnational structures generally perform better than either centralised or decentralised structures: see J.-N. Garbe and N. Richter, 'Causal analysis of the internationalization and performance relationship based on neural networks', *Journal of International Management,* vol. 15, no. 4 (2009), pp. 413–31.

10. The classic article on project-based organisations is by R. DeFillippi and M. Arthur, 'Paradox in project-based enterprise: the case of film-making', *California Management Review,* vol. 40, no. 2 (1998), pp. 125–45. For some difficulties, see M. Bresnen, A. Goussevskaia and J. Swann, 'Organizational routines, situated learning and processes of change in project-based organisations', *Project Management Journal,* vol. 36, no. 3 (2005), pp. 27–42.

11. For a discussion of more permanent team structures, see Thomas Mullern, 'Integrating the team-based structure in the business process: the case of Saab Training Systems', in A. Pettigrew and E. Fenton (eds), *The Innovating Organisation,* Sage, 2000.

12. A.D. Chandler, *Strategy and Structure,* MIT Press, 1962.

13. M. Goold and A. Campbell, *Designing Effective Organisations,* Jossey-Bass, 2002. See also M. Goold and A. Campbell, 'Do you have a well-designed organisation?', *Harvard Business Review,* vol. 80, no. 3 (2002), pp. 117–224.

14. A.D. Chandler, *Strategy and Structure,* MIT Press, 1962.

15. This practice of 'patching' or reconfiguring parts of the organisation onto each other according to changing market needs is described in K. Eisenhardt and S. Brown, 'Patching: restitching business portfolios in dynamic markets', *Harvard Business Review,* vol. 75, no. 3 (1999), pp. 72–80. See also S. Girod and R. Whittington, 'Reconfiguration, restructuring and firm performance: dynamic capabilities and environmental dynamism', *Strategic Management Journal,* forthcoming.

16. On the reverse logic of strategy and structure, see T.L. Amburgey and T. Dacin, 'As the left foot follows the right? The dynamics of strategic and structural change', *Academy of Management Journal,* vol. 37, no. 6 (1994), pp. 1427–52.

17. M. Goold and A. Campbell, *Strategies and Styles,* Blackwell, 1987.

18. E.C. Wenger and W.M. Snyder, 'Communities of practice: the organized frontier', *Harvard Business Review,* vol. 78, no. 1 (2000), pp. 139–46.

19. A. Maté, J. Trujillo and J. Mylopoulos, 'Conceptualizing and specifying key performance indicators in business strategy models', *Proceedings of the 2012 Conference of the Center for Advanced Studies on Collaborative Research,* IBM Corp., 5–7 November, pp. 102–15.

20. The value of goals and performance targets has been debated vigorously: see L. Ordonez, M. Schweitzer, A. Galinksy and M. Bazerman, 'Goals gone wild: the systematic side effects of overprescribing goal setting', *Academy of Management Perspectives,* vol. 23, no. 1 (2009), pp. 6–16; and E. Locke and G. Latham, 'Has goal setting gone wild?', *Academy of Management Perspectives,* vol. 23, no. 1 (2009), pp. 17–23.

21. See R. Kaplan and D. Norton, 'Having trouble with your strategy? Then map it', *Harvard Business Review,* vol. 78, no. 5 (2000), pp. 167–76; and R. Kaplan and D. Norton, *Alignment: How to Apply the Balanced Scorecard to Strategy,* Harvard Business School Press, 2006.

22. See Gary Hamel, 'Bringing Silicon Valley inside', *Harvard Business Review,* vol. 77, no. 5 (1999), pp. 70–84. For a discussion of internal market challenges, see A. Vining, 'Internal market failure', *Journal of Management Studies,* vol. 40, no. 2 (2003), pp. 431–57.

23. R. Waterman, T. Peters and J. Phillips, 'Structure is not organization', *Business Horizons,* June (1980), pp. 14–26.

24. R.A. Burgelman, 'Managing the new venture division: implications for strategic management', *Strategic Management Journal,* vol. 6, no. 1 (1985), pp. 39–54.

25. R. Whittington, A. Pettigrew, S. Peck, E. Fenton and M. Conyon, 'Change and complementarities in the new competitive landscape: a European panel study, 1992–1996', *Organization Science,* vol. 10, no. 5 (1999), pp. 583–600.

26. J. Galbraith, 'Organising to deliver solutions', *Organizational Dynamics,* vol. 31, no. 2 (2002), pp. 194–207.

27. Y.L. Doz and M. Kosonen, 'Embedding strategic agility: a leadership agenda for accelerating business model renewal', *Long Range Planning,* vol. 43, no. 2 (2010), pp. 370–82; P.P. Tallon and A. Pinsonneault, 'Competing perspectives on the link between strategic information technology alignment and organizational agility: insights from a mediation model', *MIS Quarterly,* vol. 35, no. 2 (2011), pp. 463–86.

28. G. Hamel and L. Valikangas, 'The quest for resilience', *Harvard Business Review,* vol. 81, no. 9 (2003), pp. 52–65; L. Välikangas and A.G.L. Romme, 'Competing perspectives on the link between strategic information technology alignment and organizational agility: insights from a mediation model', *MIS Quarterly,* vol. 35, no. 2 (2011), pp. 463–86; P. Tallon and A. Pinsonneault, 'Capabilities at "Big Brown Box, Inc."', *Strategy & Leadership,* vol. 4, no. 4 (2012), pp. 43–5.

29. P. Puranam and D. Håkonsson, 'Valve's Way', *Journal of Organization Design,* vol. 4, no. 2 (2015), pp. 2–4; T. Felin, 'Valve Corporation: strategy tipping points and thresholds', *Journal of Organization Design,* vol. 4, no. 2 (2015), pp. 10–11.

CASE EXAMPLE

One Sony?

Kazuo Hirai's April 2012 appointment as Chief Executive Officer of Sony Corporation would probably have surprised his younger self. After all, Hirai had started out as Japanese translator to the American hip-hop band the Beastie Boys. He had then become a video games designer and later led Sony's PlayStation business in the USA. However, by the time he finally became CEO at the age of 51, Sony was in deep trouble. One of Hirai's first moves was to change Sony's organisational structure. The aim was to create a more integrated business – 'One Sony'. With some adjustments over time, Sony retained this basic structure to at least until 2016.

Business background

Sony's businesses spanned professional electronics such as semiconductors and medical devices, consumer electronics from televisions and mobile phones to computers and the PlayStation, together with 'content' businesses such as movies and music. As such, Sony was pitching against companies like the American success-story Apple and the Korean high-technology giant Samsung. Despite a proud history associated with such brands as the Sony Walkman audio devices or Sony Trinitron televisions, Sony was being left far behind. By 2012, Sony's stock price was less than half it had been five years before, while Apple and Samsung were two or three times as valuable (see Figure 1).

Sony's relative decline has not been for want of trying. In 2003, the company had suffered the so-called 'Sony shock', when both earnings and stock price had plunged simultaneously following a weak response to cheaper Asian electronics firms. The company reduced costs by cutting its workforce by nearly 20 per cent. In 2005, Sony had taken the then-revolutionary step of appointing its first foreigner as CEO, Howard Stringer, a Welsh-American with a background in the music and movie business. Stringer had announced that he would break down the company's vertical management system, which he described as a set of separate 'silos' with little coherence. He sought

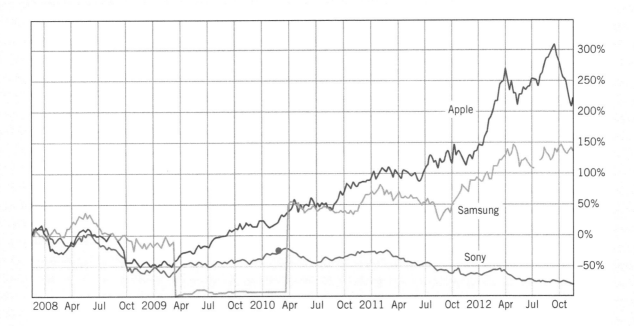

Figure 1 Sony's stock price performance relative to Apple and Samsung, 2008–12

Source: Yahoo Finance. For comparison of price changes, all prices standardised to zero in 2008.

to integrate the company's hardware business, based in Japan, with its various content businesses, led by music and movies in the USA. Stringer's slogan had been 'Sony United'. But Stringer had been neither an engineer nor a Japanese speaker. It was reported that many of his diktats to the Japanese hardware businesses were largely ignored.

The financial results for 2011–12 confirmed Stringer's failure. Without a striking new product to compare with the original Walkman or Trinitron and still heavily reliant on an expensive Japanese manufacturing base, Sony's sales were down nearly ten per cent while profits were negative. The 69-year-old Stringer became Company Chairman. Hirai, Sony's youngest ever CEO and the second non-engineer in a row, set to work.

New strategy and new structure

Hirai insisted that the new Sony would be focused predominantly on five key strategic initiatives. First of all was a strengthening of the core business, by which he meant digital imaging, games and mobile devices, including phones, tablets and laptops. Second, Hirai committed himself to returning the television business back to profitability, after eight years of consistent losses. Third, Sony would develop faster in emerging markets such as India and South America. The fourth initiative was to accelerate innovation, particularly by integrating product areas. Finally, Sony was preparing to realign its business portfolio, with divestments expected of non-core businesses (e.g. the legacy chemicals business).

Hirai supported these strategic initiatives with a new organisational structure, designed to support his concept of 'One Sony'. The old structure had been based on two big groups centred on Japan and predominantly in hardware: the Professional, Device and Solutions Group, responsible for about half of all sales; and the Consumer Products and Services Group, responsible for another fifth of sales. Alongside these two major groups were several stand-alone businesses mostly based abroad, including Music, Pictures (movies) and the Sony–Ericsson joint venture in mobile phones (see Figure 2).

The new structure broke up the big groups, creating 12 stand-alone businesses in all (see Figure 3). The ending of the Sony–Ericsson joint venture in late 2011 allowed the mobile phone business to be brought closer to the VAIO and mobile computing business. Sony's medical-related businesses, previously dispersed across multiple units but now targeted for rapid growth, were folded into a dedicated medical business unit led by an executive at corporate level. The device and semiconductor businesses, including image sensors, became a single business group, Device Solutions. Sony Network Entertainment was strengthened, with all Sony's online offerings now included.

Hirai completed his structural changes by reinforcing headquarters resources and oversight, with several new senior management appointments. The aim was to leverage the company's broad portfolio by creating exclusive content for Sony's own devices. A single corporate-level executive was made responsible for User Experience ('UX'), Product Strategy and the Creative Platform, charged with strengthening horizontal integration and enhancing the experience across Sony's entire product and network service line-up. The same executive would

Figure 2 Sony's organisational structure, 2011

Source: Adapted from www.sony.net.

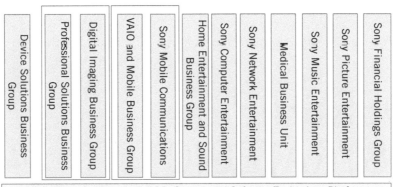

Sony Corporate: Corporate R&D; System and Software Technology Platform; Advanced Device Technology Platform; UX, Product Strategy and Creative Platform; Global Sales and Marketing Platform; Headquarters

Figure 3 Sony's organisational structure, 2012
Source: Adapted from www.sony.net.

oversee the mobile businesses, including smartphones, tablets and PCs (indicated by the box around the two relevant business groups). Digital Imaging and the Professional Solutions likewise came under the oversight of a single corporate-level executive. Hirai himself was to take direct responsibility for the Home Entertainment Business Group, including the troubled television business, pledging to give it the majority of his time in the coming months.

At an investors' meeting in April 2012, Hirai went beyond strategic and structural changes:

'The other thing is . . . the One Sony/One Management concept. That is really important, because I made sure that as I built my new management team, that everybody in the team is 100 per cent fully committed and also aligned as to what needs to get done and how we're going to get that done. And so we have a lot of discussions internally amongst the management team. Once we make that decision, then everybody moves in the same direction and we execute with speed. And I think that is another area that is quite different from some of the restructurings or the changes that we have made perhaps in the past.'

Results did not come quickly, however. In November 2012, the *Wall Street Journal* observed of Sony's new organisational chart: 'Far from providing clarity of purpose, the diagram should leave investors tearing their hair out. While new Chief Executive Kazuo Hirai shuffles the deckchairs on board the one-time electronics titan, Sony's stock is plunging into deep waters.'

Main sources: Wall Street Journal, 2 February 2012; Nikkei Report, 2 March 2012; Sony Corporation press release, Tokyo, 27 March 2012; CQ FD Disclosure, Sony Corporate Strategy Meeting Conference Call for Overseas Investors – Final, 12 April 2012; *Wall Street Journal,* 15 November 2012.

Questions

1 Assess the pros and cons of Hirai's structural changes.

2 What other initiatives beyond structural change might be necessary in order to create 'One Sony'?

7

LEADERSHIP AND STRATEGIC CHANGE

Learning outcomes

After reading this chapter you should be able to:

- Identify and assess different *leadership styles,* as related to strategic change.
- Use the *change kaleidoscope* and *forcefield analysis* to analyse how *organisational context* might affect strategic change.
- Identify *types* of strategic change, according to speed and scope.
- Assess the value of different *levers* for strategic change.
- Identify the approaches, pitfalls and problems of leading different types of strategic change.

Key terms

forcefield analysis

leadership

organisational ambidexterity

situational leadership

transactional leader

transformational leader

turnaround strategy

7.1 INTRODUCTION

Amazon, the internet retailer, has been led by founder Jeff Bezos for more than two decades. Bezos lays down 'Fifteen Leadership Principles' for the 230,000 people who work for his company around the world. According to these principles, Amazonians should 'Think Big', 'Dive Deep', follow a 'Bias for Action' and 'Have Backbone'. Such principles appear to have helped Bezos manage Amazon's strategic change from online bookstore to diversified technology giant, with interests ranging from cloud infrastructure for business to mobile phones.

The theme of strategic change runs through much of this part of the text. Part I of this book examined pressures for strategic change arising from the organisation's environment and its internal position; Part II looked at the kinds of strategic option that might form part of strategic change, such as diversification, internationalisation or innovation. However, central to strategic change is the leadership task of ensuring that people deliver whatever strategic options are finally chosen. While this leadership role is most often associated with chief executives it may, in fact, occur at different levels in organisations: other senior managers and middle managers too may take leadership roles in change. Indeed, at Amazon, the company's leadership principles are supposed to be followed by all.

Figure 7.1 provides a structure for the chapter. The chapter opens (Section 7.2) by explaining different roles of leaders and different leadership styles. A key task of leadership is strategic change. Leaders need to address two issues in considering their approach to change. First, they have to diagnose the organisational context, the extent to which it is receptive or resistant to change: Section 7.3 particularly addresses the forces blocking or facilitating change. Second, leaders have to identify the type of strategic change required: Section 7.4 differentiates types of change according to speed and scope. Understanding the context, and identifying the required type of change, should help leaders select the appropriate levers for change: Section 7.5 considers levers ranging from symbolic management to political action. Section 7.6 draws many of the issues together by considering common reasons for the failure of strategic change programmes and pointing to the importance of informal change.

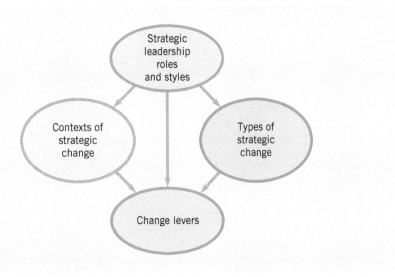

Figure 7.1 Key elements in leading strategic change

7.2 LEADERSHIP AND STRATEGIC CHANGE

Leadership is the process of influencing an organisation (or group within an organisation) in its efforts towards achieving an aim or goal.[1] Without effective leadership the risk is that people in an organisation are unclear about its purpose or lack motivation to deliver the strategy to achieve it. Leadership is associated particularly with strategic change. For example, Harvard's John Kotter argues that 'good management' is about bringing order and consistency to operational aspects of organisations, such as quality and profitability of products and services. Leadership, 'by contrast is about coping with change'.[2] Thus strategic change is a crucial underlying theme in this discussion of leadership.

7.2.1 Strategic leadership roles

While leading strategic change is often associated with top management, and chief executives in particular, in practice it typically involves managers at different levels in an organisation.

Top managers

There are three key roles that are argued to be especially significant for top management, especially a CEO, in leading strategic change:

- *Envisioning future strategy*.[3] Effective strategic leaders at the top of an organisation need to ensure there exists a clear and compelling vision of the future and communicate clearly a strategy to achieve it both internally and to external stakeholders. In the absence of their doing so, those who attempt to lead change elsewhere in an organisation, for example middle managers, are likely to construct such a vision themselves. This may be well-intentioned but can lead to confusion.

- *Aligning* the organisation to deliver that strategy. This involves ensuring that people in the organisation are committed to the strategy, motivated to make the changes needed and empowered to deliver those changes. In doing so, there is a need for leaders to build and foster relationships of trust and respect across the organisation. It can, however, also be necessary to change the management of the organisation to ensure such commitment, which is a reason that top teams often change as a precursor to or during strategic change.

- *Embodying change*. A strategic leader will be seen by others, not least those within the organisation, but also other stakeholders and outside observers, as intimately associated with a future strategy and a strategic change programme. A strategic leader is, then, symbolically highly significant in the change process and needs to be a role model for future strategy (see Section 7.5.4 below on symbolic levers for change).

Middle managers

A top-down approach to managing strategy and strategic change sees middle managers as implementers of top management strategic plans. Here their role is to ensure that resources are allocated and controlled appropriately and to monitor the performance and behaviour of staff. However, middle managers have multiple roles in relation to the management of strategy.[4] In the context of managing strategic change there are four roles to emphasise:

- *Advisers* to more senior management on requirements for change within an organisation. This is because they are often the closest to indications of market or technological changes that might signal the need for change. They are also well-placed to be able to identify likely blockages to change. Middle managers may also provide a useful variety of experience and views that can stimulate thinking on strategy.[5]

- '*Sense making*' of strategy. Top management may set a strategic direction, but how it is explained and made sense of in specific contexts (e.g. a region of a multinational or a functional department) may, intentionally or not, be left to middle managers. If misinterpretation of that intended strategy is to be avoided, it is therefore vital that middle managers understand and feel an ownership of it. They are therefore a crucial *relevance bridge* between top management and members of the organisation at lower levels.[6]

- *Reinterpretation* and *adjustment* of strategic responses as events unfold (e.g. in terms of relationships with customers, suppliers, the workforce and so on). Middle managers are uniquely qualified to reinterpret and adjust strategy because they are in day-to-day contact with such aspects of the organisation and its environment.

- *Local leadership of change*. Middle managers therefore have the roles of aligning and embodying change, as do top management, but at a local level. This can be particularly important in decentralised organisations, such as chains of retail stores or multinational corporations.

Recognising the leadership role of middle managers can help balance the heroic, top-down and individualist image often associated with leaders, particularly in Anglo-American business cultures. Of course, middle managers can be heroic individuals. However, because they do not have the power or legitimacy of top managers, middle managers are often obliged to adopt more collective or collaborative approaches to leadership.[7] Leaders may need to harness the support and ideas of colleagues in teams. Many top managers also prefer this collaborative approach. In other words, leaders are not always individualistic. There are different styles of leadership.

7.2.2 Leadership styles

Leaders tend to adopt characteristic 'styles' of behaving and intervening. These leadership styles are often categorised in two broad ways:

- **Transformational (or charismatic) leaders emphasise building a vision for the organisation,** creating an organisational identity around collective values and beliefs to support that vision and energising people to achieve it. Organisational founders are often particularly charismatic. Evidence suggests that this approach to leadership has beneficial impact on people's motivation and job performance,[8] and is particularly positive for wider business performance when organisations face uncertainty.[9]

- **Transactional leaders emphasise 'hard' levers of change such as designing systems and controls.** The emphasis here is more likely to be on changes of structures, setting targets to be achieved, financial incentives, careful project management and the monitoring of organisational and individual performance.

In practice, transformational and transactional leadership styles are two ends of a continuum, with many feasible points between. Leaders typically combine elements of the two styles, rather than identifying exclusively with one (see Illustration 7.1). Indeed, the notion of **situational leadership encourages strategic leaders to adjust their leadership style to the context they face.**[10] In other words, there is not just one best way of leading: appropriate leadership style changes according to the specific demands of the situation. The next two sections examine two aspects of such situations: contexts of change and types of change.

ILLUSTRATION 7.1 — Leadership styles

Successful top executives talk about their leadership styles.

Learn to lead

'Leadership is a learned skill. Some people are innately good at it, but all can become better. However, this is not to be confused with becoming a great leader – a Ghandi or a Nelson Mandela. . . . [It is] not about how many people report to you, but about how you behave, act, and endeavour to do the right thing. . . . If you are trying to solve complex problems creatively, you can be collaborative . . . If the house is on fire, you don't suggest forming a committee.'

Antony Jenkins, CEO Barclays Bank, 2012–15,
Saïd Business School, Oxford

Select and empower

Interview question: 'What are the most important things that leaders can do to create the conditions for high performance?'

Ursula Burns: 'First, they define the possibilities. They set the agenda, the tone of the organization.

Second, they select. They select the key leaders in the next echelon of the company, help to select the leaders after that, and so on. So, they have a big, big people component.

Third, they empower. After selecting correctly, they have to empower these people to actually do the job.

Next, they set the correct expectation for what excellence looks like, what greatness looks like . . . What's greatness? Greatness is growing a customer base. Greatness is distinguishing ourselves by innovation. Greatness is hitting a certain EPS or revenue growth target or cash target.'

Ursula Burns, Chairman and CEO Xerox Corporation,
December 3, 2012, *triplecrownleadership*

Vision and grit

A leader should never compare his technical skills with his employee's. Your employee should have superior technical skills than you. If he doesn't, it means you have hired the wrong person.

What, then, makes the leader stands out?

1 A leader should be a visionary and have more foresight than an employee.
2 A leader should have higher grit and tenacity, and be able to endure what the employees can't.
3 A leader should have higher endurance and ability to accept and embrace failure.

Jack Ma, Founder of Chinese eCommerce giant,
Alibaba, *VulkanPost*, 25 February 2015

Confidence when you don't know

'One of my favorite episodes of "Star Trek: The Next Generation" is when the captain and the doctor are stranded alone on this planet, and their brains are linked by some kind of alien device so they can read each other's thoughts. They're trying to get somewhere and the captain says, "We're going this way," and the doctor says, "You don't know which way to go, do you?" Because she can read his thoughts.'

'He explains to her that sometimes part of being a leader is just picking a way and being confident about it and going, because people want to be led. I remember that episode, because it rang really true to me. Sometimes you just have to lead, even if you don't have all the answers. In fact, you shouldn't have all the answers. If you think you have all the answers, then you're probably doing something wrong. Good leadership means being willing to have the confidence to move forward, even if you don't have all the answers.'

Biz Stone, Founder of Twitter, 27 May, 2014,
Washington Post

Questions

1 Which leaders are more transformational, which more transactional and which situational (see Section 7.2.1)?

2 Compare the different views of leadership, particularly with regard to knowledge, courage and people. What are the commonalities and differences?

7.3 DIAGNOSING THE CHANGE CONTEXT

The effectiveness of different leadership styles is shaped by the *organisational context* in which change is to occur.[11] A small entrepreneurial business is a very different context to a large, bureaucratic organisation. The 'change kaleidoscope' and forcefield analysis are two ways of assessing organisational receptiveness to change. This will help in the diagnosis of types of change required.

7.3.1 The change kaleidoscope

Julia Balogun (University of Liverpool) and Veronica Hope-Hailey (University of Bath) propose the 'change kaleidoscope' (summarised in Figure 7.2) as a framework for identifying key contextual features to take into account when designing change programmes. Just as a toy kaleidoscope rearranges a set of elements into different patterns, the change kaleidoscope highlights how a set of contextual features can take various forms supporting or resisting change. Figure 7.2 identifies eight contextual features:

- The *time* available for change can differ dramatically. A business may face immediate decline in turnover or profits from rapid changes in its markets. This is a quite different context for change compared with a business where the management may see the need for change as years away and have time to plan it carefully.

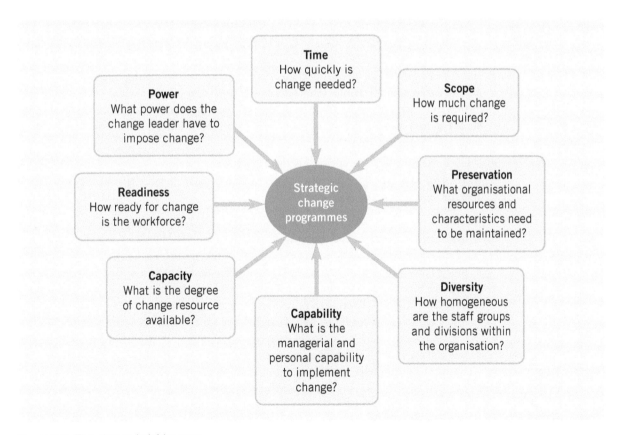

Figure 7.2 The change kaleidoscope

Source: Adapted from J. Balogun and V. Hope Hailey, *Exploring Strategic Change,* 3rd edn, Prentice Hall, 2008.

- The *scope* of change might differ in terms of either the *breadth* of change across an organisation or the *depth* of culture change required. For example, a global business with multiple brands is likely to involve a high breadth of change, while an established organisation with a long cultural heritage is likely to demand depth of change.

- *Preservation* of some aspects of an organisation may be needed. For example, some capabilities may need to be built upon in order to achieve change, while others can simply be abandoned. Alternatively, some established parts of the organisation may need to be retained in order to generate revenues, while waiting for newer parts to build up strength and economic effectiveness. This combination of preservation and change relates to the notion of organisational ambidexterity (Section 7.4).

- A *diversity* of experience, views and opinions within an organisation may help the change process, providing the seeds from which new initiatives can grow. However, if an organisation has followed a strategy for many decades, such continuity may have led to a very homogeneous way of seeing the world, which could hamper change.

- *Capacity* for change in terms of available resources will also be significant. Change can be costly, not only in financial terms, but also in terms of management time. It is likely to be the responsibility of top management (or perhaps owners) to provide such resources.

- Who has the *power* to effect change? Often it is assumed that the chief executive has such power, but in the face of resistance from below, or perhaps resistance from external stakeholders, this may not be the case. It may also be that the chief executive supposes that others in the organisation have the power to effect change when they do not, or do not see themselves as having it. In organisations with *hierarchical power structures* a directive style may be common and it may be difficult to break away from it, not least because people expect it. On the other hand, in '*flatter*' power structures, a more networked or learning organisation described elsewhere in this text (see Section 14.2.3), it is likely that collaboration and participation will be common, indeed desirable.

- Is there a *capability* of managing change in the organisation? Change is complex to manage, so larger organisations especially need to have access to skilled and experienced change managers, whether in the form of in-house organisation development professionals or external consultants. It helps too if the workforce is experienced with change, rather than being set in its ways.

- What is the *readiness* for change? Is there a felt need for change across the organisation, widespread resistance or pockets or levels of resistance in some parts of the organisation and readiness in others?

As in the notion of situational leadership (Section 7.2), the appropriate leadership style will vary according to the contextual factors illuminated by the change kaleidoscope. Urgency, a lack of diversity and low readiness to change might all encourage a transactional style, for instance. However, Balogun and Hope-Hailey highlight particularly how the change approach needs to differ according, in particular, to (i) the capability and (ii) the readiness of employees to change. Bearing in mind these two contextual features, Figure 7.3 suggests that, where there is high readiness but low capability for change, *persuasion,* involving education, training and coaching, may be an appropriate approach to emphasise. Where both readiness and capability are high, an effective focus may be *collaboration,* involving extensive consultation and teamwork in defining the change. Where capability is high but readiness is low, controlled *participation* in managing the change process may help to win over employee support. Where there is both low readiness and capability for change, top-down *direction* may be the most appropriate style, especially if change is urgent. The role of these factors in defining appropriate leadership styles is shown in Illustration 7.2, on Indian banking.

ILLUSTRATION 7.2   Challenges of change in Indian banking

India's public sector banks provide a challenging context for change.

In 2015, India had no less than 27 public-sector banks. Each typically had private investors, but the government owned majority stakes in them all. These banks were enormously important to the Indian economy, lending to large businesses, entrepreneurs, farmers, home-buyers and students needing to fund their education. Comparing India's fragmented state banks with the giant banks of China and Japan, the reformist Indian Prime Minister Narendra Modi demanded 'transformation'.

Indeed, the public-sector banks were failing. New private banks – paying higher salaries to their staff, with greater technological expertise and free of political interference – had driven the public banks' domestic market share down from over 90 per cent in the early 1990s to about 70 per cent by 2015. Return on total assets at private-sector banks was 1.6 per cent compared with just 0.5 per cent for state-run ones, while the state bank non-performing loans were more than five per cent of total loans, against two per cent in the non-state sector. The government directed the public banks to lend into sectors such as steel, power and sugar that were seen as strategically important to India's development but which were also suffering economically. The poorly-paid workforce – 850,000 strong, spread across 50,000 bank branches – was heavily trade-unionised and frequently threatened to strike. Top management was weak, with positions in the smaller banks seen as temporary stepping-stones to more senior positions in the larger banks.

In January 2015, Prime Minister Modi, his finance minister and senior regulators and public officials met with about 60 heads of both private and public financial institutions to discuss reform during a two-day 'retreat'. The official brief for the retreat was to search for 'out-of-the-box' ideas. The Prime Minister insisted that participants arrive in shared coaches rather than private cars, and yoga lessons were scheduled for the second day. Attendees heard presentations from McKinsey & Co management consultants and from the corporate guru Swami Sukhbodhanandji, author of the 'Relax' series of business books, as well as working in round-table teams.

Over the following months, the Modi government considered the various proposals from the retreat, while also heading off a national strike by public bank employees with a new pay settlement. In August 2015, the Finance Minister announced a raft of reforms including: (i) the appointment of more private-sector managers as heads of public-sector banks; (ii) the creation of a Bank Board Bureau to act as a watchdog for public banks' performance and managerial appointments; (iii) the injection of $1.9bn (€1.1bn, €1.4bn) new capital to meet international standards; (iv) allowing public banks to offer managers Employee Stock Ownership Plans to give them a stake in financial success. The Prime Minister announced that he was 'against political interference in the banks, but supports political intervention in the interests of the people'.

Many commentators were disappointed at the modesty of these reforms. The investment bank JP Morgan estimated that the public banks needed $15bn of new capital. Some argued that a proper restructuring of the fragmented sector required ownership by a single holding company with the power to merge smaller banks. Others argued for greater privatisation. The head of one leading private-sector financial institution commented: 'This is purposeful incrementalism. It is not big bang but it is helpful.' There was anxiety about the future of reform, as the Prime Minister's legislative programme faced fierce opposition in the Indian Parliament and the governing party had lost local elections in the Delhi region.

Key sources: *Economic Times*, 3 January 2015; *CNBC-TV*, 14 August 2015; *Financial Times*, 15 August 2015.

Questions

1 In terms of the eight contextual features in the change kaleidoscope (Figure 7.2), how receptive is the context for strategic change?

2 In the light of capability and readiness (Figure 7.3), what leadership style would be most appropriate to bringing about change?

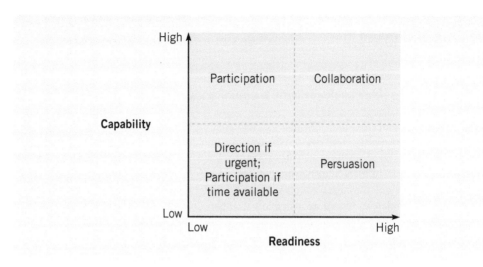

Figure 7.3 Styles of change leadership according to organisational capability and readiness

7.3.2 Forcefield analysis

A second means of approaching the context for change is analysing the balance of forces supporting or resisting change. A **forcefield analysis compares the forces at work in an organisation acting either to prevent or to facilitate change.** Thus forcefield analysis involves identifying those who favour change, those who oppose it and those are more or less neutral. Identifying allies and opponents (actual or potential) helps in the politics of strategic change. The task is to persuade those who are neutral or even against change to move into the camp of those who favour it. The relative weight of the forces finally favouring or opposing change helps also in estimating the effort required to achieve change. The more forces are arrayed against change, the more effort is needed.

Forcefield analysis helps ask some further key questions:

- What aspects of the current situation would block change, and how can these blocks be overcome?

- What aspects of the current situation might aid change in the desired direction, and how might these be reinforced?

- What needs to be introduced or developed to add to the forces for change?

Illustration 7.3 shows how a forcefield analysis was used by managers considering the intention to devolve strategic decisions within the European division of a global manufacturer.

A forcefield analysis can be informed by the change kaleidoscope but also by other concepts and frameworks in the text:

- *Stakeholder mapping* (Section 5.2.2) can provide insight into the power of different stakeholders to promote change or to resist change.

- *The cultural web* (Section 6.3.5). Strategic change often goes hand-in-hand with a perceived need to change the culture of the organisation. The culture web is a means of diagnosing organisational culture and therefore an understanding of the symbolic, routinised as well as structural and systemic factors that may be taken for granted and can act for or against change. It can also be used to envisage what the culture of an organisation would need to look like to deliver future strategy.

- *The 7-S framework* (Section 14.4.1) can highlight aspects of the infrastructure of an organisation that may act to promote or block change.

ILLUSTRATION 7.3

A forcefield analysis for devolving strategy

A forcefield analysis can be used to identify aspects of the organisation that might aid change, blockages to change and what needs to be developed to aid change.

A Japanese multinational manufacturer had always been centralised in terms of strategic direction and, in particular, new product development. It had been hugely successful in Japan and had also developed a global footprint, largely through acquisitions of local manufacturers related to its core business. These acquired businesses operated largely independently of each other as manufacturing units reporting to Japan. Regionally based sales offices were responsible for selling the range of company products and identifying customer needs and, again, reported through to Japan.

In 2012, top management in Japan took the decision to devolve strategic decisions to geographic regional divisions. The decision was based on the desire to grow non-Japanese markets given the changing competitive landscape, especially the growing power of European customers in the world market, but also the need to understand and respond to local markets better. The view was that competitive strategy and innovation

needed to originate and develop nearer to regionally based customers rather than centrally in Japan.

Managers in Europe were charged with developing a plan to implement this devolution of strategy. They undertook a forcefield analysis to identify the key issues to be addressed, a summary of which is shown here.

It was market forces and a head office decision that were the main 'pushing forces' for change. But local managers also recognised that their career prospects could be enhanced. The 'resisting forces' were not only a function of the existing organisational structure, but also the lack of any pan-European infrastructure and the lack of European managers with strategic, as distinct from operational, expertise. The forcefield underlined the importance of establishing such an infrastructure and highlighted the need for IT systems to share information and ideas. It also raised the strategic importance of management development at the strategic level.

PUSHING — **RESISTING**

PUSHING	RESISTING
LOCAL COMPETITOR GROWTH	SPECIALIST SILOS
CUSTOMER PRESSURE	RESIDUAL JAPANESE INFLUENCE
HEAD OFFICE DECISION AND SUPPORT	NO EUROPEAN IT NETWORK
CAREER ENHANCEMENT	WARINESS OF SHARING DATA
OPPORTUNITIES FOR EUROPEAN SYNERGIES	NO PAN-EUROPEAN LOCAL MANAGEMENT

ADDITIONS

MANAGEMENT DEVELOPMENT	LACK OF STRATEGIC EXPERIENCE

Questions

1 What might the problems be in devolving strategy to a European division?

2 Undertake a forcefield analysis for an organisation of your choice.

As well as helping to identify the current forces acting for and against change, each of these frameworks can also be used to help think through what else might be needed as additional forces to promote change.

7.4 TYPES OF STRATEGIC CHANGE

Julia Balogun and Veronica Hope-Hailey[12] identify four generic types of strategic change. The axes in Figure 7.4 are concerned with (i) the *extent* of change, in other words the desired end result and (ii) the *nature* of the change process, particularly the speed. These two axes relate to the time and scope features of the change kaleidoscope (Figure 7.2).

	End result (extent)	
	Transformation	Realignment
Incremental	**Evolution**	**Adaptation**
Big bang	**Revolution**	**Reconstruction (or turnaround)**

(Nature of change (speed) labels the vertical axis; Incremental / Big bang are the rows.)

Figure 7.4 Types of change
Source: Adapted from J. Balogun, V. Hope Hailey and S. Gustafsson, *Exploring Strategic Change*, 4th edn, Pearson, 2016, p. 23.

In terms of the *extent* of change, change that occurs in line with the current business model and culture is considered a *realignment* of strategy. More extensive change, going beyond the current business model or culture, is *transformational* change. Many of the tools of analysis in Part I of the text can help identify the extent of change required. For example, does the change require a substantial reconfiguration of the value chain (Section 4.4.2), significant changes in the activities underpinning strategic capabilities (Section 4.4.3) or major cultural change (Section 6.3.5)? Care does, however, need to be taken in considering the significance of new strategies on the extent of change required. For example, a business may launch new products without requiring fundamental changes in the business model or culture of the organisation. On the other hand, some changes in strategy, even if they do not take the form of dramatic product changes, may require culture change. For example, the shift from a production focus for a manufacturer to a customer-led, service ethos may not entail major product changes, but may require significant culture change.

On the other axis in Figure 7.4, the nature of change is concerned with the speed at which change needs to happen. Arguably, it is often beneficial for change in an organisation to be *incremental* since this allows time to build on the skills, routines and beliefs of those in the organisation. It also allows for learning as the change proceeds, enabling adjustments to be made in the light of experience. However, if an organisation faces crisis or needs to change direction fast, a '*big bang*' approach to change might be needed: here everything is attempted all at once.

Together, Figure 7.4's two axes of extent of change and urgency of change define four basic types of strategic change, as follows.

7.4.1 Adaptation

As explained in Section 6.4 and Section 13.3, strategy development is often *incremental* in nature. It builds on rather than fundamentally changes prior strategy. It is what Figure 7.4 refers to as *adaptation*. Change is gradual, building on or amending what the organisation has been doing in the past and in line with the current business model and organisational culture. This might include changes in product design or methods of production, launches of new products or related diversification. This is the most common form of change in organisations. Though less common, the leadership of change is more often associated with the other more fundamental types of change identified in Figure 7.4.

7.4.2 Reconstruction

Reconstruction is rapid change involving a good deal of upheaval in an organisation, but which still does not fundamentally change the culture or the business model. Thus reconstruction might include changes in organisational structure or the introduction of a cost-cutting programme. For a diversified corporation, reconstruction could also involve the acquisition or divestment of a business, something that might involve large assets but which could still be compatible with the basic organisational structure and systems.

The classic reconstruction is a turnaround strategy in the face of radical performance decline. **Turnaround strategies emphasise rapidity in change, cost reduction and/or revenue generation, with the aim of fast recovery.** The priority in turnarounds is actions that give quick and significant improvements. Situations calling for turnarounds include economic recessions, the failure of major investment projects or the sudden collapse of important markets. Turnaround actions go beyond simple cost-cutting. Five key elements of turnaround strategies are:[13]

- *Crisis stabilisation.* The aim is to regain control over the deteriorating position. This requires a short-term focus on cost reduction and/or revenue increase, typically involving some of the steps identified in Table 7.1. There is nothing novel about these steps: many of them are good management practice. The differences are the speed at which they are carried out and the focus of managerial attention on them. The most successful turnaround strategies focus on long-term improvements in direct operational costs and productivity, rather than just cuts to apparent overhead costs, such as research and development or marketing spend.

Table 7.1 Turnaround: revenue generation and cost reduction steps

Increasing revenue	Reducing costs
- Ensure marketing mix tailored to key market segments - Review pricing strategy to maximise revenue - Focus organisational activities on needs of target market sector customers - Exploit additional opportunities for revenue creation related to target market - Invest funds from reduction of costs in new growth areas	- Reduce labour costs and reduce costs of senior management - Focus on productivity improvement - Reduce marketing costs not focused on target market - Tighten financial controls - Tight control on cash expenses - Establish competitive bidding for suppliers; defer creditor payments; speed up debtor payments - Reduce inventory - Eliminate non-profitable products/services

- *Management changes.* Changes in management may be required, especially at the top. This usually includes the introduction of a new chairman or chief executive, as well as changes to the board, especially in marketing, sales and finance, for three main reasons; first, because the old management may well be the ones that were in charge when the problems developed and be seen as the cause of them by key stakeholders; second, because it may be necessary to bring in management with experience of turnaround management; and third, management changes provide the opportunity to bring in new skills and approaches from outside the organisation, different to the old skills and approaches that had led to the original crisis.

- *Gaining stakeholder support.* Poor-quality information may have been provided to key stakeholders. In a turnaround situation it is vital that key stakeholders, perhaps the bank or key shareholder groups, and employees are kept clearly informed of the situation and improvements as they are being made. It is also likely that a clear assessment of the power of different stakeholder groups (see Section 5.2.2) will become vitally important in managing turnaround.

- *Clarifying the target market(s) and core products.* Central to turnaround success is ensuring clarity on the target market or market segments most likely to generate cash and grow profits. A successful turnaround strategy involves getting closer to customers and improving the flow of marketing information, especially to senior levels of management, so as to focus revenue-generating activities on key market segments. Of course, a reason for the poor performance of the organisation could be that it had this wrong in the first place. Clarifying the target market also provides the opportunity to discontinue or outsource products and services that are not targeted on those markets, eating up management time for little return or not making sufficient financial contribution.

- *Financial restructuring.* The financial structure of the organisation may need to be changed. This typically involves changing the existing capital structure, raising additional finance or renegotiating agreements with creditors, especially banks. Reducing debt will increase an organisation's robustness in the face of future crises.

7.4.3 Revolution

Revolution is change that requires rapid and major strategic and cultural change. This could be in circumstances where the strategy has been so bounded by the existing culture that, even when environmental or competitive pressures might require fundamental change, the organisation has failed to respond. This might have occurred over many years (see the discussion of strategic drift in Section 6.4) and resulted in circumstances where pressures for change are extreme – for example, a takeover threatens the continued existence of a firm.

Revolutionary change therefore differs from turnaround (or reconstruction) in two ways that make managing change especially challenging. First, the need is not only for fast strategic change but, very likely, also for deep cultural change. Second, it may be that the need for change is not as evident to people in the organisation as in a turnaround situation, or that they have reasons to deny the need for change. This situation may have come about as a result of many years of relative decline in a market, with people wedded to products or processes no longer valued by customers – the problem of strategic drift. Or it could be that the problems of the organisation are visible and understood by its members, but that people cannot see a way forward. Leading change in such circumstances is likely to involve:

- *Clear strategic direction.* The need to give a clear strategic direction and to undertake decisive action in line with that direction is critical. This may of course include some of the decisions outlined above for turnaround: for example, portfolio changes and greater market focus. This is the type of change where individual CEOs who are seen to provide such direction are often credited with making a major difference. They may well also become the symbol of such change within an organisation and externally.

- *Top management changes.* The replacement of the CEO, senior executives or, perhaps, changes in board membership is common. Existing top management may be embedded within the past culture and their network of colleagues, customers or suppliers. New top managers do not have these established networks, nor are they embedded in the existing culture, so it is more likely that they will bring a fresh perspective and initiate or be ready to adopt new ideas and initiatives.[14] The introduction of new top management also signals the significance of change internally and externally. For similar reasons consultants may also be used not only to provide an analysis of the need for change, but also to signal how meaningful the change process is.

- *Culture change.* It may be possible to work with elements of the existing culture rather than attempt wholesale culture change. This involves identifying those aspects of culture that can be built upon and developed and those that have to be changed – in effect a forcefield approach (see Section 7.3.2).

- *Monitoring change.* Revolutionary change is likely to require the setting and monitoring of unambiguous targets that people have to achieve. Often these will be linked to overall financial targets and in turn to improved returns to shareholders. Although revolutionary change is urgent, some parts of the change – for instance, cultural change – may take longer to bed down than others.

7.4.4 Evolution

Evolution is change in strategy that results in transformation, but gradually. Arguably this is the most challenging type of strategic change since it involves building on and exploiting existing strategic capabilities while also developing new strategic capabilities. As Chapter 6 explains, however, in successful organisations many will see no pressing need for change and there will be a tendency to stick to historic bases of success, so the exploration for new ways of doing things may be limited. Managers and scholars alike have sought to identify ways in which the effective evolution of strategy might occur: how an organisation can change its business model (see Chapter 7) and culture gradually *and* keep pace with a changing environment, thus avoiding strategic drift. One approach is to cultivate organisational ambidexterity.

Human ambidexterity is the ability to use both hands with equal facility. **Organisational ambidexterity is the capacity both to exploit existing capabilities and to search for new capabilities.** It is, of course, appropriate and necessary that an organisation should seek to exploit the capabilities it has built up over time in order to achieve and sustain competitive advantage. However, exploitation will tend to allow only incremental change, since strategy is being built on established ways of doing things. If transformational change is to be achieved, there needs also to be exploration in order to innovate and build new capabilities. This is in line with the lesson from Section 4.5 that organisations need the ability to renew and re-create their capabilities; they need to develop dynamic capabilities.

However, organisational ambidexterity can be challenging because the different processes associated with exploitation and exploration raise contradictory pressures: ambidexterity involves being both focused and flexible, efficient yet innovative, looking forward and looking backward.[15] Four kinds of approach can help manage the pressures of ambidexterity:

- *Structural ambidexterity.* Organisations may maintain the main core of the business devoted to exploitation with tighter control and careful planning but create separate units or temporary, perhaps project-based, teams for exploration (see Section 14.2.5). These exploratory units will be smaller in size, less tightly controlled with much more emphasis on learning and processes to encourage new ideas. As in Illustration 14.2, Alphabet thus restructured in 2015 to place its large and mature search and advertising businesses in the Google subsidiary, while keeping its more exploratory activities apart in the separate Ventures and X subsidiaries.

- *Diversity rather than conformity.* Maintaining a diversity of views within the organisation can help promote ambidexterity, in line with the concept of *organisational learning* (see Section 13.3.1). Such diversity might be based on managers with different experience or different views on future strategy, giving rise to useful debate. Such contesting of strategy may come to be 'normal' at senior levels in an organisation.[16] Stanford University's Robert Burgelman[17] also argues that diverse views can be found close to the market and therefore perhaps at junior levels in an organisation; senior executives need to channel this market or junior-level 'dissonance' into a 'searing intellectual debate' until a clearer strategic pattern emerges.

- *The role of leadership.* In turn this has implications for leadership roles in organisations. Leaders need to encourage and value different views and potentially contradictory behaviours rather than demanding uniformity.[18] This may mean running with new ideas and experiments to establish just what makes sense and what does not. However, they also need to have the authority, legitimacy and recognition to stop such experiments when it becomes clear that they are not worthwhile pursuing and make decisions about the direction that is to be followed, which, once taken, are followed by everyone in the organisation – including those who have previously dissented.

- *Tight and loose systems.* All this suggests that there needs to be a balance between 'tight' systems of strategy development that can exploit existing capabilities – perhaps employing the disciplines of strategic planning – and 'looser' systems that encourage new ideas and experimentation. This combination of loose and tight systems can be given coherence so long as there is some overall common 'glue', perhaps in the form of an organisational mission or vision that allows different units to express the organisation's overall purpose in different ways.

Identifying the type of strategic change in hand will assist in selecting the detailed levers for change to be considered in Section 7.5. Meanwhile, following the logic of situational leadership, it should be noted that appropriate leadership styles are likely to vary according to the types of change being sought. Urgent and limited change – especially the kind of reconstruction associated with turnaround – tend to require a more transactional approach, focused on short-term targets and tight monitoring of performance. Transformational leadership styles are usually more important in broad and longer-term change programmes, for instance evolutionary change.

However, one challenge for leaders is that often one type of change leads to another type of change, requiring different leadership styles. Sometimes this shift between types of change can be managed in stages. For example, short-term turnaround can set the stage for sustained evolutionary change, obliging leaders to transition from a transactional style to a more transformational style. Sometimes, small-scale changes can actually destabilise organisations, leading to larger-scale changes whether or not originally planned or required. It is because changes are not necessarily discrete stand-alone alternatives that Balogun and Hope-Hailey refer to types of change as 'paths', underlining how changes of one kind are liable to lead to more changes of a different kind.[19]

7.5 LEVERS FOR STRATEGIC CHANGE

Having identified both the type of change required and the receptiveness of the context, change leaders must choose between the various levers (or means) for change. Most successful change initiatives rely on multiple levers.[20]

Sometimes these levers are presented as a sequence, as for example in Harvard Business School professor John Kotter's Eight Steps for Change (Figure 7.5).[21] Here the process of change is described as a series of steps, starting from establishing a sense of urgency in the organisation, leading eventually to the institutionalisation of change. These steps provide leaders with a clear progression in the managing of change. However, in practice, many of these levers are likely to be used simultaneously rather than in the kind of logical sequence in Figure 7.5. There are also other levers that can be drawn upon. Some levers for change have already been discussed elsewhere in the text. The importance of strategic vision (a major feature of Figure 7.5) was discussed in Section 6.2 together with the importance of other goals and objectives. The consolidating and institutionalising of change involves the kinds of adjustments of organisational structures and systems described in Chapter 14. This section focuses on seven further levers of change.

7.5.1 A compelling case for change

A starting point must be presenting a convincing case for change. This equates to Kotter's first step, establishing a sense of urgency. However, McKinsey & Co, the consultants,[22] warn that too often the case for change is made in terms of top management's perception of what is important: for example, meeting expectations of shareholders or beating competition. When most managers and employees are asked, however, there are many more factors that motivate them: for example, the impact on society, on customers, on the local working team, or on employees' personal well-being. In making the case for change, transformational leaders especially need to speak to these different bases of motivation, not just to top management perceptions of why change is needed. It may, of course, be difficult for top management

Figure 7.5 Kotter's Eight Steps for Change
Source: J. Kotter, 'Leading change: why transformation efforts fail', *Harvard Business Review*, March–April 1996, p. 61.

to understand and relate to these different needs. In this case, it may make sense to involve employees, themselves, in the creation of stories of change that, in effect, 'translate' corporate imperatives of change into local motivating messages. It is also important that the case for change does not just focus on the understanding of why change is needed, but the action required to deliver it.

7.5.2 Challenging the taken for granted

Often another early key step in managing strategic change is challenging what can be long-standing mindsets or taken-for-granted assumptions – the organisational paradigm, in the terms of Chapter 6. There are different approaches to challenging the paradigm. One view is that gathering enough objective evidence, perhaps in the form of careful strategic analysis, will be enough to challenge and therefore change the paradigm. However, assumptions can be very resistant to change: people find ways of questioning, reconfiguring and reinterpreting objective analyses in order to bring it in line with the existing paradigm. It may take much persistence to overcome this. Another view is that encouraging people to question and challenge each other's assumptions and received wisdom by making them explicit is valuable.[23] Scenario planning (see Section 2.4) is similarly advocated as a way of overcoming individual biases and cultural assumptions by getting people to see possible different futures and the implications for their organisations. There is also research that shows that successful firms able to enact significant strategic changes while also maintaining high levels of performance have questioning and 'contestation' embedded within their cultures: this, for example, has been the case for the French cosmetics firm L'Oréal, where they actually have a presentation theatre called the 'contestation room' (*salle de contestation*).[24]

7.5.3 Changing operational processes and routines

Another lever for strategic change is to start at the bottom, with the basic day-to-day processes and routines of the organisation's operations. These processes and routines might be formalised and codified or they might be less formal 'ways we do things around here'. The ways in which colleagues simply communicate with each other, or interact with customers, or respond to mistakes can all be serious blockages to change. The relationship between strategic change and day-to-day processes and routines is therefore important to consider in at least three respects:

- *Planning operational change.* The planning of the implementation of an intended strategy requires the identification of the key changes in the routines required to deliver that strategy. In effect, strategic change needs to be considered in terms of the re-engineering of organisational processes.
- *Challenging operational assumptions.* Changing organisational processes and routines may also have the effect of challenging the often taken-for-granted assumptions underpinning them. In turn this may have the effect of getting people to question and challenge deep-rooted beliefs and assumptions in the organisation. Richard Pascale argues: 'It is easier to act your way into a better way of thinking than to think your way into a better way of acting';[25] in other words, it is easier to change behaviour and by so doing change taken-for-granted assumptions than to try to change taken-for-granted assumptions as a way of changing behaviour. If this is so, the style of change employed (see Section 7.2.2 above) needs to take this into account: it suggests that attempting to persuade people to change may be less powerful than involving people in the activities of changing.

- *Bottom-up changes to routines.* Even when changes in routines are not planned from the top, people do change them and this may result in wider strategic change. This may occur through trial and error learning as people experiment with different routines associated with doing their jobs.[26] Or it could occur as people learn from and adapt the routines in other organisations.[27] Or it may occur more proactively by managers deliberately and persistently 'bending the rules of the game' till they achieve enough support from different stakeholders such that new routines supporting a shift in strategy become acceptable.[28]

The overall lesson is that changes in routines may appear to be mundane, but they can have significant impact.

7.5.4 Symbolic management[29]

Change levers are not always of an overt, formal nature: they may also be symbolic in nature. Symbols may be everyday things which are nevertheless especially meaningful in the context of a particular situation or organisation. Changing symbols can help reshape beliefs and expectations because meaning becomes apparent in the day-to-day experiences people have of organisations, such as the symbols that surround them (e.g. office layout and décor), the type of language and technology used and organisational rituals. Consider some examples:

- Many *rituals*[30] of organisations are concerned with effecting or consolidating change. Table 7.2 identifies and gives examples of such rituals and suggests what role they might play in change processes. New rituals can be introduced or old rituals done away with as ways of signalling or reinforcing change.

- Changes in *physical aspects* of the work environment are powerful symbols of change. Typical here is a change of location for the head office, relocation of personnel, changes in dress or uniforms, and alterations to offices or office space.

- The *behaviour of managers,* particularly strategic leaders, is perhaps the most powerful symbol in relation to change. So, having made pronouncements about the need for change, it is vital that the visible behaviour of change agents be in line with such change.

- The *language* used by change agents is also important.[31] Either consciously or unconsciously language and metaphor may be employed to galvanise change. Of course, there

Table 7.2 Organisational rituals and change

Types of ritual	Role	Examples in change initiatives
Rites of passage	Signify a change of status or role	Induction to new roles Training programmes
Rites of enhancement	Recognise effort benefiting organisation	Awards ceremonies Promotions
Rites of renewal	Reassure that something is being done Focus attention on issues	Appointment of consultant Project teams and workshops
Rites of integration	Encourage shared commitment Reassert rightness of norms	Celebrations of achievement or new ways of doing things
Rites of conflict reduction	Reduce conflict and aggression	Negotiating committees
Rites of challenge	'Throwing down the gauntlet'	New CEO setting challenging goals

is also the danger that strategic leaders do not realise the significance of their language and, while espousing change, use language that signals adherence to the status quo, or personal reluctance to change.

However, there is an important qualification to the idea that the manipulation of symbols can be a useful lever for managing change. The significance and meaning of symbols are dependent on how they are interpreted. Since they may not be interpreted as intended, their impact is difficult to predict.

7.5.5 Power and political systems

Section 5.2.2 explained the importance of understanding the political context in and around an organisation. Strategic change particularly can be a political process. Illustration 7.4 also gives examples of political processes. To effect change, powerful support may be required from individuals or groups or a reconfiguration of *power structures* may be necessary, especially if transformational change is required. This is equivalent to Kotter's second step in the change process (Figure 7.5), forming a powerful guiding coalition. Table 7.3 shows some of the mechanisms associated with managing change from a political perspective:[32]

- *Controlling or acquiring resources,* being identified with important resource areas or areas of expertise. Such resources might include for example funds, information, key organisational processes or key people. In particular the ability to withdraw or allocate such resources can be a powerful tool in overcoming resistance, persuading others to accept change or build readiness for change.

- *Association with powerful stakeholder groups* (or *elites*), or their supporters, can help build a power base or help overcome resistance to change. Or a manager facing resistance to change may seek out and win over someone highly respected from within the very group resistant to change. It may also be necessary to *remove individuals or groups* resistant to change. Who these are can vary – from powerful individuals in senior positions to whole layers of resistance, perhaps executives in a threatened function or service.

- *Building alliances* and *networks* of contacts and sympathisers may be important in overcoming the resistance of more powerful groups. Attempting to convert the whole organisation to an acceptance of change is difficult. There may, however, be parts of the organisation, or individuals, more sympathetic to change than others with whom support for change can be built. Marginalisation of those resistant to change may also be possible. However, the danger is that powerful groups in the organisation may regard the building of support coalitions, or acts of marginalisation, as a threat to their own power, leading to further resistance to change. An analysis of power and interest using the stakeholder mapping (Section 5.2.2) can, therefore, be useful to identify bases of alliance and likely resistance.

Cynthia Hardy of the University of Melbourne[33] also points out that change leaders may gain power through 'meaning power' by which she means the ability to use symbols, rituals and language to legitimise change, make change appear desirable, inevitable or help build excitement or optimism about change (see Section 7.5.4).

However, the political aspects of change management are potentially hazardous. Table 7.3 also summarises some of the problems. In overcoming resistance, the major problem may simply be the lack of power to undertake such activity. Trying to break down the status quo may become so destructive and take so long that the organisation cannot recover from it. If the process needs to take place, its replacement by some new set of beliefs and the implementation of a new strategy is vital and needs to be speedy. Further, as already identified, in

ILLUSTRATION 7.4   Change levers in action

Emotional change

Karen Addington, 2015 UK Charity Leader of the Year, remembered her third board meeting as CEO of a leading children's diabetes research charity: 'I went into the meeting all fired up to put across a clear business case and persuade the board to invest significant amounts of money in fundraising. But I suddenly realised that I had to manage people's emotional responses as well as their business responses, because at the time the board were all parents of children with diabetes. . . . I was asking them to take money from research in the short term to invest in our mission in the long term. Logically it made sense, but of course our donors hope that the next penny is the one that finds the cure for their children. I realised that it was a huge leap of faith for our trustees and learnt that I must always link the business case back to the impact that it could have on our beneficiaries – their children.'[1]

Not wasting crisis

When Mary Barra became CEO of General Motors at the beginning of 2014, she was immediately confronted by a scandal over faulty switches that, over 12 years, had caused 13 deaths. The company had avoided taking responsibility for all that time, symptomatic of an evasive corporate culture. Barra declared: 'I don't want to set it [the scandal] aside and explain it away, because . . . it uncovered some things in the company that it's critical we challenge . . . ' She continued: 'We didn't have to work too hard to make the case for change because clearly it was deeply troubling. Anytime you want to drive change, you have to have a catalyst . . . and it [the scandal] did provide that. I will also tell you it's made me more impatient.'[2]

Force for change

In November 2015, Ash Carter became new Defense Secretary, determined to reform the Pentagon's personnel systems to create a twenty-first century 'Force for the Future'. Rather than tackling the heated topic of the military's promotion system, he declared his priority to be the 'low hanging fruit'. He approved for immediate action 20 out of the 80 proposals on his desk. Carter said of his plans for change: 'Throughout this process, we've always been mindful that the military is a profession of arms. It's not a business. The key to doing this successfully is to leverage both tradition and change.'[3]

My way or the highway

Since 2013, CEO Tony Hsieh has been trying to reduce management and increase self-organisation at his online retailer, Zappos. Frustrated by slow progress, in 2015 he declared it was time to 'rip the bandaid'. In an internal memo, he told staff to back change or quit: '. . . self-management and self-organization is not for everyone . . . Therefore, there will be a special version of "the offer" on a company-wide scale, in which each employee will be offered at least 3 months' severance . . . if he/she feels that self-management [and] self-organization . . . are not the right fit.'[4]

Designer in Chief

In 2015, Zhang Ruimin, CEO of the giant electricals company Haier, launched a radical decentralization of power in his company. With Haier now a mass of 'micro-enterprises', Zhang would have a reduced role. He commented: 'If one day companies no longer exist, CEOs will also disappear. But I believe organisations will still exist and there may be some role for a person to design the way organisations work and how they grow. Maybe my title can be changed to something like "designer for the organisation".'[5]

Sources: (1) *Third Sector*, 25 June 2015; (2) *Fortune*, 18 September 2014; (3) J. Garamone, 'Carter details force of the future initiatives', US Department of Defense, 18 November 2015; (4) *Quartz*, 26 March 2015; (5) *Financial Times*, 25 November 2015.

Questions

1 Identify the various change levers (Section 7.5) used by these five leaders.

2 Do you think that a diabetes charity or the US military have anything to teach business organisations about change?

Table 7.3 Political mechanisms in organisations

Activity areas	Mechanisms			Problems
	Resources	Elites	Building alliances	
Building the power base	Control of resources Acquisition of/identification with expertise Acquisition of additional resources	Sponsorship by an elite Association with an elite	Identification of change supporters Alliance building Team building	Time required for building Perceived duality of ideals Perceived as threat by existing elites
Overcoming resistance	Withdrawal of resources Use of 'counter-intelligence'	Breakdown or division of elites Association with change leader Association with respected outsider	Foster momentum for change Sponsorship/reward of change leaders	Striking from too low a power base Potentially destructive: need for rapid rebuilding
Achieving compliance	Giving resources	Removal of resistant elites Need for visible 'change hero'	Partial implementation and collaboration Implantation of 'disciples' Support for 'young Turks'	Converting the body of the organisation Slipping back

implementing change, gaining the commitment of a few senior executives at the top of an organisation is one thing; it is quite another to convert the body of the organisation to an acceptance of significant change.

7.5.6 Timing

How much time is available for strategic change has already been considered as part of the change kaleidoscope (Section 7.3). However, choosing the precise time at which to launch strategic change is another variable. The timing of change is often neglected. Choosing the right time can be tactically vital. For example:

- *Building on actual or perceived crisis* is especially useful the greater the degree of change needed. If there is a higher perceived risk in maintaining the status quo than in changing it, people are more likely to change. Change leaders may take advantages of performance downturns, competitive threats or threatened takeover as catalysts for strategic change.

- *Windows of opportunity* in change processes may exist. The arrival of a new chief executive, the introduction of a new, highly successful product, or the arrival of a major competitive threat on the scene may provide opportunities to make more significant changes than might normally be possible. Since change will be regarded nervously, it may also be important to choose the time for promoting such change to avoid unnecessary fear and nervousness. For example, if there is a need for the removal of executives, this may be best done before rather than during the change programme. In such a way, the change programme can be seen as a potential improvement for the future rather than as the cause of such losses.

- *The symbolic signalling of time frames* may be important. In particular, conflicting messages about the timing of change should be avoided. For example, if rapid change is required, the maintenance of procedures or focus on issues that signal long time horizons may be counter-productive.

7.5.7 Visible short-term wins

A strategic change programme will require many detailed actions and tasks. It is important that some are seen to be successful quickly. In Kotter's model of change (Figure 7.5), creating short-term wins is the sixth step. Identifying some 'low-hanging fruit' – changes that may not be big but can be made easily and yield a quick payoff – can be useful. This could take the form, for example, of a retail chain introducing a new product range and demonstrating its success in the market or the breaking down of a long-established routine and the demonstration of a better way of doing things. In themselves, these may not be especially significant aspects of a new strategy, but they may be visible indicators of a new approach associated with that strategy. The demonstration of such wins can therefore galvanise commitment to the wider strategy.

One reason given for the inability to change is that resources are not available to do so. This may be overcome if it is possible to identify '*hot spots*' on which to focus resources and effort. For example, William Bratton, famously responsible for the 'zero tolerance' policy of the New York Police Department, began by focusing resource and effort on narcotics-related crimes. Though associated with 50–70 per cent of all crimes, he found they only had five per cent of the resources allocated by NYPD to tackle them. Success in this field led to the roll-out of his policies into other areas and to gaining the resources to do so.

In sum, there are many kinds of change lever available. Which levers are most appropriate depends on the type of change being sought and the context in which it is being carried out. Similarly, leadership style needs to be consistent. For example, political approaches are associated with a more transactional leadership style and are more likely to work in unreceptive contexts seeking limited types of change. On the other hand, symbolic management and transformational leadership styles are particularly important when seeking evolutionary or revolutionary change in receptive contexts.

7.6 PROBLEMS OF FORMAL CHANGE PROGRAMMES

Strategic change is often launched as a top-down initiative supported by formal methods of programme and project management. Kotter's Eight Steps for Change (Figure 7.5), with its clear and logical sequence, can lend itself to this kind of formal, top-down approach. However, there are two kinds of potential problem with this formal programmatic approach. First, problems can arise from the process itself. Second, managers may mistake the relative importance of formal and informal change.

7.6.1 Problems in the process

In designing change programmes, it is useful to know in advance common reasons for failure. Researchers identify seven factors that can go wrong in formal change processes, as follows:[34]

- *Death by planning*. The emphasis is put on planning the change programme rather than delivering it. There is a continuous stream of proposals and reports, each one requiring agreement among managers affected by the changes. Subcommittees, project teams and working groups may be set up to examine problems and achieve buy-in. The result can be 'analysis paralysis' and a discourse about change rather than the delivery of change. This may also be linked to the politicisation of the change programme where meetings about change become forums for debate and political game-playing.

- *Loss of focus*. Change is often not a one-off process; it might require an ongoing series of initiatives, maybe over years. However, the risk is that these initiatives are seen by employees as 'change rituals' signifying very little. There is also the risk that the original intention of the change programme becomes eroded by other events taking place: for example, a redundancy programme.

- *Reinterpretation.* The attempted change becomes reinterpreted according to the old culture. For example, an engineering company's intended strategy of achieving differentiation by building on what customers valued was interpreted by the engineers within the firm as providing high levels of technical specification as determined by them, not by the customers.

- *Disconnectedness.* People affected by change may not see the change programme connecting to their reality. Senior executives, as proponents of the change, might not be seen to be credible in terms of understanding the realities of change on the ground. Or perhaps new systems and initiatives introduced are seen as out of line with the aims of the intended change.

- *Behavioural compliance.* There is the danger that people comply with the changes being pursued in the change programme without actually 'buying into' them. Change leaders see specified changes in behaviour, but this is merely superficial compliance. This is like following the letter of the law, rather than its spirit. Because employees do not believe in the behaviours, the result is cynicism and rigid compliance to the rules even when circumstances do not precisely call for them.

- *Misreading scrutiny and resistance.* Change leaders are likely to face either resistance to the change or critical scrutiny of it. Often their response is to see such behaviour as negative and destructive. However, scrutiny and resistance can be seen as ways in which 'change recipients' in the organisation engage with what the changes mean for them. Even if resistance occurs, this is a way of keeping the agenda for change on the table. Moreover, resistance that is explicit is more capable of being addressed than that which is passive or covert. So managers should see scrutiny and resistance as potential positives rather than only negatives. Scrutiny and resistance can be the basis for engaging recipients in the change programme.

- *Broken agreements and violation of trust.* The need for a clear message about the need for and direction of change has been emphasised in this chapter. However, if senior management fail to provide honest assessments of the situation or provide undertakings to employees on which they subsequently renege, then they will lose the trust and respect of employees and, very likely, ensure heightened resistance to change.

7.6.2 What formal programmes forget

Not only can formal change programmes fail, but they often forget what else is going on in the organisation. According to Hari Tsoukas and Robert Chia, from the Universities of Warwick and Glasgow, respectively, a lot of change happens regardless of formal programmes.[35] They argue that change is an inherent property of organisations, as employees continually adapt and learn in response to changing conditions on the ground. Managers are liable not to recognise this inherent, unmanaged change. Indeed, hierarchy and management control often dampen such change. Thus managers underestimate spontaneous, emergent change, while overestimating formal change programmes.

The implication is that top-down planned change programmes can actually get in the way of the local adaptations that employees are always making anyway, and that can be more effective because they are closer to market needs. It is important to remember that strategic change can bubble up from the bottom of the organisation. In this view, management's job is to encourage and multiply successful local adaptations, not just impose strategic change from the top.

THINKING DIFFERENTLY | Women as leaders

Do women lead differently – and better – than men?

Traditionally men have been associated with leadership: think of Winston Churchill or Nelson Mandela. Men too tend still to dominate leadership roles in important spheres from politics to business: in 2015, women still held less than five per cent of CEO roles in the Fortune 500 list of largest American corporations. The implication might seem to be that if women aspire to leadership positions, they should act more like men.

However, increasingly women are taking CEO positions in large corporations across a wide range of industries: for example, Mary Barra at General Motors, Indra Nooyi at PepsiCo, Ginni Rometty at IBM and Cheryl Sandberg at Facebook. Such women leaders do not by any means necessarily lead like men. And their companies tend to perform better than those led by men: over the period 2002–14, leading American companies with women CEOs outperformed those with male CEOs by more than 200 per cent.[36]

Indeed, research suggests that women leaders do lead differently. Women are associated with transformational leadership styles, concerned with collective achievement and energising people, rather than transactional styles, more concerned with structures, systems and incentives (see Section 7.2.2).[37] Moreover, it is often argued that contemporary business, reliant on cooperation between knowledge-workers, demands more transformational leadership styles. Transactional styles do not fit organisations where trust and creativity are important. However, the research also finds very substantial overlaps between male and female leadership styles. Many male leaders display the same traits as women leaders.

Question

Consider two female leaders, in any sphere whether business, politics, education, sport or the arts. How similar are they in style and in what ways is gender important to their style? Could you imagine men leading similarly?

SUMMARY

A recurrent theme in this chapter has been that styles and levers of change need to be tailored to the nature of that change. Bearing in mind this general point, this chapter has emphasised the following:

- There are two main types of leadership style, *transactional* and *transformational*.
- *Situational leadership* suggests that leaders need to adapt their *styles* according to different types and contexts of change.
- The *types of strategic change* can be thought of in terms of the *extent* of change required and its *urgency* – whether it can be achieved through incremental change or requires immediate action (the 'big bang' approach).
- The context for change can be analysed in terms of the *change kaleidoscope* and *forcefield analysis*.
- *Levers* for managing strategic change include building a compelling case for change, challenging the taken for granted, changing operational processes, routines and symbols, political processes, timing and quick wins.

WORK ASSIGNMENTS

✳ Denotes more advanced work assignments.
* Refers to a case study in the Text and Cases edition.

7.1   Compare and contrast the different styles of leading change you have read about in the press or in this text (e.g. Sergio Marchionne at Fiat and Chrysler and Steve Jobs and Tim Cook at Apple*).

7.2   Drawing on Section 7.2.2, assess the key contextual dimensions of an organisation (such as Barclays in Chapter 6) and consider how they should influence the design of a programme of strategic change.

7.3   Use a forcefield analysis to identify blockages and facilitators of change for an organisation (such as one for which you have considered the need for a change in strategic direction in a previous assignment). Identify what aspects of the changes suggested by this analysis can be managed as part of a change programme and how.

7.4✳ In the context of leading strategic change in a large corporation or public-sector organisation, to what extent, and why, do you agree with Richard Pascale's argument that it is easier to act ourselves into a better way of thinking than it is to think ourselves into a better way of acting?

7.5✳ There are a number of books by (or about) renowned senior executives who have led major changes in their organisation (for example, Karren Brady, Alex Ferguson, Elon Musk). Read one of these and note the levers and mechanisms for change they employed, using the approaches outlined in this chapter as a checklist. How effective do you think these were in the context that the change leader faced, and could other mechanisms have been used?

Integrative assignment

7.6✳ What would be the key issues for the corporate parent of a diversified organisation with a multi-domestic international strategy (see Chapter 9) wishing to change to a more related portfolio? Consider this in terms of (a) the strategic capabilities that the parent might require (Chapters 4 and 8), (b) the implications for organising and controlling its subsidiaries (Chapter 14), (c) the likely blockages to such change and (d) how these might be overcome (Chapter 15).

RECOMMENDED KEY READINGS

- For a succinct summary of research on effective leadership, including the leadership of change, see G. Yukl, 'Effective leadership behaviour: what we know and what questions need more attention', *Academy of Management Perspectives,* vol. 26, no. 4 (2012), pp. 66–85.

- J. Balogun and V. Hope-Hailey, *Exploring Strategic Change,* Prentice Hall, 4th edn, 2016, builds on and extends many of the ideas in this chapter. In particular, it emphasises the importance of tailoring change programmes to organisational context and discusses more fully many of the change levers reviewed in this chapter.

- For an understanding of different approaches to leading change, see M. Beer and N. Nohria, 'Cracking the code of change', *Harvard Business Review,* vol. 78, no. 3 (May–June 2000), pp. 133–41. For an understanding of organisational ambidexterity, see G. Johnson, G. Yip and M. Hensmans, 'Achieving successful strategic transformation', *MIT Sloan Management Review,* vol. 53, no. 3 (2012), pp. 25–32.

REFERENCES

1. This definition of leadership is based on the classic by R.M. Stodgill, 'Leadership, membership and organization', *Psychological Bulletin*, vol. 47 (1950), pp. 1–14. Recent reviews of the leadership literature include G. Yukl, 'Effective leadership behavior: What we know and what questions need more attention', *Academy of Management Perspectives*, vol. 26, no. 4 (2012), pp. 66–85; and Jessica E. Dinh, Robert G. Lord, William L. Gardner, Jeremy D. Meuser, Robert C. Liden and Jinyu Hu, 'Leadership theory and research in the new millennium: current theoretical trends and changing perspectives', *Leadership Quarterly*, vol. 25, no. 1 (2014), pp. 36–62.

2. J. Kotter, 'What leaders really do', *Harvard Business Review*, December 2001, pp. 85–96.

3. See D. Ulrich, N. Smallwood and K. Sweetman, *Leadership Code: the five things great leaders do*, Harvard Business School Press, 1999.

4. See S. Floyd and W. Wooldridge, *The Strategic Middle Manager: how to create and sustain competitive advantage*, Jossey-Bass, 1996.

5. See E. Mollick, 'People and process, suits and innovators: the role of individuals in firm performance', *Strategic Management Journal*, vol. 33, no. 9 (2012), pp. 1001–15.

6. See for example J. Balogun and G. Johnson, 'Organizational restructuring and middle manager sensemaking', *Academy of Management Journal*, August 2004, pp. 523–49; and J. Sillence and F. Mueller, 'Switching strategic perspective: the reframing of accounts of responsibility', *Organization Studies*, vol. 28, no. 2 (2007), pp. 155–76.

7. J.A. Raelin, 'Imagine there are no leaders: reframing leadership as collaborative agency', *Leadership* (2014) DOI 1742715014558076.

8. See T.A. Judge and R.F. Piccolo, 'Transformational and transactional leadership: a meta analytic test of their relative validity', *Journal of Applied Psychology*, vol. 89 (2004), pp. 755–68.

9. For this evidence, see D.A. Waldman, G.G. Ramirez, R.J. House and P. Puranam, 'Does leadership matter? CEO leadership attributes and profitability under conditions of perceived environmental uncertainty', *Academy of Management Journal*, vol. 44, no. 1 (2001), pp. 134–43.

10. The discussion on different approaches of strategic leaders and evidence for the effectiveness of the adoption of different approaches can be found in D. Goleman, 'Leadership that gets results', *Harvard Business Review*, vol. 78, no. 2 (March–April 2000), pp. 78–90; and C.M. Farkas and S. Wetlaufer, 'The ways chief executive officers lead', *Harvard Business Review*, vol. 74, no. 3 (May–June 1996), pp. 110–12.

11. For an interesting example of how different contexts affect receptivity to change, see J. Newton, J. Graham, K. McLoughlin and A. Moore, 'Receptivity to change in a general medical practice', *British Journal of Management*, vol. 14, no. 2 (2003), pp. 143–53. And for a discussion of the problems of importing change programmes from the private sector to the public sector, see F. Ostroff, 'Change management in government', *Harvard Business Review*, vol. 84, no. 5 (May 2006), pp. 141–7.

12. This part of the chapter draws on Chapter 3 of *Exploring Strategic Change* by J. Balogun and V. Hope-Hailey, 3rd edn, Prentice Hall, 2008.

13. Turnaround strategy is extensively explained in D. Lovett and S. Slatter, *Corporate Turnaround*, Penguin Books, 1999; and P. Grinyer, D. Mayes and P. McKiernan, 'The sharpbenders: achieving a sustained improvement in performance', *Long Range Planning*, vol. 23, no. 1 (1990), pp. 116–25. Also see V.L. Barker and I.M. Duhaime, 'Strategic change in the turnaround process: theory and empirical evidence', *Strategic Management Journal*, vol. 18, no. 1 (1997), pp. 13–38.

14. See J. Battilana and T. Casciaro, 'Change agents, networks and institutions: a contingency theory of organizational change', *Academy of Management Journal*, vol. 35, no. 2 (2012), pp. 381–98.

15. See W.K. Smith and M. Tushman, 'Senior teams and managing contradictions: on the team dynamics of managing exploitation and exploration', *Organization Science*, vol. 16, no. 5 (2005), pp. 522–36. See also M.L. Tushman and C.A. O'Reilly, 'Ambidextrous organizations: managing evolutionary and revolutionary change', *California Management Review*, vol. 38, no. 4 (1996), pp. 8–30.

16. M. Hensmans, G. Johnson and G. Yip, *Strategic Transformation: changing while winning*, Palgrave, 2013.

17. Robert Burgelman and Andrew Grove, 'Strategic dissonance', *California Management Review*, vol. 38, no. 2 (1996), pp. 8–28.

18. R.A. Burgelman and A.S. Grove, 'Let chaos reign, then rein in chaos – repeatedly: managing strategic dynamics for corporate longevity', *Strategic Management Journal*, vol. 28 (2007), pp. 965–79: also C.A. O'Reilly and M.L. Tushman, 'Organizational ambidexterity in action: how managers explore and exploit', *California Management Review*, vol. 53, no. 4 (2011), pp. 5–22.

19. *Exploring Strategic Change* by J. Balogun and V. Hope-Hailey, 3rd edn, Prentice Hall, 2008. For how incremental changes can tip into transformational change, see S. Girod and R. Whittington, 'Change escalation processes and complex adaptive systems: from incremental reconfigurations to discontinuous restructuring', *Organization Science*, vol. 26, no. 5 (2015), pp. 1520–35.

20. For a review of research that makes this point, see D. Buchanan, L. Fitzgerald, D. Ketley, R. Gallop, J.L. Jones, S.S. Lamont, A. Neath and E. Whitby, 'No going back: a review of the literature on sustaining organizational change', *International Journal of Management Reviews*, vol. 7, no. 3 (2005), pp. 189–205.

21. J. Kotter, 'Leading change: why transformation efforts fail', *Harvard Business Review*, March–April 1995, pp. 59–66.

22. See C. Aiken and S. Keller, 'The irrational side of change management', *McKinsey Quarterly*, no. 2 (2009), pp. 101–9.

23. For an example of this approach, see J.M. Mezias, P. Grinyer and W.D. Guth, 'Changing collective cognition: a process model for strategic change', *Long Range Planning*, vol. 34, no. 1 (2001), pp. 71–95. Also for a systematic approach to strategy making and change based on such surfacing, see

F. Ackermann and C. Eden with I. Brown, *The Practice of Making Strategy*, Sage, 2005.

24. See G. Johnson, G. Yip and M. Hensmans, 'Achieving successful strategic transformation', *MIT Sloan Management Review*, vol. 53, no. 3 (2012), pp. 25–32.

25. This quote is on page 135 of R. Pascale, M. Millemann and L. Gioja, 'Changing the way we change', *Harvard Business Review*, vol. 75, no. 6 (November–December 1997), pp. 126–39.

26. See C. Rerup and M.S. Feldman, 'Routines as a source of change in organizational schemata: the role of trial and error learning', *Academy of Management Journal*, vol. 54, no. 3 (2011), pp. 577–610.

27. See H. Bresman, 'Changing routines: a process model of vicarious group learning in pharmaceutical R&D', *Academy of Management Journal*, vol. 56, no. 1 (2013), pp. 35–61.

28. See G. Johnson, S. Smith and B. Codling, 'Institutional change and strategic agency: an empirical analysis of managers' experimentation with routines in strategic decision-making', in D. Golsorkhi, L. Rouleau, D. Seidl and E. Vaara (eds), *The Cambridge Handbook of Strategy as Practice*, Cambridge University Press, 2010.

29. For a fuller discussion of this theme, see J.M. Higgins and C. McCallaster, 'If you want strategic change don't forget your cultural artefacts', *Journal of Change Management*, vol. 4, no. 1 (2004), pp. 63–73.

30. For a discussion of the role of rituals in change, see D. Sims, S. Fineman and Y. Gabriel, *Organizing and Organizations: an Introduction*, Sage, 1993.

31. See C. Hardy, I. Palmer and N. Phillips, 'Discourse as a strategic resource', *Human Relations*, vol. 53, no. 9 (2000), p. 1231.

32. Table 7.3 is based on observations of the role of political activities in organisations by, in particular, H. Mintzberg, *Power in and around Organizations*, Prentice Hall, 1983; and J. Pfeffer, *Power in Organizations*, Pitman, 1981.

33. C. Hardy, 'Understanding power; bringing about strategic change', *British Journal of Management*, vol. 7, special issue (1996), pp. 3–16.

34. The observations and examples here are largely based on L.C. Harris and E. Ogbonna, 'The unintended consequences of culture interventions: a study of unexpected outcomes', *British Journal of Management*, vol. 13, no. 1 (2002), pp. 31–49; and J.D. Ford, L.W. Ford and A.D. Amelio, 'Resistance to change: the rest of the story', *Academy of Management Review*, vol. 23 (2008), pp. 362–77.

35. H. Tsoukas and R. Chia, 'On organizational becoming: rethinking organizational change', *Organisation Science*, vol. 13, no. 5 (2002), pp. 567–82.

36. *Fortune Magazine*, 'Women-led companies perform three times better than the S&P 500', 3 March 2015.

37. A. Eagly, 'Female leadership advantage and disadvantage: resolving the contradictions', *Psychology of Women Quarterly*, vol. 31 (2007), pp. 1–12; I. Cuadrado, C. García-Ael, and F. Molero, 'Gender-typing of leadership: evaluations of real and ideal managers', *Scandinavian Journal of Psychology*, vol. 56, no. 2 (2015), pp. 236–44.

CASE EXAMPLE

Sergio Marchionne – motor of change

In 2009, two of America's three largest automotive makers, General Motors and Chrysler, were bankrupt. General Motors was rescued by the US government, with loans and a substantial equity stake. Chrysler was rescued by an Italian company with a decidedly mixed reputation, Fiat. At the head of Fiat was Sergio Marchionne, an Italian–Canadian accountant with just four years' experience in the auto industry. Marchionne undertook radical change at Chrysler, but six years later ended up offering the company for sale to General Motors – and was rejected.

Nonetheless, Marchionne had transformed Chrysler through his energetic leadership style. He is famous for his constant smoking, his heavy consumption of espresso coffees and his informal dress sense, based on sweaters rather than traditional suits. At the same time, Marchionne is a notorious workaholic: no lower than 42 executives report directly to him, he carries six mobile phones, and he works 14–18 hour days, seven days a week. Regarding leadership, he explained to the *Harvard Business Review*: 'My job as CEO is not to make decisions about the business but to set stretch objectives and help our managers work out how to reach them.'[1]

Marchionne at Fiat

When Marchionne took over as CEO at Fiat in 2004, he was the fifth CEO since 2001. The company was unprofitable, the products had a reputation for poor quality, its most recent new car launch had been unsuccessful and relationships with the unions were poor.

At Fiat, Marchionne spent his first 50 days touring the business, listening to people and analysing the situation. He found that senior executives were unused to taking responsibility for decisions; everything was referred upwards to the CEO. Executives communicated with each other via their secretaries and spent their time fire-fighting or avoiding problems. The company was dominated by engineers, who would work on new models in isolation. They then passed on their finished designs to sales and marketing, complete with sales targets and price. As well as being inefficient, this procedure caused fierce tensions between departments.

Following initial measures to reduce Fiat's debt level, Marchionne turned his attention to the leadership of the

Sergio Marchionne, CEO Fiat Chrysler

Source: Bloxham/LAT/REX/Shutterstock.

business. Many senior executives were dismissed and 2000 other managers and staff were retired early. On the other hand, as he toured the company, he had identified young talented managers, often in areas such as marketing that were not the traditional routes to the top, or in geographic areas such as Latin America that were less influenced by head office and where managers tended to behave more autonomously. He drew on this 'talent spotting' to make 20 new leadership appointments as well as other promotions.

Marchionne took a close interest in high potential talent and regarded his personal engagement with them as more valuable than more formal assessment. He also believed that such personal engagement helped develop a top team with strongly held common values. His expectation of this new top cadre of leaders was that they should be given responsibility. He recognised that this was demanding:

'As I give people more responsibility, I also hold them more accountable. A leader who fails to meet an objective should suffer some consequences, but I don't believe that failing to meet an objective is the end of the world . . . (but) if you want to grow leaders, you can't let explanations and excuses become a way of life. That's a characteristic of the old Fiat we've left far behind.'[2]

To achieve greater integration and speed business up, Marchionne also took out several layers of management, eliminated committees and replaced them with a Group Executive Council that brought together executives from disparate operations such as tractors and trucks. To run Fiat Auto he also established a 24-person team with the aim of getting all parts of the company to talk to one another. To further encourage the sharing of ideas, he also began to move executives from one part of the business to another and required his top managers to accept multiple responsibilities for different parts of the business.

Marchionne saw one of his own major roles as the challenging of assumptions. He cites how he asked why it took Fiat four years to develop a new model. The question helped identify processes that could be removed, which meant that the new Cinquecento car was developed and launched in just 18 months in 2006. 'You start removing a few bottlenecks in this way, and pretty soon people catch on and begin ripping their own processes apart.'[3] Such challenging of assumptions and processes was also aided by recruiting managers from outside the car industry and by benchmarking, not just against other car makers but also companies like Apple. At the same time, Marchionne introduced 'World Class Manufacturing', the Japanese approach to lean production.

In 2004, Marchionne's new team had produced a business plan with a stretch target of €2bn (£1.6bn, $2.6bn) profits in 2007. Many thought the target unrealistic, but Marchionne believed that it forced managers to think differently and challenge old ways of doing things. By 2006, Fiat was profitable again. In 2007, Fiat made over €3bn profits. Soon it would be Chrysler's turn to experience Marchionne's leadership style.

Marchionne at Chrysler

By 2009, Chrysler was bankrupt, with potentially 300,000 jobs on the line. Supported by the US government, Fiat Group formed a strategic alliance with Chrysler, taking a 20 per cent ownership stake. Marchionne was appointed CEO, while retaining his role at Fiat. His vision was that Fiat and Chrysler together could create a leading global player in the automobile sector, exploiting synergies in terms of purchasing power, distribution capabilities and product portfolios – Chrysler's Jeeps, mini-vans and light trucks and Fiat's small cars and fuel-efficient engines.

When Marchionne took over at Chrysler in 2009, not only did he inherit a $6bn high-interest government loan, he also found a fearful workforce and a company riddled with bureaucracy. One of his first acts was to point out, in a memo to Chrysler employees, the parallels with Fiat: 'Five years ago, I stepped into a very similar situation at Fiat. It was perceived by many as a failing, lethargic

automaker that produced low-quality cars and was stymied by endless bureaucracy.'[4] Like Fiat, Chrysler was highly hierarchical with managers reluctant to take decisions: 'This place was run by a chairman's office . . . the top floor (known as the Tower). It's empty now . . . Nothing happens there. I'm on the floor here with all the engineers.'[5]

Again Marchionne changed the management. As well as bringing in three senior managers from Fiat, Marchionne identified 26 young leaders from two or three levels below top management and made them direct reports in a new flatter organisation structure. One brief for the new managers was to introduce the Japanese-style manufacturing processes that Fiat had already used in its Italian plants. Marchionne also emphasised cost control; for example, the 2009 plan identified savings of $2.9bn by 2014 by sharing parts and engines with Fiat. But there was also an emphasis on product development. Here he drew on the experience of his new executive team to focus on improvements to the product range:

> **'Everyone knew what was wrong with the cars. You ask any employee in the company, they could list ten things that they would do better. And when you're given the chance to do those ten things better, you end up with a product that exceeds the sum of its parts.'[5]**

Another key ambition was to improve product quality. Chrysler had been organised such that each brand had its own quality department. These separate departments were merged and new ways to measure quality introduced to provide greater oversight across all the brands. This attention to product and quality improvement went hand-in-hand with plant modernisation. The result was improved quality ratings for 16 models in 18 months.

An example of Marchionne's bold approach on the ground was the Ram pick-up truck business. In 2009, it had been languishing as part of the Dodge car division, with just 11 per cent share of the US pick-up market. While many expected him to merge brands to save costs, Marchionne made the Ram business a division on its own. A conference room in the basement of Chrysler's headquarters was turned into a 'Ram war room'. Mr Marchionne met monthly with the Ram executives for detailed updates on progress. The Ram division could now approach the market as a truck business rather than part of a car business, and introduced innovations such as fuel-efficient engines, luxury interiors and superior transmission systems that had been denied before. The new manufacturing methods gave a previously alienated workforce a voice in operating decisions. By 2014, Ram held 33 per cent market share.[6]

Ram's success was reproduced elsewhere. Already by 2011 Chrysler was able to announce an operating profit of $2bn (compared with a net loss of $652mn in 2010) and repay all government loans. Fiat increased its stake in Chrysler to 53.5 per cent and in September 2011, Marchionne became the company's Chairman as well as Chief Executive. Chrysler's share in the US automobile market rose from 8.8 per cent in 2009 to 12.2 per cent in 2014. In 2014, Fiat and Chrysler merged entirely to form a new corporation, FCA, headquartered in London and with Marchionne in overall control.

The last lap?

The creation of FCA was marked by the launch in May 2014 of a new five-year plan. Vehicle sales were due to rise from 4.4m in 2013 to 6.3m in 2018, building particularly on the internationalisation of production and marketing of the famous Jeep line of products. However, a stagnant European market was weighing heavily on FCA's performance, with losses at Fiat leading to the accumulation of €10bn debt. Profit margins even in the USA were low, at about four per cent, half those of rivals Ford and General Motors. In 2015, the influential J.D. Powers quality survey rated three FCA brands – Chrysler, Jeep and Fiat – amongst the worst five automotive brands for reliability.

Quality requires investment, and investment requires scale. The *Financial Times* pointed out that, even after the merger, the new FCA was still half the size of world leaders Volkswagen and Toyota.[7] Its US rivals General Motors and Ford were each roughly 50 per cent larger than FCA. Volkswagen was spending more than five times as much as FCA on research and development, and twice as much on capital investment. At the same time, car prices were falling and worrying new entrants such as Google and Tesla were emerging on the margins. In 2015, Marchionne approached General Motors for a merger. He was turned down. Rumour had it that perhaps a Far Eastern manufacturer would finally take over FCA.

References
1. Sergio Marchionne, 'Fiat's extreme makeover', *Harvard Business Review*, December 2008, p. 46.
2. *Harvard Business Review*, December 2008, p. 46.
3. *Harvard Business Review*, December 2008, p. 47.
4. Peter Gumbe, 'Chrysler's Sergio Marchionne: the turnaround artista', *Time Magazine*, 18 June 2009.
5. Resurrecting Chrysler, *60 minutes,* CBS; interview with Steve Kroft, 25 March 2012, http://www.youtube.com/watch?v=h3ppoyWNN7s.
6. *New York Times*, 18 September 2014.
7. *Financial Times*, 26 May 2015.

Questions

1 In relation to Section 7.3, what were the types of change pursued at Fiat and Chrysler? Were these appropriate to the change contexts?

2 How would you describe the leadership style of Sergio Marchionne? Was this appropriate to the change contexts?

3 What levers for change were employed by Sergio Marchionne? What others might have been used and why?

4 By what criteria would you assess the effectiveness of the change programmes at Fiat and Chrysler?

8

HISTORY AND CULTURE

Learning outcomes

After reading this chapter you should be able to:

- Analyse how *history* influences the strategic position of an organisation, especially via *path dependence.*

- Distinguish different kinds of cultures, *national-geographical, field-level* and *organisational.*

- Analyse the influence of an *organisation's culture* on its strategy using the *cultural web.*

- Identify organisations which may be experiencing the symptoms of *strategic drift.*

Key terms

cultural web

legitimacy

organisational culture

organisational identity

paradigm

path dependency

recipe

strategic drift

8.1 INTRODUCTION

The preceding chapters in this section of the book have considered various implications of position for strategy, including the influences of the environment, organisational capabilities and stakeholder expectations. This chapter considers two last important and interconnected aspects of position: organisational history and culture.

Many organisations have long histories. The large Japanese Mitsui Group was founded in the seventeenth century; automobile company Daimler was founded in the nineteenth century; the University of Bologna was founded in the eleventh century. But even newer organisations are marked by their histories: for instance, the airline and consumer group Virgin is still influenced by its hippy origins from the early 1970s (see Chapter 8 end case). Such histories become embedded in organisational cultures, shaping strategic options and decisions. Virgin's culture is very different to that of its rival airline British Airways, which had its origins as a state-owned airline in the 1940s. Sometimes an organisation's cultural heritage can give it a unique advantage, but sometimes it can be a significant barrier to change. Either way, if an organisation's strategy is to be understood, so must the history and culture that influenced it. This is the focus of this chapter, as summarised in Figure 8.1.

The chapter starts in Section 2.2 with history, examining its influence on organisational strategy and considering how that history can be analysed. History shapes culture, so Section 8.3 moves on to examine cultural aspects of organisations, in particular how cultural influences at geographical, institutional and organisational levels impact current and future strategy. This section also explores how a culture can be analysed and its influence on strategy understood. Section 8.4 explains the phenomenon of *strategic drift,* a frequent consequence of historical and cultural influences and hard for managers to correct. Finally, Thinking Differently introduces the conflicts and diversity introduced *institutional logics.*

Figure 8.1 The influence of history and culture

The theme of this chapter, then, is the significance of history and culture for strategy. A sense of history is important for environmental analysis, particularly understanding positions on economic cycles (Chapter 2) or industry life cycles (Chapter 3). History and culture are relevant to the capabilities of an organisation (Chapter 4), especially those that have built up over time in ways unique to that organisation. The power and influence of different stakeholders (Chapter 5) are also likely to have historical origins. An understanding of an organisation's history and culture also helps explain how strategies develop (Chapter 12) and informs the challenges of strategic change (Chapter 15).

8.2 WHY IS HISTORY IMPORTANT?

This section starts by introducing the concept of path dependency as one way of examining how history can shape organisations over time. It then brings out positive aspects of history, in terms of it being a managerial resource. The section concludes by describing several ways of analysing an organisation's history.

8.2.1 Path dependency

A useful way of thinking of the influence of history is the concept of **path dependency, where early events and decisions establish 'policy paths' that have lasting effects on subsequent events and decisions.**[1] This suggests that organisational strategies may be historically conditioned. Path dependency has been described as like the ruts made in a dirt track by the passing of vehicle wheels over time. These ruts become deeper and deeper as more and more vehicles go along. Once that happens, vehicles have no option but to continue along those ruts. Future direction is dependent on the paths laid down in the past.

Examples of path dependency often relate to technology. There are many instances where the technology we employ is better explained by path dependency than by deliberate optimisation. A famous example is the layout of keyboard characters in most English-speaking countries: QWERTY. This originated in the nineteenth century as a way of reducing the problem of the keys on mechanical typewriters getting tangled when sales people demonstrated the machine at maximum speed by typing the word 'typewriter'. There are more optimal layouts, but QWERTY has remained with us for over 150 years despite radical changes in keyboard technology with the development of computers, tablets and mobile phones.[2]

Path dependency is not only about technology. It also relates to any form of behaviour that has its origins in the past and becomes so entrenched that it becomes locked-in. '*Lock-in*' occurs where the infrastructure of an organisation (or even whole industry) is so strongly entrenched around a technology, product or service that the costs of switching from the established offering become prohibitive. Lock-in could begin with a decision which, of itself, may not appear especially significant, but which then has unforeseen and hard to reverse consequences. For example, airlines easily become 'locked-in' on particular aircraft types (e.g. Boeing), because once systems for crew-training and spare parts availability have become optimised for that particular aircraft type, it is extremely disruptive to start switching to another aircraft type (e.g. Airbus). Thus an initial, maybe chance, decision leads to the development of self-reinforcing mechanisms that lock-in on a particular path.

As Figure 8.2 shows, lock-in can be reinforced by a system of technologies, material objects (such as infrastructure or standardised forms), customers and suppliers in the value system, the day-to-day habits of managers, employees and users, formal and informal industry or professional standards, and the training systems that reproduce appropriate patterns of behaviour.[3] An example is the accounting business, where particular approaches are reinforced by

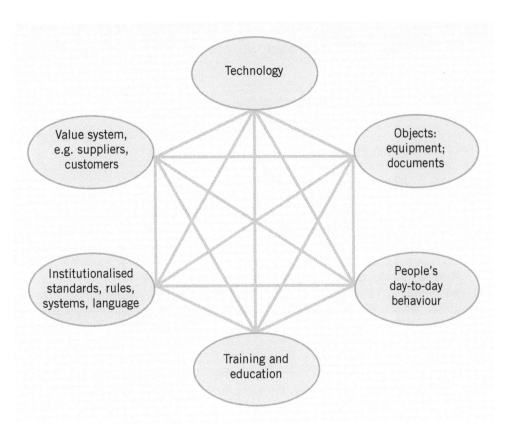

Figure 8.2 Path dependency and lock-in

technologies such as specialised software, by fixed-format forms such as capital expenditure proposals, by the ingrained expectations of customers, by the habits of accountants, by professional standards and by the training of successive generations of accounting practitioners. All these have developed over time and mutually reinforce each other. They also persist despite increasing numbers of experts, both in the accountancy profession and elsewhere, who point to fundamental weaknesses in such systems, not least the failure of accounting to provide measures for many of the factors that account for the market value of firms.[4]

Path dependency tends to reinforce the importance of three aspects of strategy:

- *Comprehensive change.* Because of the system of reinforcing elements, trying to change just one aspect without changing the others is likely to fall short. For an airline to switch from Boeing planes to Airbus planes without changing training and spare parts systems would be highly inefficient and dangerous.

- *Conservatism.* Because the reinforcing elements may make an otherwise maladapted approach work fairly well, it is often not worth the costs of changing everything to gain a small improvement in the performance of one particular element. In India, Japan and the UK roads retain left-hand drive, even though there might be cost advantages for automobile importers and exporters of standardising on the world's dominant right-hand drive approach.

- *Path creation.* Because initial decisions (such as starting with Boeing) can have longstanding repercussions, it is important for managers to recognise that what they choose to do at the start of an initiative or enterprise may lock them into a long-term path. Apple's original investment in graphics capabilities for its computers in the 1980s, and Microsoft's prioritisation of business users in the same period, still resonate in relative market positions three decades or so later.

ILLUSTRATION 8.1   Indian Railways and Empire

The history of an organisation can define culture and strategy.

India's first train journey in April 1853 took 75 minutes to travel 39km on a stretch of rail near Mumbai. More than a century and a half later, the journey still takes 57 minutes. But the Indian railway system has grown enormously since its origins. The network is 64,000km long, with 21,000 trains carrying about 23 million passengers and three million tonnes of freight per day.

The railway system originated under the British Empire (the Raj) and its dependent princely states. It gained impetus with the Indian Mutiny of 1857, when the British learnt the importance of rail for ferrying troops around their vast domain. The railway's restaurant wagons still reflect these origins in the British Empire, with 'Anglo-Indian' food such as omelettes, 'cutlets' and baked beans on the menu. Station baggage carriers are known as 'coolies', the derogatory name for the indentured labourers who served the Raj. Just as colonial officers would travel and stay in railway hotels for free, so too do contemporary politicians and their associates today.

Soon after independence, the various regional railway companies were brought together to form the state-owned Indian Railways in 1951. Socialist-style politics left an enduring mark on the new Indian Railways. Price rises for passengers were extremely rare, with freight used to subsidise transport for 'the common man'. Continuing policies that had been started to support privileged British staff under the Raj, Indian Railways developed a vast social system of employee housing, sports stadia, nursing homes and hospitals, with 2500 doctors by the second decade of this century. Many jobs were passed on almost by family inheritance. All was presided over by a Delhi headquarters (Bhavan) with 140 senior managers. There were 13 levels of hierarchy in every department. Bhavan jobs were sold illegally and many senior managers had never worked outside the Delhi headquarters building. It was said that it took approval from ten departments to change the soap in the first-class carriages.

Although there were pockets of excellence and innovation – for example, the Delhi metro – Indian Railways as a whole stagnated. Its share of passenger traffic declined from 74 per cent in 1951 to 12 per cent in 2011. Indian Railways' productivity trailed international peers: traffic units/employee was 0.84 for India, 1.4 for China and 15.1 for the USA. Bribes were necessary for seat reservations. There were 27,000 railway related deaths in 2014, many involving unguarded crossings and people falling off over-laden trains.

The problems of Indian Railways were well-recognised. A government report of 2015 noted with some irony that there had been 21 government inquiries into the railways since 1951: 'On the positive side, this large number illustrates the importance attached to the railways. On the negative side, repeated reports highlight the non-implementation of recommendations'.

Nonetheless, the government was determined to reform the railways. In 2014, the Chairman of the Railway Board declared: 'The need of the hour is to bring in a total change in the work culture and delivery of railway services by going in for large scale integrated computerisation of major functions of Indian Railways'. A new accounting system was introduced, which began for the first time to record outcomes as well as expenditures. Coolies would be given uniforms, trained in soft skills and renamed as 'sahayaks' ('helpers' in Hindi). Dozens of senior managers were moved out of the Delhi Bhavan. Deloitte Consulting was brought in to do comprehensive work studies. Private investors were allowed to operate services on Indian Railways track. After 16 years of price-freezes and years of financial losses, small price increases were approved.

Sources: Guardian, 30 December 2011; *Economic Times*, 8 July 2014; S. Debroy, 'Interim Report of the Committee for Mobilization of Resources for Major Railway Projects and Restructuring of Railway Ministry and Railway Board', Indian Government publication, 2015.

Questions

1 How would you sum up (i) the strategy (ii) the culture of Indian Railways in the early years of this century?

2 In what ways can you trace this strategy and culture to the Indian Railways' history?

Path dependency is a useful concept because it provides an explanation for why apparently inefficient historical patterns are allowed to continue: in the short term at least, it can be more costly to change than keep things the same. Sometimes though history continues to influence because of managerial inertia or self-interest. These too contribute to the phenomenon of 'strategic drift', as described in Section 8.4. Either way, the hand of history can be heavy. Illustration 8.1 illustrates the lingering influence on Indian Railways of events and strategies from the British Empire, nearly three quarters of a century after independence.

8.2.2 History as a resource

Although historical lock-in does create inflexibility, history can be a useful managerial resource as well. There are at least three ways that managers can use history:[5]

- *Learning from the past*. Understanding the current strategic position of an organisation in terms of the past can provide useful lessons. For example, have there been historical trends or cycles that may repeat themselves? The construction industry for instance has a regular pattern of boom and crisis. Managers in this industry should not expect that good times will continue forever. How have competitors responded to strategic moves in the past? Consumer good companies Unilever and Procter & Gamble have nearly a century's history of move and counter-move from which to learn. These companies' managers can examine past experience in order to predict their rival's likely response to any competitive move.

- *Building capabilities*. In the BMW museum in Munich there is a quote: 'Anyone who wants to design for the future has to leaf through the past.'[6] While the museum is about the history of BMW, it is also about how the lessons of the past can give rise to new ideas and innovation. Indeed the Innovation and Technology Division of BMW is sited next to the museum and the archives of BMW. Innovation may build on historic capabilities in at least two ways. First, as technologies change, firms with experience and skills built over time that are most appropriate to those changes tend to innovate more than those that do not.[7] Or it could be that there are new combinations of knowledge as capabilities built up in adjacent technologies are adapted in innovative ways to new technological opportunities. For example, successful firms in the creation of the TV industry were previously radio manufacturers. They were more effective innovators than the non-radio producers because of their historic capabilities in assembling small components and in mass distribution.[8]

- *Legitimising strategy and change*. History can be used as a resource to legitimise strategies or strategic change. For example, at technology enterprise Hewlett Packard, CEO Carly Fiorina legitimised her strategy by summarising it in terms of 'rules for the garage', referring to the company's famous origins in Dave Packard's garage.[9] Past successes effecting strategic change may also be used as evidence of the organisational potential in managing change and innovation or to encourage commitment to future changes. Thus Microsoft appealed to its earlier success in overcoming the challenge of the internet as it faced the threat of mobile computing.

8.2.3 Historical analysis

If history matters so much, how might managers undertake an historical strategic analysis of their own organisation or of their competitors? There are four ways this may be done:[10]

- *Chronological analysis*. This involves setting down a chronology of key events showing changes in the organisation's environment – especially its markets – how the organisation's strategy itself has changed and with what consequences – not least financial. Organisations will often provide a basic chronology on their websites, but crises and strategic reversals are likely to be underplayed on these, so further analysis using media and other sources will normally be useful.

- *Cyclical influences.* Is there evidence of cyclical influences? These include economic cycles, but perhaps also cycles of strategic activity, such as periods of high levels of mergers and acquisitions. Understanding when these cycles might occur and how industry and market forces can change during such cycles can inform decisions on whether to build strategy in line with those cycles or in a counter-cyclical fashion.

- *Key events and decisions.* History may be regarded as continuous, but historical events can also be significant for an organisation at particular points in time. These could be particularly significant events, in terms of either industry change or an organisation's strategic decisions: for example, Apple remembers the return of founder Steve Jobs in 1997, 12 years after he had previously been sacked. Or they might be policies laid down by a founder or defining periods of time that have come to be seen as especially important: for example, Alex Ferguson's successful years at Manchester United. Key events or decisions could, of course, be for the good: they may help provide a clear overall strategic direction that contributes to the sort of vision discussed in the previous chapter. They can, on the other hand, be a major barrier to challenging existing strategies or changing strategic direction. A famous example is Henry Ford's maxim 'You can have any colour provided it's black', which set a trajectory for mass production and low variety that inhibited the Ford company's response to the more varied cars eventually produced by General Motors and Chrysler in the 1930s.

- *Historical story-telling.* How do people tell their organisation's history? As above, many organisations will have parts of their websites dedicated to their histories, and some even commission business historians to write books on their histories.[11] The stories people tell can offer revealing clues about how the organisation sees its past, not least in terms of the origins of success. IKEA often tells the story of how flat-packed furniture began at the company when a worker of the company disassembled a table to fit inside of a car. And there may be implications in their stories for future strategy development. For IKEA, the story of flat-pack promotes practical improvisation in strategy. Does what people say suggest an organisation with historic capabilities relevant to current markets and customers? Is the organisation capable of innovation and change or so rooted in the glories of the past that it will be difficult to change?

History, then, is important in terms of how it influences current strategy, for better or for worse. History also feeds into organisational culture: history becomes 'encapsulated in culture'.[12] The next section goes on to explain what culture is and how it can be analysed.

8.3 WHAT IS CULTURE AND WHY IS IT IMPORTANT?

There are many ways to define culture, but typically definitions emphasise a set of taken-for-granted beliefs and values that are shared within a particular group. What individual managers believe in and value obviously influences their strategic decisions. Strategy is influenced by culture, therefore. However, because we all belong to many groups, these cultural influences can be very diverse. As in Figure 8.3, we shall analyse three kinds of cultural influences: geographical cultures, field cultures and organisational cultures and subcultures, all of which impinge on individual managers.

Figure 8.3 Cultural frames of reference

8.3.1 Geographically-based cultures

Many writers – perhaps the most well-known of whom is Geert Hofstede – have shown how attitudes to work, authority, equality and other important factors vary in different geographies, national or regional. Such differences have been shaped by powerful forces concerned with history, religion and even climate over many centuries. Hofstede traces cultural differences between the countries of southern and northern Europe to the boundaries of the Roman Empire 2000 years ago.[13]

According to Hofstede, there are at least four key dimensions upon which national cultures tend to differ:

- *Power distance,* referring to relationships with authority and acceptance of inequality. In Hofstede's studies, and those of his associates, many Asian countries are found to have high power distance, and therefore quite authoritarian management styles. Australia has a low power distance and therefore is more democratic in style.

- *Individualism–collectivism,* referring to the relationship between the individual and the group. According to Hofstede's research, some national cultures are highly individualistic, for example the USA. South American cultures are apparently more collectivist, valuing team approaches.

- *Long-term orientation,* referring to the extent to which people look to the future, something essential to strategy. Hofstede suggests that many Asian cultures tend to be long-term orientated. North American and African cultures are supposedly more short term.

- *Uncertainty avoidance,* referring to tolerance of uncertainty and ambiguity. According to Hofstede, Japan is associated with relatively high intolerance for uncertainty. Chinese culture appears more pragmatic and accepting of uncertainty.

Hofstede's research pioneered understanding about geographical variations in culture, but it has since been criticised for its generalisations about whole countries. After all, countries vary widely within themselves: consider the cultural differences between different regions in Nigeria, Southern and Northern Italy or the East and West Coasts of the USA.[14] Individuals too differ very widely within a particular geographical culture. It is important not to stereotype. Nevertheless, certain national or subnational cultural tendencies can be observed and Hofstede's four dimensions are valuable in alerting us to some of the ways in which people from different geographies may vary. When discussing strategic options in an international management team, it might be helpful to be aware that not everybody will be equally comfortable with *uncertainty,* heroic *individualism,* the use of *authority* to make final decisions, or projecting far out into the *long-term* future. For example, the joint venture between American tyre-maker Cooper and the Chinese tyre-maker Chengshan fell apart because of very different attitudes to acceptable levels of risk: the American partner, backed by billionaire hedge-fund investor John Paulson, was much more aggressive financially than the state-owned Chinese company.

8.3.2 Organisational fields[15]

As in Chapter 2, an organisational field is a community of organisations that interact more frequently with one another than with those outside the field and that have developed a shared culture. Fields can extend beyond the firms, customers and suppliers in particular industries; they can include relevant regulators, professional bodies, university researchers, specialist media and even campaign groups. An important characteristic of fields is that they involve not just economic transactions, but shared assumptions and beliefs about how the field works.

For example, in the organisational field of 'justice' there are many different types of organisation, such as law firms, police forces, courts, prisons and probation services. The roles of each are different, they all have their own specific organisational cultures and their detailed prescriptions as to how justice should be achieved differ. However, despite their differences, they are all committed to the principle that justice is a good thing which is worth striving for; they interact frequently on this issue; they have developed shared ways of understanding and debating issues that arise; and they operate a set of common routines helping them interact with each other. Similar cultural coherence is common in other organisational fields: for example, professional services such as accountancy and medicine or sectors such as software development or journalism.

Where such shared assumptions and beliefs are powerful, these organisational fields help set the institutional 'rules of the game' (Section 2.2.6) or 'institutional logics' (see final Thinking Differently). Fields influence the ways managers see their activities, define strategic options and decide what is appropriate. Three concepts are useful here:

- *Categorisation.* The ways in which members of an organisational field categorise (or label) themselves and their activities has significant implications for what they do.[16] To categorise a mobile phone as primarily a personal computer or a fashion-statement rather than a phone changes the whole strategy. Over time, members of an organisational field tend to converge on dominant categorisation schemes. For instance, the early car industry had competing categories of 'horseless carriage' and 'automobile'; in computing, there were competing categories of 'pen-computing' and 'tablets' to describe more or less the same thing. Converging on the categories of automobile and tablet helped define the respective industries' subsequent developments.

- *Recipes.* Because of their shared cultures, organisational fields tend to cohere around standard ways of doing things, or 'recipes'. A **recipe is a set of assumptions, norms and routines held in common within an organisational field about the appropriate purposes and strategies of field members.**[17] In effect, a recipe is the 'shared wisdom' about what works best. In English Premier league football, the standard approach is a 'talent-based recipe', where teams compete each year to hire the best players because they believe that individual talent is what delivers results. An alternative recipe, for instance of developing team spirit and skills over the long term as in Germany, is little contemplated in the English Premier league.

- *Legitimacy.* Where categories and recipes have become strongly institutionalised over time, they become the only legitimate way of seeing and behaving. **Legitimacy is concerned with meeting the expectations within an organisational field in terms of assumptions, behaviours and strategies.** By conforming to legitimate norms within the field, organisations secure approval, support and public endorsement, thus increasing their legitimacy. Stepping outside that strategy may be risky because important stakeholders (such as customers or bankers) may not see such a move as appropriate. Therefore, organisations tend to *mimic* each other's strategies. There may be differences in strategies between organisations, but those differences tend to be limited to the bounds of legitimacy.[18] Legitimacy helps explain why accounting firms and universities, for example, tend to follow similar strategies to each other, promote similar products and hire similar people.

8.3.3 Organisational culture

Edgar Schein defines organisational culture as the 'basic assumptions and beliefs that are shared by members of an organisation, that operate unconsciously and define in a basic taken-for-granted fashion an organisation's view of itself and its environment'.[19] Related to this are the taken-for-granted 'ways we do things around here'[20] that accumulate over time. So **organisational culture is the taken-for-granted assumptions and behaviours of an organisation's members.** This culture helps make sense of people's organisational context and therefore contributes to how they respond to issues they face.

An organisation's culture can be conceived as consisting of different layers. The four proposed by Edgar Schein[21] are (see Figure 8.4):

- *Values* may be easy to identify in terms of those formally stated by an organisation since they are often explicit, perhaps written down (see Chapter 1). The values driving a strategy may, however, be different from those in formal statements. For example, in the early 2000s, many banks espoused values of shareholder value creation, careful risk

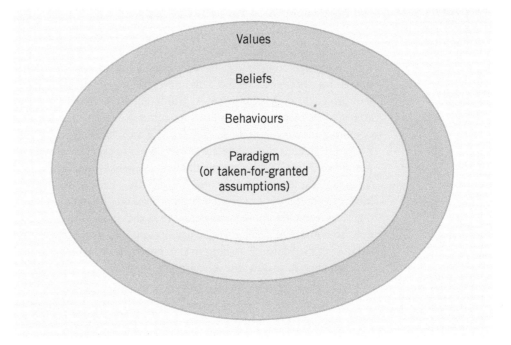

Figure 8.4 Culture in four layers

management and, of course, high levels of customer service. But in practice they indulged in highly risky lending, resulting in the need for huge government financial support in the financial crisis of 2008–09. It is therefore important to delve beneath espoused values to uncover underlying, perhaps taken-for-granted, values that can help explain the strategy actually being pursued by an organisation (see Section 8.3.6 below).

- *Beliefs* are more specific. They can typically be discerned in how people talk about issues the organisation faces; for example, a belief that the company should not trade with particular countries or a belief in the rightness of professional systems and standards.

- *Behaviours* are the day-to-day way in which an organisation operates and that be seen by people both inside and often outside the organisation. This includes the work routines, how the organisation is structured and controlled and 'softer' issues around symbolic behaviours (see Section 8.3.5 below). These behaviours may become the taken-for-granted 'ways we do things around here' that are potentially the bases for inimitable strategic capabilities (see Section 4.3.3) but also significant barriers to achieving strategic change if that becomes necessary (see Chapter 15).

- *Taken-for-granted assumptions* are the core of an organisation's culture which, in this book, we refer to as the organisational *paradigm*. The **paradigm is the set of assumptions held in common and taken for granted in an organisation.** In effect these shared assumptions represent *collective experience* about fundamental aspects of the organisation that, in turn, guide people in that organisation about how to view and respond to different circumstances that they face. The paradigm can underpin successful strategies by providing a basis of common understanding in an organisation but, again, can be a major problem when major strategic change is needed (see Chapter 15). The importance of the paradigm is discussed further in Section 8.3.5.

The concept of culture implies coherence, hence the common expression 'corporate culture'. Illustration 8.2 on the AB InBev brewery describes a company that works hard to create a coherent corporate culture. However, there are at least two ways in which cultures can be subdivided in practice:

- *Organisational subcultures.* Just as national cultures can contain local regional cultures, there are often subcultures in organisations. These subcultures may relate to the structure of the organisation: for example, the differences between geographical divisions in a multinational company, or between functional groups such as finance, marketing and operations. Differences between divisions may be particularly evident in organisations that have grown through acquisition. Also different divisions may be pursuing different types of strategy that require or foster different cultures. Indeed, aligning strategic positioning and organisational culture is a critical feature of successful organisations. Differences between business functions can also relate to the different nature of work in different functions. For example, in a major oil company differences are likely between those functions engaged in 'upstream' exploration, where time horizons may be in decades, and those concerned with 'downstream' retailing, with much shorter market-driven time horizons. Arguably, this is one reason why the oil company Shell took the decision to sell its retail outlets and other downstream activities. In strategic decision-making, therefore, it is important to recognise the different subcultural assumptions managers may be bringing to the processes: finance managers may have different subcultural assumptions to marketing managers, and so on.

- *Organisational identity.* An organisation's culture covers a wide range of aspects, for instance how it sees its environment, but an important part is how the organisation views itself. **Organisational identity refers to what members believe and understand about who they specifically are as an organisation.**[22] Managers and entrepreneurs often try to manipulate organisational identity because it is important for recruiting and guiding employees,

ILLUSTRATION 8.2   Dream. People. Culture.

'Brito', Chief Executive of the world's largest brewery, has culture as one of his three buzzwords.

AB InBev's clumsy name reflects the manner of its growth. It has its origins in the 1999 merger of two Brazilian brewers, Antarctica (founded in 1880) and Brahma (founded in 1886). The new 'AmBev' then merged with Belgian brewer InterBrew to become InBev in 2004, before taking over the American giant Anheuser-Busch in 2008. By 2015, AB InBev was the largest brewer in the world, with its headquarters in Belgium and a 25 per cent share of the global beer business. Its brands included Beck's, Budweiser, Corona and Stella Artois. AB InBev employed 155,000 people in 25 countries. The company had its eyes on taking over one of its last major rivals, the South African brewer SABMiller.

AB InBev's Chief Executive was the Brazilian Carlos Brito, known simply as 'Brito' (never Carlos, never Mr Brito). He had originally begged the former Brazilian tennis champion and investor Jorge Paolo Lemann to fund his MBA at Stanford University. On completion of his MBA, he had joined Brahma, a brewery that Lemann had just bought. By 2004, Brito was CEO of AmBev. With the InterBrew merger, he played second fiddle initially, but by 2005 – aged 45 – he emerged as CEO of the newly-created company InBev.

Brito's three buzzwords, repeated by executives throughout the company, are: 'Dream. People. Culture'. The culture he has sought to create at AB InBev is intense. He himself is away from home travelling on business more than half the year. He claims no hobbies, unless a daily 30 minutes on the treadmill counts. He and his top team fly economy class except on the longest haul flights and they all use mid-market hotels. The top team's desks are placed at the centre of open-plan offices.

Lemann (with a 12.5 per cent stake in the company) describes the culture of AB InBev thus: 'You are always running, always close to the limit. You're working very hard and being evaluated all the time. People either like it or don't like it.' Zero-based budgeting is practised, with all budgets negotiated from scratch at the beginning of each year. Costs and performance are monitored closely. On buying Anheuser-Busch, Brito fired 1400 staff, with the whole top tier of managers going: according to Brito, 'Some were too rich to care, some were too old to work, some wouldn't fit the culture anyway.' Throughout the company, employee metrics are all public and managers are subject to 360 degree feedback systems. The internal joke is that to get promoted, you have to kill three people.

But the rewards are high for good performers, and promotion fast. Young managers rarely spend more than two or three years in a single posting, moved on as soon as they start to get comfortable. In 2014, more than 100,000 people applied for 147 graduate level jobs. Brito personally addresses each class of graduate trainees, looking for talent. He always encourages his trainees to 'dream big'. Luiz Fernando Edmond, head of sales worldwide, was on the company's first management trainee programme in Brazil in 1990. He remarks: 'I came here with nothing. If you work hard, you focus on your results and you work with people, bring people together, promote people better than you, you have a chance to become a CEO of the company.'

Sources: *Fortune*, 15 August 2013; *Financial Times*, June 15 and 16, 2015.

Questions

1 Why do you think that creating a common culture might be important for a company like AB InBev?

2 What mechanisms are used to reinforce such a common culture (see also Chapter 14).

interacting with customers and dealing with regulators. Organisational identity *claims* are often prominent on websites and other official materials. Thus the Danish lager company Carlsberg went through a very deliberate process of changing its claimed identity from a brewer to a fast-moving consumer goods company, with important ramifications for the skills it required. Plausible identity claims are important for entrepreneurial start-ups also: there are significant benefits with customers and investors if they can define themselves as the next generation, rather than a 'me-too'.

8.3.4 Culture's influence on strategy

Mark Fields, President of Ford Motor Company in 2006, famously argued that 'culture eats strategy for breakfast', by which he emphasised the importance of culture for the strategy of the business. The importance of culture does not mean that strategy is irrelevant of course: culture should be seen as *part* of the strategy, something that can be a source of competitive advantage and, to some degree, something that can be adjusted.

The enduring influence of culture on strategy is shown in Figure 8.5.[23] Faced with a stimulus for action, such as declining performance, managers first try to improve the implementation of existing strategy (step 1). This might be through trying to lower cost, improve efficiency, tighten controls or improve accepted ways of doing things. If this is not effective, a change of strategy may occur, but a change in line with the existing culture (step 2). For example, managers may seek to extend the market for their business, but assume that it will be similar to their existing market, and therefore set about managing the new venture in much the same way as they have been used to. Alternatively, even where managers know intellectually that they need to change strategy, they find themselves constrained by path-dependent

Figure 8.5 Culture's influence on strategy development
Source: Adapted from P. Grinyer and J.-C. Spender, *Turnaround: Managerial Recipes for Strategic Success*, Associated Business Press, 1979, p. 203.

organisational routines and assumptions or political processes, as seems likely in the case of Kodak (see Illustration 8.4 later). This often happens, for example, when there are attempts to change highly bureaucratic organisations to be customer-orientated. Even if people accept the need to change a culture's emphasis on the importance of conforming to established rules, routines and reporting relationships, they do not readily do so. It is a fallacy to assume that reasoned argument necessarily changes deeply embedded assumptions rooted in collective experience built up over long periods of time. Readers need only think of their own experience in trying to persuade others to rethink their religious beliefs, or, indeed, allegiances to sports teams, to realise this. Changes in strategy which entail a fundamental change to an organisation's culture (step 3) are likely to be rare and triggered by dramatic evidence of the redundancy of that culture such as a financial crisis or major loss of market share.

8.3.5 Analysing culture: the cultural web

In order to understand the existing culture and its effects it is important to be able to analyse an organisation's culture. The cultural web[24] is a means of doing this (see Figure 8.6). The **cultural web** shows the behavioural, physical and symbolic manifestations of a culture that inform and are informed by the taken-for-granted assumptions, or paradigm, of an organisation. It is in effect the inner two ovals in Figure 8.4. The cultural web can be used to understand culture in any of the frames of reference discussed above, but it is most often used at the organisational and/or subunit levels in Figure 8.3.[25] The seven elements of the cultural web are as follows:

- The *paradigm* is at the core of Figure 8.6. As previously defined, the paradigm is the set of assumptions held in common and taken for granted in an organisation. The paradigmatic assumptions are, quite likely, very basic. For example, a common problem in technology and engineering firms is the propensity of people to focus on the technical excellence of products rather than customer-perceived needs. Or the paradigm of practitioners in the National

Figure 8.6 The cultural web of an organisation

Health Service in the UK is about curing illnesses. It is quite likely that, even if the rational view is to build a strategy around the engineering business' customer needs or the need for prevention (as distinct from curing) of illnesses, people in those organisations may still interpret issues and behave in line with its paradigm. So it is really important to understand the paradigm and how it informs debate on strategy. The problem is that, since it is unlikely to be talked about, or even be something that people are conscious of, trying to identify it can be difficult, especially if you are part of that organisation. Outside observers may find it easier to identify simply by listening to what people say and emphasise. One way of 'insiders' getting to see the assumptions they take for granted is to focus initially on other aspects of the cultural web because these are to do with more visible manifestations of culture. Moreover these other aspects are likely to act to reinforce the assumptions of the paradigm.

- *Rituals and routines* point to the repetitive nature of organisational cultures. *Routines* refer to 'the way we do things around here' on a day-to-day basis. At their best, routines lubricate the working of the organisation, and may provide a basis for distinctive organisational capabilities. However, they can also represent a taken-for-grantedness about how things should happen which, again, can guide how people deal with situations and be difficult to change. For example, managers trying to achieve greater customer focus in engineering firms often report that customer-facing sales engineers routinely tend to tell customers what they need rather than listening to their needs. The *rituals*[26] of organisational life are particular activities or special events that emphasise, highlight or reinforce what is important in the culture. Examples include training programmes, interview panels, promotion and assessment procedures, sales conferences and so on. An extreme example, of course, is the ritualistic training of army recruits to prepare them for the discipline required in conflict. However, rituals can also be informal activities such as drinks in the pub after work or gossiping around watercoolers. A checklist of organisational rituals is provided in Chapter 15 (see Table 15.2).

- The *stories* told by members of an organisation to each other, to outsiders, to new recruits, and so on may act to embed the present in its organisational history and also flag up important events and personalities. They typically have to do with successes, disasters, heroes, villains and mavericks (who deviate from the norm). They can be a way of letting people know what is conventionally important in an organisation.

- *Symbols* are objects, events, acts or people that convey, maintain or create meaning over and above their functional purpose. For example, offices and office layout, cars and job titles have a functional purpose, but are also typically signals about status and hierarchy. Particular people may come to represent especially important aspects of an organisation or historic turning points. The form of language used in an organisation can also be particularly revealing, especially with regard to customers or clients: defining executive education clients as 'course participants' rather than 'students' makes a significant difference to how teaching staff interact with them. Although symbols are shown separately in the cultural web, it should be remembered that many elements of the web are symbolic. So, routines, control and reward systems and structures are not only functional but also symbolic.

- *Power* was defined in Chapter 5 as the ability of individuals or groups to persuade, induce or coerce others into following certain courses of action. So *power structures* are distributions of power to groups of people in an organisation. The most powerful individuals or groups are likely to be closely associated with the paradigm and long-established ways of doing things. In analysing power, the guidance given in Chapter 5 (Section 5.2.2) is useful.

- *Organisational structures* are the roles, responsibilities and reporting relationships in organisations. These are likely to reflect power structures and how they manifest themselves. Formal hierarchical, mechanistic structures may emphasise that strategy is the province of top managers and everyone else is 'working to orders'. Structures with less emphasis on formal reporting relationships might indicate more participative strategy making. Highly decentralised structures (as discussed in Chapter 14) may signify that collaboration is less important than competition and so on.

- *Control systems* are the formal and informal ways of monitoring and supporting people within and around an organisation and tend to emphasise what is seen to be important in the organisation. They include measurements and reward systems. For example, public-service organisations have often been accused of being concerned more with stewardship of funds than with quality of service. This is reflected in their control systems, which are more about accounting for spending rather than with quality of service. Remuneration schemes are a significant control mechanism. Individually-based bonus schemes related to volume are likely to signal a culture of individuality, internal competition and an emphasis on sales volume rather than teamwork and an emphasis on quality.

Illustration 8.3 describes the culture of the American fund manager Vanguard Asset Management (see also Illustration 7.1). It can be seen that the central paradigm of low-cost investing has been supported by many mutually-reinforcing elements of the cultural web.

8.3.6 Undertaking cultural analysis

When analysing the culture of an organisation, there are important issues to bear in mind:

- *Questions to ask.* Figure 8.7 outlines some of the questions that might help build up an understanding of culture using the cultural web.
- *Statements of cultural values.* As explained in Chapter 1, organisations may make public statements of their values, beliefs and purposes, for example in annual reports, mission or values statements and business plans. There is a danger that these are seen as useful descriptions of the organisational culture. But this is likely to be at best only partially true, and at worst misleading. This is not to suggest that there is any organised deception. It is simply that the statements of values and beliefs are often carefully considered and carefully crafted statements of the aspirations of a particular stakeholder (such as the CEO) rather than descriptions of the actual culture. For example, an outside observer of a police force might conclude from its public statements of purpose and priorities that it had a balanced approach to the various aspects of police work – catching criminals, crime prevention, community relations. However, a deeper probing might reveal that (in cultural terms) there is the 'real' police work (catching criminals) and the 'lesser work' (crime prevention, community relations).
- *Pulling it together.* The detailed 'map' produced by the cultural web can be a rich source of information about an organisation's culture, but it is useful to be able to characterise the culture that the information conveys. Sometimes this is possible by means of graphic descriptors. For example, managers who undertook a cultural analysis in the UK National Health Service (NHS) summed up their culture as 'The National Sickness Service'. Although this approach is rather crude and unscientific, it can be powerful in terms of organisational members seeing the organisation as it really is – which may not be immediately apparent from all of the detailed points in the cultural web. It can also help people to understand that culture may drive strategy; for example, a 'national sickness service' will prioritise strategies that are about developments in curing sick people above strategies of health promotion and prevention. So those favouring health promotion strategies need to understand that they are facing the need to change a culture.

If managers are to develop strategies that are different from those of the past, they need to be able to challenge, question and potentially change the organisational culture that underpins the current strategy. In this context, the cultural analysis suggested in this chapter can

ILLUSTRATION 8.3   The Bogleheads and Vanguard Asset Management

Vanguard's culture of low-cost investing is supported by many elements of the cultural web.

Jack Bogle, founder of Vanguard Asset Management in 1974, tells a story about a summer job as a messenger at a Wall Street broker when he was a student. One of the other messengers said to him: "Let me tell you all you need to know about the investment business". Bogle said, "What's that?" He said, "Nobody knows nuthin'." It was on this principle that investment professionals know nothing that Bogle built what became the largest mutual fund in the world.

Bogle developed a model of index funds in which, instead of trying to pick winners, stocks were chosen simply to match the various stock market indices (for example, the S&P 500). As an investor, he did not claim to know more than other investors. All he did was make sure that his portfolio exactly reflected whatever index he was aiming to follow. There were none of the costs of stock-picking, investment research or frequent trades. His funds would never beat the index, but, unlike the vast majority of funds at the time, his expenses were significantly lower. Moreover, Bogle chose an unusual financial structure for Vanguard: it was owned by its own funds and, as a result, ultimately by the customers investing in the funds. This meant that there were no profits to be paid out to outside investors. Moreover, Bogle refused to pay fees to investment advisers for selling Vanguard products: price and performance should be enough to attract customers.

The result of these policies was what Vanguard describes as 'a culture of low-cost investing'. A Vanguard index fund would charge investors fees of only 0.2 per cent of their investment, against fees approaching 2.0 per cent for an active stock-picker. Between 1983 and 1999, a Vanguard index fund tracking the S&P 500 would turn $10,000 (£6000, €7500) into $81,900, while an active stock-picking fund, allowing for the extra charges, would only make $62,700. Jack Bogle's philosophy eventually attracted 25 million retail American investors, many of them enthusiastically describing themselves as 'Bogleheads'. Each year, these Bogleheads meet at Vanguard's Pennsylvania headquarters to, in their phrase, 'visit their money'. Even in his 80s, Jack Bogle would attend the Boglehead conferences to give his investment advice.

Vanguard's headquarters has some unusual features. There was a prominent mural reproducing a famous picture of the 1798 Battle of the Nile, in which Nelson's ship the *Vanguard* had led the British fleet to a decisive victory over Napoleon. The *Vanguard* is depicted firing upon the French ship *La Fidelité*, a reference to Bogle's great active fund rival Fidelity. All 11 buildings on the Vanguard headquarters are named after Nelson's ships and the restaurant is called the 'galley'. To emphasise the mutual nature of relationships, Bogle insisted that Vanguard employees should be called 'crew'.

The Vanguard crew are chosen carefully. For example, when Vanguard began to expand in the UK, the local head Thomas Rampulla interviewed every one of the first 250 staff personally: Bill McNabb, Vanguard's CEO from 2008, described Rampulla as Vanguard's 'culture carrier'. Employees are under careful performance management, using portfolio attribution analysis to precisely measure their results against relevant indices: low performers are asked to 'walk the plank'. Despite the continuing Bogleheads' adoration of Jack Bogle, who still works in a research role at the headquarters and is sometimes critical of Vanguard's recent policies, Bill McNabb is firmly in control. While his predecessor as CEO fought bitterly with Bogle when the latter retained the executive chairmanship position, McNabb combines the roles of chief executive and company chairman, even though this contradicts the corporate governance arrangements Vanguard preaches for the companies it invests in. McNabb's remuneration is secret and he is politely dismissive of Bogle's criticisms.

Sources: New York Times, 11 August 2012; *Financial Times,* 27 May 2015; *Reuters,* 16 September 2014.

Questions

1 Map Vanguard's corporate culture to the cultural web elements of paradigm, stories, symbols, power, organisation structure, control styles and rituals and routine.

2 How do the various elements of the web interrelate? Do any of the elements not fit together?

Stories
- What core beliefs do stories reflect?
- What stories are commonly told, e.g. to newcomers?
- How do these reflect core assumptions and beliefs?
- What norms do the mavericks deviate from?

Symbols
- What objects, events or people do people in the organisation particularly identify with?
- What are these related to in the history of the organisation?
- What aspects of strategy are highlighted in publicity?

Routines and rituals
- Which routines are emphasised?
- Which are embedded in history?
- What behaviour do routines encourage?
- What are the key rituals?
- What assumptions and core beliefs do they reflect?
- What do training programmes emphasise?
- How easy are rituals/routines to change?

Power structures
- Where does power reside? Indicators include:
  (a) status
  (b) claim on resources
  (c) symbols of power
- Who 'makes things happen'?
- Who stops things happening?

Control systems
- What is most closely monitored/controlled?
- Is emphasis on reward or punishment?
- Are controls rooted in history or current strategies?
- Are there many/few controls?

Organisational structures
- What are the formal *and* informal structures?
- How rigid are the structures?
- Do structures encourage collaboration or competition?
- What types of power structure do they support?

Overall
- What do the answers to these questions suggest are the (few) fundamental assumptions that are the paradigm?
- How would you characterise the dominant culture?
- How easy is this to change?
- How and to what extent do aspects of the web inter relate and re-enforce each other?

Figure 8.7 The cultural web: some useful questions

inform aspects of strategic management discussed in other parts of this book. These include the following:

- *Strategic capabilities.* As Chapter 4 makes clear, historically embedded capabilities are, very likely, part of the culture of the organisation. The cultural analysis of the organisation therefore provides a complementary basis of analysis to an examination of strategic capabilities. In effect, such an analysis of capabilities should end up digging into the culture of the organisation, especially in terms of its routines, control systems and the everyday way in which the organisation runs.

- *Strategy development.* An understanding of organisational culture sensitises managers to the way in which historical and cultural influences will likely affect future strategy for good or ill. It therefore relates to the discussion on strategy development in Chapter 13.

- *Managing strategic change.* An analysis of the culture also provides a basis for the management of strategic change, since it provides a picture of the existing culture that can be set against a desired strategy so as to give insights as to what may constrain the development of that strategy or what needs to be changed in order to achieve it. This is discussed more extensively in Chapter 15 on managing strategic change.

- *Leadership and management style.* Chapter 15 also raises questions about leadership and management style. If one of the major requirements of a strategist is to be able to encourage the questioning of that which is taken for granted, it is likely to require a management style – indeed a culture – that allows and encourages such questioning. If the leadership style is such as to discourage such questioning, it is unlikely that the lessons of history will be learned and more likely that the dictates of history will be followed.

- *Culture and experience.* There have been repeated references in this section to the role culture plays as a vehicle by which meaning is created in organisations. This is discussed more fully in the Commentary on the experience lens and provides a useful way in which many aspects of strategy can be considered (see the Commentaries throughout the book).

8.4 STRATEGIC DRIFT

The influence of an organisation's history and culture on its strategic direction is evident in the pattern of strategy development depicted in Figure 8.8. **Strategic drift[27] is the tendency for strategies to develop incrementally on the basis of historical and cultural influences, but fail to keep pace with a changing environment.** An example of strategic drift in Kodak is given in Illustration 8.4. The reasons for and consequences of strategic drift are important to understand, not only because it is common, but also because it helps explain why organisations often seem to stagnate in their strategy development and their performance. Strategic drift also highlights some significant challenges for managers that, in turn, point to some important lessons.

Figure 8.8 Strategic drift

ILLUSTRATION 8.4   Kodak: the decline and fall of a market leader

Knowledge of technological and market changes may not be enough to avoid strategic drift.

In the twentieth century, Kodak, the manufacturer of photographic film and cameras, was one of the world's most valuable brands. Based in Rochester in New York State, by 1976 Kodak had 90 per cent of film and 85 per cent share of camera sales in the USA, and by 1996 turnover was $16bn (£9.6bn, €12bn) and in 1999 profits nearly $2.5bn. Initially known for its innovative technology and marketing, it had developed digital camera technology by 1975, but did not launch digital cameras until the late 1990s by when it was too late.

By 2011, its traditional photography business had been almost entirely eroded, first by digital cameras and then by smartphones. Turnover was only $6bn, it was loss making, the share price had plummeted and in 2012 it filed for bankruptcy protection. How did Kodak miss such a fundamental shift in the market?

According to Steve Sasson, the engineer who invented the first digital camera, the response to his invention in Kodak was dismissive because it was filmless photography. There were similar responses to early internal intelligence reports on digital technology: 'Larry Matteson, a former Kodak executive . . . recalls writing a report in 1979, detailing fairly accurately how different parts of the market would switch from film to digital, starting with government reconnaissance, then professional photography and finally the mass market, all by 2010.'[1] Another internal report in the early 1980s concluded that digital technology would take over the camera industry in about ten years; ten years in which Kodak could work out its response.

The Kodak response was to use digital to enhance the film business. For example, in 1996 Kodak launched a film system using digital technology to provide users with a preview of shots taken and indicate the number of prints required. It flopped.

It was executives in the film division who carried most weight and they were over-confident about Kodak's brand strength. They also misjudged the speed of the change in customer buying preferences. For example, they believed that people in fast-developing markets such as China would buy lots of film, but many moved from no camera at all to digital. The profit margin on digital was also tiny compared with film and there was a real fear of product cannibalisation. Rosabeth Moss Kanter of Harvard Business School also pointed to the Kodak culture: 'Working in a one company town did not help ... Kodak's bosses in Rochester seldom heard much criticism ... '. Moreover, 'executives suffered from a mentality of perfect products, rather than the hi-tech mindset of make it, launch it, fix it.'[1] They also moved slowly: 'Even when Kodak decided to diversify, it took years to make its first acquisition.'[1] Kodak's attempts to diversify by developing the thousands of chemicals its researchers had created for use in film for the drug market also failed.

In 1989, the Kodak board needed to choose a new CEO. The choice was between Kay R. Whitmore, a long-serving executive in the traditional film business, and Phil Samper, who was more associated with digital technology. The board chose Whitmore, who insisted that he would make sure Kodak stayed closer to its core businesses in film and photographic chemicals.[2]

As late as 2007, a Kodak marketing video announced that 'Kodak is back' and 'wasn't going to play grab ass anymore' with digital.[3]

Sources: (1) *The Economist*, 14 January 2012; (2) *New York Times*, 9 December 1989; (3) *Forbes*, 18 January 2012.

Questions

1 Which of the reasons for strategic drift are evident in the Kodak story?

2 Drawing on the lessons from Part I of the book as a whole, how might Kodak's problems have been avoided?

Figure 8.8 identifies four phases in the process of strategic drift, leading either to the organisation's death or to transformational change:

- *Incremental strategic change* is the first phase, involving small changes. In many organisations, there are long periods of relative continuity during which established strategy remains largely unchanged or changes very incrementally. After all, where the environment is changing slowly (as in Figure 8.8 at this point), there is no need for more radical change. Where the pace of environmental change is slow, managers can also experiment with a variety of small-scale responses to change, waiting to see what works before adopting the best solution.

- *Strategic drift* emerges when the rate of environmental change starts to outpace the rate of the organisation's strategic change. Phase 2 of Figure 8.8 shows environmental change accelerating. However, the organisation's rate of change is still incremental, leading to a growing gap with the accumulated environmental change.

- *Flux* is the third phase, triggered by the downturn in performance caused by the growing gap between organisation and environment. In this phase, strategies may change but in no very clear direction: changes may even be reversed, so that strategies loop back on themselves. There may be internal disagreements amongst managers as to which strategy to follow, quite likely based on differences of opinion as to whether future strategy should be based on historic capabilities or whether those capabilities are becoming redundant.

- *Transformation or death* is the final phase in Figure 8.8. As things get worse, there are two possibilities: (a) The organisation may die, either through bankruptcy – as Kodak did in 2012 – or by takeover by another organisation; or (b) the organisation may go through a period of *transformational change,* which brings it back to the level of cumulated environmental change. Such change could take the form of multiple changes related to the organisation's strategy or perhaps a change to its whole business model (see Section 7.4), as well as changes in top management, organisational culture and organisation structure.

Strategic drift is a common phenomenon. The consultants McKinsey & Co. point out that the tendency is for 'most companies to allocate the same resources to the same business units year after year'.[28] It usually takes significant performance decline to prompt transformational change: a study of 215 major UK firms over the 20-year period 1983–2003 identified only four that could be said to have *both* maintained consistently high levels of performance and effected major transformational change over that period.[29] There are three main groups of reasons why it is hard to avoid strategic drift:

- *Uncertainty.* Strategic drift is not easy to see at the time. Chapters 2 and 3 provided ways of analysing the environment, but such analyses are rarely unambiguous. It takes time for managers to be sure of the direction and significance of environmental changes. Changes may be temporary, for instance the result of cyclical downturns that will soon be reversed or fashions that may soon pass. It is easier to see major and irreversible changes with hindsight; it is less easy to grasp their significance as they are happening.

- *Path dependency and lock-in.* As in Section 8.2, the historical trajectory of the organisation might lock organisations into strategies that are costly to change, at least in the short term. For example, capabilities that have historically been the basis of competitive advantage can be difficult to abandon in favour of developing new and untested capabilities. In this sense, old capabilities can become *core rigidities,* rather than core competences capable of supporting new businesses.[30] Similarly, *existing relationships* can become shackles that inhibit significant change.[31] Thus managers may be reluctant to break relationships

THINKING DIFFERENTLY | Institutional logics versus organisational cultures

Societal-level institutional logics can be both sources of conflict and sources of inspiration for organisational cultures.

Institutional logics are socially constructed sets of material practices, assumptions, values and beliefs that shape human cognition and behaviour across domains of activity, typically at a societal level.[33] To put it more simply, what we think and how we behave are shaped by the informal rules of the society we live in. These rules come in distinct and coherent sets: for instance, every society has informal rules about how to behave in the different domains of business, the family, national politics and professions. However, we remain sensitive to all these rules even when we are operating in one particular domain.

This notion of institutional logics comes from the institutional theory tradition associated with the concept of organisational fields, with its emphasis on legitimate behaviour (see Section 8.3.2). It has at least two radical implications for the notion of organisational culture. First, organisational cultures can never be wholly 'organisational': they will certainly be impacted – and sometimes distorted – by logics from outside the organisation. Second, organisational cultures can never be entirely coherent and unified: they will always be 'plural', i.e. cross-cut by multiple logics from external society, such as those of the family or profession.

These institutional logics mean that business decisions are rarely purely business decisions. Familial responsibilities may be influential in a family business; professional identities and standards may be influential in a law firm or architectural practice; patriotism or home-country culture may shape local strategic moves in a multinational. These pluralistic logics can be a source of conflict, of course. But institutional logics can also be a source of inspiration for organisations: professionalism or family spirit can be powerful ingredients in organisational cultures.

Question

How might institutional logics shape such strategic choices as diversification, innovation and internationalisation (see Chapters 8, 9 and 10) for (i) a family-business owner looking to pass on the business to the next generation of children; (ii) a state-owned enterprise from a commodity-hungry country such as China; (iii) a growth-seeking professional services firm, in law for example, considering new businesses and new countries to operate in?

with important customers, suppliers and employees built up over many years for the sake of some emerging and uncertain opportunity.

- *Cultural entrenchment.* As in Section 8.3, culture can exert a strong influence over strategy. The paradigmatic set of taken-for-granted assumptions may prevent managers from seeing certain issues: organisational *identities* (such as 'we are a brewing company', not a 'fast-moving consumer goods company') can shape views of environmental opportunities and threats. Performance measures embedded in the organisation's *control systems* can obscure the need for change. Thus many performance measures are lagged: in the early stages of strategic drift, sales figures may hold up because of customer loyalty or long customer waiting lists; profits may be buttressed by simple cost-cutting or staff working harder in an unsustainable way.

- *Powerful people*, whose skills and power bases relate to the old strategy, may naturally resist change too. These kinds of issues are explored further in Chapter 15.

Thus history, culture and genuine uncertainty can easily support strategic drift. Rebecca Henderson of MIT suggested how a Kodak executive might have responded to reports on the threat of digital technology (see Illustration 8.4): '... you are suggesting that we invest millions of dollars in a market that may, or may not exist but that is certainly smaller than our existing market, to develop a product that customers may or may not want using a business model that will almost certainly give us lower margins than our existing product lines ... Tell me again just why we should make this investment?'[32]

SUMMARY

- Historical, *path-dependent processes* may play a significant part in the success or failure of an organisation and need to be understood by managers. There are historical analyses that can be conducted to help uncover these influences.

- *Cultural and institutional influences* both inform and constrain the strategic development of organisations.

- *Organisational culture* is the basic taken-for-granted assumptions, beliefs and behaviours shared by members of an organisation.

- The seven elements of the *cultural web* are useful for analysing organisational cultures and their relationships to strategy.

- Historic and cultural influences may give rise to *strategic drift* as strategy develops incrementally on the basis of such influences and fails to keep pace with a changing environment.

WORK ASSIGNMENTS

✻ Denotes more advanced work assignments.
* Refers to a case study in the Text and Cases edition.

8.1✻ In the context of Section 8.2, undertake a historical analysis of the strategy development of an organisation of your choice and consider the question: When has history mattered for strategy; when has it appeared not to matter?

8.2 Identify an organisation that describes its culture publicly (use a Google search on 'our culture' plus 'business', for example). What do they mean by culture and how does it fit with the description of culture in this chapter?

8.3 Identify a company reputed to have a strong and positive culture (e.g. via Fortune's 'Best Companies', Glassdoor's 'Best Places to Work' or LinkedIn's 'Most In-Demand Employers'). What is attractive about this company's culture, how is it sustained and to what extent is it a competitive advantage?

8.4 Use the questions in Figure 8.8 to identify elements of the cultural web for Barclays Investment Bank (end of chapter case), Adnams* or an organisation of your choice (for example, your business school).

8.5 Identify an organisation that, in your view, is in one of the phases of strategic drift described in Section 8.4 (Google search 'disappointing results' or 'slow growth' plus 'business' or 'company'). How and why did it get into this state?

Integrative assignment

8.6✻ Choose an example of a major change in strategy of an organisation. Explain to what extent and how its strategic capabilities and its organisation culture changed. (Refer to Chapters 4, 6 and 15.)

RECOMMENDED KEY READINGS

- For a historical perspective on strategy, see Manuel Hensmans, Gerry Johnson and George Yip, *Strategic Transformation: Changing while Winning,* Palgrave Macmillan, 2013 (summarised in G. Johnson, G. Yip and M. Hensmans, 'Achieving successful strategic transformation', *MIT Sloan Management Review,* vol. 53, no. 3 (2012), pp. 25–32); and John T. Seaman Jr and George David Smith, 'Your company's history as a leadership tool', *Harvard Business Review* (December 2012), pp. 1–10.

- For a summary and illustrated explanation of institutional theory, see Gerry Johnson and Royston Greenwood, 'Institutional theory and strategy', in *Strategic Management: A Multiple-Perspective Approach,* M. Jenkins and V. Ambrosini (eds), Palgrave, 2007.

- For a comprehensive and critical explanation of organisational culture see Mats Alvesson, *Understanding Organisational Culture,* 2nd edn, Sage, 2012.

REFERENCES

1. W.B. Arthur, 'Competing technologies, increasing returns and lock in by historical events', *Economic Journal,* vol. 99 (1989), pp. 116–31.

2. P.A. David, 'Clio and the economics of QWERTY', *American Economic Review,* vol. 75, no. 2 (1985), pp. 332–7, but also for a challenge to David's argument see S.J. Liebowitz and S.E. Margolis, 'The fable of the keys', *Journal of Law & Economics,* vol. 30, April (1990), pp. 1–26.

3. For discussions of path dependency in an organisational context, see Jorg Sydow, George Schraeyogg and Jochen Koch, 'Organisational path dependance: opening the black box', *Academy of Management Review,* vol. 34, no. 4 (2009), pp. 689–708. L. Dobusch and E. Schüssler discuss path dependence at Intel and Microsoft in 'Theorizing path dependence: a review of positive feedback mechanisms in technology markets, regional clusters, and organizations', *Industrial and Corporate Change,* vol. 22, no. 3 (2013), pp. 717–46.

4. The world's biggest accounting firms have called for radical reform: 'Big four in call for real time accounts', *Financial Times* (8 November 2006), p. 1.

5. See J.T. Seaman Jr and G.D. Smith, 'Your company's history as a leadership tool', *Harvard Business Review,* December 2012, pp. 1–10.

6. This quote by André Malroux and the story of the BMW museum was provided by the business historian Mary Rose.

7. See D. Holbrook, W. Cohen, D. Hounshell and S. Klepper, 'The nature, sources and consequences of firm differences in the early history of the semiconductor industry', *Strategic Management Journal,* vol. 21, no. 10–11 (2000), pp. 107–42.

8. S. Klepper and K.L. Simons, 'Dominance by birthright: entry of prior radio producers and competitive ramifications in the US television receiver industry', *Strategic Management Journal,* vol. 21, no. 10–11 (2000), pp. 987–1016.

9. S. Paroutis, M. Mckeown and S. Collinson, 'Building castles from sand: unlocking CEO mythopoetical behaviour in Hewlett Packard from 1978 to 2005', *Business History,* vol. 55, no. 7 (2013), pp. 1200–27. See also O. Brunninge, 'Using history in organization: how managers make purposeful reference to history in strategy processes', *Journal of Organizational Change Management,* vol. 22, no. 1 (2009), pp. 8–26.

10. Also see D.J. Jeremy, 'Business history and strategy', in A. Pettigrew, H. Thomas and R. Whittington (eds), *The Handbook of Strategy and Management,* pp. 436–60, Sage, 2002.

11. For good examples of corporate histories see G. Jones, *Renewing Unilever: Transformation and Tradition,* Oxford University Press, 2005; R. Fitzgerald, *Rowntrees and the Marketing Revolution, 1862–1969,* Cambridge University Press, 1995; and T.R. Gourvish, *British Railways 1948–73,* Cambridge University Press, 1986.

12. This quote is from S. Finkelstein, 'Why smart executives fail: four case histories of how people learn the wrong lessons from history', *Business History,* vol. 48, no. 2 (2006), pp. 153–70.

13. See G. Hofstede, *Culture's Consequences,* Sage, 2nd edn, 2001; and M. Minkov and G. Hofstede, 'The evolution of Hofstede's doctrine', *Cross Cultural Management: An International Journal,* vol. 18, no. 1 (2011), pp. 10–20.

14. For a critique of Hofstede's work, see B. McSweeney, 'Hofstede's model of national cultural differences and their consequences: a triumph of faith – a failure of analysis', *Human Relations,* vol. 55, no. 1 (2002), pp. 89–118. For example, differences in regional cultures impacted on the integration of banking mergers in Nigeria, as shown by E. Gomes, D. Angwin and K. Melahi, 'HRM practices throughout the mergers and acquisition (M&A) process: a study of domestic deals in the Nigerian banking industry', *International Journal of Human Resource Management,* vol. 23, no. 14 (2012), pp. 2874–900.

15. A useful review of research on this topic is T. Dacin, J. Goodstein and R. Scott, 'Institutional theory and institutional change: introduction to the special research forum', *Academy of Management Journal,* vol. 45, no. 1 (2002), pp. 45–57. For a more general review, see G. Johnson and R. Greenwood, 'Institutional theory and strategy', in M. Jenkins and V. Ambrosini (eds), *Strategic Management: a Multiple-Perspective Approach,* Palgrave, 2007.

16. For discussion of a classic case, see J.F. Porac, H. Thomas and C. Baden-Fuller, 'Competitive groups as cognitive communities: the case of Scottish knitwear manufacturers revisited', *Journal of Management Studies*, vol. 48, no. 3 (2011), pp. 646–64. See also F.F. Suarez, S. Grodal and A. Gotsopoulos, 'Perfect timing? Dominant category, dominant design, and the window of opportunity for firm entry', *Strategic Management Journal*, vol. 36, no. 3 (2015), pp. 437–48.

17. The term 'recipe' was introduced to refer to industries by J.-C. Spender, *Industry Recipes: the Nature and Sources of Management Judgement*, Blackwell, 1989. We have broadened its use by applying it to *organisational fields*. For a recent application, see P. McNamara, S. I. Peck and A. Sasson, 'Competing business models, value creation and appropriation in English football', *Long Range Planning*, vol. 46, no. 61 (2013), pp. 475–487.

18. D. Deephouse, 'To be different or to be the same? It's a question (and theory) of strategic balance', *Strategic Management Journal*, vol. 20, no. 2 (1999), pp. 147–66.

19. This definition of culture is taken from E. Schein, *Organisational Culture and Leadership*, 3rd edn, Jossey-Bass, 2004, p. 6.

20. This is how Terrence Deal and Alan Kennedy define organisational culture in *Corporate Cultures: the Rites and Rituals of Corporate Life*, Addison-Wesley, 1982.

21. E. Schein (see end note 19) and A. Brown, *Organisational Culture*, Financial Times Prentice Hall, 1998 are useful in understanding the relationship between organisational culture and strategy. For a useful critique of the concept of organisational culture see M. Alvesson, *Understanding Organizational Culture*, Sage, 2002.

22. M.J. Hatch, M. Schultz and A.-M. Skov, 'Organizational identity and culture in the context of managed change: transformation in the Carlsberg Group, 2009–2013', *Academy of Management Discoveries*, vol. 1, no. 1 (2015), pp. 56–87; T. Wry, M. Lounsbury and M.A. Glynn, 'Legitimating nascent collective identities: coordinating cultural entrepreneurship', *Organization Science*, vol. 22. no. 2 (2011), pp. 449–63.

23. Figure 8.5 is adapted from the original in P. Grinyer and J.-C. Spender, *Turnaround: Managerial Recipes for Strategic Success*, Associated British Press, 1979, p. 203.

24. A fuller explanation of the cultural web can be found in G. Johnson, *Strategic Change and the Management Process*, Blackwell, 1987; and G. Johnson, 'Managing strategic change: strategy, culture and action', *Long Range Planning*, vol. 25, no. 1 (1992), pp. 28–36.

25. A practical explanation of cultural web mapping is a 'white paper' by Gerry Johnson, 'Mapping and Re-mapping Organisational Culture: a Local Government Example', www.strategyexplorers.com.

26. See A.C.T. Smith and B. Stewart, 'Organizational rituals: features, functions and mechanisms', *International Journal of Management Reviews*, vol. 13, no. 2 (2011), pp. 113–33; and G. Islam and M.J. Zyphur, 'Rituals in organizations: a review and expansion of current theory', *Group & Organization Management*, vol. 34 (2009), pp. 114–39.

27. For an explanation of strategic drift, see G. Johnson, 'Rethinking incrementalism', *Strategic Management Journal*, vol. 9 (1988), pp. 75–91; and 'Managing strategic change – strategy, culture and action', *Long Range Planning*, vol. 25, no. 1 (1992), pp. 28–36. Also see E. Romanelli and M.T. Tushman, 'Organizational transformation as punctuated equilibrium: an empirical test', *Academy of Management Journal*, vol. 7, no. 5 (1994), pp. 1141–66. They explain the tendency of strategies to develop incrementally with periodic transformational change.

28. S. Hall, D. Lovallo and R. Musters, 'How to put your money where your strategy is', *McKinsey Quarterley* (March 2012).

29. See G. Yip, T. Devinney and G. Johnson, 'Measuring long-term superior performance: the UK's long term superior performers 1984–2003', *Long Range Planning*, vol. 43, no. 3 (2009), pp. 390–413.

30. See D. Leonard-Barton, 'Core capabilities and core rigidities: a paradox in managing new product development', *Strategic Management Journal*, vol. 13 (1992), pp. 111–25.

31. This is a term used by Donald S. Sull in accounting for the decline of high-performing firms (see 'Why good companies go bad', *Harvard Business Review*, July/August 1999, pp. 42–52).

32. John Naughton, 'The lessons we can learn from the rise and fall of Kodak', *Observer Discover*, 22 January 2012.

33. M.L. Besharov and W.K. Smith, 'Multiple institutional logics in organizations: explaining their varied nature and implications', *Academy of Management Review*, vol. 39, no. 3 (2014), pp. 364–81; and for a case of an international law firm, M. Smets, T. Morris and R. Greenwood, 'From practice to field: a multilevel model of practice-driven institutional change', *Academy of Management Journal*, vol. 55, no. 4 (2012), pp. 877–904.

Culture clashes at Barclays Bank

Barclays Bank is an international retail and investment bank based in London. It ranks amongst the ten largest banks in the world and has 130,000 employees. In the four years to 2015, it had four separate bosses: the aggressive investment banker Robert Diamond ('Diamond Bob'), the reformist 'Saint' Antony Jenkins, ex-insurance titan John 'Mack the Knife' McFarlane; and lately another American investment banker James ('Jes') Staley.

Quaker origins – and beyond

Barclays Bank traces its origins to 1690. Its early address in Lombard Street – the heart of London's financial district – was 'the Sign of the Black Spread Eagle'. The Spread Eagle remains Barclays' corporate logo even today. The bank's founding families were from the Quaker religious movement, who emphasised sobriety, pacifism and high ethical standards. Their descendants were still in important executive positions in the mid-twentieth century: the last family member served as Chairman during the 1980s. Reinforced by mergers, the company became one of the big four retail bankers in the UK. As the *Financial Times* observed:

> 'In many ways the bank resembled a club and, as so often with British clubs, the thing worked surprisingly well despite its flaws ... It was, in fact, the most innovative of the British clearing banks in the post-war period. In 1967 it installed the world's first automated cash teller machine ... Barclays also came up with the first plastic payment device, Barclaycard, still outstandingly successful.'

Since the early 1800s, Barclays had been accepting bills from other banks to reinvest in businesses – an early form of investment banking. The investment banking business received a huge impetus after the 1986 Big Bang, the liberalisation of London's stock market. Barclays embarked on acquisitions including a leading stock broker, de Zoete Wedd. This became the core of an investment bank, BZW. However, in common with other investment banks who got involved in equities trading, Barclays had great difficulty combining conventional and investment banking in a coherent model. As the *Financial Times* put it:

Bob Diamond, Barclays CEO 2011–12

Source: Jerome Favre/Bloomberg/Getty Images.

'The chief problem was culture. As Michael Lewis, author of *Liar's Poker,* a commentary on Wall Street in the 1980s, memorably put it, a commercial banker was someone who had a wife, a station wagon, 2.2 children and a dog that brought him his slippers when he returned home from work at 6 pm. An investment banker, by contrast, was a breed apart, a member of a master race of dealmakers. He possessed vast, almost unimaginable talent and ambition. If he had a dog it snarled. He had two little red sports cars yet wanted four. To get them, he was, for a man in a suit, surprisingly willing to cause trouble.'

Investment banking was notorious for its 'hard work and hard play'. It was common for investment bankers to work through the night, or at least to be seen to be doing so – stories had it that they would own two suit jackets so they could leave one on the back of the chair to pretend they were still in the office working. It was also a 'can-do' mentality which legitimated, for example, a day trip to Australia for a one-hour meeting. No expense was spared on flights, entertainment or accommodation provided a big deal was signed. There was also much visible excess with traders spending thousands of pounds a night at champagne bars. Long hours and intense pressure tended to foster strong loyalties to team-mates, with bankers identifying with their work group rather than with the bank as a whole.

Diamond Bob

The American investment banker Bob Diamond joined Barclays in 1996, with a reputation as a successful trader earned in leading US banks. Throughout the first decade of this century, Bob Diamond grew in influence, becoming head of Barclays' investment banking businesses. A past employee of Barclays' investment arm, interviewed in a BBC *Panorama* programme, claimed that Bob Diamond 'installed Wall Street values into Barclays; it was every man for himself ... It was all about doing ever bigger deals' and being willing to take 'extreme risks' to make 'super profits' and generate huge bonuses for the traders involved. In 2008, Diamond was responsible for buying the failed Lehman Brothers Wall Street investment bank. Diamond also grew the much criticised Structured Capital Markets 'tax planning' business, which many saw as just about tax avoidance. Employing only 100 people, by 2010 this business was generating £1 (€1.2, $1.5) billion a year in profits. Bob Diamond also succeeded in growing the trading arm of the bank into a major profit contributor, accounting for 58 per cent of Barclays' overall pre-tax earnings by 2011. Diamond became known as 'Diamond Bob', a reference both to his financial success and to a rather flashy lifestyle which included hanging out with Mick Jagger of the Rolling Stones.

In 2011, Diamond's success was rewarded by appointment as chief executive of the whole bank. But problems were emerging. There were investigations into the mis-selling of payment protection insurance by the retail bank and into the manipulation of the inter-bank lending rate, Libor, in the investment bank. Traders at Barclays were accused of manipulating Californian electricity prices. A mysterious rescue package involving Qatari capital that had saved Barclays from nationalisation during the financial crisis of 2008 came under growing scrutiny. Barclays was criticised for continuing to pay high bonuses to staff even after the financial crisis of 2008–09. BBC's *Panorama* calculated that in 2010–11 payments to shareholders had amounted to £1.4bn while payment of bonuses for staff amounted to £6bn. There was widespread criticism of the bank's tax minimisation activities and public outrage at Bob Diamond's huge remuneration package, estimated to be around £120m between 2007 and 2012. Barclays' reputation was in tatters. Bob Diamond resigned in 2012.

Saint Antony

Antony Jenkins was appointed Chief Executive of Barclays in August 2012. He had actually begun his career in the bank's UK retail business in the early 1980s, before a time at Citigroup. He had returned to Barclays to run the credit card division in 2006, becoming head of retail and business banking in 2009. Jenkins was not an investment banker and declared himself determined to clean up Barclays' reputation.

Jenkins commissioned a prominent City lawyer, Anthony Salz, to review Barclays' culture. The review concluded:

> 'We believe that the business practices for which Barclays has rightly been criticised were shaped predominantly by its cultures, which rested on uncertain foundations. There was no sense of common purpose in a group that had grown and diversified significantly in less than two decades. And across the whole bank, there were no clearly articulated and understood shared values – so there could hardly be much consensus among employees as to what the values were and what should guide everyday behaviours. And as a result there was no consistency to the development of a desired culture.'

The review specifically identified pay, especially in the investment bank, as a source of many problems:

> 'Most but not all of the pay issues concern the investment bank. . . . Based on our interviews, we could not avoid concluding that pay contributed significantly to a sense among a few that they were somehow unaffected by the ordinary rules. A few investment bankers seemed to lose a sense of proportion and humility. . . . Elevated pay levels inevitably distort culture, tending to attract people who measure their personal success principally on compensation. . . . Many interviewees [reported] a sense of an entitlement culture.

Antony Jenkins' concurred with the criticisms of the Salz review, issuing a memo to all Barclays' staff as follows:

> 'Over a period of almost 20 years, banking became too aggressive, too focused on the short term, too disconnected from the needs of our customers and clients, and wider society. We were not immune at Barclays from these mistakes ... Performance assessment will be based not just on what we deliver but on how we deliver it. We must never again be in a position of rewarding people for making the bank money in a way which is unethical or inconsistent with our values.'

All Barclays' staff would receive training on the central importance of five core values: respect, integrity, service, excellence and stewardship. Jenkins became known in the bank as 'Saint Antony', wearing crisp white shirts and plain ties in the Barclays' colour blue. In a saintly gesture, Jenkins waived his first year bonus of £2.75m. He also told his employees that anybody who did not like the new culture should leave.

In his first strategic review, Jenkins examined the performance and reputation of Barclays' 75 business units. The review concluded that 39 business units were in good shape, 15 needed some attention, 17 needed serious attention to avoid closure or sale and four would definitely be sold or closed, one of which was its tax-avoiding Structured Capital Markets unit. Basically though, investment banking would remain intact.

Nonetheless, Jenkins promised to bring pay at the investment bank down as a percentage of income to the mid-thirties. During 2014, however, rival banks started to poach top performers. Jenkins publicly warned of a 'death spiral' if pay did not match competitors'. The investment banking pay ratio increased from 39.6 to 43.2 per cent.

Mack the Knife

In May 2015, John McFarlane took over as Barclays chairman on the retirement of his predecessor. McFarlane had acquired his nickname 'Mack the Knife' when he had despatched his CEO within a few weeks of arriving as chairman of Aviva, the large insurance company. Matters quickly came to a head at Barclays when the board had an off-site meeting in June at an exclusive country house hotel near Bath.

The investment bankers were already disgruntled with Jenkins. The latest irritation was when Jenkins had sent a letter to all staff celebrating the bank's 325th anniversary without mentioning the investment banking division. The Bath meeting was divided between Jenkins and the investment bankers about strategy for the next five years. McFarlane sided mostly with the investment bankers. Consulting with the non-executive directors present, McFarlane decided to dismiss Jenkins. McFarlane declared himself as executive chairman, filling the CEO role until another one could be put in place.

McFarlane did not commit himself to major changes in strategy, only to focus more on execution. He declared that Barclays was only halfway through its cultural change 'journey'. But in almost the same breath, he added: 'What we really need is a high energy, supercharged performance driven approach.' He promised to double the Barclay's share price in three to four years.

The Staley strategy

James Staley joined Barclays as CEO at the end of 2015, with McFarlane returning to a non-executive chairman role. Although recently working at a hedge-fund, Staley had spent his career mostly at JPMorgan, the largest bank in the USA and an investment banking powerhouse since the late nineteenth century. Staley quickly appointed former JPMorgan colleagues as chief operating officer and chief risk officer.

In March 2016, Staley presented his first strategic review to shareholders and analysts. He committed himself to simplifying the international businesses, including the sale of the major African retail business and peripheral international investment banking operations. In order to strengthen the bank's financial position, he cut the dividend payments for the next two years by 50 per cent. The Barclays share price fell by eight per cent on the news. Barclays' market valuation was little more than half what it had been in 2014.

Sources: Barclays Bank, *Salz Review: an Independent Review of Barclays' Business Practices*, April 2013; *Financial Times*, 6 July 2012, 12 February 2012, 12 July 2013, 10 July 2015, 1 March 2016; *Guardian*, 28 June 2012; *Panorama: Inside Barclays: Banking on Bonuses*, 11 February 2013; *Telegraph*, 17 January 2013.

Questions

1 With an eye to elements of the cultural web (Section 8.3.5), analyse the culture of Barclays' investment banking business.

2 Reformist Antony Jenkins could have used Barclays' Quaker history as a resource for change (Section 8.2.2). What might have been the advantages and disadvantages of drawing on this history?

COMMENTARY ON
PART I THE STRATEGY LENSES

The strategy lenses aim to help you explore strategy 'critically'. Critical here is meant constructively: it is about asking better questions, generating new options, building stronger evidence and being more aware of different points of view. Ultimately, thinking critically should help you be more persuasive with regard to your own chosen positions, helping you convince your teachers, your fellow students or your work colleagues.[1] Using the strategy lenses to explore strategic issues critically will help you both to generate additional insights and respond to possible counter-arguments against your own position.

The last few chapters have already introduced many points of view, each offering different insights into what matters in strategy. Some of these reflect a strong economics orientation, for instance macro-economic cycles and the Five Forces in Chapters 2 and 3. Others are more sociological, such as the highlighting of legitimacy in Chapters 2 and 5. Some concepts and frameworks emphasise opportunities for innovation, as in the strategy canvas of Chapter 3. Others stress conservatism in organisations, for example strategic drift and organisational culture in Chapter 6. Generally, the chapters assume objectivity in analysis, but issues such as the principal–agent problem in Chapter 5 warn of the scope for divergent political interests in organisations, while organisational culture too can be a source of bias. What should be clear from these chapters, therefore, is that there are many different ways of seeing strategy. Each of them suggests different questions, generates different kinds of insights and demands different types of evidence.

The strategy lenses organise many of these different perspectives into four basic approaches to exploring strategic issues. Each of these lenses will help you generate distinct kinds of questions, options and evidence. They each have distinct implications for practice too.

The four strategy lenses are as follows:

- **The design lens views strategy development as a logical process of analysis and evaluation.** This is the most commonly held view about how strategy is developed and what managing strategy is about. Options and evidence here are generated by objective analysis using formal concepts and frameworks.

- **The experience lens views strategy development as the outcome of people's taken-for-granted assumptions and ways of doing things.** Strategy through the experience lens puts people, culture and history centre stage in strategy development. Options need to respect the past, and evidence is likely to draw heavily on previous experience.

- **The variety lens* views strategy as the bubbling up of new ideas from the variety of people in and around organisations.** According to this lens, strategy emerges not just from the top, but also from the periphery and bottom of the organisation. It is important to question top management views, and recognise the potential value of options coming from all round the organisation, and even from outside.

- **The discourse lens views language as important both for understanding and changing strategy and for managerial power and identity.** Through this lens, unpicking managers' language can uncover hidden meanings and political interests. Choosing the right language is also important to legitimating options and evidence.

* In earlier editions the variety lens was called the 'ideas lens'. The authors believe that the word 'variety' more accurately encapsulates the concepts explained in this section.

The critical exploration of strategy through these four lenses is useful because they all raise different questions and suggest different approaches. Think of everyday discussions you have. It is not unusual for people to say: 'But what if you looked at it this way instead?' Taking just one view can lead to a partial and perhaps biased understanding. Looking at an issue another way can give a much fuller picture, generating new and different insights. For example, is a proposed strategy the result of objective analysis or is it rather the reflection of the proposer's personal experience or political self-interest? The lenses can also prompt different options or solutions to strategic problems. For example again, should organisations rely just on top managers to create new strategies, or rather look towards the bottom of the organisation to uncover existing experiments and initiatives that have greater potential? Thus, taking a critical perspective on strategy can help managers and students consider a wider range of issues and responses.

The rest of this Commentary explains the lenses in more detail, showing how they each relate to the following three key dimensions of managing strategy:

- *Rationality*: the extent to which the development of strategy is rationally managed. The design lens assumes high rationality, but the other lenses question this.

- *Innovation*: the extent to which strategy is likely to develop innovative, change-oriented organisations, or alternatively consolidate past experience and existing power structures.

- *Legitimacy*: the extent to which strategy analysis and discourse is involved in sustaining managers' power and identities in organisations.

This Commentary concludes with a short case on Nokia, illustrating how the four lenses can be used to explore a real company's strategy. There will be shorter Commentaries later in the book helping readers to reflect on the concepts and frameworks highlighted in Parts II and III. Meanwhile, this Commentary relates mostly to the material in the first six chapters of this book.

The design lens

The design lens evokes an image of the strategist as detached designer, drawing up precise blueprints distant from the messy realities of action. In terms of the three key dimensions, the design lens therefore puts a strong premium on rational analysis and decision-making (see Figure C.i).[2] Because of its overt commitment to optimising the performance of

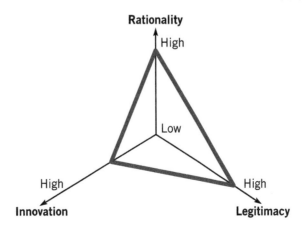

Figure C.i Design lens

organisations, the design lens tends also to be highly legitimate. Rational analysis is what counts, not passion or intuition. However, this commitment to dry analysis can sometimes work against innovation.

The design lens is associated broadly with strategy theorists such as the former Lockheed Corporation strategic planner Igor Ansoff or the economics-trained Harvard Business School Professor Michael Porter.[3] It has its origins in traditional economists' expectations about perfect information and 'rational economic man', and is further informed by management science techniques for resource optimisation. The design lens is also how strategy is often explained in textbooks, by teachers and indeed by managers. The design lens makes the following three assumptions about how strategic decisions are made:

- *Systematic analysis is key.* Although there are many influences on an organisation's performance, careful analysis can identify those that are most significant. In this view, calculating the attractiveness of an industry using Porter's Five Forces (Chapter 3), and identifying strategic capabilities using Valuable, Rare, Inimitable and Organisational support criteria (Chapter 4), would be standard processes for estimating future performance.

- *Analysis precedes action.* In the design lens, strategy is generally seen as a linear process. Decisions about strategy are separate from and precede implementation. From this point of view, therefore, environmental analysis – for example projecting scenarios or forecasting industry life cycles (Chapters 2 and 3) – is the crucial first step in strategy-making.

- *Objectives should be clear.* Rational analysis and decision-making need unambiguous criteria by which to evaluate options. Missions and visions (Chapter 1) should be set in advance as precisely as possible, with little scope for adjustment as new opportunities or constraints are discovered in action.

These design lens assumptions about how decisions should be made are in turn associated with two key views about the nature of organisations:

- *Organisations are hierarchies.* It is the responsibility of top management to plan the destiny of the organisation. The responsibility of the rest of organisation is simply to implement the strategy decided at the top.

- *Organisations work mechanically.* This hierarchical approach implies a view of organisations as engineered systems or even machines. Pulling the right organisational levers should produce predictable results. Principal–agent problems can be controlled by the appropriate gearing of incentives (Chapter 5). Even organisational cultures (Chapter 6) can be designed from above.

Implications

The design lens has practical implications for both managers and students. From the design point of view, it is worth investing extensive time in formal analysis, especially economic forms of analysis. Formal strategic planning and financial calculations are crucial parts of the design lens approach. But even if strategic plans do not always produce the expected results, there are two further reasons for taking a design lens approach:

- *Dealing with complexity and uncertainty.* The design lens provides a means of talking about complex and uncertain issues in a rational, logical and structured way. Even if rational analysis can sometimes over-simplify or convey undue precision, it is usually better than just concluding that everything is all much too complicated for any kind of plan or calculation. Strategy is more than guesswork.

- *Meeting stakeholder expectations.* As well as the sheer analytical value of a design approach, adopting rational procedures is something that important stakeholders (see Chapter 5) such as banks, financial analysts, investors and employees typically expect. For these audiences, analysis is highly legitimate. Taking a design lens approach is therefore an important means of gaining the support and confidence of significant internal and external actors.

Technical and elitist forms of strategy analysis can also have implications for managerial power and personal identity. These side-effects will be discussed further with the discourse lens later.

In summary, the design lens is useful in highlighting the potential value of systematic analysis, step-by-step sequences and the careful engineering of organisational objectives and systems. However, the design lens does have its limits. In particular, a narrow design lens tends to underestimate the positive role of intuition and experience, the scope for unplanned and bottom-up initiatives, and the power effects of strategy analysis. Different lenses can provide useful insights into these other elements of strategy.

Strategy as experience

The experience lens sees strategy as coming less from objective analysis on a clean sheet of paper and more from the prior experience of the organisation's managers. History and culture matter. Strategy is shaped by people's individual and collective taken-for-granted assumptions and ways of doing things. As indicated in Figure C.ii, the experience lens therefore places less emphasis than the design lens on rationality. It also sets low expectations in terms of innovation and change. Legitimacy is important, but this is defined in terms of tradition, routines and culture rather than simple appeal to analysis and 'the facts'.

The experience lens is based on a good deal of research about how strategies actually develop in the real world. As early as the 1950s, Nobel prize winner Herbert Simon was developing the so-called Behavioral Theory of the Firm, based on how managers really behave.[4] Contemporary researchers into 'Behavioral Strategy' underline two kinds of problem for rational analysis in practice:

- *External constraints:* Behavioral Theory points to real-world barriers to rationality: for example, it is difficult to obtain all the information required for comprehensive analysis; it is hard to forecast accurately in an uncertain future; and there are cost and time limits to undertaking complete analyses. In these conditions, managers often 'satisfice' when analysing strategic options: in other words, they settle for adequate solutions rather than the rational optimum.

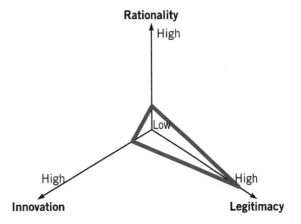

Figure C.ii Experience lens

- *Internal psychological limitations:* Behavioral Theory underlines how managers suffer from 'bounded rationality', human limitations on the intellectual ability to process information and carry out analysis. They are also liable to 'cognitive bias': in other words, managers tend to be selective in the attention they give to issues and often automatically favour some types of solutions rather than others.

Cognitive bias is often based on managers' experience, both individual and collective:

- *Individual experience* can particularly shape managers' taken-for-granted assumptions about what is important and what kinds of actions work best. Influential sources of experience can be education and training. For example, accountants tend to see things differently to engineers; MBAs are often accused of favouring excessively analytical approaches to solving problems. Other kinds of influential individual experience are personal careers. Thus a manager who had spent his or her career in the traditional automobile industry (for instance, Ford or BMW) might find it difficult to take seriously new entrants such as Google or Tesla. Differences in individual experience within an organisation can lead to debate and negotiation between managers with divergent views about what is important and what should be done. Sometimes such negotiation can slow decision-making down and lead to excessive compromise. Stakeholder mapping (Chapter 5) of different managers' power and attention can be useful in resolving divergent views.

- *Collective experience* tends to form habitual patterns of thinking and acting, which can translate into standard responses to strategic issues. One kind of collective experience is encapsulated in organisational culture, as discussed in Chapter 6. Another kind of collective experience is reflected by national culture: so for instance Chinese and American managers may see the world differently (see also Chapter 10). A third kind of collective experience is embodied in industry 'recipes' (Chapter 6), based on years of regular interaction between existing competitors: for example, managers in the clothing industry come to believe over time that style is important to success, even though new ideas from outside the industry imply that new technologies may be the source of competitive advantage in the future. By contrast with individual experience, collective experience tends to suppress debate in management teams, and it becomes hard to challenge the consensus. A consequence can be 'strategic drift' (Chapter 6), with everybody agreeing to continue as before, even in the face of environmental change.

Implications

The experience lens has significant implications for strategy. First there are three important warnings:

- *Analysis is typically biased to some extent.* All managers – and even students – bring their own particular experience to any set of strategic issues. It is very hard to analyse a situation as if from a clean sheet of paper. You should distrust claims to complete objectivity. Ask yourself where people are coming from.

- *Watch out for undue conservatism.* Experience is likely to lead to routinised responses, even to new problems. Tried-and-tested solutions become too legitimate; managers become powerful because of successes experienced in the past. 'Path dependency' and 'lock-in' are enduring risks (Chapter 6). Organisations can end up like old-fashioned generals, always fighting the last war.

- *Change is hard.* Because of conservatism, strategic change is liable to require long and difficult processes of persuasion (see Chapter 15). Continuity is often the default option. Relying on the 'objective analysis' in the business case for change will rarely win over hearts as well as minds.

On the other hand, the experience lens has some positive practical advice:

- *Analysis can cost more than it's worth.* Because good information is hard and expensive to get, and because analysis can consume too much time, sometimes it is sensible simply to cut short information search and analysis. Depending on the availability of information and the ability to analyse it, beyond a certain point it might be sensible just to drop the analysis.

- *Experience may provide the best guide.* If analysis is not going to produce good answers, then relying on the rules-of-thumb ('heuristics') and instincts of experienced managers may be at least as effective. Sometimes a quick response that is half right is better than an analytical response that is only slightly better but much slower.

- *Challenge the consensus.* While established rules-of-thumb can be effective, sometimes it is necessary to challenge the consensus in an organisation. As in Chapter 16, 'groupthink' is a risk. The need to challenge existing approaches is often the motivation for bringing in new leaders from outside the organisation in order to manage strategic change (Chapter 15).

Strategy as variety

The extent to which the design and experience lenses help explain innovation is rather limited. The variety lens, on the other hand, emphasises innovation and change. However, as indicated in Figure C.iii, the variety lens puts low value on rational analysis and tends to give little weight to what is simply legitimate in an organisation. Viewed through the variety lens, strategies are seen as emerging from the different ideas that bubble up from the variety in and around organisations.

The variety lens builds on two theoretical perspectives from the natural sciences, both emphasising spontaneity. First there is *evolutionary theory,* in which natural phenomena evolve through a Darwinian process of Variety, Selection and Retention.[5] Various genetic mutations emerge as more or less random experiments; some variations are selected for success by their environments; and these successful variations may be retained over the long term because of continuing good environmental fit. Second, there is *complexity theory*, where phenomena are characterised by complex, dynamic sets of interactions, so that small events can have surprisingly large effects.[6] An example is the famous butterfly effect, where the flap of a butterfly's wings in Brazil triggers a series of escalating knock-on effects that eventually cause a tornado in far-way Texas. In both evolutionary and complexity theories, variety in the form of many small experiments or interactions can lead to large and enduring outcomes. These outcomes are generated spontaneously, with very little top-down direction.

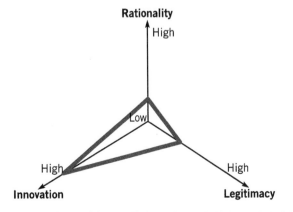

Figure C.iii Variety lens

Moving from nature to strategy, the variety lens de-emphasises the deliberate decision-making of the design lens. Likewise, the emphasis on spontaneity contrasts with the conservatism of the experience lens. For human organisations, the three elements of evolutionary theory work as follows:

- *Variety*. Organisations and their environments offer a rich 'ecology' for the generation of different ideas and initiatives. There are many kinds of people and many kinds of circumstance. Sales people working closely with customers may be able to sense new opportunities at least as well as top managers at headquarters. Since people interact with their environment throughout the organisation, new ideas often come from low down in the hierarchy, not just from the top.[7] Complexity theorist Bill McKelvey refers to this as the 'distributed intelligence' of an organisation.[8] Variety can even come from apparent mistakes, just as genetic mutations come from imperfect genes. A famous example is Post-it notes, which originated from an 'imperfect' glue being applied to paper, but resulted in a semi-adhesive for which the researcher saw market potential.

- *Selection*. In nature, selection is 'blind', determined by environmental fit rather than deliberate intervention. In organisations, selection can be nearly as blind, with strategies selected more according to how they well they match prevailing cultures or standard decision rules, rather than by objective analysis and evaluation. In this view, there is an 'internal ecology' within organisations, with ideas and initiatives winning out against competing ideas and initiatives according to their internal fit.[9] A good idea may fail simply because it does not meet existing selection rules, regardless of its overall merits: for example, a company may apply standard return on capital criteria that are outdated on the basis of the current real cost of capital (see Chapter 12 on strategy evaluation). On the other hand, as in complexity theory, ideas can gain rapid momentum as they attract 'positive feedback': the support of one important set of actors can attract the support of another, and the support of that set of actors attracts the support of still others, and so on in an escalating process. Thus selection mechanisms can be self-reinforcing, speeding the passage of both good and bad ideas.

- *Retention*. As well as processes of selection, there are processes of retention. Retention refers to the preservation and reproduction over time of selected variations.[10] Retention may happen as particular policies or preferences become embedded in the organisation. Retention may be achieved by instituting formal procedures: for example, job descriptions, accounting and control systems, management information systems, training and organisation structure. Often it is done through more informal processes of routinisation, in which simple repetition of certain routine behaviours leads to the eventual imprinting of such routines in the culture and capabilities of the organisation.

Implications

A key insight from the variety lens is that managers need to be wary of assuming that they can wholly control the generation and adoption of new ideas. However, there are a number of things managers can do to foster initiatives and prevent the undue suppression of good ideas. At the same time, the variety lens points both managers and students to distinctive sources of innovation in organisations. We highlight three key implications:

- *Allow for emergence*. Rather than being deliberately designed, strategies often emerge from the bottom and the periphery of organisations, accumulating coherence over time. As in Chapter 1, Henry Mintzberg's definition of strategy as an emergent 'pattern' rather than an explicit statement is widely relevant. Managers and students should not necessarily trust in the stated strategic vision and mission (Chapter 1), but rather look to what is actually happening, especially on the ground. The future of an organisation may well be emerging from somewhere far beyond headquarters' formal initiatives. Indeed, in many industries, large firms frequently watch the interesting experiments and initiatives of small independent firms, and then buy them up.[11]

- *Encourage interaction, experiment and change.* From a variety lens point of view, organisations can be too stable and ordered. To generate variety, managers should promote potentially disruptive interactions across internal and external organisational boundaries: cross-departmental initiatives are important internally and communication with customers, suppliers, partners and innovators should be extensive externally. Alphabet (formerly Google) encourages experiments by giving staff 20 per cent of their time to pursue their own projects. Complexity theorists prescribe regular change in order to stay at the dynamic 'edge of chaos', the delicate balancing point where organisations neither settle down into excessive stability nor topple over into destructive chaos.[12]

- *Attend to key rules.* If strategies tend to get adopted according to their fit with established organisational cultures or investment criteria, then managers need to attend at least as much to setting the context for strategy as to individual strategic decisions. As above, managers should create a context conducive to interaction, experiment and change. But they should particularly attend to the key selection and retention rules by which strategies are allowed to emerge. Drawing on complexity theory, Kathy Eisenhardt encourages the design of 'simple rules', a few clear guidelines for strategy selection and retention.[13] For example, the movie studio Miramax only selects movies that revolve round a central human condition (e.g. love), feature an appealing but flawed central character, and have a clear storyline. The Danish hearing aid company Oticon does not retain projects where any key team member chooses to switch from that project to another.

Strategy as discourse

In many ways, management is about discourse. Managers spend 75 per cent of their time communicating: for example, gathering information, persuading others or following up decisions.[14] In particular, strategy has a high discursive component, involving both talk and text. Strategy is debated in meetings, written as formal plans, explained in annual reports and media releases, presented on PowerPoints, and communicated to employees.[15] The discourse lens recognises this discursive component as central to strategy. Here, as indicated in Figure C.iv, the legitimacy of discourse is particularly important. The importance of legitimacy, however, can work against both objective rationality and organisational innovation.

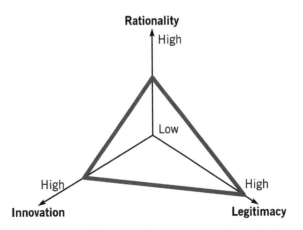

Figure C.iv Discourse lens

An important influence on the discourse lens is the work of the French philosopher Michel Foucault. Foucault stresses the subtle effects that language can have on understanding, power and personal identities. For example, he shows how changing scientific discourses in the seventeenth and eighteenth centuries redefined insanity as treatable illness rather than natural foolishness.[16] The insane now had a new identity, medically ill, and became subject to a new power, the medical doctors with the task of curing them. In a similar way, the 'financialisation' discourse emerging in the 1990s and early 2000s sought to redefine the purpose of the firm as solely about shareholder value, enhancing the power of investors to insist on short-term financial results rather than long-term strategic investments.[17] Those taking a discourse lens are therefore sensitive to how strategy discourse can shape understanding, change personal identities and disseminate power.

These three effects of strategy discourse are explored as follows:

- *Shaping understanding.* The language of strategy has characteristics that make it convincing to others.[18] Its concepts and jargon have high legitimacy in many organisations. Here the discourse lens reveals the design lens in another light. The legitimacy of strategy discourse gives the analytic apparatus of the design lens a persuasiveness that often goes beyond the technical effectiveness of the analysis itself. Drawing on established techniques such as the Porter Five Forces (Chapter 3) or fashionable concepts such as Blue Ocean strategy (Chapter 3) can add to the authority of strategic recommendations. The ability to write inspiring vision and mission statements (Chapter 1) can help motivate a whole organisation. The justification of strategic change by the radical rhetoric of hypercompetition (Chapter 3) or disruptive innovation (Chapter 10) may give legitimacy to radical actions that might otherwise be rejected as excessive. In other words, managers draw on the rhetoric of strategy and the apparent 'rightness' of strategy concepts to convince others they should comply.

- *Defining identities.* How managers talk about strategy also positions them in relation to others, either by their own deliberate choice or as a result of how they are perceived.[19] Discourse therefore influences the identity and legitimacy of managers as 'strategists'. The ability to use the rational analytical language of the design lens helps define managers as legitimate participants in the strategy process. Of course, sometimes other kinds of discursive identity may be appropriate. For example, in some contexts the language of the heroic leader (Chapter 15) or the innovative entrepreneur (Chapter 10) might offer more support for the decision-maker's identity than simple rational analysis. Whatever the precise identity, the assumptions built into strategy discourse are liable to affect behaviour. For example, lower-level managers and professionals who internalise the strategy discourse of competitiveness and performance as part of their identities come to prioritise those values in their everyday work, subordinating to some degree the administrative or professional values (such as equity or care) that might otherwise be important in their roles.

- *Instrument of power.* Here strategy discourse is linked to power and control.[20] By understanding the concepts of strategy, or being seen to do so, top managers or strategy specialists are positioned as having the knowledge about how to deal with the really difficult problems the organisation faces. The possession of such knowledge gives them power over others who do not have it. Design lens discourse, with its commitment to demanding forms of technical analysis, can be particularly elitist and exclusive. Thus mastering the discursive language of the design lens offers a political advantage as well as an analytical one. At the same time, the internalisation of strategy discourse by employees renders them more compliant to the strategy: they see pursuing the strategy as a natural part of their role. In this sense, discourse is associated with power when it attracts followers and is self-reproducing and self-reinforcing. Insofar as strategy discourse serves the interests of the powerful, it may suppress innovation and change and distort objective rational analysis from the point of view of the organisation as a whole.

Implications

The discourse lens suggests the importance of the appearance, as well as the reality, of rational argument. Through the discourse lens, strategies need to be legitimate, not simply correct. Strategy discourse, moreover, helps define legitimate participants in strategic decision-making and gives power to the decisions that are ultimately made. The fundamental lesson for managers and students is that the language of strategy matters.

The implications of the discourse lens have both instrumental and critical aspects:

- *Use strategy discourse skilfully.* The right discourse can add legitimacy to particular strategies or individuals in an organisation.[21] This discourse needs to match particular contexts and circumstances. Justifying a strategy to a potential investor may call for a logical, highly quantitative financial case; explaining the same strategy to employees may involve emphasising implications for job security and career growth. For some organisations, the analytic discourse of the design lens will be a legitimate mode of justification; in other organisations, appeal to technical or professional values may be more effective. The instrumental value of the discourse lens lies in this: using the right language matters both for justifying and imposing strategies and for participating in strategy discussions in the first place.

- *Treat strategy discourse sceptically.* Just as strategy discourse can be used instrumentally, so should managers and students be ready to take a critical perspective towards such discourse. Are concepts and frameworks being used as a smokescreen for some particular individuals or groups to advance their sectional power and interests, as for example 'financialisation' discourse did for investors? Are strengths and weaknesses, threats and opportunities (Chapter 4) being mystified or exaggerated? Are the grandiose ambitions of vision and mission statements just empty rhetoric (Chapter 1)? Seeing strategy as discourse can prompt the healthy questioning of concepts, ideas and rhetorics that might otherwise be taken for granted. The discourse lens encourages managers and students to see through the surface language of strategy to uncover the deeper interests and motives behind it. Adopters of the discourse lens are naturally sceptical.

Conclusion

The core assumptions and the key implications of the four lenses of design, experience, variety and discourse are summarised in Table C.i. They are not offered here as an exhaustive list, but to crystalise the distinctive perspectives of each lens. Indeed, this Commentary as a whole is merely an introduction and you may usefully explore each of the lenses further yourself. After all, each of the lenses presented here actually includes several perspectives themselves. For example, the variety lens builds on both evolutionary theory and complexity theory, each of which offers distinctive points of their own. So, within these lenses there are finer-grained insights to discover. The references at the end of this Commentary should help with deeper exploration of the lenses. In addition, there are whole books written that provide multiple perspectives on strategy, from the four different ones that Richard Whittington offers, to the ten of Henry Mintzberg and his co-authors, or even the 13 'images' provided in the collection by Stephen Cummings and David Wilson.[22]

However, the overarching message that comes from all four lenses is this: in considering a topic like strategy, it is useful to take a critical approach. Being critical involves recognising that one lens is probably not enough, and that every lens has its own value and its own limitations. You should not necessarily be satisfied with just the rational analysis of the design lens. Use the experience lens to consider sources of unconscious bias; take a variety lens approach to be sensitive to spontaneous initiatives from the bottom or periphery; stay sceptical by

Table C.i A summary of the strategy lenses

	Strategy as:			
	Design	Experience	Variety	Discourse
Strategy develops through . . .	A logical process of analysis and evaluation	People's experience, assumptions and taken-for-granted ways of doing things	Ideas bubbling up from the variety of people in and around organisations	Managers seeking influence, power and legitimacy through the language they use
Assumptions about organisations	Mechanistic, hierarchical, rational systems	Cultures based on experience, legitimacy and past success	Complex, diverse and spontaneous systems	Arenas of power and influence shaped by discourse
Role of top management	Strategic decision-makers	Enactors of their experience	Creators of context	Manipulators of language
Key implications	Undertake careful and thorough analysis of strategic issues	Recognise that people's experience is central but also needs challenging	Be sensitive to ideas from the bottom, the periphery and even outside the organisation	See through strategy language to uncover hidden assumptions and interests

interpreting strategy talk through the discourse lens. It is because different perspectives are important that we shall return to the four lenses in the Commentaries at the ends of Parts II and III of this book. Throughout your course, we encourage you to approach the topics of strategy with eyes open to different points of view. To get into the habit, you might now want to consider the short Nokia case through the four strategy lenses.

REFERENCES

1. For a good discussion of the meaning of critical thinking, see S. Michailova and A. Wright, 'Criticality in management learning and education: what it is and what it is not', *Academy of Management annual conference*, Vancouver, Canada, 2015.

2. A useful review of the principles of rational decision making can be found in J.G. March, *A Primer on Decision Making: How Decisions Happen*, Simon & Schuster, 1994, Chapter 1, pp. 1–35.

3. An introduction to Ansoff's thought is R. Moussetis, 'Ansoff revisited', *Journal of Management History*, vol. 17, no. 1 (2011), pp. 102–25. Porter discusses his thinking in N. Argyres and A. McGahan 'An interview with Michael Porter', *Academy of Management Executive*, vol. 16, no. 2 (2002), pp. 43–52.

4. An updated view of the *Behavioral Theory of the Firm* is in G. Gavetti, D. Levinthal and W. Ocasio, 'The behavioral theory of the firm: assessment and prospects', *Academy of Management Annals*, vol. 6, no. 1 (2012), pp. 1–40. A contrast with traditional economics is provided in M. Augier, 'The early evolution of the foundations for behavioral organization theory and strategy', *European Management Journal*, vol. 28 (2012), pp. 84–102.

5. W. P. Barnett and R. Burgelman, 'Evolutionary perspectives on strategy', *Strategic Management Journal*, vol. 17.S1 (2007), pp. 5–19.

6. S. Girod and R. Whittington, 'Change escalation process and complex adaptive systems: from incremental reconfigurations to discontinuous restructuring', *Organizational Science*, vol. 26, no. 5 (2015), pp. 1520–535.

7. See G. Johnson and A.S. Huff, 'Everyday innovation/everyday strategy', in G. Hamel, G.K. Prahalad, H. Thomas and D. O'Neal (eds), *Strategic Flexibility – Managing in a Turbulent Environment*, Wiley, 1998, pp. 13–27. Patrick Regner also shows how new strategic directions can grow from the periphery of organisations in the face of opposition from the centre; see 'Strategy creation in the periphery: inductive versus deductive strategy making', *Journal of Management Studies*, vol. 40, no. 1 (2003), pp. 57–82.

8. Bill McKelvey, a complexity theorist, argues that the variety within this distributed intelligence is increased because individual managers seek to become better informed about their environment: see B. McKelvey, 'Simple rules for improving corporate IQ: basic lessons from complexity science', in P. Andriani and G. Passiante (eds), *Complexity, Theory and the Management of Networks*, Imperial College Press, 2004.

9. R. Burgelman and. A. Grove, 'Let chaos reign, then rein in chaos – repeatedly: managing strategic dynamics for corporate longevity', *Strategic Management Journal*, vol. 28, no. 10 (2007), pp. 965–79.

10. B. McKelvey and H. Aldrich, 'Populations, natural selection, and applied organizational science', *Administrative Science Quarterly*, vol. 28, no. 1 (1983), pp. 101–128.

11. P. Puranam, H. Singh and M. Zollo, 'Organizing for innovation: managing the coordination-autonomy dilemma in technology acquisitions', *Academy of Management Journal*, vol. 49, no. 2 (2006), pp. 263–80.

12. K.M. Eisenhardt and S. Brown, 'Competing on the edge: strategy as structured chaos', *Long Range Planning*, vol. 31, no. 5 (1998), pp. 786–89.

13. C.B. Bingham and K.M. Eisenhardt, 'Rational heuristics: the "simple rules" that strategists learn from process experience', *Strategic Management Journal*, vol. 32, no. 13 (2011), pp. 1437–64.

14. H. Mintzberg, *The Nature of Managerial Work*, Harper & Row, 1973.

15. See A. Spee and P. Jarzabkowski, 'Strategic planning as communicative process', *Organization Studies*, vol. 32, no. 9 (2011), pp. 1217–45. Also W. Küpers, S. Mantere and M. Statler, 'Strategy as storytelling: a phenomenological collaboration', *Journal of Management Inquiry*, vol. 22, no. 1 (2013), pp. 83–100.

16. M. Foucault, *Discipline and Punish*, Vintage, 1995.

17. P. Thompson and B. Harley, 'Beneath the radar? A critical realist analysis of "the knowledge economy"and "shareholder value"as competing discourses', *Organization Studies*, vol. 33, no. 10 (2012), pp. 1363–81.

18. D. Barry and M. Elmes, 'Strategy retold: toward a narrative view of strategic discourse', *Academy of Management Review*, vol. 22, no. 2 (1997), pp. 429–52.

19. S. Mantere and E. Vaara, 'On the problem of participation in strategy: a critical discursive perspective', *Organization Science*, vol. 19, no. 2 (2008), pp. 341–58.

20. C. Hardy and R. Thomas, 'Strategy, discourse and practice: the intensification of power', *Journal of Management Studies*, vol. 51, no. 2 (2014), pp. 320–48.

21. R. Whittington, B. Yakis-Douglas and K. Ahn, 'Cheap talk: strategy presentations as a form of Chief Executive Officer impression management', *Strategic Management Journal* (forthcoming).

22. R. Whittington, *What is Strategy – and Does it Matter?*, Thompson, 2000; H. Mintzberg, B. Ahlstrand and J. Lampel, *Strategy Safari*, Prentice Hall, 1998; S. Cummings and D. Wilson, *Images of Strategy*, Sage, 2003.

CASE EXAMPLE

Nokia's evolving strategy through the lenses

Nokia, the Finnish telecommunications firm, has pursued a trajectory that, over time, has exemplified all four of the Strategy Lenses.

Nokia started out in 1865 as a Finnish paper pulp mill. The company only began to take its modern form in 1966 when it had merged with the Finnish Rubber Works and the Finnish Cable Company to form a conglomerate with businesses ranging from rubber boots to aluminium parts. The Finnish Cable Works had established a small electronics department in 1960 in one corner of its main factory. This electronics department in turn spawned several businesses, including a mobile phone unit launched in 1979 through a joint venture with another Finnish company, Salora.

During the 1980s, Nokia became committed to an active diversification strategy, especially internationally. Businesses were acquired in the television and computer industries, and Salora itself was taken over in 1984. By 1987, an internal strategic planning document identified over 30 strategic business units in a Boston Consulting Group portfolio matrix (see Chapter 8), with mobile phones labelled one of several 'star' businesses ripe for investment.

But Nokia then hit a very rough patch. Its chairman and CEO committed suicide in 1988, and many of its industrial markets were hit hard by the collapse of the then Soviet Union. There was a period of losses and top management turmoil, from which finally emerged a new CEO, Jorma Ollila. Ollila had only arrived at Nokia in 1985, after an early career in the American investment bank Citibank. Since 1990, he had been head of the mobile phones business, then accounting for only ten per cent of Nokia's total sales.

On appointment as CEO, Ollila had promised continuity. In fact, the company rapidly focused on mobile phones. By 1996, mobile phones accounted for 60 per cent of Nokia sales and two years later Nokia became the world's largest mobile phone company. Other businesses were divested, so that soon the only other substantial business was Nokia telecommunications networks and infrastructure business, merged into a joint venture with Siemens in 2007.

Nokia's phone business flourished for more than a decade, until two cataclysmic events: first, Apple's launch of the iPhone in 2007 and then the 2009 launch of Google's Android operating system supported by companies such as HTC and Samsung. At the same time,

Stephen Elop and Steve Ballmer
Source: Simon Dawson/Bloomberg via Getty Images.

Chinese manufacturers began to attack Nokia's position in low-cost phones, especially in developing markets. In 2010, Nokia responded to the growing pressure by appointing its first non-Finnish CEO, the Canadian Stephen Elop.

Elop's previous company had been Microsoft, another company struggling in the phone market, though he himself had been responsible for Microsoft's Office products business. The new CEO launched a wide-ranging strategic review: 'The very first day I began, I sent out an email to all of the employees and I asked them: what do you think I need to change? What do you think I need not or should not change? What are you afraid I'm going to miss?' A key issue that he and his management team struggled with during the first year was whether Nokia should continue with its own operating system. Operating systems are highly expensive to develop and sustain and need to be attractive to external software developers in order to secure a competitive range of apps. Within a few months, Elop and his team had decided to abandon Nokia's own operating system. There were two alternative operating systems available: Google's or Microsoft's. Elop inclined towards Microsoft. His reasoning was that Microsoft was the weaker of the two, and therefore needed Nokia more than Google did. Nokia also feared being just another Android phone manufacturer competing on the same basis as HTC or Samsung.

In February 2011, Elop released what would become his famous 'burning platform' memo to all employees. Nokia was compared to a man on a burning oil platform, who could only survive by leaping into the sea. Nokia had been too slow, and must now make a dramatic move. Elop told his employees: 'We poured gasoline on our own burning platform. I believe we have lacked accountability and leadership to align and direct the company through these disruptive times. We had a series of misses. We haven't been delivering innovation fast enough. We're not collaborating internally. Nokia, our platform is burning.' Several days later, he announced to the world that he was abandoning Nokia's own operating systems in favour of Microsoft's, sealed by a public handshake with his old boss, Steve Ballmer, CEO of Microsoft. A senior Google executive commented on the Nokia–Microsoft alliance: 'two turkeys do not make an eagle'.

Nokia's first phones with the new operating system were not an immediate success and Nokia's losses deepened. By spring 2012, Stephen Elop was describing Nokia in terms of a famous Finnish long-distance runner, Lasse Virén, who had tripped during a race in 1972 but still won in the end: 'like Virén we are off the grass, on the track and running again.' But Nokia soon ran out of breath. In the autumn of 2013, it was announced that Nokia would be selling its mobile phone business to Microsoft, and that Stephen Elop would be returning to his old company.

Key sources: J. Aspara, J.A. Lamberg, A. Laukia and H. Tikkanen, 'Strategic management of business model transformation: lessons from Nokia', *Management Decision*, vol. 49, no. 4 (2011), pp. 622–647; *Financial Times*, 11 April 2011, 3 May 2012 and 3 September 2013; *Engadget*, 2 August 2011. T. Laamanen, J.-A. Lamberg and E. Vaara, 'Explanations of success and failure in management learning: what can be learnt from Nokia's rise and fall?', *Academy of Management Learning and Education*, vol. 15, no. 1 (2016), pp. 2–25.

Questions

1 How could you use the design lens, the experience lens and the variety lens to account for the development of the mobile phone business within Nokia?

2 How could you use the design lens and the experience lens to explain Stephen Elop's adoption of the Microsoft operating system?

3 Comment on Stephen Elop's changing language from a discourse lens perspective.

9

CORPORATE STRATEGY AND DIVERSIFICATION

9.1 INTRODUCTION

Chapter 7 was concerned with *competitive strategy* – the ways in which a single business unit or organisational unit can compete in a given market space, for instance through cost leadership or differentiation. However, organisations may choose to enter many new product and market areas (see Figure II.1 in Part II introduction). For example Tata Group, one of India's largest companies, began as a trading organisation and soon moved into hotels and textiles. Since that time, Tata has diversified further into steel, motors, consultancy, technologies, tea, chemicals, power, communications. As organisations add new units and capabilities, their strategies may no longer be solely concerned with *competitive strategy* in one market space at the business level, but with choices concerning different businesses or markets. Corporate strategy is about what business areas to be active in, and this will determine which business unit(s) to buy, the direction(s) an organisation might pursue and how resources may be allocated efficiently across multiple business activities. For Tata, the corporate strategy questions are whether it should add any more businesses, whether it should exit some, and how far it should integrate the businesses it retains. For large public-sector organisations and charities these choices also have to be made. These choices, indicated in Figure 9.1, inform decisions about how broad an organisation should be. This 'scope' of an organisation is central to *corporate strategy* and the focus of this chapter.

Scope is concerned with how far an organisation should be diversified in terms of two different dimensions: products and markets. As the opening example shows, an organisation may increase its scope by engaging in market spaces or products different to its current ones. Section 9.2 introduces a classic product market framework that uses these categories for identifying different growth directions for an organisation. This indicates different *diversification* strategies open to an organisation, according to the novelty of products or markets. Underpinning diversification choices are a range of drivers, which are discussed in Section 9.3, including increasing market power, reducing risk and exploiting superior internal processes. The performance implications of diversification are, then, reviewed in Section 9.4.

Another way of increasing the scope of an organisation is *vertical integration,* discussed in Section 9.5. It allows an organisation to act as an internal supplier or a customer to itself (as

Figure 9.1 Strategic directions and corporate-level strategy

for example an oil company supplies its petrol to its own petrol stations). The organisation may decide to *outsource* certain activities – to 'dis-integrate' by subcontracting an internal activity to an external supplier – as this may improve organisational efficiency. The scope of the organisation may therefore be adjusted through growth or contraction.

Diversified corporations that operate in different areas of activity will have multiple strategic business units (SBUs) with their own strategies for their specific markets for which they can be held accountable in terms of success or failure. SBUs thus allow large corporations to vary their business strategies according to the different needs of the various external markets they serve. Nevertheless, corporate head office, the 'corporate level', needs to manage the selection of SBUs and establish their boundaries, perhaps by market, geography or capability, so they add value to the group.[1] The value-adding effect of head office to individual SBUs, that make up the organisation's portfolio, is termed **parenting advantage** (see Section 9.6). Their ability to do this effectively may make them competitive amongst other corporate parents in acquiring and manage different businesses. But just how do corporate-level activities, decisions and resources add value to businesses? As will be seen at the end of the chapter in the 'Thinking Differently' section, some are sceptical about headquarters' ability to add value.

In order to decide which industries and businesses organisations should invest in or dispose of, the corporate centre needs to assess whether the *portfolio* of businesses is worth more under its management than the individual businesses would be worth standing alone. Section 9.7 reviews portfolio matrices, which are useful techniques to help structure corporate-level choices about businesses in which to invest and those to divest.

This chapter is not just about large commercial businesses. Small businesses may also have different business units. For example, a local building company may be undertaking contract work for local government, industrial buyers and local homeowners. Not only are these different market segments, but the mode of operation and capabilities required for competitive success in each are also likely to be different. Moreover, the owner of that business has to take decisions about the extent of investment and activity in each segment. Public-sector organisations such as local government or health services also provide different services, which correspond to business units in commercial organisations. Corporate-level strategy is also highly relevant to the appropriate drawing of organisational boundaries in the public sector. Privatisation and outsourcing decisions can be considered as responses to the failure of public-sector organisations to add sufficient value by their parenting.

9.2 STRATEGY DIRECTIONS

A central corporate strategy choice is about in which areas a company should grow. **Ansoff's** product/market **growth matrix**[2] **is a classic corporate strategy framework for generating four basic directions for organisational growth** – see Figure 9.2. Typically an organisation starts in zone A. It may choose between *penetrating* still further within zone A (sometimes termed 'consolidation'), or increasing its diversity along the two axes of increasing novelty of markets or increasing novelty of products. This process of increasing the diversity of products and/or markets is known as 'diversification'. **Diversification involves increasing the range of products or markets served by an organisation. Related diversification involves expanding into products or services with relationships to the existing business.** Thus on Ansoff's axes the organisation has two related diversification strategies available: moving to zone B, *developing new products* for its existing markets, or moving to zone C by bringing its existing products into *new markets*. In each case, the further along the two axes, the more diversified the strategy. Alternatively, the organisation can move in both directions at once, following

Figure 9.2 Corporate strategy directions

Source: Adapted from H.I. Ansoff, *Corporate Strategy*, Penguin, 1988, Chapter 6 . Ansoff originally had a matrix with four separate boxes, but in practice strategic directions involve more continuous axes. The Ansoff matrix itself was later developed – see Reference 2.

a *conglomerate diversification* strategy with altogether new markets and new products (zone D). Thus **conglomerate (unrelated) diversification involves diversifying into products or services with no relationships to existing businesses.**

Ansoff's axes can be used for brainstorming strategic options, checking that all four zones have been properly considered. Illustration 9.1 traces the evolution of a social enterprise, raising questions about how businesses might think about Ansoff's matrix in choosing their strategic direction. The next section will consider each of Ansoff's four main directions in some detail. Section 9.5 will examine the additional option of *vertical integration*.

9.2.1 Market penetration

For a simple, undiversified business, the most obvious strategic option is often increased penetration of its existing market, with its existing products. Market penetration implies increasing share of current markets with the current product range. This strategy builds on established strategic capabilities and does not require the organisation to venture into uncharted territory. The organisation's scope is exactly the same. Moreover, greater market share implies increased power vis-à-vis buyers and suppliers (in terms of Porter's five forces), greater economies of scale and experience curve benefits.

However, organisations seeking greater market penetration may face two constraints:

● *Retaliation from competitors.* In terms of the five forces (Section 3.2), increasing market penetration is likely to exacerbate industry rivalry as other competitors in the market defend their share. Increased rivalry might involve price wars or expensive marketing battles, which may cost more than any market-share gains are actually worth. The dangers of provoking fierce retaliation are greater in low-growth markets, as gains in volume will be more at the expense of other players. Where retaliation is a danger, organisations seeking market penetration need strategic capabilities that give a clear competitive advantage. In low-growth or declining markets, it can be more effective simply to acquire competitors. Some companies have grown quickly in this way. For example, in the steel industry the Indian company LNM (Mittal) moved rapidly in the 2000s to become the largest global steel producer by acquiring

ILLUSTRATION 9.1   Baking change into the community

How Greyston's diversification transforms a depressed community.

Probably best known for producing the brownies in the famous Ben and Jerry's ice creams, the Greyston Bakery is part of the Greyston Foundation – a $15m (£9m; €11.25m) integrated network of for-profit and not-for-profit entities. The Foundation provides a wide array of services to benefit its local depressed community.

A Zen Buddhist meditation group started the bakery in 1982. They located in the poor neighbourhood of Yonkers, New York, where they perceived a need to create jobs for people in the community who were 'hard to employ' – the homeless, those with poor employment histories, prison records and past substance-abuse problems. Radically they used an 'open hiring' practice that continues today, in which anybody who applies for a job has an opportunity to work, on a first-come, first-hired basis. Employees have to show up for work on time, perform the job and have an appropriate attitude for three months and are then automatically made permanent employees. As SVP David Rome says, 'we judge people based on their performance in the operation, not on their background'. There is high initial turnover but the average tenure is about three years. Greyston considers it a success when an employee moves onto a new job using his or her new skills. According to CEO Julius Walls, 'The company provides opportunities and resources to its employees so they can be successful not only in the workplace but in their personal lives. We don't hire people to bake brownies; we bake brownies to hire people.'

As the bakery expanded it realised that providing jobs to the community was not enough. In 1991, working with governmental agencies, Greyston Family Inn was opened to provide permanent housing for homeless people. Currently there are three buildings, providing 50 housing units. A child day-care centre was also started as after-school care was one of the most pressing needs in the community for working parents. In 1992, Greyston Health Services was formed and in 1997, Issan House opened with 35 permanent housing units for those with HIV/AIDS, mental illness or chemical dependency. Other ventures included Greyston Garden Project, five community-run gardens on neglected properties, and a technology education centre. In 2011, a local retail bakery/café was opened and in 2012, with the help of the Foundation's real-estate division, a new bakery was constructed, for $10m in a public–private partnership project with the city, on a long-dormant brownfield (contaminated) site.

The Foundation is an umbrella for all Greyston organisations, providing centralised management, fund-raising, real-estate development and planning services. It now comprises four interrelated organisations: bakery, healthcare services, child and family programmes and real-estate development. The Foundation's social mission of supporting low-income people to forge a path to self-sufficiency and community transformation is blended with business collaboration to enable continual growth.

In 2012, Greyston Bakery celebrated its 30th anniversary, and New York State made it a Benefit Corporation, allowing Greyston to demonstrate higher standards of corporate purpose, accountability and transparency. As CEO Steven Brown said, 'Really, we were a benefit corporation long before the term was coined. You're in business for a much larger community that has a stake in what you are doing. Creating value and opportunity is the path out of distress for communities.' Since then Greyston has continued to grow, opening new multi-family housing developments for local working families.

Sources: www.greyston.com; http://1596994.sites.myregisteredsite.com/levpoints/lp52.html#face; *Huffington Post*, 9 December 2012. http://www.youtube.com/watch?v=2WLzV7JfVSc.

Questions

1 What were the motivation(s) for Greyston Bakery's diversifications?

2 Referring to the Ansoff matrix, how would you classify these diversifications?

struggling steel companies around the world. Acquisitions may reduce rivalry, by taking out independent players and controlling them under one umbrella.

- *Legal constraints.* Greater market penetration can raise concerns from official competition regulators concerning excessive market power. Most countries have regulators with the powers to restrain powerful companies or prevent mergers and acquisitions that would create such excessive power. In the UK, the Competition Commission can investigate any merger or acquisition that would account for more than 25 per cent of the national market, and either halt the deal or propose measures that would reduce market power. The European Commission has an overview of the whole European market and can similarly intervene. For example, when it gave approval for the acquisition of the vaccines business of Novartis by GSK, and the creation of a new entity, the decision was conditional upon the divestiture of certain related assets. The Commission had concerns the transaction would have eliminated an important competitor to GSK for the supply of several vaccines and consumer health products, which might lead to price increases for European consumers.[3]

Market penetration may also not be an option where economic constraints are severe, for instance during a market downturn or public-sector funding crisis. Here organisations will need to consider the strategic option of *retrenchment*: withdrawal from marginal activities in order to concentrate on the most valuable segments and products within their existing business. However, where growth is still sought, the Ansoff's axes suggest further directions, as follows.

9.2.2 Product development

Product development is where organisations deliver modified or new products (or services) to existing markets. This can involve varying degrees of diversification along the horizontal axis of Figure 9.2. For Apple, developing its products from the original iPod, through iPhone to iPad involved little diversification: although the technologies differed, Apple was targeting the same customers and using very similar production processes and distribution channels. Despite the potential for benefits from relatedness, product development can be an expensive and high-risk activity for at least two reasons:

- *New resources and capabilities.* Product development strategies typically involve mastering new processes or technologies that are unfamiliar to the organisation. For example, the digital revolution is forcing universities to reconsider the way learning materials are acquired and provided to students and the nature of the student/academic interface. High-quality content available free online and virtual engagement with students now raise the question of how universities should consider redeploying their resources in the future. Success is likely to depend on a willingness to acquire new technological capabilities, to engage in organisational restructuring and new marketing capabilities to manage customer perceptions. Thus product development typically involves heavy investments and can have high risk of project failures.

- *Project management risk.* Even within fairly familiar domains, product development projects are typically subject to the risk of delays and increased costs due to project complexity and changing project specifications over time. For example, Boeing's Dreamliner 787 aircraft made innovative use of carbon-fibre composites but had a history of delays even before launch in 2010, and required $2.5bn (£1.5bn, €1.9bn) write-offs due to cancelled orders. Since then, batteries catching fire has resulted in fleets being grounded.

Strategies for product development are considered further in Chapter 10.

9.2.3 Market development

Product development can be risky and expensive. Market development can be more attractive by being potentially cheaper and quicker to execute. Market development involves offering existing products to new markets. Again, the degree of diversification varies along Figure 9.2's downward axis. Typically, of course, market development entails some product development as well, if only in terms of packaging or service. Nonetheless, market development remains a form of related diversification given its origins in similar products. Market development takes two basic forms:

- *New users*. Here an example would be aluminium, whose original users, packaging and cutlery manufacturers, are now supplemented by users in aerospace and automobiles.
- *New geographies*. The prime example of this is internationalisation, but it would also include the spread of a small retailer into new towns.

In all cases, it is essential that market development strategies be based on products or services that meet the *critical success factors* of the new market (see Section 3.4.3). Strategies based on simply off-loading traditional products or services in new markets are likely to fail. Moreover, market development faces similar problems to product development. In terms of strategic capabilities, market developers often lack the right marketing skills and brands to make progress in a market with unfamiliar customers. On the management side, the challenge is coordinating between different users and geographies, which might all have different needs. *International* market development strategy is considered in Chapter 9.

9.2.4 Conglomerate diversification

Conglomerate (or unrelated) diversification takes the organisation beyond both its existing markets and its existing products (i.e. zone D in Figure 9.2). In this sense, it radically increases the organisation's scope. Conglomerate diversification strategies can create value as businesses may benefit from being part of a larger group. This may allow consumers to have greater confidence in the business units products and services than before and larger size may also reduce the costs of finance. However, conglomerate strategies are often not trusted by many observers because there are no obvious ways in which the businesses can work together to generate additional value, over and above the businesses remaining on their own. In addition, there is often an additional bureaucratic cost of the managers at headquarters who control them. For this reason, conglomerate companies' share prices can suffer from what is called the 'conglomerate discount'–in other words, a lower valuation than the combined individual constituent businesses would have on their own. For instance, shares in Old Mutual, an international financial services group, traded at a 25 per cent discount to its peers since the recession. This underperformance occurred since it moved its business to the UK from South Africa and diversified away from its core focus on Africa and emerging markets. Speculation that the CEO will announce a break-up saw Old Mutual shares rise 7 per cent in trading.

However, it is important to recognise that the distinction between related and conglomerate (unrelated) diversification is often a matter of degree. Relationships that might have seemed valuable in related diversification may not turn out to be as valuable as expected. Thus the large accounting firms have often struggled in translating their skills and client contacts developed in auditing into effective consulting practices. Similarly, relationships may change in importance over time, as the nature of technologies or markets change: see, for example, the decision by TomTom to move into different product offerings (Illustration 9.2).

ILLUSTRATION 9.2   From sat nav to driverless cars

Sat nav manufacturer TomTom diversifies to survive.

Dutch manufacturer TomTom's fortunes dived in 2008 with sales down 36 per cent to €959m (£767m, $1.2bn) (2014) and profits down 71 per cent to €25.4m (2014). From its peak of $15bn, multinational TomTom's market value was just €2.3bn by 2015. How did this decline come about and what could management do about it?

Originally a software developer for business-to-business mobile applications and personal digital assistants (PDAs), TomTom became market leader in PDA software in just two years with navigation applications RoutePlanner and Citymaps. In 2002, the TomTom Navigator was launched, providing European customers for the first time with an easy-to-use, affordable, portable navigation device (PND). Demand was strong for the PND which was not just a new product, but an entirely new consumer electronics category. TomTom GO, launched in 2004, revolutionised the way millions of drivers got from A to B. Affordable and accessible to everyone, it became the fastest selling consumer technology device ever. Since then, over 75 million devices have been sold in 35 countries, guiding drivers over 280 billion kilometres.

During 2008, TomTom's sales fell dramatically due to an increasingly saturated sat nav market, plus smartphone alternatives from Google and Nokia. TomTom was forced to reconsider its business and diversified into fleet management and vehicle telematics, where it is now a recognised leader. TomTom evolved from just a hardware business, selling sat navs to stick on windscreens, to a software and services provider that offered free mapping on smartphones and integrated traffic management systems used by governments to quell traffic and manage roads.

After partnering with Nike on the Nike+ Sport-Watch, TomTom launched its own TomTom Runner and TomTom Multi-Sport watches in 2013, to help runners, cyclists and swimmers keep moving towards their fitness goals, by providing essential performance information at a glance. Both have GPS sensors, allowing them to tap into TomTom's navigation platform. TomTom is now straying further from its roots by launching Bandit, an action camera, to challenge American market leader GoPro. It will contain GPS sensors allowing users to find and tag exciting moments in their video footage, based on speed, altitude, G-force and acceleration. Bandit's real selling point is its video-editing and -sharing capabilities.

Although sat nav devices, sports watches and action cameras may seem unlikely bedfellows, co-founder Vigreux explains that 'TomTom is a bit like a collection of startups under one umbrella. Employees are actively encouraged to be entrepreneurial in product development. . . . We're a tech brand at the end of the day – the only consumer electronics brand to come out of Europe in the last 15 years with a global footprint' and if there is one thing that unites Tomtom products its 'we make things easy for consumers'.

TomTom still feels there is a market for a stand-alone sat nav for people to avoid roaming charges on mobile phones and the need to buy a new car if they want an in-built system. They are also working with car manufacturers to build embedded navigation systems into their vehicles as the era of the 'connected car' – where manufacturers do everything from updating car entertainment to suspension adjustment – has forced automakers into partnerships with technology companies. Competitive concerns mean manufacturers are unwilling to share data with rivals and so rely on third parties for services such as traffic management as it is not always cost-effective for them to make the investment themselves. TomTom is currently collaborating with Volkswagen on real-time map updates for driverless cars although they will face tough competition from Google and Apple.

Sources: http://corporate.tomtom.com; *Telegraph*, 20 August 2015; *Financial Times*, 12 February 2015.

Questions

1 Explain the ways in which relatedness informed TomTom's post-2008 strategy.

2 Were there alternative strategies open to TomTom post 2008?

9.3 DIVERSIFICATION DRIVERS

Diversification might be chosen for a variety of reasons, some more value-creating than others.[4] Growth in organisational size is rarely a good enough reason for diversification on its own: growth must be profitable. Indeed, growth can often be merely a form of 'empire building', especially in the public sector. Diversification decisions need to be approached sceptically.

Four potentially value-creating drivers for diversification are as follows:

- *Exploiting economies of scope.* **Economies of scope refer to efficiency gains made through applying the organisation's existing resources or competences to new markets or services.**[5] If an organisation has under-utilised resources or competences that it cannot effectively close or sell to other potential users, it is efficient to use these resources or competences by diversification into a new activity. In other words, there are economies to be gained by extending the scope of the organisation's activities. For example, many universities have large resources in terms of halls of residence, which they must have for their students but which are under-utilised out of term time. These halls of residence are more efficiently used if the universities expand the scope of their activities into conferencing and tourism during holiday periods. Economies of scope may apply to both *tangible* resources, such as halls of residence, and *intangible* resources and competences, such as brands or staff skills.

- *Stretching corporate management competences ('dominant logics').* This is a special case of economies of scope, and refers to the potential for applying the skills of talented corporate-level managers (referred to as 'corporate parenting skills' in Section 9.6) to new businesses. The **dominant logic is the set of corporate-level managerial competences applied across the portfolio of businesses.**[6] Corporate-level managers may have competences that can be applied even to businesses not sharing resources at the operating-unit level.[7] Thus the French luxury-goods conglomerate LVMH includes a wide range of businesses – from champagne, through fashion, jewellery and perfumes, to financial media – that share very few operational resources or business-level competences. However, LVMH creates value for these specialised companies by applying corporate-level competences in developing classic brands and nurturing highly creative people that are relevant to all its individual businesses. See also the discussion of dominant logic at Berkshire Hathaway in Illustration 9.4 later.

- *Exploiting superior internal processes.* Internal processes within a diversified corporation can often be more efficient than external processes in the open market. This is especially the case where external capital and labour markets do not yet work well, as in many developing economies. In these circumstances, well-managed conglomerates can make sense, even if their constituent businesses do not have operating relationships with each other. For example, China has many conglomerates because it is able to mobilise internal investment, develop managers and exploit networks in a way that stand-alone Chinese companies, relying on imperfect markets, cannot. For example, China's largest privately owned conglomerate, the Fosun Group, owns steel mills, pharmaceutical companies and China's largest retailer, Yuyuan Tourist Mart.[8]

- *Increasing market power.*[9] Being diversified in many businesses can increase power vis-à-vis competitors in at least two ways. First, having the same wide portfolio of products as a competitor increases the potential for *mutual forbearance*. The ability to retaliate across the whole range of the portfolio acts to discourage the competitor from making any aggressive moves at all. Two similarly diversified competitors are thus likely to forbear from competing aggressively with each other. Second, having a diversified range of businesses increases the power to *cross-subsidise* one business from the profits of the others. The ability to cross-subsidise can support aggressive bids to drive competitors out of a particular market and, being aware of this, competitors without equivalent power will be reluctant to attack that business.

Where diversification creates value, it is described as 'synergistic'.[10] **Synergies are benefits gained where activities or assets complement each other so that their combined effect is greater than the sum of the parts** (the famous $2 + 2 = 5$ equation). Thus a film company and a music publisher would be synergistic if they were worth more together than separately – if the music publisher had the sole rights to music used in the film company productions for instance. However, synergies are often harder to identify and more costly to extract in practice than managers like to admit.[11]

Indeed, some drivers for diversification involve negative synergies, in other words value destruction. Three potentially value-destroying diversification drivers are:

- *Responding to market decline* is one common but doubtful driver for diversification. Rather than let the managers of a declining business invest spare funds in a new business, conventional finance theory suggests it is usually best to let shareholders find new growth investment opportunities for themselves. For example, Kodak (see Illustration 6.4), the US photo film corporation, spent billions of dollars on diversification acquisitions such as chemicals, desktop radiotherapy, photocopiers, telecommunications and inkjet printers in order to compensate for market decline in its main product. Many of these initiatives failed and the decline of the core business continued until Kodak went bankrupt. Shareholders might have preferred Kodak simply to hand back the large surpluses generated for decades beforehand rather than spending on costly acquisitions. If shareholders had wanted to invest in the chemicals, telecommunications or printers, they could have invested in the original dominant companies themselves.

- *Spreading risk* across a range of markets is another common justification for diversification. Again, conventional finance theory is very sceptical about risk-spreading by diversification. Shareholders can easily spread their risk by taking small stakes in dozens of very different companies themselves. Diversification strategies, on the other hand, are likely to involve a limited range of fairly related markets. While managers might like the security of having more than one market, shareholders typically do not need each of the companies they invest in to be diversified as well – they would prefer managers to concentrate on managing their core business as well as they can. However, conventional finance theory does not apply to private businesses, where owners have a large proportion of their assets tied up in their company: here it can make sense to diversify risk across a number of distinct activities, so that if one part is in trouble, the whole business is not pulled down.

- *Managerial ambition* can sometimes drive inappropriate diversification. For example Vijay Mallya, CEO of UB Group, an Indian conglomerate involved in alcoholic beverages, aviation infrastructure, real estate and fertiliser, diversified further into airlines with Kingfisher Airlines (see Chapter 5 end case). This seemed in keeping with his extravagant lifestyle and pursuit of glamour; fitting his reputation as 'the King of Good Times'. However, there were no obvious synergies, and the airline industry was not competitive – leading to the collapse of Kingfisher and the loss of other key group assets. Managers such as Mallya might gain short-terms benefits in terms of prestige and financial rewards from diversification, but going beyond his areas of true expertise soon brought financial disaster.

9.4 DIVERSIFICATION AND PERFORMANCE

Because most large corporations today are diversified, but also because diversification can sometimes be in management's self-interest, many scholars and policy-makers have been concerned to establish whether diversified companies really perform better than undiversified companies. After all, it would be deeply troubling if large corporations were diversifying simply to spread risk for managers, to save managerial jobs in declining businesses or to generate short-term benefits for managers, as in the case of UB group.

Research studies of diversification have particularly focused on the relative benefits of related diversification and conglomerate or unrelated diversification. Researchers generally find that related or limited diversifiers outperform both firms that remain specialised and those that have unrelated or extensively diversified strategies.[12] In other words, the diversification–performance relationship tends to follow an inverted (or upside-down) U-shape, as in Figure 9.3. The implication is that some diversification is good – but not too much.

However, these performance studies produce statistical averages. Some related diversification strategies fail – as in the case of some accounting firms' ventures in consulting – while some conglomerates succeed – as in the case of LVMH. The case against unrelated diversification is not solid, and effective dominant logics or particular national contexts can play in its favour. For instance, easyGroup, with interests including planes, pizza, cars and gyms, has a strong dominant logic around business model innovation in mature industries. In terms of national contexts, conglomerate diversification may be particularly effective in developing economies as a form of protection against institutional weaknesses such as poor law enforcement, lack of quality labour, capricious political contexts. The conclusion from the performance studies is that, although on average related diversification pays better than unrelated, any diversification strategy needs rigorous questioning on its particular merits.

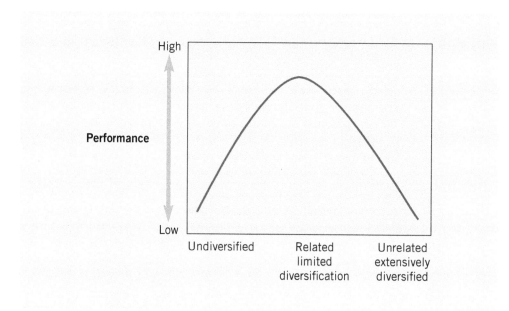

Figure 9.3 Diversity and performance

9.5 VERTICAL INTEGRATION

As well as diversification, another direction for corporate strategy can be vertical integration. **Vertical integration describes entering activities where the organisation is its own supplier or customer.** Thus it involves operating at another stage of the value network (see Section 4.4.2). This section considers both vertical integration and vertical dis-integration, particularly in the form of outsourcing.

9.5.1 Forward and backward integration

Vertical integration can go in either of two directions:

- *Backward integration* is movement into input activities concerned with the company's current business (i.e. further back in the value network). For example, acquiring a component supplier would be backward integration for a car manufacturer.
- *Forward integration* is movement into output activities concerned with the company's current business (i.e. further forward in the value network). For a car manufacturer, forward integration would be into car retail, repairs and servicing.

Thus vertical integration is like diversification in increasing corporate scope. The difference is that it brings together activities up and down the same value network, while diversification typically involves more or less different value networks. However, because realising synergies involves bringing together different value networks, diversification (especially related diversification) is sometimes also described as *horizontal integration*. For example, a company diversified in cars, trucks and buses could find benefits in integrating aspects of the various design or component-sourcing processes. The relationship between horizontal integration and vertical integration is depicted in Figure 9.4.

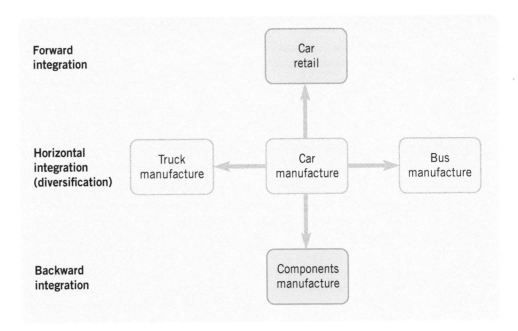

Figure 9.4 Diversification and integration options: car manufacturer example

Vertical integration often appears attractive as it seems to 'capture' some of the profits gained by retailers or suppliers in a value network – the retailers' or suppliers' profits. However there are two dangers. First, vertical integration involves investment. Expensive investments in activities that are less profitable than the original core business will be unattractive to shareholders because they are reducing their *average* or overall rate of return on investment. Second, even if there is a degree of relatedness through the value network, vertical integration is likely to involve quite different strategic capabilities. Thus car manufacturers forwardly integrating into car servicing found managing networks of small service outlets very different to managing large manufacturing plants. Growing appreciation of both the risks of diluting overall returns on investment and the distinct capabilities involved at different stages of the value network has led many companies in recent years to vertically *dis*-integrate.

9.5.2 To integrate or to outsource?

Where a part of vertically integrated operations is not adding value to the overall business, it may be replaced through outsourcing or subcontracting. **Outsourcing is the process by which activities previously carried out internally are subcontracted to external suppliers.** Outsourcing can refer to the subcontracting of components in manufacturing, but is now particularly common for services such as information technology, customer call centres and human resource management (see Illustration 9.3). The argument for outsourcing to specialist suppliers is often based on strategic capabilities. Specialists in a particular activity are likely to have superior capabilities than an organisation for which that particular activity is not a central part of its business. A specialist IT contractor is usually better at IT than the IT department of a steel company.

However, Nobel prize-winning economist Oliver Williamson has argued that the decision to integrate or outsource involves more than just relative capabilities. His *transaction cost framework* helps analyse the relative costs and benefits of managing ('transacting') activities internally or externally.[13] Assessing whether to integrate or outsource an activity, Williamson warns against underestimating the long-term costs of *opportunism* by external subcontractors (or indeed any other organisation in a market relationship). Subcontractors are liable over time to take advantage of their position, either to reduce their standards or to extract higher prices. Market relationships tend to fail in controlling subcontractor opportunism where:

- there are *few alternatives* to the subcontractor and it is hard to shop around;
- the product or service is *complex and changing,* and therefore impossible to specify fully in a legally binding contract;
- investments have been made in *specific assets,* which the subcontractors know will have little value if they withhold their product or service.

Both capabilities and transaction cost reasoning have influenced the outsourcing decisions of the Royal Bank of Scotland, see Illustration 9.3.

This transaction cost framework suggests that the costs of opportunism can outweigh the benefits of subcontracting to organisations with superior strategic capabilities. For example, mining companies in isolated parts of the Australian outback typically own and operate housing for their workers. The isolation creates specific assets (the housing is worth nothing if the mine closes down) and a lack of alternatives (the nearest town might be 100 miles away). Consequently, there would be large risks to both partners if the mine subcontracted housing to an independent company specialising in worker accommodation, however strong its capabilities. Transaction cost economics therefore offers the following advice: if there are few alternative suppliers, if activities are complex and likely to change, and if there are

ILLUSTRATION 9.3   'Out of sight – out of mind'? Outsourcing at Royal Bank of Scotland

In 2012, Royal Bank of Scotland (RBS) experienced a major crisis when its customers could not withdraw cash. Was this the consequence of outsourcing?

In June 2012, RBS encountered severe problems when ten million retail and business customers suddenly found they could not access their cash. This was highly damaging to the bank's reputation and could result in significant customer loss. The problem was faulty updating of CA-7 – critical software that controls the batch processing systems dealing with retail banking transactions. Generally regarded as 'a very common and reliable product, it processes accounts overnight via thousands of pieces of work' such as ATM transactions, bank-to-bank salary payments and so on, and finishes by updating the account master copy with the definitive balance. Described as a huge game of Jenga (the tower game played with interlaced wood blocks), all transactions are related, so everything needs to be processed in order. Thus Tuesday's batch must run before Wednesday's to avoid, for example, penalising someone who has a large sum of money leave their account on Wednesday that might put them in debt but which would be covered by money arriving on Tuesday. In updating CA-7, files were deleted or corrupted so the master copy was wrong for three nights – meaning millions of transactions were not processed. RBS branches had to extend their opening hours to reassure customers about their accounts.

Unions argued that the disaster was due to 'offshoring' UK IT jobs to India. 'RBS has 40 years' experience running this system and banks as a rule don't drop the ball like this,' remarked one bank employee. However, the general banking crisis had pressured UK banks to reduce their costs. RBS, which had suffered badly from the banking crisis, let thousands of UK staff go and transferred their roles to Chennai, India. As one former employee complained, 'We were having to pass 10–20+ years worth of mainframe knowledge onto people who'd never heard of a mainframe outside of a museum . . . '.

Offshore outsourcing was once heralded as the saviour of UK IT departments, cutting costs without compromising quality. Thousands of IT jobs were axed in the name of 'efficiency', many outsourced to India with much lower wages than the UK. Indeed in February 2012, RBS advertised it was urgently seeking computer graduates with several years' experience of using CA-7.

However, India's staff attrition rates in 2012 were at an all-time high with people changing jobs very quickly for just a few extra rupees, leaving insufficient time for adequate cultural awareness training. Quality at call centres suffered. At the same time, the UK was in recession with a devaluing pound greatly reducing wage disparity between India and the UK.

RBS's overseas problems were not uncommon with other banks experiencing loss of private data and in some instances criminal activity. Spanish-owned Santander UK – a bank created from Abbey National, Alliance & Leicester and Bradford & Bingley – also found that outsourced IT systems for these banks could not be trusted and so became the first of the major UK financial institutions to bring back its call centres and software from India to the UK, so that it could take care of its customer base. Ana Botin, Santander UK's Chief Executive, said the move was 'the most important factor in terms of satisfaction with the bank.' This 'inshoring' of strategic assets raises the question of whether strategic assets can afford to be 'out of sight and out of mind'.

Sources: *Guardian*, 25 June 2012; http://www.hrzone.co.uk/topic/business-lifestyle/shoring-new-shoring-call-centres-come-back-uk/112654.

Questions

1 In terms of transaction and capability costs, why might outsourcing be attractive to companies?

2 What might be the risks of 'insourcing'?

significant investments in specific assets, then it is likely to be better to vertically integrate rather than outsource.

In sum, the decision to integrate or subcontract rests on the balance between:

- *Relative strategic capabilities*. Does the subcontractor have the potential to do the work significantly better?

- *Risk of opportunism*. Is the subcontractor likely to take advantage of the relationship over time?

9.6 VALUE CREATION AND THE CORPORATE PARENT

Sometimes corporate parents do not add value to their constituent businesses. Where there is no added value, it is usually best to divest the relevant businesses from the corporate portfolio. Thus in 2016, Toyota Boshoku agreed to sell the automotive interior business of Polytec Holding that the Japanese parts maker had acquired in 2011, at a substantial loss. In the public sector too, units such as schools or hospitals are increasingly being given freedom from parenting authorities, because independence is seen as more effective. Some theorists even challenge the notion of corporate-level strategy altogether. The following section examines how corporate parents can both add and destroy value, and considers three different parenting approaches that can be effective.

9.6.1 Value-adding and value-destroying activities of corporate parents[14]

Corporate parents need to demonstrate that they create more value than they cost. This applies to both commercial and public-sector organisations. For public-sector organisations, privatisation or outsourcing is likely to be the consequence of failure to demonstrate value. Companies whose shares are traded freely on the stock markets face a further challenge. They must demonstrate they create more value than any other rival corporate parent could create. Failure to do so is likely to lead to a hostile takeover or break-up. Rival companies that think they can create more value out of the business units can bid for the company's shares, on the expectation of either running the businesses better or selling them off to other potential parents. If the rival's bid is more attractive and credible than what the current parent can promise, shareholders will back it at the expense of incumbent management.

In this sense, competition takes place between different corporate parents for the right to own and control businesses. In this 'market for corporate control', corporate parents must show that they have *parenting advantage,* on the same principle that business units must demonstrate competitive advantage. They must demonstrate that they are the best possible parents for the businesses they control. Parents therefore must be clear on how they create value. In practice, however, parenting activities can be value-destroying as well as value-creating.

Value-adding activities[15]

There are five main types of activity by which a corporate parent can add value:

- *Envisioning*. The corporate parent can provide a clear overall vision or *strategic intent* for its business units.[16] This should guide and motivate business unit managers to maximise corporation-wide performance through commitment to a common purpose. Envisioning should also provide stakeholders with a *clear external image* about what the organisation as a whole is about: to reassure shareholders about the rationale for having a diversified strategy in the first place.[17] Finally, a clear vision provides a *discipline* on the corporate parent to stop its wandering into inappropriate activities or taking on unnecessary costs.

- *Facilitating synergies.* The corporate parent can facilitate cooperation and sharing across business units, so improving *synergies* from being within the same corporate organisation. This can be achieved through incentives, rewards and remuneration schemes.

- *Coaching.* The corporate parent can help business unit managers develop strategic capabilities, by coaching them to improve their skills and confidence. Corporate-wide management courses are one effective means of achieving these objectives, as bringing managers across the business to learn strategy skills also allows them to build relationships between each other and perceive opportunities for cooperation.

- *Providing central services and resources.* The centre can provide capital for *investment* as well as central services such as treasury, tax and human resource advice. If these are centralised they may have *sufficient scale* to be efficient and can build up *relevant expertise*. Centralised services often have greater *leverage*: for example, combining many business unit purchases increases bargaining power for shared inputs such as energy. This leverage can be helpful in *brokering* with external bodies, such as government regulators, or other companies in negotiating alliances. Finally, the centre can have an important role in managing expertise within the corporate whole, for instance by *transferring managers* across the business units or by creating shared *knowledge management* systems via corporate intranets.

- *Intervening.* Finally, the corporate parent can also intervene within its business units to ensure appropriate performance. The corporate parent should be able to closely *monitor* business unit performance and *improve performance* either by replacing weak managers or by assisting them in turning around their businesses. The parent can also *challenge and develop* the strategic ambitions of business units, so good businesses are encouraged to perform even better.

Value-destroying activities

However, there are three ways in which the corporate parent can inadvertently destroy value:

- *Adding management costs.* Most simply, corporate staff and facilities are expensive. Corporate staff are typically the best-paid managers with the most luxurious offices. It is the actual businesses that have to generate the revenues that pay for them and if corporate centre costs are greater than the value they create, then corporate staff are net value-destroying.

- *Adding bureaucratic complexity.* As well as these direct financial costs, there is the 'bureaucratic fog' created by an additional layer of management and the need to coordinate with sister businesses. These typically slow down managers' responses to issues and lead to compromises between the interests of individual businesses.

- *Obscuring financial performance.* One danger in a large diversified company is that the under-performance of weak businesses can be obscured. Weak businesses might be cross-subsidised by stronger ones. Internally, the possibility of hiding weak performance diminishes the incentives for business unit managers to strive as hard as they can for their businesses: they have a parental safety net. Externally, shareholders and financial analysts cannot easily judge the performance of individual units within the corporate whole. Diversified companies' share prices are often marked down, because shareholders prefer the 'pure plays' of stand-alone units, where weak performance cannot be hidden.[18]

Figure 9.5 Portfolio managers, synergy managers and parental developers
Source: Adapted from M. Goold, A. Campbell and M. Alexander, *Corporate Level Strategy,* Wiley, 1994.

These dangers suggest clear paths for corporate parents that wish to avoid value destruction. They should keep a close eye on centre costs, both financial and bureaucratic, ensuring that they are no more than required by their corporate strategy. They should also do all they can to promote financial transparency, so that business units remain under pressure to perform and shareholders are confident that there are no hidden disasters.

Overall, there are many ways in which corporate parents can add value. It is, of course, difficult to pursue them all and some are hard to mix with others. For example, a corporate parent that does a great deal of top-down intervening is less likely to be seen by its managers as a helpful coach and facilitator. Business unit managers will concentrate on maximising their own individual performance rather than looking out for ways to cooperate with other business unit managers for the greater good of the whole. For this reason, corporate parenting roles tend to fall into three main types, each coherent within itself but distinct from the others.[19] These three types of corporate parenting role are summarised in Figure 9.5.

9.6.2 The portfolio manager

The **portfolio manager** operates as an active investor in a way that shareholders in the stock market are either too dispersed or too inexpert to be able to do. In effect, the portfolio manager is acting as an agent on behalf of financial markets and shareholders with a view to extracting more value from the various businesses than they could achieve themselves. Its role is to identify and acquire under-valued assets or businesses and improve them. The portfolio manager might do this, for example, by acquiring another corporation, divesting low-performing businesses within it and intervening to improve the performance of those with potential. Such corporations may not be much concerned about the relatedness (see Section 9.2) of the business units in their portfolio, typically adopting a conglomerate strategy. Their role is not to get closely involved in the routine management of the businesses, only to act over short periods of time to improve performance. In terms of the value-creating activities identified earlier, the portfolio manager concentrates on intervening and the provision (or withdrawal) of investment.

Portfolio managers seek to keep the cost of the centre low, for example by having a small corporate staff with few central services, leaving the business units alone so that their chief executives have a high degree of autonomy. They set clear financial targets for those chief executives, offering high rewards if they achieve them and likely loss of position if they do not. Such corporate parents can, of course, manage quite a large number of such businesses because they are not directly managing the everyday strategies of those businesses. Rather they are acting from above, setting financial targets, making central evaluations about the well-being and future prospects of such businesses, and investing, intervening or divesting accordingly.

Some argue that the days of the portfolio manager are gone. Improving financial markets mean that the scope for finding and investing cheaply in underperforming companies is much reduced. However, some portfolio managers remain and are successful. Private equity firms such as Apax Partners or Blackstone operate a portfolio management style, typically investing in, improving and then divesting companies in loosely knit portfolios. For example, in 2015, Blackstone, with $300bn in assets, owned companies in energy, real estate, water treatment, camera manufacture, banking, railway operation and seed development with more than 616,000 employees around the world. Illustration 9.4 includes a description of the portfolio parenting approach of Warren Buffett at Berkshire Hathaway.

9.6.3 The synergy manager

Obtaining synergy is often seen as the prime rationale for the corporate parent.[20] The **synergy manager is a corporate parent seeking to enhance value for business units by managing synergies across business units.** Synergies are likely to be particularly rich when new activities are closely related to the core business. In terms of value-creating activities, the focus is threefold: envisioning building a common purpose; facilitating cooperation across businesses; and providing central services and resources. For example, at Apple, Steve Jobs' vision of his personal computers being the digital hub of the new digital lifestyle guided managers across the iMac computer, iPod, iPhone and iPad businesses to ensure seamless connections between the fast-developing offerings. The result is enhanced value through better customer experience. A metals company diversified into both steel and aluminium might centralise its energy procurement, gaining synergy benefits through increased bargaining power over suppliers.

However, achieving such synergistic benefits involves at least three challenges:

- *Excessive costs.* The benefits in sharing and cooperation need to outweigh the costs of undertaking such integration, both direct financial costs and opportunity costs. Managing synergistic relationships tends to involve expensive investments in management time.

- *Overcoming self-interest.* Managers in the business units have to want to cooperate. Especially where managers are rewarded largely according to the performance of their own particular business unit, they are likely to be unwilling to sacrifice their time and resources for the common good.

- *Illusory synergies.* It is easy to overestimate the value of skills or resources to other businesses. This is particularly common when the corporate centre needs to justify a new venture or the acquisition of a new company. Claimed synergies often prove illusory when managers actually have to put them into practice.

ILLUSTRATION 9.4   Eating its own cooking: Berkshire Hathaway's parenting

The challenge of managing a highly diverse set of businesses for shareholders.

From a small struggling textile business in the 1960s Warren Buffet, Berkshire Hathaway's 85-year-old billionaire Chairman and CEO, had built a $356bn (£219bn; €274bn) conglomerate in 2015. Its businesses were highly diverse including insurance companies (GEICO, General Re, NRG), carpets, building products, clothing and footwear manufacturers, retail companies and private jet service, NetJets. It also held significant long-term minority stakes in Coca-Cola and General Electric and continued to make major cash acquisitions, including BNSF for $34bn in 2009 (the second largest US railway company), Lubrizol (speciality chemicals, $9bn, 2011), Heinz ($23.3bn, 2013), Duracell (batteries, $4.7bn, 2014). In 2015, Precision Castparts, an aircraft components company suffering from falling revenues, profits and a 30 per cent decline in share price, was acquired for $37bn. But, as Buffet remarked, the size of Berkshire Hathaway made finding deals that make a difference, difficult – a bit like 'elephant hunting'.

Annual reports explained how Buffet and Deputy Chairman Charlie Munger ran the business:

'Charlie Munger and I think of our shareholders as owner-partners, and of ourselves as managing partners. (Because of the size of our shareholdings we are also, for better or worse, controlling partners.) We do not view the company itself as the ultimate owner of our business assets but instead view the company as a conduit through which our shareholders own the assets . . . In line with Berkshire's owner-orientation, most of our directors have a major portion of their net worth invested in the company. We eat our own cooking.'

Berkshire has a clear 'dominant logic':

'Charlie and I avoid businesses whose futures we can't evaluate, no matter how exciting their products may be. In the past, it required no brilliance for people to foresee the fabulous growth that awaited such industries as autos (in 1910), aircraft (in 1930) and television sets (in 1950). But the future then also included competitive dynamics that would decimate almost all of the companies entering those industries. Even the survivors tended to come away bleeding. Just because Charlie and I can clearly see dramatic growth ahead for an industry does not mean we can judge what its profit margins and returns on capital will be as a host of

competitors battle for supremacy. At Berkshire we will stick with businesses whose profit picture for decades to come seems reasonably predictable. Even then, we will make plenty of mistakes.'

Explaining how they managed their subsidiary businesses, Buffet said:

'We subcontract all of the heavy lifting to the managers of our subsidiaries. In fact, we delegate almost to the point of abdication: though Berkshire has about 340,000 employees, only 25 of these are at headquarters. Charlie and I mainly attend to capital allocation and the care of our key managers. Most are happiest when they are left alone to run their businesses, and that is just how we leave them. That puts them in charge of all operating decisions and of dispatching the excess cash they generate to headquarters. By sending it to us, they don't get diverted by the various enticements that would come their way were they responsible for deploying the cash their businesses throw off. Furthermore, Charlie and I are exposed to a much wider range of possibilities for investing these funds than any of our managers could find.'

Berkshire Hathaway's 50th birthday had financial commentators reviewing its astonishing success. Buffet's investment genius is often cited alongside 'a weirdly intense contagious devotion of shareholders and media' (Munger). Many would like to fully understand the success formula that has stood Berkshire Hathaway in such good stead for so long. In the meantime, Berkshire Hathaway still had a huge cash pile in 2016. Should the ageing billionaire investor reload his 'elephant gun' for another acquisition?

Sources: 'Berkshire Hathaway Owner's Manual', http://brkshr.com/owners.html; http://www.berkshirehathaway.com/letters/2009ltr.pdf.

Questions

1 In what ways does Berkshire Hathaway fit the archetypal portfolio manager (see Section 9.6.2)?

2 Warren Buffet still had $73bn to invest. Suggest industries and businesses he would be unlikely to invest in.

The failure of many companies to extract expected synergies from their businesses has led to growing scepticism about the notion of synergy. Synergistic benefits are not as easy to achieve as would appear. For example, lawsuits between Hewlett Packard and former Autonomy employees following the former's €6.6bn (£5.3bn, $8.8bn) write down of Autonomy, a British software company, have resulted from failure to achieve anticipated integration benefits. Hewlett Packard blamed the former management team of Autonomy for fraudulent misrepresentation during the acquisition process. Nevertheless, synergy continues to be a common theme in corporate-level strategy, as Illustration 9.2 on TomTom shows.

9.6.4 The parental developer[21]

The **parental developer seeks to employ its own central capabilities to add value to its businesses**. This is not so much about how the parent can develop benefits *across* business units or transfer capabilities between business units, as in the case of managing synergy. Rather, parental developers focus on the resources or capabilities they have as parents which they can transfer *downwards* to enhance the potential of business units. For example, a parent could have a valuable brand or specialist skills in financial management or product development. It would seem that McDonald's believed it had identified a parenting opportunity in its acquisition of Chipotle as shown in Illustration 9.5. Parenting opportunities tend to be more common in the case of related rather than unrelated diversified strategies and are likely to involve exchanges of managers and other resources across the businesses. Key value-creating activities for the parent will be the provision of central services and resources. For example, a consumer products company might offer substantial guidance on branding and distribution from the centre; a technology company might run a large central R&D laboratory.

There are two crucial challenges to managing a parental developer:

- *Parental focus*. Corporate parents need to be rigorous and focused in identifying their unique value-adding capabilities. They should always be asking what others can do better than them, and focus their energy and time on activities where they really do add value. Other central services should typically be outsourced to specialist companies that can do it better.

- *The 'crown jewel' problem*. Some diversified companies have business units in their portfolios which are performing well but to which the parent adds little value. These can become 'crown jewels', to which corporate parents become excessively attached. The logic of the parental development approach is: if the centre cannot add value, it is just a cost and therefore destroying value. Parental developers should divest businesses[22] they do not add value to, even profitable ones. Funds raised by selling a profitable business can be reinvested in businesses where the parent can add value.

9.7 PORTFOLIO MATRICES

Section 9.6 discussed rationales for corporate parents of multi-business organisations. This section introduces models by which managers can determine financial investment and divestment within their portfolios of business.[23] Each model gives more or less attention to at least one of three criteria:

- the *balance* of the portfolio (e.g. in relation to its markets and the needs of the corporation);
- the *attractiveness* of the business units in terms of how strong they are individually and how profitable their markets or industries are likely to be; and

ILLUSTRATION 9.5   Chipotle: doing things differently

Struggling to find parenting advantage.

Chipotle Mexican Grill had always done things rather differently to the rest of the restaurant industry. Its outlets were not in the busiest locations, it spent lots on food, rarely added to the menu, didn't serve breakfast, do drive-throughs, franchises, or much advertising. And yet by 2015 it was a $22bn (£13.2bn, €16.5 bn) burrito empire. Despite its success, why did owner McDonald's sell it, especially when McDonald's own sales and stock price had dropped, as it became associated with America's obesity epidemic?

Founded 1993 in Denver, USA by Steve Ells, and relying initially on parents and wealthy friends for initial funding, Chipotle's fast casual dining business soon needed significant capital to expand beyond its 13 stores. In 1998, McDonalds made a $50m investment in Chipotle as part of the group's expansion that included Boston Market, Donatos Pizza, Pret a Manger and Aroma Cafe. It also investigated other businesses such as dry cleaning, a maid service and mowing the lawn.

McDonald's brought distribution systems, real estate expertise, construction knowledge and organisational structure along with its capital investment. To McDonald's, Chipotle brought new products – fresh cilantro, red onions and avocados. One McDonald's executive said: '[Our] Portland distribution centre smelled like a produce house. McDonald's product is fresh, but it's sealed in bags for shelf-life purposes.' Only one product was common to both companies – a five-gallon bag of Coca-Cola syrup.

Coming from a standardised, rules-based, efficiency-oriented culture, McDonald's executives were startled when they first visited Chipotle's headquarters. People brought their dogs into the office and Steve Ells walked around in blue jeans. Shown by Chipotle employees how they scrubbed the grill by hand, one McDonald's executive complained, saying, 'There's got to be a better system. You can't do this by hand all the time,' then suggested a power tool. They showed food could be customised as customers walked down the line. 'If you just want a little bit more salsa or a little bit less rice . . . nobody ever says no to you. . . . They might charge you for it . . . but that customization doesn't slow the throughput.'

By 2005, McDonald's owned 90 per cent of Chipotle. They pressed Chipotle to do drive-throughs, breakfasts and advertising, and suggested the name Chipotle Fresh Mexican Grill. Steve Ells hated the idea and was beginning to be resented at McDonald's for rejecting everything.

Chipotle did franchise eight restaurants for McDonald's, but they didn't succeed, costing a lot to be bought back. Steve Ells explained: 'there are two big things that we do differently. . . . the way we approach food . . . the way we approach our people culture.' McDonald's invited Steve to visit their chicken farm in Arkansas, but he was repelled and soon realised sourcing from small farms dramatically improved the taste of his food. Chipotle food costs ran at 30–32 per cent of total costs, similar to up-market restaurants, and McDonald's executives found this difficult to accept: 'That's ridiculous: that's like a steakhouse.' But Steve Ells was now focusing on ingredients and food integrity.

After seven years, Chipotle's contribution to McDonald's bottom line was small, despite 500 restaurants which investors wanted co-branded. Franchisees were getting distracted and Chipotle's was increasingly unhappy about McDonald's supply chain. Jim Cantalupo, McDonald's CEO, had already begun to sell off partner brands and the stock price had begun to rise. It was time for a McSplit.

Since leaving McDonald's, Chipotle's worth had risen to $15bn (2015), with 1,800 locations and business was booming. Although McDonald's pocketed $1.5bn (after $360m investment), McDonald's shareholders angrily questioned Steve Easterbrook, McDonald's CEO, on Chipotle's disposal.

Sources: Chipotle: the Definitive Oral History, http://www.bloomberg.com/graphics/2015-chipotle-oral-history.

Questions

1 What parenting advantages did McDonald's perceive it might bring to Chipotle?

2 Despite its success, why was Chipotle spun-off?

- the '*fit*' that the business units have with each other in terms of potential synergies or the extent to which the corporate parent will be good at looking after them.

9.7.1 The BCG (or growth/share) matrix[24]

One of the most common and longstanding ways of conceiving of the balance of a portfolio of businesses is the Boston Consulting Group (BCG) matrix (see Figure 9.6). The **BCG matrix uses market share and market growth criteria for determining the attractiveness and balance of a business portfolio.** High market share and high growth are, of course, attractive. However, the BCG matrix also warns that high growth demands heavy investment, for instance to expand capacity or develop brands. There needs to be a balance within the portfolio, so that there are some low-growth businesses that are making sufficient surplus to fund the investment needs of higher-growth businesses.

The growth/share axes of the BCG matrix define four sorts of business:

- A *star* is a business unit within a portfolio that has a high market share in a growing market. The business unit may be spending heavily to keep up with growth, but high market share should yield sufficient profits to make it more or less self-sufficient in terms of investment needs.

- A *question mark* (or problem child) is a business unit within a portfolio that is in a growing market, but does not yet have high market share. Developing question marks into stars, with high market share, takes heavy investment. Many question marks fail to develop, so the BCG advises corporate parents to nurture several at a time. It is important to make sure that some question marks develop into stars, as existing stars eventually become cash cows and cash cows may decline into dogs.

- A *cash cow* is a business unit within a portfolio that has a high market share in a mature market. However, because growth is low, investment needs are less, while high market share means that the business unit should be profitable. The cash cow should then be a cash provider, helping to fund investments in question marks.

- *Dogs* are business units within a portfolio that have low share in static or declining markets and are thus the worst of all combinations. They may be a cash drain and use up a disproportionate amount of managerial time and company resources. The BCG usually recommends divestment or closure.

Figure 9.6 The growth share (or BCG) matrix

The BCG matrix has several advantages. It is a good way of visualising different needs and potentials of all the diverse businesses within the corporate portfolio. It warns corporate parents of the financial demands of what might otherwise look like a desirable portfolio of high-growth businesses. It also reminds corporate parents that stars are likely eventually to wane. Finally, it provides a useful discipline to business unit managers, underlining the fact that the corporate parent ultimately owns the surplus resources they generate and can allocate them according to what is best for the corporate whole. Cash cows should not hoard their profits.

However, there are at least four potential problems with the BCG matrix:

- *Definitional vagueness.* It can be hard to decide what high and low growth or share mean in particular situations. Managers are often keen to define themselves as 'high-share' by defining their market in a particularly narrow way (e.g. by ignoring relevant international markets).

- *Capital market assumptions.* The notion that a corporate parent needs a balanced portfolio to finance investment from internal sources (cash cows) assumes that capital cannot be raised in external markets, for instance by issuing shares or raising loans. The notion of a balanced portfolio may be more relevant in countries where capital markets are under-developed or in private companies that wish to minimise dependence on external shareholders or banks.

- *Unkind to animals.* Both cash cows and dogs receive ungenerous treatment, the first being simply milked, the second terminated or cast out of the corporate home. This treatment can cause *motivation problems,* as managers in these units see little point in working hard for the sake of other businesses. There is also the danger of the *self-fulfilling prophecy.* Cash cows will become dogs even more quickly than the model expects if they are simply milked and denied adequate investment.

- *Ignores commercial linkages.* The matrix assumes there are *no commercial ties to other business units* in the portfolio. For instance, a business unit in the portfolio may depend upon keeping a dog alive. These commercial links are less important in conglomerate strategies, where divestments or closures are unlikely to have knock-on effects on other parts of the portfolio.

9.7.2 The directional policy (GE–McKinsey) matrix

Another way to consider a portfolio of businesses is by means of the *directional policy matrix*[25] which categorises business units into those with good prospects and those with less good prospects. The matrix was originally developed by McKinsey & Co. consultants in order to help the American conglomerate General Electric manage its portfolio of business units. Specifically, the directional policy matrix positions business units according to (i) how attractive the relevant market is in which they are operating, and (ii) the competitive strength of the SBU in that market. Attractiveness can be identified by PESTEL or five forces analyses; business unit strength can be defined by competitor analysis (for instance, the strategy canvas; see Section 3.4.3. Some analysts also choose to show graphically how large the market is for a given business units activity, and even the market share of that business unit, as shown in Figure 9.7. For example, managers in a firm with the portfolio shown in Figure 9.7 will be concerned that they have relatively low shares in the largest and most attractive market, whereas their greatest strength is in a market with only medium attractiveness and smaller markets with little long-term attractiveness.

The matrix also offers strategy guidelines given the positioning of the business units. It suggests that the businesses with the highest growth potential and the greatest strength are those

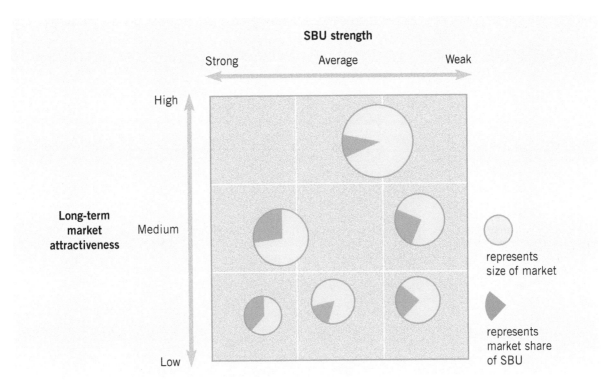

Figure 9.7 Directional policy (GE–McKinsey) matrix

in which to invest for growth. Those that are the weakest and in the least attractive markets should be divested or 'harvested' (i.e. used to yield as much cash as possible before divesting).

The directional policy matrix is more complex than the BCG matrix. However, it can have two advantages. First, unlike the simpler four-box BCG matrix, the nine cells of the directional policy matrix acknowledge the possibility of a difficult middle ground. Here managers have to be carefully selective. In this sense, the directional policy matrix is less mechanistic than the BCG matrix, encouraging open debate on less clear-cut cases. Second, the two axes of the directional policy matrix are not based on single measures (i.e. market share and market growth). Business strength can derive from many other factors than market share, and industry attractiveness does not just boil down to industry growth rates. On the other hand, the directional policy matrix shares some problems with the BCG matrix, particularly about vague definitions, capital market assumptions, motivation and self-fulfilling prophecy and ignoring commercial linkages. Overall, however, the value of the matrix is to help managers invest in the businesses that are most likely to pay off.

So far, the discussion has been about the logic of portfolios in terms of balance and attractiveness. The third logic is to do with 'fit' with the particular capabilities of the corporate parent.

9.7.3 The parenting matrix

The *parenting matrix* (or Ashridge Portfolio Display) developed by consultants Michael Goold and Andrew Campbell introduces parental fit as an important criterion for including businesses in the portfolio.[26]

Businesses may be attractive in terms of the BCG or directional policy matrices, but if the parent cannot add value, then the parent ought to be cautious about acquiring or retaining them.

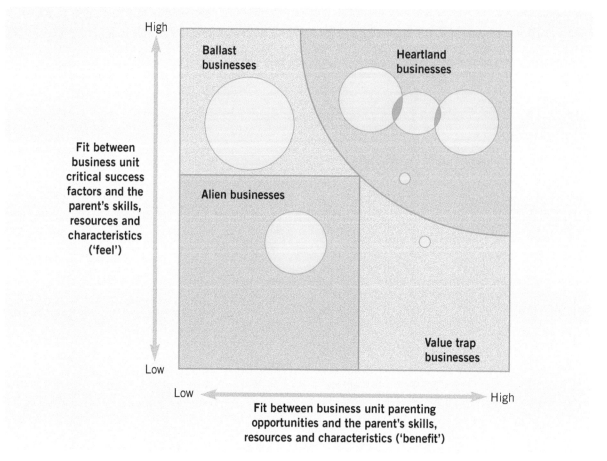

Figure 9.8 The parenting matrix: the Ashridge Portfolio Display

Source: Adapted from M. Goold, A. Campbell and M. Alexander, *Corporate Level Strategy*, Wiley, 1994.

There are two key dimensions of fit in the parenting matrix (see Figure 9.8):

- *'Feel'*. This is a measure of the fit between each business units critical success factors (see Section 3.4.3) and the capabilities (in terms of competences and resources) of the corporate parent. In other words, does the corporate parent have the necessary 'feel', or understanding, for the businesses it will parent?

- *'Benefit'*. This measures the fit between the parenting opportunities, or needs, of business units and the capabilities of the parent. Parenting opportunities are about the upside, areas in which good parenting can benefit the business (for instance, by bringing marketing expertise). For the benefit to be realised, of course, the parent must have the right capabilities to match the parenting opportunities.

The power of using these two dimensions of fit is as follows. It is easy to see that a corporate parent should avoid running businesses that it has no feel for. What is less clear is that parenting should be avoided if there is no benefit. This challenges the corporate parenting of even businesses for which the parent has high feel. Businesses for which a corporate parent has high feel but can add little benefit should either be run with a very light touch or be divested.

Figure 9.8 shows four kinds of business along these two dimensions of feel and benefit:

- *Heartland* business units are ones that the parent understands well and can continue to add value to. They should be at the core of future strategy.

THINKING DIFFERENTLY   Corporate strategy is a fool's errand

Is there a need for corporate strategy at all?

Although this chapter has argued that corporate strategy adds value to the multi-business (see Section 9.6.1), a recent *Harvard Business Review* article by Frank Vermeulen fundamentally challenges this position by asking 'does the headquarters actually add any value?'[27] Other commentators also worry that corporate functions do not generate the value from their activities they expect.[28] Although today's multi-businesses seem to have somewhat related businesses, in reality the various divisions operate completely independently from one another.[29] Also a third of the largest companies in North America and Europe have reported increased numbers of corporate functions with growing influence and yet complaints about that function's performance have increased.[30]

Disparate businesses come from companies growing into adjacent business areas each then requiring their own strategy, management teams and profit and loss responsibility. Corporate top management teams then aim to find synergies between the different divisions, by promoting cooperation, to create extra value as recommended by corporate finance. If none can be found, then headquarters is just managing a portfolio. The alternative view is that those businesses should be spun-off, as investors can diversify for themselves, and money would be saved on expensive headquarters.

Corporate top management may have advantages over external investors, including greater in-depth understanding of their businesses, and they are less likely to be fooled by numbers and charismatic SBU CEOs. They can act as the company's governance mechanism ensuring shareholder funds are wisely spent and strategies are genuine and they can staff divisional management teams with experts they know. However, this may just be rhetoric to conceal portfolio management. Or it may be a genuine attempt to contrive an overarching corporate strategy that seeks to proclaim cross-divisional synergies and cooperation, but is really an expensive illusion, as value is often not created. If the latter, corporate managers should really get out of the way of divisional strategies, rather than trying to set them. And if they are acting as portfolio managers, external investors can do this more efficiently. Therefore corporate strategy is a fool's errand.

> **Question**
>
> Evaluate the arguments for and against corporate strategy for Berkshire Hathaway or the Greystone Foundation.

- *Ballast* business units are ones the parent understands well but can do little for. They would probably be at least as successful as independent companies. If not divested, they should be spared as much corporate bureaucracy as possible.

- *Value trap* business units are dangerous. They appear attractive because there are opportunities to add value (for instance, marketing could be improved). But they are deceptively attractive, because the parent's lack of feel will result in more harm than good (i.e. the parent lacks the right marketing skills). The parent will need to acquire new capabilities if it is to be able to move value trap businesses into the heartland. It might be easier to divest to another corporate parent that could add value, and will pay well for the chance.

- *Alien* business units are clear misfits. They offer little opportunity to add value and the parent does not understand them anyway. Exit is definitely the best strategy.

This approach to considering corporate portfolios places the emphasis firmly on how the parent benefits the business units. This is the question that observers are asking of the Virgin Group in the end of chapter case. It requires careful analysis of both parenting capabilities and business unit parenting needs. The parenting matrix can therefore assist hard decisions where either high-feel or high-parenting opportunities tempt the corporate parent to acquire or retain businesses. Parents should concentrate on actual or potential heartland businesses, where there is both high feel and high benefit.

The concept of fit has equal relevance in the public sector. The implication is that public-sector managers should control directly only those services and activities for which they have special managerial expertise. Other services should be outsourced or set up as independent agencies (see Section 9.5).

SUMMARY

- Many corporations comprise several, sometimes many, business units. Corporate strategy involves the decisions and activities above the level of business units. It is concerned with choices concerning the scope of the organisation.

- Organisational *scope* is often considered in terms of *related* and *unrelated* diversification.

- Corporate parents may seek to add value by adopting different parenting roles: the *portfolio manager*, the *synergy manager* or the *parental developer*.

- There are several portfolio models to help corporate parents manage their businesses, of which the most common are: the *BCG matrix*, the *directional policy matrix* and the *parenting matrix*.

- *Divestment* and *outsourcing* should be considered as well as diversification, particularly in the light of relative strategic capabilities and the transaction costs of *opportunism*.

WORK ASSIGNMENTS

✻ Denotes more advanced work assignments.
* Refers to a case study in the Text and Cases edition.

9.1 Using the Ansoff axes (Figure 9.2), identify and explain corporate strategic directions for any one of these case organisations: CRH*, Air Asia and the Tune Group*, Severstal* and SABMiller or AB InBev in the Megabrew* case.

9.2 Go to the website of any large multi-business organisation (e.g. Alphabet, Google, Megabrew*, Siemens, Tata Group, Virgin Group – see end of chapter case) and assess the degree to which its corporate-level strategy is characterised by (a) related or unrelated diversification and (b) a coherent 'dominant logic' (see Section 9.3).

9.3 For any large multi-business corporation (as in Section 9.2), Alphabet, the Tune Group*, Siemens* or Severstal*, explain how the corporate parent should best create value for its component businesses (as portfolio manager, synergy manager or parental developer: see Section 9.6). Would all the businesses fit equally well?

9.4✻ For any large multi-business corporation (as in 9.2), Megabrew* or the Virgin Group (end of chapter case), plot the business units on a portfolio matrix (e.g. the BCG matrix: Section 9.7.1). Justify any assumptions about the relative positions of businesses on the relevant axes of the matrix. What managerial conclusions do you draw from this analysis?

Integrative assignment

9.5 Take a case of a recent merger or acquisition (see Chapter 11), and assess the extent to which it involved related or unrelated diversification (if either) and how far it was consistent with the company's existing dominant logic. Using share price information (see www.bigcharts.com or similar), assess shareholders' reaction to the merger or acquisition. How do you explain this reaction?

RECOMMENDED KEY READINGS

- An accessible discussion of corporate strategy is provided by A. Campbell and R. Park, *The Growth Gamble: When Leaders Should Bet on Big New Businesses,* Nicholas Brealey, 2005.
- M. Goold and K. Luchs, 'Why diversify: four decades of management thinking', in D. Faulkner and A. Campbell (eds), *The Oxford Handbook of Strategy,* vol. 2, Oxford University Press, pp. 18–42, 2003, provides an authoritative overview of the diversification option over time.

- L. Capron and W. Mitchell, *Build, Borrow or Buy: solving the growth dilemma,* Harvard Business Press, 2012, provides a good review of the arguments for and against different modes of growth.
- A good review of the current state of corporate portfolio management research is provided by M. Nippa, U. Pidua and H. Rubner, 'Corporate portfolio management: appraising four decades of academic research', *Academy of Management Perspectives,* November 2011, pp. 50–66.

REFERENCES

1. For a detailed discussion as to how organisational structures might 'address' an organisation's mix of SBUs, see M. Goold and A. Campbell, *Designing Effective Organizations: How to Create Structured Networks*, Jossey-Bass, 2002. Also K. Eisenhardt and S. Brown, 'Patching', *Harvard Business Review*, vol. 77, no. 3 (1999), p. 72.

2. This figure is an extension of the product/market matrix: see I. Ansoff, *Corporate Strategy*, 1988, Chapter 6. The Ansoff matrix was later developed into the one shown below.

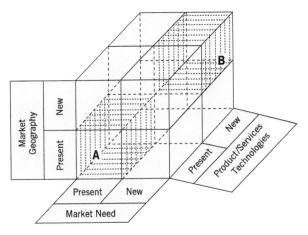

3. For the European Commission competition authority, http://ec.europa.eu/comm/competition; for the UK Competition Commission, see http://www.competition-commission.org.uk/.

4. For discussions of the challenge of sustained growth and diversification, see A. Campbell and R. Parks, *The Growth Gamble*, Nicholas Brealy, 2005; and D. Laurie, Y. Doz and C. Sheer, 'Creating new growth platforms', *Harvard Business Review*, vol. 84, no. 5 (2006), pp. 80–90.

5. On economies of scope, see D.J. Teece, 'Towards an economic theory of the multi-product firm', *Journal of Economic Behavior and Organization*, vol. 3 (1982), pp. 39–63.

6. See R. Bettis and C.K. Prahalad, 'The dominant logic: retrospective and extension', *Strategic Management Journal*, vol. 16, no. 1 (1995), pp. 5–15.

7. F. Neffke and M. Henning, 'Skill relatedness and firm diversification', *Strategic Management Journal*, vol. 34, no. 3 (2013), pp. 297–316 show that internal skills may aid in the diversification process.

8. See C. Markides, 'Corporate strategy: the role of the centre', in A. Pettigrew, H. Thomas and R. Whittington (eds), *Handbook of Strategy and Management*, Sage, 2002. For a discussion of Chinese diversification patterns, see A. Delios, N. Zhou and W.W. Xu, 'Ownership structure and the diversification and performance of publicly-listed companies in China', *Business Horizons*, vol. 51, no. 6 (2008), pp. 802–21. See M.C. Mayer, C. Stadler and J. Hautz, 'The relationship between product and international diversification: the role of experience', *Strategic Management Journal*, vol. 36, no. 10 (2015), pp. 1458–68 for a discussion of the importance of experience in driving diversification.

9. These benefits are often discussed in terms of 'multimarket' or 'multipoint' competition: see J. Anand, L. Mesquita and R. Vassolo, 'The dynamics of multimarket competition in exploration and exploitation activities', *Academy of Management Journal*, vol. 52, no. 4 (2009), pp. 802–21.

10. M. Goold and A. Campbell, 'Desperately seeking synergy', *Harvard Business Review*, vol. 76, no. 2 (1998), pp. 131–45. See also Y.M. Zhou, 'Synergy, coordination costs, and diversification choices', *Strategic Management Journal*, vol. 32, no. 6 (2011), pp. 624–39.

11. A. Pehrson, 'Business relatedness and performance: a study of managerial perceptions', *Strategic Management Journal*, vol. 27, no. 3 (2006), pp. 265–82. See also F. Neffke and M. Henning, 'Skill relatedness and firm diversification', *Strategic Management Journal*, vol. 34, no. 3 (2013), pp. 297–316.

12. L.E. Palich, L.B. Cardinal and C. Miller, 'Curvilinearity in the diversification-performance linkage: an examination of over three decades of research', *Strategic Management Journal*, vol. 21 (2000), pp. 155–74. The inverted-U

relationship is the research consensus, but studies often disagree, particularly finding variations over time and across countries. For recent context-sensitive studies, see M. Mayer and R. Whittington, 'Diversification in context: a cross national and cross temporal extension', *Strategic Management Journal*, vol. 24 (2003), pp. 773–81; and A. Chakrabarti, K. Singh and I. Mahmood, 'Diversification and performance: evidence from East Asian firms', *Strategic Management Journal*, vol. 28 (2007), pp. 101–20. There are also variations by type of diversification – see M. Geoffrey, G.M. Kistruck, I. Qureshi and P.W. Beamish, 'Geographic and product diversification in charitable organizations', *Journal of Management*, vol. 39, no. 2 (2011), pp. 496–530.

13. For a discussion and cases on the relative guidance of transaction cost and capabilities thinking, see R. McIvor, 'How the transaction cost and resource-based theories of the firm inform outsourcing evaluation', *Journal of Operations Management*, vol. 27, no. 1 (2009), pp. 45–63. See also T. Holcomb and M. Hitt, 'Toward a model of strategic outsourcing', *Journal of Operations Management*, vol. 25, no. 2 (2007), pp. 464–81.

14. For a good discussion of corporate parenting roles, see Markides in endnote 8 above. A recent empirical study of corporate headquarters is D. Collis, D. Young and M. Goold, 'The size, structure and performance of corporate headquarters', *Strategic Management Journal*, vol. 28, no. 4 (2007), pp. 383–406.

15. M. Goold, A. Campbell and M. Alexander, *Corporate Level Strategy*, Wiley, 1994, is concerned with both the value-adding and value-destroying capacity of corporate parents.

16. For a discussion of the role of clarity of mission, see A. Campbell, M. Devine and D. Young, *A Sense of Mission*, Hutchinson Business, 1990.

17. T. Zenger, 'Strategy: the uniqueness challenge,' *Harvard Business Review*, November 2013, pp. 52–8.

18. E. Zuckerman, 'Focusing the corporate product: securities analysts and de-diversification', *Administrative Science Quarterly*, vol. 45, no. 3 (2000), pp. 591–619.

19. The first two rationales discussed here are based on M. Porter, 'From competitive advantage to corporate strategy', *Harvard Business Review*, vol. 65, no. 3 (1987), pp. 43–59.

20. See A. Campbell and K. Luchs, *Strategic Synergy*, Butterworth–Heinemann, 1992.

21. The logic of parental development is explained extensively in Goold, Campbell and Alexander (see endnote 15 above). For more on the dynamics of organisational structure see J. Joseph and W. Ocasio, 'Architecture, attention, and adaptation in the multi-business firm: General Electric from 1951 to 2001', *Strategic Management Journal*, vol. 33, no. 6 (2013), pp. 633–60.

22. J. Xia and S. Li, 'The divestiture of acquired subunits: a resource dependence approach', *Strategic Management Journal*, vol. 34, no. 2 (2013), pp. 131–48.

23. A good review of the current state of corporate portfolio management research is provided by M. Nippa, U. Pidua and H. Rubner, 'Corporate portfolio management: appraising four decades of academic research', *Academy of Management Perspectives*, vol. 25, no. 4 (2011), pp. 50–66.

24. For a more extensive discussion of the use of the growth share matrix, see A.C. Hax and N.S. Majluf, 'The use of the industry attractiveness business strength matrix in strategic planning', in R.G. Dyson (ed.), *Strategic Planning*: *Models and Analytical Techniques*, Wiley, 1990; and D. Faulkner, 'Portfolio matrices', in V. Ambrosini (ed.), *Exploring Techniques of Analysis and Evaluation in Strategic Management*, Prentice Hall, 1998; for source explanations of the BCG matrix, see B.D. Henderson, *Henderson on Corporate Strategy*, Abt Books, 1979.

25. Hax and Majluf (see endnote 24).

26. The discussion in this section draws on Goold, Campbell and Alexander (see endnote 15) which provides an excellent basis for understanding issues of parenting.

27. F. Vermeulen, 'Corporate strategy is a fool's errand', *Harvard Business Review*, March 2013.

28. S. Kunisch, G. Muller-Stewens and A. Campbell, 'Why corporate functions stumbles', *Harvard Business Review*, December 2014.

29. Vermeulen (see endnote 27).

30. Kunisch (see endnote 28).

CASE EXAMPLE

Virgin – is the brand more than Richard Branson?

by Marianne Sweet

Introduction

The Virgin Group is a highly diversified organisation which runs a range of businesses including mobile telephony, financial services, airlines, railways, music, holidays and health and care services. It has grown to be one of the largest private UK companies, employing around 50,000 people in 50 countries and with revenues in excess of £15bn (€18bn, $22bn). According to the Centre for Brand Analysis, in 2015 Virgin was the number three best-known brand in the UK after British Airways and Apple.

Virgin's flamboyant founder, Sir Richard Branson, is one of the UK's richest and best known entrepreneurs and at the centre of the group's growth. Branson has a flair for publicity and over the past 40 years has generated the interest and awareness that have made Virgin such a strong brand. The Group believes the Virgin brand is so well respected that it adds value to any business that bears the name.

What is difficult to unpick is how much of Virgin's success is down to Branson's entrepreneurial flair and how much is down to the group's unusual structure and business model. Virgin's strategy and business models are not widely understood and, as a result, investors have questioned its sustainability should Branson depart. The parent company describes itself as a leading international investment group. But does Virgin Group add value to the diverse portfolio of SBUs? Does the portfolio of businesses make strategic sense?

Virgin's beginnings and style

Branson founded his first business, a student magazine, after dropping out of school at the age of 15. Virgin began in 1970 when Branson sold music (vinyl records) by mail order. Able to undercut high street retailers, the business grew rapidly. He opened Virgin Record Shop – named to reflect his naivety in business – in Oxford Street, London a year later. Further expansion took the form of backward integration as he moved into recording and publishing music: his first album, *Tubular Bells* by unknown musician Mike Oldfield in 1973, became a worldwide hit. He then controversially signed the Sex Pistols, a punk rock group

Richard Branson

Source: RichardBakerFarnborough/Alamy Images.

who became notorious for their rude anti-establishment behaviour and lyrics. Those two events epitomised the business philosophy Branson would use to build a worldwide brand – a love of risk-taking, irreverence to the 'old school of business', a passion for fun and a flair for publicity.

The common threads uniting this diverse group of companies are the core values of the Virgin brand – as described by Virgin Group itself: customer-driven with an emphasis on value for money, quality, fun and innovation.[1]

Branson is not risk averse, but a core part of his business philosophy is 'protect the downside' – that is limiting possible losses before moving forward with a new business venture. It was a lesson his father taught him when he was 15. His dad agreed to let him drop out of school to start a magazine, but only if he sold £4,000 of advertising to cover printing costs.[2]

It's an approach he repeated in 1984 when launching low-cost transatlantic airline, Virgin Atlantic. To create this new venture, Branson had to battle to procure landing rights at London's Heathrow Airport. Up to that time, the routes had been dominated by British Airways, which led to an intense rivalry between the two carriers, involving a 'dirty tricks' campaign by BA and a very bitter and public court case, which Virgin won, adding fuel to the image of Richard Branson as the underdog, average businessman

Marianne Sweet is Director of Damselfly Communications Limited and lectures on business enterprise and entrepreneurship at the University of Gloucestershire, UK. This case example includes some material and sources from previous cases on Virgin which featured in earlier editions of *Exploring Strategy*, written by Urmilla Lawson and updated by Aidan McQueen and by John Treciockas.

taking on the oppressors, self-interested 'big business' and the traditional establishment.

Branson had to make some tough decisions to support the fledgling airline. At the time, Virgin Records was a profitable business and Virgin decided that selling that business was the safest way to raise funds. 'If we continued running both companies, then we risked them both. At that point, it seemed possible that Virgin Atlantic would have had to close, leaving 2,500 people without jobs and our brand's reputation in tatters. By selling Virgin Records, we left both companies in strong positions,' explained Branson in one of his Virgin blogs.[3]

Virgin Records was sold to EMI for £500m. The Group then decided to go on to the London and NASDQ stock markets, offering 35 per cent ownership. But Branson's business style did not suit the accountability needed for a chairman of a public corporation and he returned the group to private ownership in 1988.

Growth of the Virgin brand

The Virgin Group grew rapidly through a series of new start-ups, joint ventures and acquisitions. Branson, as chair of Virgin Group, has overseen approximately 500 companies during the parent group's lifetime.

The rationale behind many of the initiatives can be hard to understand and some appear to be pure whim. For Branson it all made business sense. 'Think of the world as one country – it's a lot more fun to do business that way,' he commented.[4] Initially the group focused on travel/holidays and music. Since the 1990s, it has expanded into a wide variety of businesses (Appendix 1, below, lists a selection of new businesses and key events). Virgin Group has repeatedly demonstrated that it is skilled at environmental scanning, searching for those strategic windows of opportunity – usually created by innovation or changes in legislation – and then taking the market advantage.

For instance, the development of digital technologies enabled Virgin to grow its retail interests, moving into the online sales of music, cars, wine, financial products and internet services. Virgin Mobile was the result of deregulation of the telecommunications sector in the UK and the growing advances in cellular communications. Deregulation of the railways in the UK led to Virgin launching Virgin Rail, first running the passenger train service on the West Coast of England and then, in 2014, in a joint venture with Stagecoach, winning the franchise for the East Coast line, between London and Scotland.

In 2012, Virgin purchased Northern Rock, a medium-sized UK mortgage finance provider, which the Government had temporarily nationalised at the beginning of the financial crisis in 2007. The purchase marked the growth of Virgin as a financial services provider, leading to the eventual flotation of Virgin Money on the London Stock Exchange in 2014.

Branson is also known for his taste for adventure and in 2012 launched Virgin Galactic, intending to provide a passenger service into orbital space. He has often commented that being an adventurer and being an entrepreneur is the same thing – and both involve risk. Although Virgin Galactic suffered a huge setback in 2014, when one of its test planes crashed, the following year Virgin Galactic won a $4.7m contract from NASA to carry more than a dozen satellites into orbit on board its LauncherOne.

Again identifying opportunities from deregulation, this time of health services in the UK, Virgin acquired a 75 per cent stake in Assura Medical, which in 2012 was rebranded as Virgin Care. Since then, Virgin Care has become one of the market leaders in providing healthcare, for example, in 2012 it signed a £500m five-year contract to provide community health services for the National Health Service's Surrey region. The Virgin Care website was able to claim that it was providing more than 230 NHS social care services and since 2006 had treated more than four million people.

Corporate rationale

In 2016, the Virgin Group described itself as a leading international investment group and one of the world's most recognised and respected brands. While the group does not provide an organisational structure chart, it is possible to see a discernible grouping of businesses (see Figure 1) within six categories. The operational companies are all separate strategic business units (SBUs), financed on a stand-alone basis.

Branson believes that companies should succeed within the first year or exit the market. In 2013, Virgin Atlantic launched a UK domestic airline, Little Red, linking London Heathrow with Edinburgh, Aberdeen and Manchester. After 18 months, it was scrapped. Branson claimed the venture had benefited consumers but 'the odds were stacked against us'.

Virgin looks for market opportunities where the Group believes its brand can create competitive advantage, usually in markets where existing customers are not receiving value for money, such as health clubs, cosmetics, weddings, drinks, airlines and clothing. The Virgin brand is perceived as the consumer's champion for value-for-money, good quality, brilliant customer service, innovation, being anti-establishment and fun.

Virgin is a mix of publicly listed and privately owned companies, ranging from start-up ventures through to large corporate businesses. Each is 'ring-fenced' so that lenders to one company have no rights over the assets of another. Each company may have very different strategic

Figure 1

objectives. The larger start-ups are serious strategic moves into new markets. Some may be a method of training and developing managers. Some may be to keep Virgin in the public eye.

Each company has no direct lines of reporting or control in the Group. There are minimal management layers. Companies are linked through a complex network of parent subsidiary relations involving 'holding companies' with the ultimate holding company being registered in the British Virgin Islands – a tax haven. The freedom of the companies and the employees – which mirrors Branson's disrespect for hierarchy – and their separation from the parent company, enables the group to retain a spirit of entrepreneurism.

Managers are trusted, have high levels of responsibility and have financial incentives that could turn them into millionaires. This mirrors Branson's ethos of shaping and building businesses around people. He also believes that trusting others with the day-to-day running of Virgin has enabled him to be more agile as an entrepreneur and to focus on scoping for opportunities to grow the brand. He surrounds himself with people who can turn his ideas into reality.

'The best bit of advice I think I can give to any manager of a company is find somebody better than yourself to do the day-to-day running,' Branson stated in 2015 in an interview with Business Insider UK. 'And then free yourself up to think about the bigger picture. By freeing myself up, I've been able to dream big and move Virgin forward into lots of different areas.'[2]

Virgin is known for its risk-taking when entering the market and its pragmatic approach to exiting. No business is too precious to have its role challenged within the portfolio. The underlying business logic has been summarised by Branson: 'Business opportunities are like buses . . . There's always another coming along'.[5]

Branson wrote in 2016, at the time of the sale of Virgin America: 'In 2007, when the airline started service, 60 per cent of the industry was consolidated. Today, the four mega-airlines control more than 80 per cent of the US market. Consolidation is a trend that sadly cannot be stopped.'[6] In 2015, the Group decided to sell another of its flagship companies, with 80 per cent of its share of the Virgin Active fitness chain going to South African billionaire Christo Wiese, prompting the British health-club chain to cancel plans for a share sale.[7] Of the sale, Virgin stated: 'Our investment strategy is to build businesses of scale and this sometimes means accessing external capital to build them further through sales of stakes to partners or through the public markets.'[8]

The future

While Branson does not mention his departure, he has continued to state that the company has been structured to continue without him. He says that he now devotes the majority of his time and energy to Virgin Unite – a charitable foundation which focuses on environmental and charity activities. Business observers remain divided about the essence of the group's business model: some see it as a private equity organisation (but many of the businesses are start-ups); others see it as a branded venture capital organisation (but the group incubates its own businesses); some suggest that it is a conglomerate. Some critics assert that the Virgin brand has been over-extended.

It is difficult to discover the overall financial position of Virgin because it is made up of so many individual companies and there are no consolidated accounts. Branson has agreed that he is interested in growth, not short-term profits, and builds companies for the long term. There is an emphasis on maximising returns to Virgin Group equity through high financial leverage and the use of equity partners. The financial picture is very mixed: in 2014, Virgin Money reported a £34m statutory profit before tax whereas Virgin Australia reported a AUS$356m ($276m, €245m, £193m) net loss after tax for the same year. A spokesman for Virgin Care, in 2015, said the company had not yet reached 'a state of profitability' and shareholders were still investing in the growth of the business.

Branson remains, as ever, defiant to his critics. Is Virgin a strong enough brand to survive if he steps aside? Would the Virgin Group survive? 'The Virgin brand is not a product; it's an attitude and a way of life to many,' explained Branson in 2012 in an interview for Economia. 'That attitude is about giving customers a better time and better value in a fun way that embraces life. But brands, ultimately, belong to the consumer and while a business can influence its brand by what it does and how it behaves, it is what the customer thinks at the end of the day that is the only important thing.'[9]

Questions

1 What directions of strategic development have been followed by Virgin over the period of the case (use Figure 9.2 as a guide)?

2 Which type of corporate parenting role (as per Figure 9.5) best describes the Virgin Group? Justify your choice.

3 How does the Virgin Group as a corporate parent add value to its businesses? To what extent are these parenting skills relevant to the differing business units?

4 What should the future corporate strategy be? (And how essential is Richard Branson himself to that strategy?)

References
1. http://www.virgin-atlantic.com/tridion/images/companyoverviewnov_tcm4-426059.pdf
2. http://uk.businessinsider.com/how-richard-branson-maintains-the-virgin-group-2015-2?r=US&IR=T
3. https://www.virgin.com/entrepreneur/richard-branson-how-to-find-the-right-funding-for-your-business
4. https://www.virgin.com/entrepreneur/six-things-we-learnt-business-adventure-la
5. https://www.virgin.com/richard-branson/opportunity-missed
6. https://www.virgin.com/richard-branson/virgin-america
7. http://www.bloomberg.com/news/articles/2015-04-16/brait-agrees-to-buy-80-of-virgin-active-for-about-1-billion
8. http://www.theguardian.com/business/2015/apr/16/virgin-active-stake-sold-to-south-africas-brait
9. http://economia.icaew.com/people/november-2012/out-of-this-world

Appendix 1 Strategic developments of the Virgin Group 1970–2016

1970	Branson founds the Virgin business selling records
1971	First Virgin record shop opened
1977	Virgin record label is launched
1984	Virgin Atlantic, a long-haul airline is founded
1985	Virgin Holidays is founded
1986	Virgin Group PLC formed
1987	Virgin Records America is launched
1988–90	Virgin Megastores are opened in prime city locations in Europe, USA and Japan Branson takes Virgin Group PLC private for £248 m
1991	Virgin Publishing formed through merging Virgin Books and WH Allen PLC Virgin Games formed
1992	Virgin Records sold for £510 m
1993	Virgin Games floated as Virgin Interactive Entertainment PLC Virgin Radio commences broadcasting
1994	Virgin Retail acquires Our Price chain of shops
1996	Virgin Net an internet service provider is launched
1997	Virgin Trains is founded to run West Coast rail franchise in the UK Virgin Cosmetics launches with four flagship stores Virgin Radio sold for £87m
1999	Virgin Mobile is launched in joint venture with Deutsche Telekom Virgin Health starts a network of health clubs Virgin Cinemas is sold for £215 m 49 per cent of Virgin Atlantic sold to Singapore Airlines for $500 m
2000	Virgin Mobile launches US wireless phone service (JV with Sprint) Virgin Blue launched (low-cost airline – Australia) Virgin Cars launched to sell online
2001	50 per cent of Virgin Blue sold
2004	Virgin Digital launched to sell online music Virgin Unite, a charitable foundation, launched
2006	Virgin Media is launched in partnership with NTL-Telewest Virgin Fuel launched Virgin Cars closed
2007	Last of Virgin Megastores (125) sold Virgin America (airline) launched Virgin Earth Challenge and World Citizen initiatives are launched
2009	Virgin Green Fund launched
2010	Virgin Hotels launches Virgin Racing launched (Formula One) Virgin Gaming launched Virgin Produced launched (film and TV production company) Virgin Money acquires Church House Trust to acquire UK banking licence Virgin Group acquires majority stake in Assura Medical
2011	Virgin Cosmetics and Virgin Money (USA) are closed Virgin Active acquires Esporta for £80 m Virgin Unite (charitable foundation) launches Branson's Centre for Entrepreneurship
2012	Assura Medical rebrands as Virgin Care Virgin Care signs £500m contract to run Surrey Care Services, part of NHS Surrey
2013	Virgin Money acquires Northern Rock for about £1bn Virgin Media sold to Liberty Global
2014	Virgin Money floated on Stock Exchange Virgin and Stagecoach joint venture wins East Coast mainland rail franchise Virgin Galactic spaceship crashes
2015	Virgin Active sells 80% of its stake Virgin Galactic wins $4.7m NASA contract
2016	Virgin America is sold to Alaska Air for £1.8bn Branson unveils Virgin Galactic's new space tourism rocket plane

Source: Based on www.virgin.com.